AF279184

Nāgārjuna's Advice for Buddhists

An Explanation of *Letter to a Friend*

Geshe Lhundub Sopa

With Beth Newman

Foreword by Lama Zopa Rinpoche

Wisdom Publications
199 Elm Street
Somerville, MA 02144 USA
wisdomexperience.org

Library of Congress Cataloging-in-Publication Data
Names: Sopa, Geshe Lhundub, author. | Newman, Beth, author.
Title: Nāgārjuna's advice for Buddhists: An explanation of letter to a friend /
Geshe Lhundub Sopa, with Beth Newman.
Description: First edition. | Somerville: Wisdom Publications, 2023. |
Includes bibliographical references and index.
Identifiers: LCCN 2022019367 (print) | LCCN 2022019368 (ebook) |
ISBN 9781614297857 (hardcover) | ISBN 9781614298090 (ebook)
Subjects: LCSH: Nāgārjuna, active 2nd century. Suhṛllekha. |
Religious life—Buddhism. | Buddhist priests—India—Correspondence.
Classification: LCC BQ5385.N333 S67 2022 (print) |
LCC BQ5385.N333 (ebook) | DDC 294.3/444—dc23/eng/20220711
LC record available at https://lccn.loc.gov/2022019367
LC ebook record available at https://lccn.loc.gov/2022019368

ISBN 978-1-61429-785-7   ebook ISBN 978-1-61429-809-0

27 26 25 24 23
5 4 3 2 1

Photos of Geshe Sopa by Kalleen Mortensen.
Cover image: Geshe Sopa's personal thangka of Nāgārjuna,
photographed by Kalleen Mortenson.
Cover design by Gopa & Ted 2. Interior design by Tony Lulek.

Printed on acid-free paper that meets the guidelines for permanence and durability of the Production Guidelines for Book Longevity of the Council on Library Resources.

Printed in Canada.

Contents

Foreword

EVEN BEFORE GOING INTO EXILE from Tibet, Geshe Sopa Rinpoche was known as a learned teacher in the three great monasteries of Sera, Ganden, and Drepung and their colleges—he was famed not only in Sera Mey and Jey, but also in Ganden Shartse and Jangtse, and Drepung Loseling and Gomang. He had the three qualities of being learned, strict in vows, and good-hearted. Despite having all those qualities, Geshe Sopa never showed arrogance. He was very humble. That is an incredible quality. Often when people become learned, they develop arrogance and pride, but Geshe-la was not like that. Even though he was extremely learned, whenever I took lamrim teachings or oral transmissions from him, at the beginning he would say that he may have forgotten the teaching. This was an expression of his humility—it didn't mean that in reality he was unable to remember.

Geshe Sopa was an unbelievable teacher, not only to me, but also to my guru Lama Yeshe. Geshe-la had a special way of teaching, especially when teaching philosophy. He learned this from his teacher at Sera Jey, Geshe Thabkyé. Geshe Thabkyé was one of the most famous geshes preserving Lama Tsongkhapa's lineage and spreading his profound, secret, and unmistaken knowledge throughout all the Gelukpa monasteries. Geshe Thabkyé received the lineage of teaching from his teacher, Geshe Lhundup Tsöndrü, a famous Ganden Tripa from Sera Jey's Tsangpa Khangtsen. Through this lineage, Geshe Sopa received a very clear way of understanding the teachings. In addition, he had an extremely kind way of guiding students. Geshe-la taught many learned geshes inside and outside Tibet. Due to

Geshe-la's kindness, many sentient beings were brought onto the path to enlightenment, instead of continuing to experience the ocean of samsaric suffering, which has no beginning.

When His Holiness the Dalai Lama was being examined for his geshe degree at the great monasteries, Geshe-la was one of the main teachers who debated with him at Sera. From that time, His Holiness the Dalai Lama regarded Geshe Sopa as very close to him. Many years later, Geshe-la invited His Holiness many times to Deer Park outside Madison, Wisconsin, to give various teachings and commentaries. It was there that His Holiness gave the Kālachakra initiation for the first time in America, in 1981.

I want to mention an amazing story to show the capacity of Geshe-la's memory. When a Tibetan family that lived in Chicago went to Mustang, in Nepal, their plane crashed and they died. Other members of the family came from Chicago to Deer Park to ask for prayers. Geshe Sopa called together everyone who was there at that time to join in the prayers, which were led by Geshe Sherab Thabkyé. I was also there, attending one of the summer courses at Deer Park. Geshe Thabkyé began with a recitation of one mala of the mantra Om Mani Peme Hung, and then recited the eight prayers for the dead. Geshe Sopa Rinpoche said he wasn't sure if he would remember these prayers, since he had memorized them when he was in Tibet, which meant forty or fifty years before. After we did the prayers, Geshe-la said, "Oh, I remembered them." In my view, his ability to remember all the prayers, even though he hadn't recited them for such a long time, shows that Geshe-la had lived a very pure life.

Because this book is a commentary on Ārya Nāgārjuna's *Letter to a Friend*, I feel it is important to say a few words about the author of that text. Nāgārjuna generated bodhicitta and accumulated the two collections without interruption for an incalculable eon. While he was performing deeds to actualize the aims of countless living beings in an inexpressible number of worlds, by choice he came into this world, his field of salvific activity. He held the tradition of the Bhagavān Buddha and was one of the two reopeners of the path.

There are ways that Nāgārjuna was prophesized. The *Laṅkāvatāra Sūtra* says:

> In the southern land of Vedali
> a monk famed as Śrīman

will be called the name Nāgā.
He will destroy the philosophical positions of existence and
    nonexistence.
After explaining my teachings of the unsurpassed
great vehicle throughout the world,
he will attain the first bodhisattva bhumi
and go to the pure land Sukhāvatī.

It is said that Nāgārjuna was born about four hundred years after the Bhagavān Buddha passed beyond sorrow, in a place called Vidarbha in southern India. A diviner said that the child would not live more than seven years. His parents could not bear to see their child die, so they sent him off to another place accompanied by servants. Eventually they reached the largest monastery in Maghada, Nālandā. There he met the master Brahman Saraha and requested a longevity ritual. In addition, he studied much secret mantra Dharma—the Guhyasamāja and so forth. Before the preceptor Rāhulabhadra he received monk's vows and the ordination name Śrīman. At Nalanda he studied all the ways of explaining the tripiṭaka and four branches of tantra. Primarily he heard all the holy Dharma of sutra and tantra from the bodhisattva Ratnamati.

Then a great famine occurred. In accord with the advice of the Sthavira Rāhulabhadra, he was appointed monastery manager. From another region he acquired alchemical elixirs and transformed a large quantity of base metal into gold. With that he amassed all the necessities of life—rice, other grains, and so forth—from areas not affected by the famine. For twelve years he provided the sangha's livelihood and kept them from want. Someone then said, "It contradicts the Dharma discipline to bring together the means to live by engaging in commerce without permission from the sangha." So, he was cast out of the monastery.

Then he went to the large cities of Maghada, Śrāvastī, and so forth and established many temples and stupas. He extensively taught the Dharma as an antidote to Bhikshu Śaṅkara's many treatises that were composed to criticize both the view and practice of the Great Vehicle. At the invitation of the nāga king Takṣaka he went to the land of the nāgas and extensively taught the Dharma, and he brought the 100,000 line *Perfection of Wisdom Sutra* back from there and taught it to his disciples. At Bodhgaya he had a stone balustrade erected encircling the bodhi tree. He encircled the splendid Dhānyakaṭaka stūpa with an iron fence and established 108 temples. He went to Uttarakuru and performed deeds to achieve the aims of migrating beings. In the latter part of his life, he resided at Śrīparvata in southern India and extensively set in motion the Dharma wheel of sutra and tantra. He conclusively taught the definitive-meaning sutras of the Victor such that no one could give them another meaning.

When he was extensively engaging in deeds like that for the teachings, evil maras influenced the mind of Prince Nudan, the son of Nāgārjuna's friend King Dechözangpo. The prince asked for Nāgārjuna's head. The master assented, and the prince cut off Nāgārjuna's head and he passed away. It is said that at that time blood came forth as milk, and from the mouth of that severed head came the words, "I am going from here to Sukhāvatī. Later I will reenter this body." The prince worried that the head would reconnect to the body so he threw it about a league away. The master had previously accomplished the elixir of longevity, so his body and head turned to stone. Subsequently, neither the body nor head deteriorated and gradually each year the two came closer and closer together. It is said that eventually, they will reattach, and the master himself will be just as he was when he was in the world, before and he will extensively work to accomplish the goals of the Teaching and migrating beings.

In the hagiographies it is taught that this Master proclaimed the words of the Dharma three times. The splendid protector Ārya Nāgārjuna composed the six-fold corpus of texts on reasoning to definitively establish the explicit teaching of the perfection of wisdom sūtras—the exposition of emptiness—via limitless varieties of reasoning. And he also compiled the *Sūtrasamuccaya* to definitively establish the scriptural foundation for the teaching of emptiness. The treatises this master composed were translated into Tibetan during the period of the Tibetan great king Tri Songdetson and exist in the Tengyur. Chief among Ārya Nāgārjuna's many disciples are Śākyamitra, Nāgabodhi, Āryadeva, Mātaṅga, Buddhapālita, Bhāviveka, Ācārya Śūra, and so forth.

There are two ways to explain the lifespan of this master, who is like the second Teacher, Buddha Śākyamuni: one says he lived for six hundred years, the other says he lived for three hundred years. However, Tāranātha's *History of the Dharma in India* says both systems of calculation are the same—one referring to half his lifespan, the other the full span.

Nāgārjuna's Advice for Buddhists is an incredible book. Geshe Sopa

Rinpoche's commentary on Nāgārjuna's *Letter to a Friend* is so good to study. For example, in one verse we learn that until nonvirtuous karma is exhausted, life cannot be separated from suffering. If you create the negative karma to be born in hell, there will be no time to practice Dharma. No matter how many eons it takes, you will have to experience that hellish suffering without choice. And the most excruciating human suffering is peace compared to suffering in hell. In that one verse from *Letter to a Friend*, Nāgārjuna tells us that we can't ignore the ten nonvirtues, or negative karmas, in our daily life. He is advising us, with so much compassion and care, that everything comes from the mind: hell and enlightenment, samsara and nirvana, and even each day's problems and happiness come from the mind. Therefore, we really have to watch our mind and not just blindly engage in negative karma all the time. We must put effort into not creating negative karma. And we must be careful from now up to the attainment of enlightenment. In other words, we must be careful in all our future lives. It's not just being careful in one or two lives so as not to be reborn in the lower realms. Advising us to be careful is incredible guidance. You yourself have the whole responsibility for this every year, every month, every week, every day, every hour, every second. Even though some people may know this intellectually, they don't put it into practice.

Reading this book by Geshe Sopa gives us the most practical advice about how to live our life. This advice is not for those with high tantric realizations. Nāgārjuna's down-to-earth advice was given to a busy king. It is advice about the Dharma practice to do when there is no time to meditate or do many practices. People in the West today don't easily recognize the great value of life and how to make their life meaningful. Because people think life is meaningless, they are unhappy and depressed. Studying this book and practicing its advice will help so much to alleviate this. Nāgārjuna advised the king that there are three very important things to practice: bodhicitta, rejoicing, and taking refuge in Buddha, Dharma, and Sangha. No matter how busy we are, we should practice these three too.

I hope that the precious teachings of Buddha, especially those on philosophy, that Geshe-la has taught will last for a long time and spread in the world.

Lama Zopa Rinpoche

Acknowledgments

THIS BOOK was made possible by the wise and comprehensive teachings of Geshe Lhundub Sopa. The kind instruction of my other teachers contributed greatly to my understanding of the material so that I could bring Geshe Sopa's commentary into print. This book is dedicated to all of these teachers.

John Newman shared his expertise in research, translation, and teaching to make this work better for the reader. Rodney Stevenson worked magic to improve the audio recordings. Alex Gardner of Wisdom Publications asked questions and made suggestions that improved this book. Many other friends offered encouragement that helped me throughout the composition.

Introduction

Buddhist literature is vast. The Buddha taught many things to a variety of audiences based on their individual needs and abilities. After the Buddha passed into nirvana, it is said that his followers convened to collect his teachings. To help those trying to practice the Buddhist path, many Buddhist teachers and scholars composed explanations of the founder's words and also wrote independent works to further elucidate his ideas. Soon there were commentaries on these works as well. Scholarship and composition have continued over the last two and a half millennia.

How should someone who wants to learn about Buddhism approach this enormous quantity of ideas and texts? Those willing to dedicate a great deal of time and effort can take university classes, enter a monastery, or sit at the feet of a teacher and engage in intensive study for many, many years. Even in such situations certain topics and texts have to be singled out for study and practice. But Buddhism is not just for those who have left society behind for a life dedicated solely to religious pursuits. It is a religious system of thought and practice that can benefit people still active in the world. So how can an ordinary person with an interest in Buddhism, but limited free time, get an overview of Buddhist religious practice and ideas? Simply picking a text or two from the corpus of specialized Buddhist literature will not be effective. This has been the case almost from the very beginning of the tradition. To solve this problem Buddhist teachers from early on have written works that summarize the entire system of Buddhist practice.

One of the earliest Buddhist teachers we know to have addressed this issue was the great Indian Buddhist philosopher Nāgārjuna. Two of his works, *The Precious Garland* and *Letter to a Friend* are comprehensive and practical summaries of Buddhist practice. The book you have in your hands is Geshe Lhundub Sopa's explanation of *Letter to a Friend*.

The Tibetan Buddhist tradition, following the Indian tradition, says that Nāgārjuna lived 400 years after the passing away of the Buddha. Etic scholars—in other words, those studying Buddhism as outside observers—tend to think that this master lived circa 150–225 of the common era. In fact, this dating is largely dependent upon the identification of Gautamīputra Śatakarṇi, a Sātavāhana king of Andhra, in Eastern India, for whom *Letter to a Friend* was written.[1]

While there is no historically verifiable biographical information about Nāgārjuna, there is a great deal of legend. His life and activities were prophesized in various sutras and tantras, including *the Laṅkāvatāra, Mahāmegha, Mahāberī,* and *Mañjuśrīmūlakalpa Tantra.*[2] According to a composite picture drawn from these sources, Nāgārjuna was born into a brahmin family in South-Central India in an area that is now within the state of Maharashtra. The Chinese and Tibetan traditions differ about why the boy entered monastic life. The Tibetan accounts say that a soothsayer prophesized the child would die young unless he entered religious life, whereas the Central Asian scholar and translator Kumārajīva (344–413) says that Nāgārjuna entered Nālandā monastery in order to escape punishment for indiscreet behavior at a royal court.[3] The traditional accounts of his life attest to many travels, miraculous deeds, the establishment of temples, composition of texts, and so forth. He is most famous for obtaining the Perfection of Wisdom—*Prajñāpāramitā*—texts from the nāgas and subsequently writing philosophical treatises to explain the doctrine contained within them. These works that explicate Madhyamaka philosophy and the Mahayana path are the most famous, and often considered the most important of Nāgārjuna's writings.

Nāgārjuna is one of the earliest and most important Mahayana scholars. He wrote on a wide variety of topics for varied audiences. The Tibetan tradition separates his works into three categories: a collection of works of formal philosophy, a collection of didactic discourses, and a collection of hymns.[4] *Letter to a Friend* is included in the collection of didactic discourses. Many other texts on the topics of the *Guhyasamāja Tantra,* alchemy, medicine, and even eroticism have been attributed to this master. In order to accommodate single authorship of all these texts, which even with the minimal dating possible for Indian Buddhist literature were clearly written over a period of centuries, the Buddhist tradition, based on a prophesy from the *Mañjuśrīmūlakalpa* says that the lifespan of Nāgārjuna was more than 600 years.[5] Etic scholars have said that it is reasonable to assume that a number of later scholars with the same name have been conflated with the great Madhyamaka philosopher and author of *Letter to a Friend*.[6]

Letter to a Friend stands out among Nāgārjuna's works because of its minimal philosophical content and limited discussion of Mahayana practices. *Letter to a Friend* is a comprehensive yet brief summary of the basic ideas and practices that form the substrate for all forms Buddhism: in other words, the text outlines the practices common to the Hinayana— more respectfully called the Śrāvakayāna—and the Mahayana in both its Sutrayana and Vajrayana forms. In that regard, it can be seen as a very early precursor of the presentation of the graduated path to awakening in a single text developed centuries later by Atiśa (circa 982–1055), and expanded in Tibet by the master Je Tsongkhapa (1357–1419).

Because of both its form and content, *Letter to a Friend* is included in the category of didactic letters (*lekha, spring yig*)[7] in the Tengyur (*bstan 'gyur*).[8] This type of text was often composed for elite lay sponsors, and presents Buddhist doctrine in a form accessible to those patrons. Although neither the author nor the addressee of *Letter to a Friend* are specifically mentioned within the text, the author uses an honorific form of address when exhorting the reader to behave in a certain way. Further, the content of this work suggests that it was meant for a king, an educated and powerful layperson. The Buddhist tradition has long accepted the attribution in the colophons of the Tibetan and Chinese translations that state that the author was Nāgārjuna and he wrote this for his friend, the Sātavāhana monarch. Although some modern scholars have questioned whether Nāgārjuna wrote this text,[9] the colophon in the recently discovered Sanskrit manuscript supports the traditional ascription of the text to Nāgārjuna and that he wrote it for a king of the Sātavāhana dynasty.[10]

Letter to a Friend has enjoyed widespread popularity. It was translated into Chinese three times, twice in the early fifth century.[11] The Chinese pilgrim and writer Yijing (635–713) wrote that the text was taught early in the course of a Buddhist education and that many devotees continued to work with the text throughout their lives.[12] Although only translated once into Tibetan, many Tibetan scholars wrote commentaries on the text and it is quoted many times in other independent works.[13] In recent years the root text, often with an accompanying commentary, has been translated into English and other languages multiple times from Tibetan and Chinese sources. The Tibetan and Chinese translations were used because until August of 2020, when the Tibetan scholar Dngos grub tshe ring published a monograph in Tibet that includes the original Sanskrit of this text found in a manuscript hoard in Tibet, it was thought that the Sanskrit text no longer existed.[14] The reason for *Letter to a Friend*'s renown across continents and over the centuries lies in its concise explication of the common path of Buddhism. In other words, the 123 verses of the text present the reader with the basic Buddhist teachings common to both the Śrāvakayāna and Mahayana.

The text can be divided into three broad sections: (1) advice regarding the practice of virtue; (2) developing renunciation through seeing the faults of samsara; and (3) advice on practicing the path to emancipation. Of course, each of these has many subtopics. After a brief three-verse introduction advising the reader to study the text, the first main section of the text (verses 4–64) presents fundamental doctrines, such as the cultivation of faith, how to counteract negative propensities, and how to practice ethical behavior in order to have a good rebirth. This section also includes a discussion of wisdom and the dispelling of wrong views, because it is asserted that only when ethical behavior is combined with wisdom can freedom from samsara be achieved. The second general section of the text (verses 65–103) outlines the various types of existence found in samsara. The general types of suffering as well as the particular nature of the suffering in each realm are presented so that the reader will develop renunciation—a disgust for samsara so strong that one turns away from all forms of rebirth controlled by ignorance and karma. Here we find a discussion of death, impermanence, and the opportune conditions needed for the practice of religion. The third section of the text (verses 104–123) shows the reader why liberation from samsara is to be valued and presents the path to emancipation from samsara as well. Only in the final verses of the text (119–123) is the Mahayana discussed. There the nature of the goal—perfect buddhahood—is described and the reader

is exhorted to become a buddha in order to benefit other living beings
through dedicating the merit accrued from practicing the methods outlined earlier in the text.

Thus, although *Letter to a Friend* clearly presents the practices for an
individual to attain their own liberation from samsara, it should not be
forgotten that these same practices are the foundation of the Mahayana
path. The goal of the Mahayana path is to attain perfect buddhahood
because that is the only way to help other suffering beings end their misery. In other words, through practice of the Mahayana path a practitioner
will attain their own liberation from samsara and in addition develop
superior abilities and wisdom that enable them to truly assist others. It is
within this context that Venerable Geshe Sopa explained this text.

Over the course of the last few years of twentieth century, Geshe
Sopa gave an oral exposition of Nāgārjuna's *Letter to a Friend*. This was
a continuation of his Sunday morning Dharma class that began in 1975.
Starting in his living room, Geshe Sopa began to teach a small group of
students. As time went on and the number of students increased, he taught
first in a remodeled basement and then in the temples of Deer Park, the
monastery he established in Oregon, Wisconsin. In addition to Sundays,
Thursday evening classes and intensive multiweek summer courses on the
great works of the Mahayana tradition from India and Tibet were added.
Although many other great teachers came to Deer Park Monastery to
teach, Geshe Sopa himself gave teachings on Sundays whenever he was
able to do so. By the 1990s Geshe Sopa had many commitments all over
the world; it took a long time for him to complete his teachings on *Letter
to a Friend* because he often left Wisconsin to teach in other locations.

Geshe Sopa was an exemplary Buddhist monk practitioner as well as a
superlative scholar. His quiet and compassionate traditionalism drew people in; he did not blast people with charisma. He was a recognized master
of his tradition and also knew how to reach a contemporary audience. His
teachings on *Letter to a Friend* roughly follow the commentary written
by Rendawa Shönu Lodrö (1349–1412). However, he added much, much
more. He brought in additional material from many sources: the sutras,
other texts by Nāgārjuna, works by great Indian masters such as Śāntideva,
Āryadeva, Candrakīrti, Vasubandhu and others, and from multiple works
by Je Tsongkhapa.[15] Although Nāgārjuna's text primarily teaches the common path with little emphasis on philosophy, Geshe Sopa's explanation

supplements it to teach the Mahayana path and Madhyamaka philosophy. Further, his explanation took into account the lives of the students in his audience. He made a text written almost two thousand years ago applicable to modern Buddhist lay practitioners.

I was privileged to be a student of Geshe Sopa, both at Deer Park and at the University of Wisconsin, from 1975 until his death in 2014. His teachings and example have shaped my life. His clear explanations of Buddhist thought and practice have influenced many others' lives too. I feel very fortunate to have been able to help spread his wisdom by transforming his oral teachings into written format. I hope that this condensation of his teachings on Nāgārjuna's *Letter to a Friend* conveys to you, the reader, the wisdom and loving compassion of Geshe Sopa and provides a template for your practice of the Buddhadharma.

1. Why Read This Book?

Why should you read this book? It is because you have a great opportunity to use your life to achieve something very special. You can develop your understanding of the Dharma and with that wisdom you could ensure that you and others will have positive experiences in the future. Or, your actions could be self-centered and egoistic. You could use what you have solely for your own enjoyment. Many people just want to enjoy life as much as possible. I've had people tell me they don't want to become a buddha because it'll be too lonely and dry. Attraction to the sensory pleasures of life is so powerful that Buddhist teachers spend quite a lot of time showing their students the disadvantages of ordinary life. The teachings give you a framework to contemplate the faults of samsara so that you come to feel deep disgust with any type of rebirth. Only when you feel great sorrow about having to be reborn again and again will you want to get out of that situation. If you really don't want any more samsaric suffering, you have to know what causes it. With that knowledge you can stop creating the causes that result in misery.

There is an alternative to suffering in samsara. Nirvana is emancipation from suffering; it is the permanent cessation of rebirth controlled by karma and the mental afflictions. Not only must you know that liberation is possible, you also need to learn how to achieve that state of permanent cessation. First you learn about the practices common to both the Hinayana and Mahayana. Finally, you learn about the unique goal of the Mahayana path and the practices particularly designed to achieve the state of buddhahood.

As a human you have intelligence. You can think about many things: the past and the future; what you experience; what you fear or worry about; what you want; and how to use your body, speech, and mind to get that. In general, from time without beginning up until now you have used your intelligence to work for pleasure in samsara. You have used up hundreds and thousands of lives; it looks like forever. But now you have come in contact with spiritual teachings. In short, you have a fortunate life. *Fortunate* doesn't mean that you have a lot of money, prestige, or power. It means that your life can be utilized for long-term future benefits. What you do in this life affects your next life. Through practicing the Dharma, you can block a lower rebirth. Then during one higher rebirth after another you can engage in spiritual practice. Through that you can attain freedom for yourself. And if you enter the Mahayana path you can attain enlightenment for the benefit of other sentient beings.

What happens to you, whether you will go upward or downward after your death, depends only upon you. According to Buddhism there is no one outside you that has permanent and total control over you. Your mindset and actions determine your future. Thus, when you have all the necessary internal and external conditions for religious practice, you have a great opportunity. A human life only lasts a short time. If you don't use it, or use it in the wrong way, there is no question that the result after death will be an unpleasant rebirth. You can stop that from happening by developing your positive potential.

A spiritual teaching is a method of training your mind. The purpose of a Dharma teaching is to transform your impure mind into a pure one, to make your imperfect mind become perfect, and develop your inferior mind into a superior mind. If you follow the instructions from the beginning, you will proceed to the intermediate level and then to the highest level. This training can be difficult. But if you understand its value you can joyfully accept any hardships you encounter.

The text called *Letter to a Friend* by the great scholar Nāgārjuna contains the advice you need to train your mind. The friend for whom Nāgārjuna composed this text was a ruler of the South Indian Sātavāhana dynasty during the second century of the common era. Because this king was a layperson, the advice in this short text is slightly different than that found in many other religious works. A king is the leader of a country; he is active in society and governance. If he acts well with a good motivation he can benefit many people. If he acts selfishly and cruelly he can do great harm. Therefore, Nāgārjuna shows the king how to incorporate the practice of Dharma into his responsibilities in the world. Thus, in this text the encouraged mode of practice is often directed to someone living and working in society. In that regard, these instructions apply equally to contemporary laypeople who are involved with many people and activities. However, this advice is applicable to all practitioners: laypeople and those who have renounced lay life and taken ordination. No matter who you are, if you put the instructions in this short text into practice, you can use your life in a wholesome way.

In the first three verses of *Letter to a Friend,* Nāgārjuna tells you why you need to take the time to study this text.

> 1. It is right for someone naturally suited to virtue
>   to study this short text that I have composed.
>   These special verses will lead you to aspire to the virtues
>   which arise from the teachings of the Sugata.[16]

Nāgārjuna begins by addressing the recipient of his letter as "someone naturally suited to virtue." The king, and by extension all of us, is given this appellation because we have the opportunity and ability to practice the Dharma. As a result of prior virtuous actions, we have a human life. We have the intelligence to listen to religious teachings and put them into practice. It is quite wonderful when, in addition to this ability to practice, there is a special karmic seed that ripens as an opportunity to meet a spiritual teacher and the teachings. This doesn't always happen. Sometimes people have created good karma in the past that leads to a high rebirth, but it is just an ordinary worldly rebirth. For example, a king is at a high level of society and has wealth and temporal power. However, when that kind of rebirth is finished, there is the possibility to be reborn poor, or even into a lower realm. But in this case, in addition to his superior worldly status the king has the opportunity and ability to practice the Dharma. If the king had not created a particular type of good karma in the past he wouldn't have this opportunity. So what kind of karma is necessary to obtain this kind of good life? You must be habituated to merit or virtue, things like patience, generosity, and good conduct. The nature of these virtues is that they are causes for becoming a suitable vessel for listening to the holy Dharma. The roots of virtue accumulated earlier are the cause for your current good situation.

Nāgārjuna assures us that this is a short text with succinct verses. This is important because ancient kings and contemporary Dharma students are very busy people. Kings had many obligations involving the rule of their kingdom. You have many responsibilities too: jobs, families, community, and so on. Neither the king nor most people today have much leisure time to study extensively. So Nāgārjuna offers us a brief text to show us the method to attain positive spiritual goals.

There are two kinds of spiritual goals: one is temporary and one is final. The final spiritual goal has two parts: nirvana and enlightenment. Nirvana can be described in a number of ways: it is one's own permanent cessation of ignorance; permanent liberation from uncontrolled rebirths caused by the mental afflictions; permanent freedom from suffering; and peace. In addition to these qualities, the even higher goal of enlightenment has the qualities of omniscience, perfect love and compassion, and the intention and ability to help others attain liberation. Attaining nirvana or enlightenment isn't easy; it takes a lot of effort over a long time. Most of us are not able to attain those goals in this life. So what should we do? We need to create the causes for a good rebirth in our next life, and our lives thereafter, during which we can continue to work toward the attainment of the permanent states of nirvana or enlightenment. So, our temporary spiritual goal is a high rebirth. Here *high* doesn't just refer to a human life, a life as a god, or a level of status. It indicates a life suitable for the practice of virtue and the elimination of the mental afflictions. A high rebirth is a temporary goal because it does not last. But by using this good temporary situation to study and practice, we can work toward our definite goal without much interruption. If you have that type of life for rebirth after rebirth, eventually you will never fall to a lower rebirth and you will attain your long-term permanent goal. Or, if you do go down to a rebirth in the lower realms, it is for a short time.

If the method you employ to reach your goal is incorrect, or if you have the right method but don't understand it properly, everything goes wrong. In the world, people do many things to attain a variety of goals. We need an infallible method to achieve our spiritual goals. The complete and error-free methods to attain a higher rebirth and the permanent spiritual goals are taught extensively in the Buddhist scriptures. The teachings of the Buddha show us these positive goals and the actions that lead to them. They also show us the negative things that prevent us from attaining our desired goals and lead to undesirable results. These teachings are vast and complex. We need a summary of the methods that we can understand and then apply with accuracy. In brief, the method is to engage in the practice of virtue so that we attain our spiritual goals and avoid engaging in nonvirtue that only leads to suffering. Therefore, the first thing we have to learn in order to attain our spiritual goals is: What is virtue? What is nonvirtue? What is merit? And, what is not merit? Then we can get more specific. Certain actions create the potential for their main result to be a good temporary experience within samsara; others create the potential for the definite or permanent result of emancipation or enlightenment.

The methods derived from the Buddha's teachings are without error because the Buddha completely eliminated his own ignorance and only wanted to benefit others. This is not to say that all other religions and spiritual teachings are wrong. But many of these traditions do not advocate practices that purify the karma that will cause rebirth in the lower realms or encourage other practices that lead to being reborn in the upper realms. An example of an incorrect method is the practice of various forms of asceticism. For example, some religious practitioners never cut their hair, eat very, very little, burn their body, self-flagellate, and so on. However, hardship alone isn't a cause that leads to high rebirth. Others think that taking a bath in a certain kind of water will purify them. Even today in many parts of the world some religions encourage their followers to sacrifice animals if they want to go to heaven or attain a higher rebirth. According to Buddhism, killing living beings as a religious act simply creates the negative karma of killing. The results of that action will be to be reborn in a lower rebirth and experience being killed. Now, making offerings to the upper realm—gods and buddhas—and being charitable to the lower realm—people, animals, and other living beings—is good karma. But they should be proper offerings and gifts to those in need. The result of such generosity is to naturally possess wealth and not be distressed by any scarcity.

Therefore, Nāgārjuna emphasizes that the correct method comes from the teachings of the Buddha. He says that he wrote these verses so that the king will study these instructions, come to admire them, and engage in their practice. The wisdom that comes from study and practice is invaluable.

Āryaśūra wrote,

> Hearing the teachings is the lamp that clears away the darkness
>   of ignorance.
> Study is the best form of wealth: it cannot be stolen or
>   destroyed.
> It is a staunch comrade even if you become impoverished.
> Instruction on the method is your best friend.
>   [*Garland of Birth Stories*, 31.32]

Ordinary wealth can be lost, stolen, or destroyed by various factors. When you are rich in an ordinary way you may have friends cluster around you. But if you lose that affluence they may give you up and go away. But the wisdom that you gain from studying can't be lost. That knowledge brings you great benefit. In that regard, Nāgārjuna confesses that even though his own verses may not be very eloquent, they are worthy of your attention because their meaning comes from the teachings of the Buddha.

> 2. The wise venerate statues of the Sugata
>   no matter their quality, even those made of wood.
>   Likewise, this poetry of mine may be poor
>   but do not scorn it for it expresses the holy Dharma.

You may think that unless a text is well written it isn't worth reading and considering. But a composition should be valued in the same way that a wise person honors a statue of the Buddha. It doesn't matter if a statue is made of clay or gold. It doesn't matter if the statue is well made and attractive or crudely made and of poor quality. Because it is an image of the Buddha, because of what it represents, it is worthy of veneration. Similarly, these stanzas' literary quality is not important; they are valuable because they contain instructions on the method to attain our spiritual goals.

This parallel between visual images and written compositions can be taken further. There are many types of statues and paintings: images of meditation deities may look wrathful and powerful; images of bodhisattvas and buddhas may appear peaceful; some have many arms; some have just two arms. Each figure's posture, hand positions, and implements have symbolic meaning reflecting the spiritual attainments that the figure has attained. You need to understand the symbolism and realize that you can and should attain these qualities too. It is the subject matter—what is symbolized—that is worthy of our respect and interest. When we don't know this, we may throw away or make fun of an unattractive image. That is negative karma. It doesn't hurt the statue or painting; but it does hurt the person who creates the karma. This also pertains to the subject matter of a written text. It is wholesome karma to have respectful interest. In Tibet it was very common for people, even those without a religious education, to pick up a fragmentary piece of statue or scrap of a page of scripture they found on the ground. Even though they didn't have a deep understanding of Dharma, out of respect for what this seeming bit of detritus represented, they would touch it to their head and put it in a high place. Therefore, for the purpose of accruing merit please consider these verses that contain teachings that come from Buddha.

Śāntideva says something similar at the beginning of the *Introduction to the Practice of Bodhisattvas.*[17]

> There is nothing here that has not been explained before
> and I have no skill in the art of rhetoric.
> [*Introduction to the Practice of Bodhisattvas,* 1.3 ab]

Both Nāgārjuna and Śāntideva are obliquely referencing the four types of reliance. The Buddha explained to his disciples that when you want to learn something of great importance you need to be sensible. There are four levels on which to exercise prudence. First, you should not rely upon the person; you should rely upon the teaching. Just because a person is from a good family or famous, don't assume that everything they say is reliable. Second, do not rely upon the words; rely upon the meaning. Words can be beautiful and not mean much; or they can be awkward and have great import. Third, do not rely on the provisional meaning but rely on the definitive meaning. This is more difficult to understand. Here you need to discern whether the meaning is in the context of phenomenal reality or ultimate reality.[18] And finally, do not rely on conceptual understanding; you should rely upon wisdom. To properly understand ultimate reality you first need to understand it with logic. This is inferential knowledge and it is necessary to gain this type of understanding first. But don't rely just on that. You need to meditate on your conceptual understanding so that it becomes a direct realization of ultimate reality. In short, both of these great masters are saying that although their compositions may not be beautiful, they have great meaning and so they should be relied upon.

All the subjects covered in this text have been taught before. But even if you have heard them elsewhere, it is still good to study what is presented here. It will bring more clarity to what you have understood. It certainly won't hurt you to hear it again! The third stanza is an exhortation to pay attention employing an analogy. When the moon is high in the sky and its light shines on a house that has an exterior of white plaster, the house looks even more white. The plaster is naturally white, but it looks even lovelier in the moonlight.

> 3. The words of the Great Sage are exquisite.
>   Even if you have understood them,
>   doesn't something made of white plaster
>   become even whiter in winter moon-light?

2. General Advice

Now we begin the actual instruction with instructions on cultivating and practicing virtue. The practice of virtue can be examined from the point of view of who is practicing and from the perspective of the goal of the practice. Nāgārjuna addresses both. He begins with general advice that pertains to both laypeople and the ordained. That is the subject of this chapter. In subsequent chapters we will look at the advice he directs primarily to laypeople, and then his advice for both laypeople and the ordained regarding pursuit of a higher rebirth and the states of definite, permanent liberation.

Nāgārjuna's general advice regarding the practice of virtue for both householders and those who have left home life behind follows ancient Indian organizational models that are probably unfamiliar to most people today: (1) advice on developing faith through contemplating the six recollections; (2) advice on exerting yourself in the practice of ten virtuous actions; and (3) advice on practicing the six perfections. Although the framework may not be what you are used to, I will attempt to make the content and intent clear as we go along.

Developing Faith

Any type of endeavor requires that a person have faith in the value of the goal and trust in the efficacy of the path of action necessary to reach that goal. Without this you won't strive for the goal. If you don't engage in the method you won't get anywhere. So, faith is the foundation, seed, or root of the practice of virtue. In short, religious faith is to have trust in a spiritual goal and method to reach that goal.

A sutra found in the *Heap of Jewels* collection of sutras says,

> Faith is the best vehicle
> to carry you to liberation.
> Therefore, those who are wise
> rely upon and are led by faith.
>
> Just as green sprouts do not grow
> from seeds scorched by fire,
> good qualities will not arise
> in people who lack faith.
>
> [*Ten Teaching Sutra*]

From the Buddhist point of view faith requires understanding. For example, faith in karmic causality is based on at least some appreciation of the type of causes that result in suffering and the type of causes that result in pleasant experiences. Faith in the Buddha is based upon some knowledge of a buddha's qualities, what a buddha can do, and the connection between a buddha and oneself. There are sequential levels of faith based on the nature of its underlying understanding. The first is called clear faith. Here you simply trust the religious goals and the path that leads to them without much thought about it. It is just following along, believing what someone else says about reality, the qualities of the goal, the reasons for practice, and spiritual experience. This is almost like blind faith because it isn't based on an in-depth rational understanding of the goal or the methods to reach the goal. However, it isn't completely blind. Even though you don't understand all the reasons, you have a good attitude and a pure sense of trust in the object. It can be an emotional feeling of trust, but it is correct.

The second type of faith is based on logic. From studying and learning you eliminate any doubts that you may have had. You develop an understanding based on methodical reasoning. So, this second type of faith comes from wisdom. You know about the object in which you are placing your faith; you don't just simply trust. This type of faith is almost irreversible; it is confident faith. Even if someone tries to tell you that you are wrong, you have firm confidence in your understanding. The second type of faith brings about the third type: faith that is imbued with the desire to achieve that goal. Faith based on understanding develops into strong admiration. You want to obtain the qualities that you have faith in; you want to embody them in yourself. Thus, this is no longer faith in something external, you really want to be that yourself. This faith is such a strong appreciation for the value of the goal and the method that you enthusiastically practice.

You start with the first type of faith and gradually develop the second type of faith. Dharma practice doesn't mean just sitting somewhere. You need to do lots of things, starting with study. You learn what the goals are: both the temporary goal of a high rebirth and the definite final goal of complete emancipation from suffering. Then you learn the value of the goals and the methods to achieve them. The methods involve your body, speech, and mind. You need to build confidence in these things in the beginning. Once you have confidence, you will be more and more comfortable about proceeding. Then, even if hardships and difficulties arise, you will not be daunted.

Just as all plants grow from earth, all spiritual attainments, good qualities, or virtues must be grounded in faith. Faith is like a mother who gives birth to those good things. Without a mother they cannot be born. The ideal mother nourishes her children, teaches them, and helps them to grow. Faith is similar. Your practice of virtue is as strong as your faith. If your faith is shaky, your practice is shaky and you won't achieve your goal. If you don't know what you are doing or why you are doing it you will lack confidence. You will be uncomfortable, worried that you can't do something correctly, or that you are doing something wrong. This is good discomfort! It is foolish not to be uncomfortable when you lack understanding. This discomfort can be alleviated by gaining understanding. If your faith is based on strong understanding, you will joyfully engage in meritorious behavior. That is the practice of Dharma.

Objects of Faith

What should you have faith in? What do you need to learn about? Nāgārjuna explains that there are six topics that both laypeople and the ordained should constantly bear in mind throughout their daily lives. These are called the six mindfulnesses, the six reflections, or the six recollections.[19] Through remembering these important subjects you will have faith and confidence in spiritual practice. What are these six foci of faith? They are faith in: (1) the Buddha, (2) the Dharma, (3) the Sangha, (4) generosity, (5) morality, and (6) the gods. First, we have the set of the Three Jewels: Buddha, Dharma, and Sangha. Next are the practices of generosity and the pure moral conduct of avoiding negative actions of body, speech, and mind. The last one is literally the gods or the divine. Of course, in the highest sense, the divine are buddhas. On the ordinary level it is a high rebirth as a god in the desire realm, the corporeal, and noncorporeal realms.[20] Here the point is that you need to have accumulated virtue or merit to be born there.

> 4. The Jina[21] taught six recollections:
>   Buddha, Dharma, Sangha, generosity, morality, and the
>   gods.
>   You should be mindful of the good qualities
>   of each one of these.

Whether you are a layperson or are ordained as a monk or nun, you need to live your life remembering these six. How do you remember them? There are sutras and commentaries that explain how to be mindful of each of these six in detail. Let's look at each one in brief.

Recollecting the Buddha as an Object of Faith

Dharmakīrti, an influential Indian Buddhist philosopher who flourished in the sixth or seventh centuries CE, discusses the qualities of a fully enlightened buddha in a lot of detail in the second chapter of the *Commentary on Valid Cognition*. In summary, a buddha's qualities can be discussed from the point of what they have abandoned and what they have realized.[22] A buddha is a sugata—"one who has gone to bliss"—because a buddha has both abandoned all flaws and realized all that is to be known. In terms of abandonment, buddhas have gotten to a state where they are rid of all suffering and the causes of suffering. This has three aspects. First there is the cessation itself. Second, the cessation is complete; it isn't a partial cessation. Everything that should be eliminated, even the subtlest mental afflictions, is removed. And third, this cessation is permanent.

Some things can be gotten rid of temporarily, but then they reoccur. Here the mental afflictions and obstacles cannot return. They are removed from the root; it is an everlasting abandonment.

From the perspective of realizations, buddhas have gone to a state where they have perfect wisdom. This also has three qualities. The first quality is that a buddha's wisdom is constant: nothing is ever forgotten. In contrast, we ordinary people sometimes know things, sometimes we forget. We can know something in this life but have to relearn it in the next. Second, a buddha's knowledge is complete. Since all ignorance has been removed from the root, a buddha is omniscient. They are a tathāgata, one who has *thus gone*. In other words, buddhas know the ultimate nature of all things exactly as they are.

A buddha's wisdom is complete and as such it is in contrast to the realizations of an *arhat*. This Sanskrit word can be glossed etymologically as "destroyer of the enemy." By practicing the Hinayana path one can become an arhat—become completely free from samsara by destroying the enemy, meaning the mental afflictions. From the Mahayana perspective, an arhat has permanently removed the gross mental afflictions—desire, hatred, ignorance, and so forth—but subtle predispositions remain as limitations. Arhats haven't removed the knowledge obstacles that prevent the complete omniscience of buddhahood. So compared to a buddha's knowledge, an arhat's knowledge is more limited. Although in some Buddhist scriptures a buddha is called an arhat, this refers to the arhatship of a completely enlightened being; a buddha has conquered the enemy—both the mental afflictions that are the obstacles to emancipation and the subtle knowledge obstacles to omniscience. The analogy for this is cleaning a piece of cloth that has been wrapped around a really smelly, rotten object for a long time. First you throw out the foul thing and wash the cloth; this is analogous to eliminating the mental afflictions. But even though you've completely gotten rid of the gross level of dirt, there is a subtle smell left in the cloth. You have to do more to eliminate the odor. The residual odor is analogous to the knowledge obstacles. In other words, an arhat is free of the mental afflictions; arhats' minds are far superior to ordinary living beings. But they still have knowledge obstacles in their mental continuum. A buddha has eliminated every obstacle.

Finally, a buddha's knowledge is firm. It is never reversed. Some yogis can do practices that temporarily remove the mental afflictions, but unlike in the case of a buddha, the root of ignorance and the mental afflictions is still there. Their attainment is like cutting off a poisonous plant at ground level; it is gone for a while but because the roots remain it will grow back.

Buddhas are often described as truly, completely perfect awakened ones. There is nothing left for them to do. They have cleared away all the obstacles and their knowledge is perfect and unlimited. This epithet can also be understood to mean "having woken up from the sleep of ignorance." Not only have they woken up, they also know the two modes of reality: the nature of both phenomenal and ultimate reality. They possess the base, or foundation. This can be understood two ways. One connotation of *the base* is pure ethical conduct. Moral conduct is the foundation for all mundane and supramundane spiritual attainments. Just as the earth is the foundation for all animate and inanimate things, all higher spiritual qualities are based on pure conduct. Without pure conduct you cannot have higher spiritual qualities. Another way to understand *the base* is as a meditative concentration where you can stabilize your mind on an object for as long as you wish. A buddha has both these types of bases.

A buddha is a knower of the world. Here *world* refers to the entire universe—in other words, both external and internal domains. The external world consists of different environments, the elements, the different realms of rebirth, and world systems. The external world is like a vessel that holds the internal world: this refers to the bodies and minds of sentient beings. The word *world* more specifically refers to ordinary things that are impermanent, existing in dependence upon parts, causes, conditions, and so forth. In short, this is the samsaric world of the twelve links of dependent origination. I won't go into that topic here because an extensive explanation of dependent origination comes later in the text. But in brief, from the combination of karma and the mental afflictions you take rebirth, then due to ignorance you create more karma, and then you die and take rebirth again. The Buddha explained this completely. If he didn't know this complex progression perfectly, he could not have explained it in a way that others could understand.

An experienced driver of a horse-drawn wagon knows how to control his horses and the correct way to go to the destination. Buddhas are similar because they show sentient beings the wheel of the Dharma and the path to liberation. They know when someone is ready to be trained and when they should be left alone. They know the capabilities of different beings:

some are ready for the Hinayana but not the Mahayana; some are ready for the basic Mahayana but not the more advanced Vajrayana. Buddhas do not have different attitudes towards these different people; they have compassion for all of them and the wisdom to see how each individual can be benefitted at the present time. The main way buddhas benefit sentient beings is to teach them what they themselves have realized. A buddha has mastered the process and attained the goal that we want too.

Buddhas are unsurpassable in their ability to train sentient beings in accordance with the nature and ability of each individual. In general, there are six different types, or realms, of sentient beings in the desire realm. Although a buddha has compassion and wants to liberate every living being, some—such as animals, hungry ghosts, and hell beings— have such heavy karma that they cannot be taught at present. You may have an adorable dog that you love very much. You want the best things for your pet. You can give them good food, a nice bed, and a comfortable life. But more than that you can't do. You can't teach them about spiritual practice. For the time being they are left out. The most suitable disciples are humans and some of the gods. However, many people do not have the ability and propensities to benefit from the buddhas and spiritual teachers who have come into the world. Their own karma keeps them from being a disciple. So, from a Buddhist point of view the opportunity to develop spiritually is a very rare and fortunate situation. In that regard, when we praise a buddha as *lord* we are saying that they are the best teacher. We are not using the term *lord* in the sense of a ruler or master who can keep you somewhere, block you from doing something, or make you do things.

These are the qualities you should recall when you say, "I go for refuge to the Buddha." In order to trust the Buddha and follow the path to buddhahood you must learn about these qualities. When you properly understand them, you will have irreversible faith when you hear the term *Buddha*. You will know that the Buddha isn't someone or something way up in the sky. You will take the Buddha as your object of refuge because you realize that you have problems and Buddha can teach you how to resolve them without error. That is the way a buddha can save you. That is why a buddha is compared to a trainer, a doctor, or a guide.

The second-century Indian Buddhist poet Mātṛceṭa summarizes this:

You urge people to benefit others;
discipline those who steal and do wrong;
place the dishonest in steady earnestness;
and awaken inspiration in the lazy.

You connect disciples to the path;
you make the ruthlessly vicious have equanimity.
Thus, you are the unsurpassable trainer
of sentient beings who are to be tamed.
[*One Hundred and Fifty Verses of Praise,* 102–03]

When you have a serious problem and don't have the ability to alleviate it yourself, you look for someone who can provide a solution. We are suffering in samsara and cannot find the way to liberation on our own. We need a perfect guide: someone who is already free from their own suffering and the cause of that suffering; someone free from all internal and external obstacles; someone with perfect wisdom, so that their advice contains no mistakes regarding the goal, the purpose, the path, and the obstacles; someone who has universal compassion and love for others without any type of discrimination. A buddha has all these qualities. They are like an excellent physician who knows how to diagnose every type of sicknesses and is able to precisely prescribe the medicine and course of therapy to cure them.

Śāntideva makes this analogy:

When I am anxious about an ordinary sickness
I follow a physician's prescription.
So what needs to be said about being wracked constantly
by the disease of the afflictions, desire and so forth?
[*Introduction to the Practice of Bodhisattvas,* 2.54]

When you have an ordinary illness, you are in some pain and discomfort. You try to care for yourself: you search for someone who can treat your sickness; you investigate the best methods of treatment; and then you do exactly what the experts say. Even if a medication is bitter, you have to drink it if the doctor says it is necessary. You may have to give up a favorite food if the doctor says you should not eat it. It doesn't matter how hard, how difficult, or how much you dislike it, you must do it. You have to follow the treatment plan precisely if you want to recover. Taking medicine or changing your diet is relatively simple, but if you want to be free from your disease you have to take it seriously.

You have a much deeper type of sickness; this is not a temporary illness dependent upon environmental or internal physical conditions. You suffer continuously from the disease of the mental afflictions: hatred, desire, jealousy, pride, disappointment, discouragement, and so forth. These faults are in your mind all the time. First one is dominant and then another, without any break. These mental problems lead you to act in many different ways as you try to make yourself safe and happy. Hatred makes you do certain things; jealousy makes you do certain things; and so do all the other mental afflictions. Many of your actions of body, speech, and mind harm others. You may get some small advantageous return for yourself in this life, but the consequences of your actions will be greater in future lives. These actions will make you suffer for a long, long time. They throw you into a lower rebirth. Life after life you suffer.

This disease of the mental afflictions is terrifying. An ordinary sickness cannot compare to the sickness of the mental afflictions from the perspective of duration, nature, and pain. But there is a treatment for this disease. There is a way to eliminate the mental afflictions and permanently recover from the misery of repeated rebirth. The treatment to completely cure this mental disease is the spiritual practice taught by the Buddha. In this regard, the Buddha is far superior to an ordinary doctor.

Śāntideva said,

> The omniscient physician's advice
> will alleviate all misery.
> The thought to not take it
> is deluded and disgraceful.
> [*Introduction to the Practice of Bodhisattvas*, 2.56]

Every enlightened being used to be like us; they experienced suffering and were enmeshed in samsara. However, they learned how to cure this disease. They recognized the correct method, followed it, and achieved perfection. You can call this person an enlightened being, a buddha, or a god, it doesn't matter. Buddhas recognize the problems that we face in samsara and they know how to eliminate them through the spiritual path. They have mastered every aspect of the method. If they hadn't, they could not have reached the perfect result, and they would be unable to explain the path to freedom to others. Because they are omniscient, they tell you precisely how to reach your goal. Out of love and compassion they show you how to do it.

Recollecting the Dharma as an Object of Faith

There are many different kinds of spiritual training. This is because sentient beings have many different levels of ability and capacity. Some teachings are advanced, some are intermediate, and some are for beginners. But all of them are equally important. *Equally important* here means that each kind of instruction is essential at a certain level of development. This is common sense. We know this about ordinary secular education. Books and techniques must be simple for beginners; complex textbooks aren't helpful to a child in kindergarten. When starting out, picture books with simple text are more important than great books. As you master easier material you add more complexity based on your ability. Thus, some teachings are aimed at those with the lowest level of mental capacity; some are for those at a medium level, and others with the highest level of ability. Some teachings are for laypeople, some are for novices, and some for fully ordained monks and nuns. Some teachings are only for bodhisattvas who have the capacity to sacrifice themselves for the benefit of others. Some special tantric teachings are designed for those who have even higher mental abilities.

However, most people don't want to follow any of these instructions. They want the result, but not the difficulty of practice. This is extremely childish. Children are addicted to short-term pleasure; they do not see the long-term implications of their actions. Most people think they are enjoying themselves; they are attached to limited temporary pleasures. Even if a buddha were to appear and give every instruction necessary to reach freedom, most people would probably ignore them because they do not understand their value. Even if you were to understand that this is good advice, you'd think, "this isn't for me." Even if you decided to try the method, you probably wouldn't want to do anything too difficult or unpleasant. Samsaric pleasure is like honey on the blade of a knife. It is sweet on the surface, but you will cut your tongue if you lick it. Not seeing this is ignorance.

Wisdom, the opposite of ignorance, has to be awakened; you have to cultivate your mind to gain wisdom. Dharma teachings given by holy beings will nourish your mind this way. You have a human mind. You have the capacity to follow the prescribed instructions. They are difficult, but you can do it. You can see what is right, what is wrong, what to get rid of, and what to achieve. You must train in the methods yourself; no one, not even a buddha, can simply give you liberation from suffering. To attain freedom, disciples must follow the Buddha's instructions. Through practice they gradually progress and slowly recover from their problems. As their knowledge grows, they become more peaceful and more free. There is no other way to cure your deep sickness than to take the medicine prescribed by a perfect guide.

So, when you have faith in the Buddha you will have faith in the Dharma, the second of the six recollections. The Sanskrit word *Dharma* refers to two things: conventional Dharma and actual Dharma. The words of the scriptures, which record the discourses of the Buddha and other teachers, are the conventional Dharma. The actual Dharma is an individual's realization of the meaning of what was taught. Thus, part of taking refuge in the Dharma is knowing how to attain the cessation of the mental afflictions as taught in the scriptures. In that sense, Dharma practice means virtuous activity, faith, and so forth. But the actual refuge when you say, "I go for refuge to the Dharma," isn't something external. It is faith in your own personal knowledge and the cessation of your mental afflictions. For the purpose of attaining that realization you study, learn, and meditate. So there is the causal Dharma—the teachings—and the resultant Dharma—your own realization of the cessations. Another way to understand this is that there are the things to be gotten rid of and their abandonment.

What you want to get rid of is your suffering. Your suffering is caused by negative karma, which in turn is caused by the mental afflictions. Even when these mental afflictions are not manifest there can be predispositions toward them in your mind. Until you remove them, there is no possibility of liberation. The Buddha taught that we have 84,000—a number traditionally used to indicate an enormous amount—mental afflictions.

Sometimes one is stronger; another time a different one is stronger. Sometimes a particular mental affliction is absent, but later it arises again. In order to become free of all samsaric problems you have to remove all your mental afflictions. You do this step by step, not all at once. You start with the big, most obvious ones, and work to subtler levels from there. When you permanently remove a mental affliction you attain a cessation. In other words, that mental affliction has definitely and permanently ceased. This reality, or the reality of cessation, is the real Dharma—it is the third reality for āryas.[23] A cessation is the result of the reality of the path—the fourth reality for āryas. Attaining even the smallest cessation is progress along the path to freedom. To say this in ordinary words, all definitive and unalterable spiritual attainments—in other words, any cessation of ignorance and the mental afflictions—is the result of practicing the methods to purify the mind. When you attain nirvana you have the knowledge, or realization, that you have attained perfection and have terminated the afflictions. When you attain full enlightenment you have completely terminated the afflictions and the obstacles to omniscience. Things like the major and minor marks and pure lands just come along with this complete cessation.

Just as the Buddha can be described in various ways, we have many ways to describe the Dharma. First, the conventional aspect of the Dharma is said to be *well proclaimed*. The Buddha taught incomparably valuable things, he taught them well, and his speech has special positive qualities. You listen to what was said and try to understand it. Then you develop your understanding so that it is firm. Your understanding will remove some aspect of your uncertainty; it will temporarily ease a certain problem. Then you concentrate, or we can say, meditate, on that firm understanding. As you understand more deeply and strongly you develop an unshakable understanding. Finally you will have a direct realization. A direct realization permanently removes a mental affliction. That particular affliction ceases to exist in your mind. In short, attainment of liberation begins with study.

The other ways to describe the Dharma refer to the actual Dharma that protects you from further suffering. The actual Dharma is the direct realizations that cause the cessation of the mental afflictions. What is a direct realization? It is nonconceptual understanding of reality. It is comprehension that is beyond ordinary thought. Ordinary understanding is indirect;

it is knowledge based on logic, thoughts, and concepts. You need concepts for understanding to first arise in your mind. For example, right now you can imagine your room: you know where the furniture is, what books are there, where the windows and doors are, and so forth. You can truthfully tell someone what your room is like. But you are not seeing it directly; you call up an image in your mind. The appearance in your mind and the actuality of your room are mixed together. It is correct, but it isn't totally, vividly clear. In the same way, you can have an intellectual understanding of impermanence or the ultimate nature of reality. You may understand correctly, but it is indirect; you know it through logic, concepts, images, and so forth. By becoming habituated to this understanding through repeated meditation, you can make it so customary and familiar that you know it without engaging in a thought process. At that point you have attained a direct realization. A direct realization is knowing unmediated by thought. Direct realizations eliminate the poisonous tree of ignorance by cutting out its roots.

The reality of cessation isn't something physical that you can see, nor is it some aspect of mind. It is a kind of negation: through the practice of meditation you have permanently blocked and gotten rid of an obstacle so it can never arise again. However, a cessation isn't a functional thing. It is simply a negation that occurs through the power of the antidote. It is freedom from certain obstacles reached through an individual's internal direct realization. The other terms used to describe the Dharma refer to this: it is seeing completely and perfectly; it is lacking all faults and is the antidote of faults; it is permanent; it is the path through which practitioners are led to their goal; it is clear understanding like a lamp that enables you to see; it is experiential direct realization. The final descriptor means that the Dharma is known to practitioners through their own experience.

Maitreya—the bodhisattva who will be the next fully enlightened buddha to teach in our world and whose teachings Asaṅga transcribed as *The Five Treatises of Maitreya*—expresses these qualities of the Dharma in the *Higher System of the Mahayana*.[24]

> The Dharma cannot be examined in terms of existence, non-existence, both, or as something other than existence or non-existence; nor can it be expressed in words; it is realized by an individual; and is knowledge that is peace. I bow to the holy

Dharma: the sun with illumining rays of stainless wisdom that destroys all greed, hatred, and ignorance toward every object.
[*Higher System of the Mahayana,* 1.9]

The opening clause of this quotation is a bit difficult to understand. Often a direct realization specifically refers to a realization of emptiness, the ultimate nature of reality. When talking about the emptiness of a particular phenomenon, we often discuss that thing in terms of four things that it is not: it is not existent; it is not nonexistent; it is not both existent and nonexistent; and it is not neither existent nor nonexistent. These four are the only ways things could possibly exist, and nothing really exists in any of these ways. Thinking that things really exist in any of these ways is incorrect. Direct perception of the lack of existence—the emptiness—of these four is a direct realization of emptiness. The Dharma is analogized to the sun because the sun has many powers: it illuminates, heats, and causes things to grow. The realization of the Dharma is to see ultimate reality; it causes many other good qualities, all the way up to enlightenment, to grow.

In summary, you have to remember these qualities of the Dharma when you say, "I go for refuge to the Dharma." The Dharma is the main essence of your refuge. The Buddha is like a spiritual doctor, a perfect teacher who can show you the way, but the genuine treatment to cure your disease of suffering is the actual Dharma. The actual Dharma isn't a book or someone's elegant speech—yes, those are parts of the Dharma, but they don't directly help you. Changing your mind, developing your own direct realizations of wisdom, love, compassion, altruism, and so forth, is the real Dharma. Concomitant with the development of realizations is the abandonment, or cessation, of the afflictions. So, taking refuge in the Dharma is to want these things, trust in them, and have faith in them.

Recollecting the Sangha as an Object of Faith

The Sangha, the third facet of the Three Jewels, is the third recollection. In the most general sense, the Sangha is the spiritual community. It is people who are relying on the practice of the Dharma and helping each other along the path. We talk about both an ordinary sangha and a superior sangha. The ordinary sangha is comprised of people who understand at least some of the Dharma, who hold a lineage of the teachings, who have faith in the Dharma, are practicing it themselves, and assisting others who want to practice. They may not have achieved a high level of wisdom, but they have an interest in the spiritual teachings. They try to study and practice as much as possible. They try to live according to the Dharma, not harming others mentally, physically, or verbally. They may not be completely pure, but they are trying. Their emphasis is on training themselves in order to attain a spiritual goal. So far, this description applies to laypeople as well as monks and nuns. Monks and nuns differ from the laity because they have taken vows of ordination. Engaging in ethical practice with a vow is more powerful than simply acting that way without a vow. A group of at least four people who have complete vows and are trying to live in accord with the Dharma is the ordinary sense of sangha. The superior or best sangha is the ārya sangha. This refers to even a single person who has a direct realization of ultimate reality. A Hinayana ārya has directly realized the four realities for āryas; a Mahayana ārya—an ārya bodhisattva has a direct realization of emptiness and bodhicitta.

The Sangha has numerous positive qualities. The first three traits are related to the practice of the three higher trainings: ethical discipline, meditative concentration, and wisdom. These will be explained in depth later in the text. Here I will just summarize them. First, the Sangha has entered into the practice of the training of ethical conduct or morality. They behave purely. Their conduct of body, speech, and mind is virtuous. They stay away from nonvirtuous physical, verbal, and mental actions. Why is this referred to as a higher training? It is high or superior because it is a cause leading to a permanent goal that is definitely good. The second good quality of the Sangha is that they are straight or correct. This means that their minds are free from wandering about; when they meditate they can focus continuously on a virtuous object. Their minds do not veer off under the power of wrong views or afflictions. Stabilization of the mind on a virtuous object is the second of three higher trainings. The third quality of the Sangha is that they have wisdom. They correctly understand the ultimate nature of reality and accurately phenomenal reality too.

Why are the Sangha's main activities the practice of the three higher trainings? Without ethical conduct you are distracted; your mind is wild, chasing after sensory pleasure and being repulsed by unpleasant experiences. With a mind like this you cannot concentrate peacefully on an object for as long as you wish. Only when your senses are subdued can you train the mind to be stable. So, the Sangha's ethical conduct is designed to reduce both desire and disgust with objects of the senses. When someone's primary focus is no longer sensory, they have the foundation for spiritual development. The techniques to attain meditative concentration can only be practiced on the basis of ethical conduct. Meditative concentration is necessary for developing the wisdom of direct realization of ultimate reality. Without wisdom you will have no permanent peace, cessation, nirvana, or enlightenment.

Another way to describe the Sangha's practice of the three higher trainings is in terms of their harmony with wealth, conduct, view, and action. Being harmonious with wealth means that they do not place great emphasis on money or possessions. They are satisfied with simple things; they want only enough food, clothing, housing, and so forth that are necessary for survival. They are happy to wear old patched clothes and to sit on a straw mat rather than a soft silk cushion. They don't covet a fancy house or crave lavish meals. They don't worry about getting things and maintaining them. In contrast, most people worry about their possessions; instead of their things serving them, they are the servants of their possessions. Next, the real Sangha are harmonious with the laws of ethical conduct. Following the Vinaya is to avoid all wild uncontrolled actions of body, speech, and mind. Even if the Sangha is in harmony with these first two, they need to be in harmony with correct views regarding karma, future lives, the possibility of attaining buddhahood, and so forth. They need to avoid views that are antithetical to spiritual practice: nihilism, eternalism, and rejection of moral causality. The last type of harmony, harmony of action, is to be in accord with a virtuous manner of doing things. The Sangha's actions are in harmony with positive actions of body, speech and mind.

Sangha having those qualities is worthy of worship. In this context, this means that the Sangha is worthy of both material offerings, and reverential attitudes of honor, respect, and devotion. Sangha members who have the above qualities don't need your offerings; things and praise don't matter to them. But making offerings to them makes a big difference to you. It is analogous to removing rocks and tilling a field. The field doesn't care what a farmer does, but by doing these things the farmer will get a good harvest later. A buddha doesn't want or need flowers, water bowls, or fruit. But when you make these offerings it creates great merit. It is the cause for you to be rich in a virtuous way in the future.

Worship also has the sense of acting in a way that pleases those on a high spiritual level. They look at you as if you are their child. They want to help you. In turn, you want to please them. That doesn't mean giving them all your money. They will be pleased if you avoid doing negative things and do positive virtuous things. It pleases them when you are charitable, praise the buddhas, practice morality, or engage in any positive action.

In addition to pure conduct, the ārya Sangha has the mental qualities that will remove the cause of suffering. Direct realization of the nature of reality on the foundation of meditative concentration is the antidote to uncontrolled suffering rebirth. Showing reverence to those with high realizations will lead to your own realizations. Therefore, the Sangha is even more worthy of circumambulation than a stupa, a commemorative memorial of the Buddha. (Circumambulation is to walk clockwise around an object; it is an ancient way of showing respect and veneration.)[25] Another way to show reverence to the Sangha's possession of meditative concentration and wisdom is to put your palms together as in prayer. The Buddhist way of doing this is to fold your thumbs in between your palms so your hands are not empty of an offering. Pay attention to the culture you are in; if a certain hand gesture has a rude meaning in a culture, don't do it even if in a Buddhist context we say that it is virtuous,

Taking refuge in the Sangha means that you want to and will associate with these spiritual friends. You no longer desire to be the companion of someone who does harmful things, no matter how attractive that person may seem. Associating with those who act purely and strive to help others will assist you to become a better person. In the beginning of your practice of the Dharma, taking refuge in the Sangha is very important.

Following the medical analogy in which Buddha is like a physician and the Dharma is like medicine, the Sangha are like nurses or therapists. Sangha members assist the spiritual doctor by helping patients—those attempting to follow the path—act in accord with the doctor's prescription. The doctor, a buddha, may be distant; practitioners may not be able to be in direct contact with them. But the Sangha, these helpers, stay close to the patients all the time. They directly assist others in their practice.

To summarize, developing faith in the Buddha, Dharma, and Sangha is very important. It is through faith based on recollecting their various qualities, and how each one protects you in a different way, that you come to take refuge. There are different ways to think of refuge. A refuge can be temporary protection from a particular problem: if you are hot you take refuge in the shade of a tree; if you are hungry, food is your object of refuge; if you are persecuted politically you take refuge in another country. But none of these provide real, permanent freedom from all worry, fear, and problems. The real objects of refuge liberate you entirely; they provide permanent peace. The Buddha said in the Vinaya,

> Most frightened people in the world
> go to find refuge in mountains, forests
> religious temples, or even tree shrines.
> But these are not the primary objects of refuge;
> these are not superior objects of refuge.

> Depending on those objects of refuge
> will not liberate you from all misery.
> Taking refuge in Buddha, Dharma, and Sangha
> is what will definitely liberate you
> from misery and the causes of suffering.
>   [*Minor Precepts of Religious Discipline*]

Recollecting the Practice of Generosity

The fourth recollection is to remember to be generous. There are many types of generosity: you can give material things; you can donate your body; you can offer your merit; you can give spiritual teachings; and you can provide others with protection. The best thing to give is sharing what you know of the Dharma because this can lead others to both temporary and permanent higher goals.

Generosity is a cause; it is a seed for future results; it is a way to accumulate merit. Without the accumulation of merit—in other words, without having created positive causes—you will not obtain a good result. Generosity will bring you good results now, in your next life, and all the way up to the attainment of buddhahood. If you are generous now, in your next life there is no possibility that you will lack food, clothing, and other necessities. Thus, generosity is necessary from a temporary point of view; it is a cause for good conditions in samsara. An excellent life, a human life, is the result of ethical conduct; but the good conditions you experience in that life are the results of generosity. So generosity is the way to prepare for your next life.

You can give material things to two different spheres. These are referred to as upper and lower fields of generosity. The upper field consists of the Sangha, bodhisattvas, arhats, and buddhas. Animals and ordinary people in need are the lower field. Corresponding to these two fields are two types of generosity: making offerings and charity respectively. You make offerings to the upper field because they have superior qualities. Their function is to benefit sentient beings, so giving to them creates merit. When you understand causality and the concept of merit you make offerings. People who don't understand causality may think your offerings are a waste of good food. The lower field are those who are in need, who are suffering, and who need support. Giving them what they need is charity. Charity practiced with good motivation, with a delighted mind, also creates merit.

How wonderful it is to have the opportunity to be charitable and make offerings. Being happy to give is generosity. You should be generous in a respectful manner. You should not feel that you are superior to others because of your generosity. Giving just a morsel of food with a good attitude is better than making huge offerings with a poor attitude. After you give you should feel joyful. You shouldn't regret having made a gift or an offering. Don't think, "Oh, I shouldn't have done that. If I hadn't given that away I wouldn't be poor now." You should rejoice that you were able to have done that. This is an especially wonderful attitude because we live in a world where so many are motivated by greed, miserliness, and avarice. Taking delight in finding the opportunity to make offerings to the upper field and to be charitable to the lower field is the bodhisattva attitude.

The nature of generosity is to abandon the stain of stinginess in your mental continuum. We'll examine this in more detail later in the course of a discussion of the six perfections. But even here it is important to note that the essence of generosity is to joyfully give without stinginess. Generosity isn't giving away all your material possessions; it is the mind being joyful and wanting to give. It is making an effort to give; it is going out of your way to be able to do it with your own hands.

Lay people in particular can practice generosity. Engaging in meditation and other practices may be difficult for a lay person. When you see people who are tied up in stinginess and miserliness it is a good to help them to loosen a little bit and see the benefits of generosity. You don't need to tell them about future lives, or Buddhism, in any way at all. It doesn't matter if they have no belief in karmic causality. Causality functions whether you understand it or not. You should explain that everybody wants other people to like them. If they use their wealth to please others, they will be appreciated and that will bring them joy. In this way you can lead others to practice generosity.

In conclusion, mindfulness of generosity is to remember the nature of generosity, the benefits of generosity, and the undesirable results of the opposite of generosity. You recollect this until you attain Buddhahood. The twelfth-century Indian master Dhārmika Subhūtighoṣa said,

> The wise praise those who practice generosity.
> Ordinary people prefer to accumulate things:
> but no matter how they hold on, there is nothing that isn't lost.
> But giving things away always brings excellent results.
> [*String of Lights: A Compilation of Bodhisattva Practices*]

Recollecting the Practice of Morality

Mindfulness of ethical conduct is the fifth recollection. Ethical conduct, or morality, refers to positive actions of body, speech, and mind. The actions themselves and how to engage in them will be discussed in greater detail later in this chapter. Here the point is to recollect that pure ethical conduct is praised by superior practitioners because it leads to the accomplishment of meditative concentration. Realizations and the attainment of high goals depend upon a stable and focused mind; meditative concentration depends upon ethical conduct. So good conduct is the foundation or basis of all good qualities whether mundane or supramundane. Thus, ethical conduct is like the earth in that it supports both animate and inanimate things.

Recollecting the Gods

The final recollection is to be mindful of gods or deities. What gods are we talking about here? The reference is to the gods of the desire realm. The desire realm has six levels: hells, hungry ghosts, animals, humans, demigods, and gods. Together these six are called the desire realm because all the beings therein are dominated by desire for the objects of their senses:

visual objects, smells, tastes, touch (particularly sexual), and sounds. The gods of the desire realm have more enjoyable lives than any other type of desire realm being. There are six different levels of desire realm gods: on each higher level the gods have a longer life, a more pleasant environment, and the sensual objects to which they are attached are more subtle and better quality. The two lowest levels of the desire realm gods are the realm of the Four Guardians and the Heaven of the Thirty-Three. These two realms are connected to the ground on the top of Mount Meru, the mountain that is the central axis of the universe. The next four levels are not connected to earth; they are only connected to the sky.

To be mindful of the gods is to reflect upon the good qualities of such celestial rebirths in the desire realm and the causes to be born there. Even though a rebirth as a god is within samsara, they are very peaceful and pleasurable rebirths. Yes, these high rebirths are a temporary result, but enlightenment or nirvana are far away. In the meantime you want to have a good rebirth and some of the gods of the desire realm have an opportunity to practice the Dharma. If you fall to the lower realms you lose your opportunity to practice for a long, long time. The causes for being born as a desire realm god are virtue—not killing, not stealing, not lying etc.—and the practice of generosity. Wholesome virtuous practice, generosity, with the addition of effortless and flexible single-pointed concentration can have the result of being born in the corporeal and noncorporeal realms.

This completes the discussion of the six recollections in connection to the development of faith.

Karma: The Ten Virtuous Actions

Next, Nāgārjuna introduces the topic of karma. His particular focus is on acting well—in other words, engaging in the ten virtuous actions of body, speech, and mind. Every positive action can be categorized as one of these ten. Every negative action can be categorized as the opposite of one of these ten. These ten are very important and powerful actions. We do the ten negative actions easily and on a daily basis. We should try to do ten virtuous actions.

5ab. You should always adhere to the ten paths:
         the ten virtuous actions of body, speech, and mind.

Nāgārjuna uses two words to refer to karma: "actions" and "paths." You can say that actions themselves are a path. Virtuous actions are a path that leads upward to a positive result. Nonvirtuous actions are a path to lower rebirth. Some commentaries say that karma is an action itself whereas the path is the cause for an action. In other words, the path is the basis, or the motivation for an action. It is usually one of the three poisons of desire, hatred, and ignorance. We will discuss later how even virtuous actions can come from these three poisons.

If you set out on an ordinary hiking trip without enough provisions— money, clothes, food, and so forth—you will have many problems along the way. Similarly, good actions are spiritual provisions. Creating good karma is like amassing provisions for the long journey after this life. It is preparation for the future. Those who have done good actions will joyfully traverse the path to higher rebirths. If instead you create a lot of negative karma, then after you die you travel on a path to a bad migration. All of us want our futures to be pleasant and wholesome. In order for that to happen you have to know what is virtue and what is nonvirtue. You have to know the results of virtuous actions and nonvirtuous actions.

Śāntideva said,

> Misery arises from evil actions.
> How can you become free from misery?
> You should continually, all day and all night,
> think only about its cause. This is right.
> [*Introduction to the Practice of Bodhisattvas,* 2.62]

There are many sorts of suffering in the world. There is the misery of birth, aging, sickness, death, not getting what you desire, coming in contact with what you don't want, and so forth. You don't have the freedom to decline these experiences; they all happen even if you wish for the contrary.

Why do we suffer? Is our misery accidental? Do unpleasant experiences occur without a cause? No. Each problem we face has a primary cause along with surrounding conditions. These causes and conditions can be summarized as the ten nonvirtuous actions. There are hundreds of subdivisions within these ten broad categories. These nonvirtuous actions are the source of our suffering. The undesirable experiences you unwillingly endure in this life arise from the negative actions you engaged in during your previous lives or earlier in this life. Negative actions you do in this life will cause you misery in the future. Omniscient buddhas can see in precise detail how and why each specific problem arises. A buddha knows every variety of suffering, the causes of suffering, and how to become free from suffering. This is what the Buddha taught to us. You can study logical explanations of karmic causation in the sutras and commentaries. You may not have direct and precise knowledge of the past and the future like a buddha, but you can think about your present experiences and understand in general the causes for it. When through study and contemplation you are convinced about causality, you will have the best type of faith. You are confident that your actions, positive or negative, influence your future lives, not just this life. This conviction about causality enables you to you better control your actions. That is why Śāntideva says that it is right to think about this. You should worry about the negative things you have done and may do. You should be joyful about the positive things you have done. Later in the same text, he said,

> The Buddha taught that
> the root of all virtue is aspiration.
> And, the root of that aspiration
> is constant recollection of the results of karma.
> [*Introduction to the Practice of Bodhisattvas,* 7.40]

How do you create positive wholesome actions? The source of positive activity is your mental attitude. For example, you think, "From now on, I will not kill, I will not steal, I will not lie. I will resist these and all other negative actions for they are the enemy of my future well-being. I regret and want to purify any negative actions that I have done. I will always do wholesome actions. I will always take joy in doing virtuous actions. I wish to do those virtuous actions that I have not yet done." This aspirational attitude naturally leads you to want to do wholesome actions and to dislike unwholesome actions. Where do you get this inspiration? The Buddha taught that the root of this aspiration is to be familiar with the main results of karma. Through logical reasoning, analogies, and examples you must come to understand the results that occur when an action comes to fruition.

The Power of Actions

There are four types of karmic results. The primary result, often called the fruition, or maturation result, is a rebirth in a specific realm. We distinguish two types of karmic causes for a maturation result: projecting karma and actualizing karma. Projecting karma, or a projecting cause, is like planting a seed. The analogy here is that when you plant an apple seed the full maturation of that seed will be an apple. It is called a projecting cause because the seed does not necessarily sprout right away. It will sprout in the future when it meets the proper conditions. It remains dormant until the conditions are right; if the conditions never come together the seed will never sprout. The actualizing cause is the coming together of all the other conditions. It is like the moment of a seed's germination; all the conditions are there so the seed is ready to produce the sprout. When the cause and conditions come together the result—a life—will definitely arise.

The quality of this life and the pleasant or unpleasant experiences you have during that life are the results of other lighter, or incomplete actions. Of these there are two types of results that are similar to their cause, which are the second and third type of karmic results. Experiential results similar to their cause are occurrences within a rebirth. For example, as a result of stealing you may lose your wealth or thieves may steal your property. The other type of result similar to its cause is behavioral; you tend to act in a manner that you have before. For example, one child may instinctively share with others; another child always steals from others. The fourth type of karmic result is environmental. Your negative actions may result in your rebirth in a filthy place, a place plagued by fire, or an area with unfertile land. Going back to our apple seed example to analogize these other results, prior to the maturation of that seed into an apple a sprout grows from the seed, then a stem, a trunk, leaves, branches, and flowers. The trunk could be strong or weak. The tree could be tall or stunted. The fruit could be wormy or perfect.

From the point of view of when a karmic result will arise, there are three divisions of karma: karma that will be seen in the present life; karma that will be experienced in the next life; and karma that will be experienced in the third successive life or sometime thereafter. The first category doesn't mean that the entire karma will totally ripen in this life. The result of a very powerful action may start to be seen in this life, but its main maturation, a future rebirth, will come in the next life. The second type of karma's result will occur in the next life. The third type of karma will mature sometime in the future after your next life.

All actions go through one of three doors: body, speech, or mind. You need to know when to open these doors and when to shut them. It is most important for you to open the door to the ten basic virtues and shut the door on their opposites, the ten negative actions. What makes an action nonvirtuous? If an action harms another being it is unwholesome. What are the ten basic actions that harm others? Three are created through physical activity: killing, stealing, and sexual misconduct. Four are created through speech: lying, divisive words, harsh words, and senseless speech. And three are related to your mind: desire, malice, and wrong views. The practice of virtue is to control yourself by understanding what these are and avoiding them. There is no other list of actions more essential to Dharma practice.

Not every action is equally powerful. In other words, not every action causes a result of equal intensity. What makes a particular action, say telling a lie, heavier or lighter than another instance of lying? The difference is whether the action is complete. There are four necessary factors for an action to be complete: (1) an afflicted state of mind, (2) an intention, (3) undertaking the action, and (4) completing the action. All samsaric karma, or activity, whether positive or negative, is influenced by the mental afflictions. (Buddhas engage in action, but their actions are not samsaric because they are not influenced by the three poisons.) In addition to an underlying mental affliction, to complete an action you have to have the intent to do that particular action. There are two parts to an intention: (1) your conscious thought to do an action and (2) a clear and accurate perception of the object of action. The object, or base, of an action is whatever is acted upon. For example, if the action is killing, the object is a living being; if the action is stealing, the object is the thing that you take. An accurate perception of the object means that you must correctly identify the object at the time you engage in the action. Let's say you want to kill a deer based on the mental affliction that hunting is fun and a good sport. You decide to hunt a deer. Then, you go outside, see a deer, and shoot it. In this case, you have the underlying mental affliction of ignorance, the intention to kill, and you clearly identified the object of your intent. But it is possible to misperceive an object at the time of the action. Continuing the above example, let's say you shoot a dog because you didn't clearly perceive the animal in the bushes; you thought it was a deer, but it wasn't. Or let's say your intent is to kill a particular buck but you kill a doe; you have killed a deer but not the right one. Another example of an incorrect perception of the object is to step on a bug without knowing you have done so. You didn't see the insect and had no plan to kill it, so there was no clear perception of the object and no conscious intent. In all of these cases of inaccurate perception you haven't perfectly completed the action. Of course, you have created a negative action: you killed an animal or an insect. But it isn't as heavy a karma as it would been if all the factors were complete.

Now if these first two features—the underlying mental affliction and the intent including an accurate perception of the object—are present, but you don't actually begin or finish doing the action, then the action is also not complete. Say you decide to kill something but then don't actually do it; or you try to kill a particular creature but it doesn't die: in both cases the action isn't complete. Beginning an action involves some kind of effort: either you do it yourself or you incite someone else to do it. So, in the hunting example, you don't actually have to do the shooting yourself. If on your order or due to your encouragement someone else kills a deer, it is just as if you killed the creature yourself. Concluding an action is to finish doing what you made a conscious effort to do. The completion doesn't have to be immediate. In our example, let's say the deer doesn't die right away; maybe it lives for months but eventually dies from the gunshot wound. When the deer dies, that is the conclusion of the action. In any case, when all four factors are present—the mental affliction, the intent with accurate perception, engaging in the action, and completing the action—then the path of action is complete. Keep this framework in mind as we look at each of the ten nonvirtuous actions.

The Three Physical Actions: (1) Killing, (2) Stealing, and (3) Sexual Misconduct

Killing is the destruction of the life-force of a sentient being. The object of killing is a living being with a mental continuum. Therefore, a tree is not an object of the negative action of killing because although a tree is alive it is not a sentient being with a mental continuum. Many different mental afflictions can underlie a desire to kill. People kill due to ignorance, hatred, and desire. Following the mental affliction, there can be general motivation and specific motivation. For example, wanting to kill all the cockroaches in your house is a generalized motivation; wanting to kill a particular living being is a specific motivation. As above, accurate perception of the object is critical for a complete action. If you accidentally kill without the intention to do so or inaccurately identify what you are deliberately killing, that action is incomplete. There are various opinions about whether it is negative karma if you have no desire to kill. Some say that it isn't negative karma at all; others say it is an incomplete negative karma so the result will be less severe than if it were a complete action of killing. In general, the action of killing is complete when the being you want to kill is dead. However, let's say that you want to kill someone and you engage in an action that kills the person. However, before they died you changed your mind. You wished that you had not done something to kill them, but they still died. In this case, your intention wasn't complete. It is a lighter action. Or, let's say that you die before the person that you attempt to kill dies. In this case you had the mental affliction, motivation, perception of the object, and began the action. However, you died before the action reached completion. Therefore, the last factor was not complete.

Stealing is taking for yourself property that belongs to someone else. This is a negative action because taking others' things without their permission harms the owners. The base of the action is someone else's possession. If a thing is given to you, that's not stealing. There also must be the motivation to take possession of an object. And the object must be accurately perceived to belong to someone else. It is not an accurate perception to take something while thinking that it is yours, or to take something that actually is yours thinking that it belongs to someone else. The affliction can be any of the three poisons. When is an action of stealing finished? The Vinaya provides a strict interpretation; it says stealing is complete when you remove an object from where it was originally. You don't even need to carry it any distance away. However, there is a lot of discussion in various commentaries about whether the Vinaya definition is suitable in all cases. Stealing can be done by subterfuge, by force, or by trickery: you can steal a house from someone, but you don't actually move the house; you can borrow money with no intention of paying it back. Thus, moving an object and making it your own is just an example. The main thing here in terms of finishing the action is thinking, "Now I've got it." No matter what type of effort you made, the action is complete when you think the object is in your possession. Stealing can be taking even a tiny thing, a small stick that you know belongs to someone else, but you want it, take it, and then think it is yours.

The Vinaya explication of stealing is more stringent and more specific because it is setting forth rules for monks and nuns who have taken vows. The Vinaya lays out many levels of downfalls. The differences are based on what type of thing you steal, the cost of the item, how much you steal, and how much of an impact it has on others. The Vinaya was written a long time ago so the amounts can seem very minor. A few pennies were a lot of money twenty-five hundred years ago! But here we are talking about laypeople together with those who have taken vows. Thus, when we discuss a negative action, it is an action that is naturally negative, not an action that is negative because it involves breaking a vow. So, the details are a little different regarding the completion of the action.

A similar issue comes up in terms of sexual misconduct. Here we are not talking about breaking the vows of celibacy taken by the ordained. If you have a vow of celibacy you promise to completely avoid sexual activity. The explanation of sexual misconduct is for people who have a commitment to each other and are in a sexual relationship. It is not wrong for married or otherwise committed people to have sex. However, there are commonsense things that are harmful and turn sex into misconduct. For example, engaging in sexual contact with a man or woman who is not your partner can be very painful to your spouse or the other person's spouse.

The purpose of the teaching on sexual misconduct is to contain wild and extreme desire. When your desires are out of control, you go after all the sexual partners you can reach. As a practitioner, your goal is to eliminate, or at least reduce, your desire for sensual pleasure. Because sexual activity can lead to even more desire, you intentionally try to curtail it. This is about training yourself gradually, eventually culminating in complete celibacy. Traditional Vinaya texts offer a list of types of sexual misconduct that pertain to sex even with your own partner or spouse. First, it is not proper to engage in sexual activity in the wrong location. This pertains to an external locale, say in public, in front of your guru, or at a holy site, as well as sexual contact with a non-sex organ. Next, it is not right to engage in sexual activity at the wrong time, for example, when someone is ill or has taken precepts. Traditionally it is taught that a person should not have sex with another person of the same sex. Given the last stricture, a lot of people ask me if this means that same-sex relationships are wrong. There are different cultural contexts, customs, and perspectives about sexual relationships. So, laypeople today should act in the best and least harmful way that they can. The logical limitations on sexual conduct for heterosexual relationships also apply to same-sex couples. Of course, celibacy is best for working toward freedom from the mental afflictions. But if you can't completely avoid sexual contact, you should try to control yourself in a simpler way. There are many levels of virtuous conduct; you start with rough limitations on negative actions, move on to intermediate, and then gradually add more and more subtle limitations.

The Four Verbal Actions: (1) Lying, (2) Divisive speech, (3) Harsh speech, and (4) Senseless talk

Many negative actions can be done verbally, but they can be subsumed under four general categories: (1) lying, (2) divisive speech, (3) harsh speech, and (4) senseless idle talk. Just as with physical activity, the heaviness of a verbal action depends upon the completeness of the action. The action is lighter if the four factors—the object, the thought that includes the motivation and perception of the object, the action itself, and the completion of the action—are not complete.

The purpose of telling a lie is to make someone believe something that is not the case. The object of a lie is something that you have experienced with your five physical senses or your mind. The lie is saying something contrary to what you have seen, heard, smelled, tasted, touched, or cognized. For example, if you see something but say that you didn't see it, that is a lie; if you didn't hear something but say that you did hear it, that is a lie; or, if you say you know something but you really don't know it, that is a lie. You lie when you deliberately disguise what you have actually perceived. Engaging in the action is to verbalize this misrepresentation so that someone else hears it. The completion of the action is when someone hears what you have said. It doesn't matter if that person believes you.

Even if they don't, it is still a lie. There is a lot of detail about lying in the scriptures. The worst type of lie is to tell a mistruth about having superior qualities yourself or lying about someone with those extraordinary qualities. It is important to not pretend that you are above the ordinary. Claiming, "I have realized emptiness," or "I saw Buddha," when you have not is a major lie.

The object of divisive speech is two people. They can close friends, mere associates, or even unfriendly toward each other. The motivation is to make these two people dislike each other because of what you say. Your words separate those who have harmonious relations with each other and drive those who are already unfriendly further apart. It doesn't matter if what you say is true; the intent is to create disharmony. An accurate perception of the object pertains to those two people whom you targeted for your divisive words. If you mistake who you are talking to for someone else, the heaviness of the action is a bit less. There will still be a negative result, because your intent was to utter divisive words and you did so. The action is complete when someone hears what you said.

Harsh speech stems from animosity; you want to say something that will hurt a particular person. It is shooting an arrow of words such as, "You thief!" "You snake!" The object of the action is another person, your intent is to harm them with your words and you must perceive the person correctly, the action is to speak with a desire to harm, and the completion of the action is to finish saying it. It doesn't matter if the other person doesn't hear you. It doesn't matter if the other person hears you but misunderstands you. Here, simply saying the harsh words is the final factor that completes the action.

Senseless speech is gossiping, chitchat, or telling stories without any intent to hurt or deceive. It is just idle talk. But even if you don't mean to produce desire, jealousy, or resentment in someone else, that can happen as a result of frivolous chatter. Therefore, practitioners try to avoid speaking about senseless things. They stay quiet; they do not talk too much. We have a saying in Tibetan, "If you don't control your little oval tongue, you may hurt your big round head."

The preceding seven actions involve body and speech. They all have a physical aspect; they are external actions. Those actions stem from a motivation, in other words from mental actions.

The Three Mental Actions: (1) Covetousness, (2) Malice, and (3) Wrong views

Covetousness is a desire to possess something that isn't yours. For example, you go to a big department store to buy a small pen, but once you see all the things available there you feel great desire for so much more. Some people can go into stores and are not affected. Others become so filled with covetousness they can't even sleep at night. The object of covetousness is something that belongs to someone else. The thought is wanting that item for yourself. You have to recognize the item and have desire it. The completion of the action is when a determined thought arises in your mind that you wish to appropriate it for yourself. Thus, in this context covetousness doesn't encompass every type of attraction, attachment, or desire.

The object and thought of malice are the same as those explained for harsh speech. It is a desire to harm someone else. Here it isn't about the action of hitting someone, taking up a weapon, or saying something cruel. It is simply the desire to hurt someone. The final factor that makes the action complete is to decide that you will injure the other person in some manner.

There are many types of wrong views. Some wrong views put a positive spin on things, for example, thinking impure things are pure or thinking that impermanent things will last forever. But in this context, we are talking only about views that lead you away from positive actions and instead induce you to engage in negative actions. The base of a wrong view is something that is true, for example the law of cause and effect, the four realities for āryas, or the existence of past and future lives. These are all true. The wrong view is to believe that they are false; in other words, denying the existence of karmic causality, future lives, nirvana, and so forth. You complete the action when you totally reject that virtue leads to happiness and nonvirtue is the cause of suffering; deny that there is suffering, a cause of suffering, freedom from suffering, and a path to liberation from suffering; and disallow the existence of past and future lives. These wrong ideas are all forms of nihilism. Nihilism is one of the most powerful types of ignorance because it destroys spiritual practice. For example, if you believe that after death the body and mind simply disintegrate into elements and nothing continues, you will have no impetus to pursue spiritual goals. Your potential for spiritual life is destroyed. If you do not have faith in causality, you feel free to do anything. The right view, from the conventional perspective, is that there is causality—a connection between cause and effect.

If you want to learn more about the ten nonvirtues, you should read Asaṅga's *Compendium of Determinations.*

To summarize, negative actions are those that harm others and yourself. The severity of the result of a negative action is dependent on four factors. If all of them are present, it is a heavy karma. If some are not present, the karma is lighter. A heavy, or complete karma results in rebirth in a certain realm. The pleasant or unpleasant experiences you have during that life are the results of other actions. You should always be watchful and try to avoid engaging in negative actions. Avoidance has two aspects: abstaining from doing the action and distancing yourself from the object of the action. To refrain from doing the action is clear. In order to do that sometimes you need to avoid the base or object of that action. For example, if you have a strong desire for something, you may lose control whenever you are in proximity to it. So, it is better to stay away that object. Or, if something makes you angry, you should not go near it because you might lose control and act out of annoyance.

You should conclude from this discussion that Dharma practice is not simply sitting still in meditation. Dharma practice is to be aware of your three doors of action. Mindfulness of your body, speech, and mind is most important. From understanding the nonvirtues and their results, you will decide not to engage in those actions. From understanding the virtues and their results, you will decide to do them. In short, virtue isn't done accidently; it is making a decision and then mindfully not engaging in the opposite nonvirtue. If acting virtuously were simply not doing something, then trees and rocks would have perfect ethical conduct. Realizing that you've done something wrong and feeling regret is part of purification. A useful guilty feeling makes your negative action weaker and keeps you from doing that type of action in the future. A stupid guilty feeling doesn't have any purpose. It is often something out of desire, like, "Why did I buy that?"

How to Practice Virtue

In order to successfully avoid the ten nonvirtues and engage in virtue, Nāgārjuna advises us to do two things in the final two lines of verse 5:

> 5cd. Refrain from intoxicants and likewise
>   take true delight in a virtuous livelihood.

Traditionally intoxicants were understood to be any type of drink— beer, wine, grain alcohol, etc.—that alters your mind. Nowadays we need to expand that definition to any substance that causes lack of control of your body and mind. When you are confused by intoxicants you cannot tell right from wrong. You become careless and you don't know what you are doing. You don't know what you will do when you are intoxicated. For that reason, the Buddha told his disciples—monks, nuns, and laypeople with vows—that they should not drink even the amount of alcohol equivalent to a drop of dew on a blade of grass. That tiny amount might not be intoxicating. However, the problem is that you don't know precisely how much will affect you. Most people are not aware of when they begin to be impaired; they deny that they are drunk or high on drugs.

The Buddha said that taking an intoxicant is not a negative action in and of itself. There are two types of negative actions: those that are naturally bad and those that contravene a rule of conduct. The latter type of action is bad only for those who have taken that vow of religious conduct. Drinking itself isn't naturally bad; it doesn't throw you into hell or a lower rebirth. But the loss of control from taking intoxicants might lead you to do all kinds of negative actions. The evil things you do when intoxicated will propel you to the lower realms. In that regard it can be said that intoxicants are the root of all faults. Therefore, although taking intoxicants isn't one of the ten root nonvirtuous actions, there is a religious rule against it. Because they are so dangerous, intoxicants are prohibited right from the beginning.

There is a story that illustrates this point. At the time of the Buddha, a fully ordained monk was walking along a road. A woman came up to him carrying a full bottle of liquor and leading a goat. She said to the monk, "You must do one of three things otherwise I will kill myself right in front of you. You choose: either drink the alcohol, kill this goat for me, or have sex with me. Those are your choices; if you don't do one of them then I will die." The monk had a big dilemma. He didn't want to hurt the woman or the goat. If he killed the goat, it would be a very heavy negative karma. If he engaged in sex, he would lose his vow of celibacy and no longer be a monk. So he decided that his best choice was to drink the liquor. Actually, that was the worst choice. After he drank it, he lost control of his inhibitions and had sex with the woman. Then he was hungry and killed the goat for dinner.

So, a little wine might taste sweet, but it doesn't lead to anything good. It can lead people to kill each other, harm their children, or cause fatal motor-vehicle accidents. Nowadays we should be more intelligent about what is harmful to ourselves and others. But even two millennia after the Buddha gave this advice we still are indulging in intoxicants. Monks and nuns take a vow to avoid this. Those who take lay vows also promise not to drink. When you do not have this vow, in a sense you are free to drink. But keep in mind that this opens you up to many dangerous situations. It is easier to remember to watch what you do when you take a vow. Your friends or parents might say you are crazy not to drink, but now you can make the excuse that you have a vow. No one will kill you if you don't drink, but it isn't easy to avoid. Don't justify drinking because you are tired or among friends. No matter what the situation, the time, or the context you should recollect the negative aspects of drinking. (Of course, if an intoxicant of some sort is prescribed as medication, it can be taken in controlled amounts and conditions.) When the negative consequences of intoxicants strongly come to mind anytime you are tempted to indulge, you will have the confidence and ability to refrain.

The second recommendation Nāgārjuna gives us to help us practice the ten virtues and avoid nonvirtues, is to have a good livelihood. This doesn't simply mean how you earn an income. It also includes advice regarding how to maintain your health, eat properly, and protect your body. You should enjoy things that do not harm yourself or others. Partake of food, beverages, exercise, and so forth that are not causes of carelessness, do not lead to harmful actions, and that promote a virtuous life. The purpose of Dharma practice is not to punish yourself. You need to nourish your body and mind so that you can maintain and use your life. In this regard, right livelihood means you should take care of your body in order to provide a good support for your mind.

Spiritual Goals

The next verse provides additional advice regarding how to attain positive goals beyond this life. There are two spiritual goals for your future: a mundane temporary goal and a supramundane permanent goal. To attain both these goals, Nāgārjuna introduces the practices of the six perfections: (1) generosity, (2) ethical discipline, (3) patience, (4) enthusiastic perseverance, (5) concentration, and (6) wisdom. Although usually understood as unique to the Mahayana, these six practices are common to every form of Buddhism.

How to Attain Your Temporary Goal

The first goal is a high rebirth in samsara. You don't strive for a high rebirth in order to obtain the comforts of a pleasant life; you want this good situation so that you can continue to work for your permanent goals. You need a series of high rebirths suitable for practicing the Dharma in order to completely escape from samsara by attaining either nirvana or enlightenment. If you do not work hard to attain the temporary goal, you might create masses of negative karma. Then after death you will fall to one of the three lower realms and lose for a long, long time the opportunity to make progress toward your ultimate goal.

To obtain a result you must create the cause for it. The cause for a high rebirth is pure ethical conduct. There is no other cause for a life as a human, demigod, or god than creating positive karma and avoiding negative karma. But attaining a life as a human or god through the practice of ethical conduct is not enough; not every life in the upper realms is conducive to practice. What makes a high rebirth suitable for Dharma practice? The necessary conditions can be described as possession of four excellent qualities. First, you need some wealth. It doesn't have to be a lot, but if you are impoverished all your time and energy goes into searching for food and other necessities. Second, you need a healthy body and fully functional mind. Third, you need associates and friends who are helpful. Finally, you need perseverance, the ability to successfully complete whatever you start. When you have a human rebirth with these qualities there are no obstacles to practice: your body and mind are serviceable; you are not sidetracked by a need for sustenance; your associates naturally assist you; and you have the determination and tenacity to succeed. What are the causes for these excellent qualities? By practicing generosity, you will have wealth in your next life. The practice of patience results in having friends and helpers. Taking joy in acting virtuously is the practice of diligence; it is the cause for you to follow through in the future.

In the next verse Nāgārjuna emphasizes adding the practice of generosity to pure conduct.

> 6. Knowing that wealth is ephemeral and insubstantial,
>   exert yourself to properly engage in generosity
>   toward the ordained, brahmins, the poor, and friends.
>   There is no better friend for your future than generosity.

Usually, we are stingy. We want more and more, and newer and better things no matter how much we have. We don't want to give away anything that we have accumulated. Not wanting to share the smallest thing even though you are wealthy is the cause to be reborn as a hungry ghost. And even if you are reborn human, the result of stinginess is to be poor, to live in a filthy place, and suffer scarcity. Why would you want to be reborn like that? The antidote to stinginess is to understand that things are impermanent. Things change every moment and soon will disintegrate. This is obvious with food: one day it is fresh and the next day it is rotten. This is true for every possession; your clothing, house, furniture, and so on get older moment by moment. Nothing will last forever. Right now, you may have great wealth, but no matter how much you accumulate it is only temporary. In addition, although you think your possessions are truly wonderful, these things do not have a definitive perfect essence, purpose, or meaning. They can give you a small amount of pleasure here and there, they can look nice and shiny on the surface temporarily, but there is not much gained from having them. By nature they are hollow and can bring a lot of suffering. You eat food for nourishment, but that very food might make you deathly ill. Something that you enjoyed when you were young can be very dangerous when you are older. Protecting your possessions causes you anxiety and worry. You engage in all sorts of squabbles and fights over your possessions, but they will not help you at the time of your death. Knowing this will reduce your attachment to your possessions. You become able to share what you have with others.

Once you want to share your wealth, how do you properly engage in generosity? You must consider the recipients of your generosity, your attitude when being generous, and the manner in which you give. The power of generosity to create a result partially depends upon to whom you give. Generosity toward those with higher spiritual qualities creates more merit than giving to those with fewer qualities. The practice of generosity is like planting a seed for your future lives. Farmers plant seeds in expectation of a harvest. If the soil is good, rich with fertilizer and moisture, then the result will be much better than if a field is sandy and rocky. In spiritual terms, we can plant the seed of generosity in the higher field by making offerings to those with an altruistic mind, those who have spiritual attainments, and so forth. Or you can plant in the lower field: the elderly, the sick, the impoverished, and animals. Nāgārjuna lists a variety of potential recipients, starting with two on a higher level. The ordained are monks and nuns with a complete set of vows; men and women dedicating themselves to the practice of virtue are not ordinary. Brahmins, here, also indicates a higher level of spiritual being. Bodhisattvas and āryas are not mentioned but they are included implicitly. The next two categories of recipients are ordinary. Although he only mentions the poor, this implies the entire lower field. Last, he mentions friends. This category includes more than your peers. Your parents were your first friends. They gave you your life and protected and nourished you when you were young and helpless. It also includes your other relatives and other people who have benefitted you in either a worldly or spiritual way.

Proper generosity also includes a positive attitude. You should make offerings and give charitable donations with compassion, love, and faith. If instead your motivation is anger or annoyance, you are not practicing properly. The physical manner in which you give is also important. It is not pleasant for your recipient if you give in a sloppy way, just throwing down some food in front of them. Instead, you should respectfully set out what you give in a way that makes your recipient happy. When done properly you will create great merit even if you give something small.

Wealth is good if you can use it. Wealth in itself has no essence, but you can make it have a valuable purpose by making offerings to those practicing religion, being charitable to those in need, and helping your friends. If you do this, in your next life everything you need will arise naturally. Ordinary friends can turn away when you need help. The practice of generosity is never like that. Your best friend, the thing that can help you the most in the future, is being generous.

But beware. Do not focus solely on the practice of generosity. Candrakīrti, the great Madhyamaka scholar of the seventh century, warned,

> From generosity, wealth is found even in inferior migrations;
> this occurs when a person breaks the legs of ethical discipline.
> This is like spending the capital along with its interest;
> no further wealth arises from then on.
> [*Entering the Middle Way*, 2.4]

Remember, you want the results of your generosity to occur in a higher rebirth. Even if you are very generous, you will take a lower rebirth if your conduct isn't pure, in other words, if you "break the legs" of your ethical discipline. If you practice generosity but don't at the same time create a foundation of ethical discipline, you could end up like a pet dog in the United States. Being reborn as a dog is the result of negative karma. But a pet dog experiences the result of a previous practice of generosity. The dog is given a nice house, served food and drink, kept warm, petted, and cared for in all sorts of ways. The dog lives like a king. The dog didn't do anything in its current life to get all this. It enjoys these physical comforts as a result of the practice of generosity in a past life. So, what's wrong with that? The problem is that a dog cannot create merit. Its positive experience uses up the power of past virtuous actions, but no further practice of virtue is done for the future. It is like capital and interest. If you use up the capital, then no more interest will accrue. Better than you use your life in a way that increases this capital of virtue.

Candrakīrti goes on to say,

> When good qualities grow in the field of ethical discipline
> there will be an uninterrupted enjoyment of their fruit.
> [*Entering the Middle Way*, 2.6cd]

As a result of the practice of ethical discipline, along with the practice of generosity, you will have a good rebirth in a nice environment, you will be free from poverty, and you will have associates who serve and help you. Every worldly thing you need will be there: food, clothing, shelter, possessions, health, beauty, and others' love and respect. With all this you have the intelligence, resources, and capacity for further practice of virtue. You can continue, and do even better than what you have previously done.

Śāntideva cautions us to not waste this opportunity:

If I don't engage in virtuous activities,
when I have a fortunate situation for creating virtue,
then what can I possibly do when experiencing
all types of suffering and ignorance in the lower realms?
[*Introduction to the Practice of Bodhisattvas,* 4.18]

You can learn what is right and what is wrong. You can use your life to gain peace for yourself and others. This is a rare opportunity. If you don't use it, your situation is hopeless. After death you will fall to a bad rebirth. In addition to suffering there, you will be completely ignorant. You won't know that there is the possibility of permanent peace and happiness, nor will you know the method to get there. You will naturally do evil and destructive things thinking that they are for your own benefit. Trying to satisfy your desires, you will create the causes for further bad rebirths. In short, you will be stupid. This isn't stupidity in the common sense. Here it means that you will be completely ignorant of how to create the causes for liberation from suffering. A human life is the opportunity to create the causes for the attainment of permanent peace. If you can't reach that high goal in this lifetime, at least you can protect yourself in future lives. That is why the practices of morality and generosity are so important for both laypeople and the ordained.

With that in mind, Nāgārjuna says to the king,

7. You should practice morality that is unimpaired,
    not degraded, unsullied, and free from contamination.
    Just as the earth supports all animate and inanimate things,
    ethical conduct is the foundation for all good qualities.

There are a lot of adjectives describing proper ethical conduct here! They are derived from a traditional list of the qualities of good conduct. First, ethical conduct should be unimpaired. This means that you are careful to not break any of the rules or vows you have taken. Second, ethical conduct should not be degraded. This is a way of saying that your motivation to engage in ethical discipline should be without flaws. The flaws are any of the three poisons. In the *Treasury of Knowledge* (4.123) Vasubandhu says that pure morality is not tainted with immorality or the causes of immorality. The three poisonous attitudes—desire, hatred, and ignorance—are the main causes of immoral activity. You try not to act under their influence.

Next, ethical conduct should be unsullied or unmixed. Superficially this sounds like it repeats the prior quality—that your conduct should not be mixed with faults. But here "unsullied" indicates an antidote to those faults. An antidote is a meditation or realization that reduces or completely eliminates a mental affliction. For example, one antidote to desire is to meditate on the impurity of bodies. The point here is that your conduct is not only unmixed with a mental affliction but instead it is powered by an antidote to a mental affliction. If greed, hatred, ignorance, or any other mental affliction arises you should meditate on the appropriate antidote. If you reduce the mental affliction, then you will not engage in actions motivated by that mental affliction. Most negative actions are undertaken because of a variety of the mental afflictions. For example, killing can be motivated by hatred. Another person's reason to kill may not be anger; they might desire an animal's skin or flesh. Stupidity can motivate killing too: for example, thinking that you will become famous for catching a big fish. Killing is the negative action in all these cases but the antidote to apply is different in each instance.

The next quality is that ethical conduct should be free from contamination. In other words, your good conduct should not be smeared or tainted by a worldly motivation. To engage in ethical conduct because you think that by doing so you will gain a good reputation or get something in return is to act with a worldly motivation. We usually do things for worldly reasons; and in that sense, when we act, we are the servants of samsara. When your conduct is wrapped up in a desire to get something in this life, you are not motivated by a spiritual incentive. The quality of being free from contamination implies that your motivation is positive. For example, you avoid killing because you are motivated by a wish to be free from samsara. If you are practicing morality properly it is independent of, or uncontaminated by, samsara. In short, the *Treasury of Knowledge* says your actions should be motivated by the antidotes to the three poisons, and your motivation for engaging in ethical conduct should be a desire for nirvana, everlasting peace.

Ethical discipline is the basis for higher samsaric rebirths as well as nirvana and enlightenment. So, no matter what situation you find yourself in, you should keep your ethical discipline pure. There is story in the great Indian poet Āryasūra's *Garland of Birth Stories* about stealing, but it applies to avoiding the other nonvirtues too. In one of the Buddha's past lives, he was a student of a brahmin. The teacher was testing his students' knowledge, so he said, "If a brahmin is in poverty, then stealing to gain wealth is a correct practice of Dharma." In response, the student who would eventually become the Buddha said,

> It would be better to be a beggar,
> wearing rough clothes, having only a clay pot,
> and begging for food at the luxurious house of my enemy,
> than to have no shame and act contrary to the Dharma
> in order to become a powerful lord of the gods.
>
> [*Garland of Birth Stories,* 12.19]

You might be poor, your possessions may be destroyed in a fire or flood, or your wealth might be stolen by thieves, but despite these difficulties you should avoid the ten nonvirtues and keep your ethical conduct pure. A religious practitioner makes a choice. Even if they could take others' possessions, they would rather beg for food than steal. It would be better to have to beg for food from your worst enemy than to have a high worldly position because of worldly motivation and negative action.

How to Obtain Your Permanent Supramundane Goal: The Practice of the Six Perfections

The final section of Nāgārjuna's general advice regarding the practice of virtue for both laypeople and the ordained is to abide on the path of the six perfections. While the practices included in the list of six perfections are also part of the common path, here I will explain them from the Mahayana perspective.

> 8. Develop the immeasurable perfections: generosity, ethical
>   discipline,

> patience, enthusiastic perseverance, meditative stabiliza-
> tion, and wisdom.
> You will become a supreme victor after crossing
> to the far shore of the ocean of samsaric existence.

Everything you need to do to attain enlightenment is included in the six perfections. In other words, the six perfections comprise all the practices of the Mahayana path. What makes something a Mahayana practice? If whatever you practice, whether sutra or tantra, is done with the motivation of bodhicitta, it is the Mahayana. Bodhicitta is the desire to attain enlightenment in order to be able to help all other sentient beings. This motivation makes any practice of the six perfections immeasurable. The number of sentient beings is incalculable, and a Mahayana practitioner's goal is to liberate all of them. Further, because Mahayana practitioners have no selfish motivation when engaging in the countless activities necessary to attain that goal, they create an immeasurable amount of merit when they practice. Nāgārjuna advises us to develop these perfections in order to cross to the far shore of the ocean of samsara. Someone who attains enlightenment is called a *victor*. In an ordinary sense we say a king is victorious in battle. A buddha's victory is far beyond this. They have attained victory over all obstacles, mental afflictions, and undesirable experiences. Although a Hinayana arhat's victory is less complete, in that they have succeeded in conquering only the mental afflictions, they too are sometimes called *victorious ones*.

Candrakīrti explains the difference between ordinary actions and the perfection of those actions in *Entering the Middle Way*. I'll talk about this in terms of generosity, the first perfection, but this discussion pertains to all the other perfections too. You can give gifts in an ordinary way, a Hinayana way, or a Mahayana way. Ordinary generosity can be tinged with selfishness: you give hoping to get something back later. But even if generosity is practiced with a virtuous motivation, it is not necessarily a Mahayana practice. Whether it is a Mahayana practice is not based on the item that you give nor on the recipient to whom you give. It is based on a how you understand the world. There are two aspects to this manner of understanding: method and wisdom.

The method side is the bodhicitta motivation; you do certain activities because you want enlightenment, but not for just yourself. You realize that all sentient beings are suffering. You feel unbearable compassion and love for them because they have been suffering from time without beginning and even now see no relief. Therefore, you want to attain enlightenment quickly because it is the only way to help them. Sometimes in shorthand we say that bodhicitta is the *mind of enlightenment* or the *mind of awakening*. In Tibetan we say that actions *held by* bodhicitta are Mahayana activity; in English it is clearer to say that an action motivated by, or governed by, bodhicitta is a Mahayana action.

There is a story in the sutras illustrating the importance of motivation. During his lifetime the Buddha became quite famous. So, a powerful king decided to invite the Buddha and his retinue to the palace for a meal. He thought that by doing this he too would become more famous. He expected that his generosity to the Buddha would garner him even more respect and honor from others. It would even increase his power. In short, his motivation for generosity was completely worldly. At this time there was a very poor beggar who would lie down outside the palace gates every day hoping to get something to eat. Seeing the lavish preparations the king made for the Buddha, the beggar thought, "I am so poor. I cannot make an offering like this. The king is so fortunate! Not only does he have a wonderful life but now he is accumulating great merit by offering a meal to the Buddha and his Sangha." The beggar spent the whole day rejoicing in the virtue of the king. It was customary that at the conclusion of an offering the Buddha would say a prayer dedicating the merit gained. On this day he mentioned the merit of the beggar but didn't mention the king. One of his disciples asked, "Why didn't you mention the king who made such a magnificent offering? Why did you say the name of that beggar?" The Buddha responded, "The king didn't create much merit today. The beggar created a lot of merit because he spent the day rejoicing in the offering. In that way he made far more merit than the king."

Wisdom is the other factor that determines whether an action is a perfection. Wisdom is understanding the true nature of all phenomena. It is knowing that all things are empty of ultimate existence, that they have a dependent or relative nature, that there is cause and effect, and that things are like an illusion. (This will be discussed in more detail in chapter 4. Here I'll just give a summary.) To apply this understanding to the perfection of generosity, you think about the emptiness of the three spheres: the recipient to whom you give, the things that are given, and the giver. Alternatively, sometimes the three spheres are listed as the recipient to whom you give, the things that are given, and the action of giving. Both lists encompass every aspect of the act of generosity. Whenever a bodhisattva practices generosity, they should understand that these three spheres do not have a permanent or absolute intrinsic identity. Giving done with the understanding of the emptiness of the three spheres is pure and perfect giving.

It is not the perfection of generosity to give, thinking, "I'm absolutely existent, I am giving an intrinsically real thing, and the recipient of my gift is also ultimately real." To conceive of something as *real* means that you believe that thing exists as it appears, under the misapprehension that things have an autonomous intrinsic identity or essence. I'm not saying that you shouldn't give at all if you don't understand the true nature of reality. However, giving without understanding that the ultimate nature of the gift, the recipient, and the giver is ordinary generosity. Ordinary generosity always has a subtle level of desire. Even ordinary generosity is good, but it isn't the perfection of generosity. The mundane perfection of generosity is to give with a bodhicitta motivation. The supramundane perfection of generosity is giving while understanding reality.

When talking about the perfection of generosity on the first level of the bodhisattva path, Candrakīrti said,

> Giving while understanding that the gift, the recipient, and the
>   giver
> are empty is called a supramundane perfection.
> If desire for these three elements arises
> it is called a mundane perfection.
> [Entering the Middle Way, 1.16]

A supramundane perfection is a combination of the bodhicitta motivation, the wisdom understanding emptiness, and an action. All the perfections—for example, ethical conduct and patience—differ from ordinary actions because the supramundane perfections are motivated by bodhicitta and done with the understanding of the ultimate nature of reality. You can't get enlightened just by a mere wish. It is a very nice to think, "I want to attain enlightenment as soon as possible for the benefit of sentient beings." But to attain enlightenment you have to do something to fulfil that wish. What do you need to do? You do all the bodhisattva practices of the six perfections. You think, "By giving may I easily attain enlightenment as soon as possible for the benefit of others." That is the background attitude, the motivation of bodhicitta. Then when you actually give you must have wisdom. You don't perceive the gift, giver, and recipient as intrinsically real; you understand that the way things appear is not the way that they ultimately exist; you understand that all phenomena lack an independent, substantive substrata or identity. In short you understand emptiness. You give with method and wisdom combined. Then even a tiny gift, just a mouthful of food, is huge. In contrast, if you give a palace full of treasure because you want to garner praise, worldly power, or a bigger return later, and if you think these things exist as they appear, then it is just a small gift.

It is difficult to practice generosity with a good, compassionate motivation and an understanding of reality. So where do you start? The first step in the practice of generosity is to give mentally. There are many steps between imagining giving something and actually physically doing it. When you reach a certain level, you can give your body and your merit. But doing so is complicated. Don't try this for the time being! Bodhisattvas can make those gifts all the time because they have bodhicitta and wisdom. But until you attain that state you can't give your body directly. However, you can mentally practice giving without any stinginess or miserliness. Even this is difficult. Usually, people have some desire for their own benefit.

The perfection of generosity doesn't mean that you have given everyone everything that they need or desire. Śāntideva said,

> If the perfection of generosity were
> the elimination of poverty in the world,
> in what manner did previous buddhas perfect it
> since there are still impoverished beings now?
>
> The perfection of generosity is said to be
> the intention to give to all beings everything,
> along with what results from such a thought.
> Hence it is basically a state of mind.
>
> [*Introduction to the Practice of Bodhisattvas, 5.9–10*]

Another way to describe the causes necessary for enlightenment are the two types of accumulation: the accumulation of merit and the accumulation of wisdom. Merit, or virtue, is wholesome action. Just one merit won't get you to enlightenment; you need a vast amount. It will take more than one day to create this much merit, perhaps life after life over many eons. Along with merit you need the accumulation of wisdom. Wisdom is the realization of emptiness that comes from continuously concentrating on ultimate reality. You need both of these two accumulations to attain enlightenment. To generate the two accumulations all you need to do is to practice the six perfections. The perfections of generosity, ethical discipline and patience are for the accumulation of merit. The perfections of meditative stabilization and wisdom are for the accumulation of wisdom. The perfection of perseverance applies to both.

In the method of practice taught in the sutras, to accumulate the merit required for attainment of the physical, or form, body of a Buddha ordinary beings and bodhisattvas practice for three countless eons. (*Countless* is the name for a very large number that is virtually beyond calculation.) While they are in samsara for this long period of time, the first three perfections are the causes for a high rebirth. In other words, the practices of generosity, ethical discipline, and patience result in a human life with all the requisite conditions for practice. For this reason, laypeople are strongly urged to practice generosity, ethical discipline, and patience. Laypeople must engage in so many activities; they don't have the time to sit and meditate much. They have so many responsibilities in connection with owning a house, having a job, rearing children, and so forth. They have less opportunity than monks or nuns to develop meditative stabilization and wisdom. However, they can easily practice generosity. But generosity without restraint from harmful actions can lead to rich life in the lower realms. The essence of ethical conduct is deliberate nonviolence. It is the conscious avoidance of harming others with your body, speech, and mind either directly or indirectly. But what about when someone else harms you? We all get angry and upset if someone treats us poorly. When someone hits you once, you tend to want to hit back twice. Thus, a lack of patience makes you unable to keep your pure conduct. Therefore, the practice of patience, the ability to bear whatever others do, is also a critical layperson's practice. In short, these three practices—generosity, ethical conduct, and patience—are closely intertwined.

A bodhisattva's motivation, whether they are ordained or are a layperson, is to attain enlightenment in order to help other sentient beings. To progress on the path to enlightenment they need some kind of vehicle. So, until they attain enlightenment, bodhisattvas strive to have the kind of body and mind suitable for practice. They work for the temporary goal of a high rebirth on the way to the perfection of buddhahood. It is the practice of the first three perfections that will result in this type of life and eventually will result in the ultimate perfect physical body of a buddha. In other words, the accumulation of merit is the cause for both a higher rebirth and a buddha's perfect form body. The latter includes the thirty-two major marks and eighty minor marks of their body, speech, and environment or pure land. It encompasses every aspect of a buddha's physical form. Candrakīrti said,

> The Sugata praised the three practices, generosity
> and so forth, as being for householders primarily.
> These constitute the collection of merit;
> they are the cause for a buddha's physical embodiment.
> [*Entering the Middle Way*, 3.12]

To accumulate wisdom, you practice the final two perfections: meditative stabilization and wisdom. These practices are primarily for those who have dedicated their lives to the practice of the Dharma. This doesn't mean that laypeople do not practice them, but in general laypeople are like the king that Nāgārjuna is addressing in this text. They can do many things that are beneficial for others, but sitting on a cushion and meditating probably will not be their principal practice. This certainly doesn't mean that laypeople cannot practice the latter two perfections; nor does it mean that the ordained don't need to practice the first three perfections. Neither should exclude the other; it is simply a matter of the main emphasis in their practice.

Meditative stabilization enables you to temporarily control and subdue the mental afflictions. It is on this basis that you can develop wisdom. Wisdom is understanding the true nature of reality and so permanently eliminates ignorance and the mental afflictions from the root. These two practices are the cause for a buddha's perfect mind, the dharmakāya. The dharmakāya is a buddha's perfect gnosis: it is perfect emptiness; it is perfect freedom; it is the complete cessation of mental afflictions. Without wisdom the other qualities of a buddha's mind would not exist. It is wisdom that is the cause for a buddha's omniscience, perfect love, and permanent peace. In order to develop that wisdom, you need the ability to concentrate on a single object for as long as you wish.

Nāgārjuna said,

> The physical body of a buddha
> arises from the accumulation of merit.
> In brief, the dharmakāya arises from the king:
> the accumulation of wisdom.
>
> [*Precious Garland,* 3.121]

In this verse "the king" isn't an ordinary king, it is a particular type of meditative concentration, called śamatha, used to develop wisdom. Śamatha is the ability of the mind to remain focused on an object of observation with complete freedom from distraction and mental laxity for as long as desired. This effortless mental flexibility and control is accompanied by physical and mental pliancy and bliss. It is complete control and calmness of mind. Just as a king has total control of his kingdom, śamatha is firm and peaceful domination of the mind. With a stable mind you can focus upon ultimate reality, emptiness. In combination, mental stability and the wisdom that understands ultimate reality are the main antidote to ignorance and the mental afflictions. Together they bring about the dharmakāya.

While meditative concentration and wisdom are the causes for a buddha's perfect mind, in another sense they are also causes for a temporary goal while still in samsara. While taking rebirth in samsara, wisdom is understanding the difference between right and wrong. We usually mix things up because we lack wisdom. Ignorance and stupidity cause us to do all kinds of negative things. Wisdom clears away stupidity; when you properly understand what is good and what is evil you won't act incorrectly. Your actions will not be the cause of misery and suffering. Bodhisattvas' miraculous activities to help others are also a result of their practice of meditation. From meditational techniques they develop the special single-pointed concentration of śamatha; they attain the effortless ability and flexible control to focus their mind on an object for as long as desired without distraction or sleepiness. When they have developed this level of meditative concentration, they will obtain five higher types of knowledge: clairvoyance, clairaudience, telepathy, some limited ability to see past lives, and limited ability to know others' next life. Bodhisattvas use these abilities to help others on a temporary basis before they attain buddhahood. From knowing others' mental dispositions, they discern the kind of training that the disciples need. From knowing where the disciples are coming from and where they are going, they can help them successfully without making mistakes. You can try to help others without knowing these things, but what you do may or may not work. Nowadays miracles aren't seen much, but in the past magical activities were more common. When people saw someone perform miracles they were inclined to follow and trust that person's instructions.

These five higher knowledges are still an ordinary level of wisdom. Even non-Buddhist yogis can get these powers through developing śamatha. Ultimate wisdom is understanding the true nature of reality. The sixth higher knowledge is supramundane; it is knowing the extinction of your own mental afflictions. When you attain nirvana, you know that you are completely free of all deluded mental states. Until you achieve that complete cessation you don't have this sixth type of knowledge.

The fourth perfection is diligence or enthusiastic perseverance. Diligence is perseverance in the practice of virtue; it is joy in the practice of wholesome activities. It is never a special enthusiasm in doing unwholesome activities. It is explained last because it pertains to both accumulations. Candrakīrti said,

> All higher qualities follow after joyous effort.
> It is the cause for both the collections of merit and wisdom.
> [*Entering the Middle Way*, 4.1ab]

It requires diligence to develop both the form-body—the rūpakāya—and the wisdom body—the dharmakāya. All good qualities, virtues, and meritorious activity follow from diligence. Without enthusiastic perseverance you cannot develop any of them. If you are happy to do something, you will engage in it. This is the case for the countless activities summarized as the six perfections. A lot more can be said on the topic of the six perfections. In *Ornament for the Mahayana Sutras*, Maitreya extensively explains why Mahayana practice is condensed into the six perfections, the nature of each perfection, the divisions of each perfection, the order of perfections, who practices them, the goals for oneself and for others, along with many other topics. We won't go into that detail here. For now, suffice it to say these are excellent practices for bodhisattvas to attain their ultimate goal but also to attain their temporary goals while they are in samsara.

Even laypeople, like the king for whom Nāgārjuna wrote this text, can turn toward religious activity. You have that great opportunity. The next chapter is directed primarily to laypeople and explains how to practice the six perfections in the context of an ordinary, everyday life.

3. Advice Primarily for Laypeople

THE CHAPTER TITLE, "Advice Primarily for Laypeople," doesn't mean that this advice is only for laypeople. It is advice for everyone—men and women, laypeople and the ordained—but principally the recommendations are for how a layperson can best use their life. The question is, you have obtained a human life as a result of your past actions, so now what are you going to do with it? You can use it to achieve anything that you want: ordinary pleasure for your own temporary enjoyment, a better situation in a future life, or even the attainment of nirvana or enlightenment. Unfortunately, many people spend all their time in pursuit of small and meaningless goals. They see no further than this current life. In that sense, most people are not much different from animals. Animals can find food and shelter, defeat their enemies, protect themselves, defend their offspring, and experience sensual pleasure. Some animals do these things more skillfully than humans! Animal enjoyment may not be the same as human pleasure, but many animals are very clever about what they want and how to get it. The ability to make the most of current circumstances is not a rare or uniquely human trait. However, Śāntideva said that it is a waste to spend your life pursuing goals only for bettering this life.

> Those suffering in samsara due to previous karma
> destroy this fortunate opportunity that is so difficult to find
> for the sake of a trivial meaningless purpose—
> something that even an animal can attain.
> [*Introduction to the Practice of Bodhisattvas,* 8.81]

If you die after using your life this way, you will have no chance for a life similar to or better than this one. You will be like a merchant who has traveled to a land full of treasure but comes back empty-handed. Ordinary people become anxious, worry, and fight when they don't achieve what they want in their daily lives. They don't see that in pursuit of these small goals they are destroying their opportunity to achieve something with a greater purpose: a human life can be used to defeat the power of karma that binds you to samsara. It doesn't matter if you are lay or ordained. It is up to each person how they use their life. It is dangerous if you do not work to develop your mind. Candrakīrti said,

> If someone does not work to hold onto his status
> when he can act freely while living in a conducive state,
> he will fall into the abyss and be under others' sway.
> What can lift him up from that state in future?
>
> [*Entering the Middle Way*, 2.5]

The meaning of this is clear. When you have a perfect human life you have a great deal of freedom and independence. You have the opportunity to create the causes for another human life or even for complete freedom from misery. The everlasting goal of emancipation from samsara is achievable. But there are many conditions needed to achieve it. Some humans have sophisticated minds conducive to practice. Some, but not all, have the external conditions favorable for practice. Look around you right now. There are so many types of living beings: insects, animals, and humans. Animals and those in other lower realms don't have the opportunity to practice. Very few humans have all the necessary internal and external conditions. When you look, you'll see that you have a very rare and wonderful opportunity.

Having a human life is like walking along the edge of a high cliff. It is very dangerous; you need to walk carefully so that you don't fall. You are in a high rebirth right now. From this state you can rise way up or throw yourself way down. You need to put effort into the proper method to secure another high rebirth in your next life. Then you can develop further and further until you achieve your ultimate spiritual goal. If you don't take advantage of this great opportunity, in your next life you will fall into the abyss of the three lower realms. Once that happens, you'll be under the sway of other causes and conditions, both internal and external. You will have no opportunity to create virtue. You will continuously create negative karma due to ignorance. You will continuously cycle down into miserable conditions. It is almost impossible to rise up again. It isn't totally impossible; from a Buddhist point of view some positive karma will eventually ripen. But it may be far, far in the future. It is like climbing a mountain: it is difficult to walk up, but if you fall you will quickly roll down. Śāntideva asked, if you don't work to hold yourself up now, what can bring you back up later?

> The leisure and fortune of a human life is difficult to find.
> Having obtained it you can bring about the welfare of all beings.
> How will such a fortunate opportunity arise again
> if you don't make use of the advantages you have now?
> [*Introduction to the Practice of Bodhisattvas*, 1.4]

Even among humans there is a great variety in the quality of life. The life you have is traditionally described as possessing leisure and fortune. "Leisure" means that you have the freedom to work for a spiritual goal. In other words, you are able to do what you want; you are not completely dominated by others; and you have the potential to achieve what you want, temporarily or absolutely. "Fortune" means that you have the necessary conditions to practice. You are no different in that way from the historical Buddha. You have wealth, functional physical organs, a good mind, and other conditions such as a teacher, the teachings, and helpful friends. Everything you need in order to use your life for a spiritual purpose is available. The opportunity is here; using it depends upon you. There is no excuse.

There is a lot of detail about how difficult it is to obtain this sort of life in the stages of the path literature. I won't go into that here. But you can easily see how temporary life is. Once you lose your life, where you'll go next is dependent upon your karma. Who knows where you'll end up. Down? Up? All the Buddhist teachings say that you need an enormous amount of merit to obtain a human life. Can you look at what you have done in your life and expect a life like this one, much less a better life, in the future? Or, have you created negative karma most of the time? This is a very important message. You should think about it every day, otherwise you are finished!

Right now, you have the wish-fulfilling jewel of a human life. With it you can satisfy yourself and grant all sentient beings the object of their desire. What do they want? Like you, in the short term they want comfort, food, sensual pleasure, and freedom from misery; ultimately, they want everlasting freedom from suffering, peace, and happiness. So, what should you do? To benefit yourself and others you practice the Dharma. Even a layperson can devote every one of their actions toward spiritual goals if they know how to do it. In general, Dharma practice is doing wholesome activities, avoiding unwholesome activities, purifying past negativities, and eliminating the causes that lead to the creation of karma. Nāgārjuna presents nine ways a layperson can do this: (1) respecting your parents, (2) observing the one-day lay vows, (3) avoiding wrong thoughts, (4) being conscientious, (5) practicing patience, (6) abandoning negative actions, (7) understanding the characteristics of those with whom you should associate, (8) abandoning desire for another person, and (9) choosing a proper spouse.

RESPECTING YOUR PARENTS

Someone who recognizes that their current life is incredibly important respects and honors their parents.

> 9. Someone who reveres their father and mother is noble.
> The gods and spiritual teachers will be with them.
> Their respectful attitude will bring them fame,
> and in future lives they will have a high rebirth.

Acting with deference and appreciation toward your parents indicates that you are a person of high quality. Your filial devotion will please the worldly gods; and in return the gods will support you. Your actions will also please your spiritual teachers, enabling you to stay in your teachers' presence. This will be the case both in this life and in your future lives. You will be looked upon favorably; you will be recognized as a good person, someone who is honorable and humble.

Until recent times, most people lived in extended families. Traditionally the eldest person was the most respected. The grandparents were cared for and served. Children saw their parents honoring their grandparents.

As they grew up, they learned that their parents too were worthy of reverence. What was the rationale for this? Consider the fact that your parents brought you into existence. Your mental continuum comes from your prior life, but your parents provided the physical cause for this rebirth. The combination of your mind, the sperm from your father, and egg from your mother was the start of your human life. Parental love extends from before a child's birth until the parent dies. Even before you were born your parents worried about your future. Your mother nourished you in her womb. When you were born you were totally dependent on your parents. Newborns are like little worms. They don't even know how to eat. Your parents cared for you until you could stand on your own two feet. When a child is sick, it is almost as if their parents are suffering the illness. Young children view their mother and father as protectors and saviors. If someone insults or hits a child, the child will say, "I'm going to tell my mother." There is no one else like this. Later in life, when you are looking at things from a karmic perspective, others can be more important. But in a conventional way your parents are your first and most significant friends.

Therefore, when your parents get old and infirm, you must take care of them. In your early life they took care of you, later you take care of them. It is most dishonorable to not recognize and repay this debt. Of course, children don't see this, but adults should be able to remember the kindness of their parents. Most parents aren't buddhas; they act out of ignorance and other mental afflictions. Sometimes their actions alienate their children, and they no longer cherish each other as time goes on. But this is a great disaster from the spiritual point of view. Even if your parents treated you harshly, you should treat them with respect. In general, parents wish the best for their children: they want them to have wealth, fame, health, happiness, education, and success. Parents have to socialize and educate their children. This can't always be done in a sweet way; their heart may be filled with love, but outside they appear wrathful. Even if their actions were misguided, they thought that what they were doing was for the benefit of their children.

Because of the great kindness of your parents, the Abhidharma says that killing your father or mother is an action of immediate retribution. It is such a negative action that you will take birth in hell as soon as you die, no matter what other karma you have created. The only comparable actions are injuring a buddha, killing an arhat, and causing a schism in the Sangha. The contrary is also true, caring for your parents is extremely powerful good karma. It is more powerful than caring for others.

There are many different family customs throughout the world. Cultural values and material wealth have disturbed the traditional type of family life. In contemporary Western cultures there is more stress on independence than loving respect. Over time parents and children may have many differences; sometimes they don't seem to trust each other. When children grow up, they want to live totally separate lives. Everyone in the family goes their own way. When the parents need help, they may have to go to a nursing home because their children aren't there. (It is good that there are places to get help, but loving care should be part of their children's attitude.)

So, you need to think carefully about what your parents or other caregivers did for you when you were young. People often don't think about their parents' kindness. They only remember the scolding. Traditionally, parental love for a child was presented as an example of pure love. This isn't like love in the sense of lustful desire or a strong desire for material wealth. Pure love is akin to a parent wishing that their child will have happiness, peace, and enjoyment. Pure compassion is like a parent's sincere wish to alleviate their child's suffering. Bodhisattvas develop love based on this type of example. If you can't respect your parents, if you can't recollect their kindness, it will be very difficult to respect and remember the kindness of others.

Observing the One-Day Lay Vows

In order to be able to extend a loving and respectful attitude toward others, Nāgārjuna advises laypeople to observe the eight one-day vows. The Buddha offered his followers a progressive series of vows, called the *pratimokṣa*, as a gradual path leading to individual emancipation. Step by step, you can take more and more vows to control your conduct. The Buddha's teachings on the rules governing the Buddhist community fill twelve extensive volumes. In this collection, the Vinaya, he explained the purpose of taking a vow; how to obtain a vow; how to maintain a vow; the obstacles to a particular vow; what to do if you break or lose a vow; and how to repair it if you break it. There are eight types of prātimokṣa vows: (1) eight-part upoṣadha vows are one-day vows for the laity; the next two, (2) upāsaka and (3) upāsikā vows, are vows for laymen and lay-women taken for life; the next two, (4) śrāmaṇera vows for men and (5) śrāmaṇerī for women, are novice vows taken when you enter a religious order; (6) bhikṣu and (7) bhikṣuṇī are full ordination vows for men and women. (8) The eighth type of prātimokṣa vow is only for women. It is an additional level between śrāmaṇerī and full bhikṣuṇī. In addition to these eight sets of prātimokṣa vows, there are the bodhisattva vows and tantric vows. You take these when you expand your practice beyond just yourself and your goal becomes attaining enlightenment in order to help all other beings become free from samsara.

The first set of prātimokṣa vows for individual emancipation, the eight one-day lay vows, is a very handy practice. You aren't taking these vows for life, just for one day. It is difficult for laypeople to undertake keeping vows all the time. But even people with many responsibilities can do something for one day. If they have a brief break in the usual demands upon them, they can live a spiritual life by taking these eight precepts for twenty-four hours. The Buddha gave this option to lead people toward a pure life. He advised that laypeople should do this as often as possible.

These particular one-day vows for individual emancipation are only for laypeople who have not taken any other vows. In other words, the eight-part uposadha vows aren't for everyone. Those who have taken other precepts for life—fully ordained monks and nuns, novice monks and nuns, and even laypeople who have taken lay vows for life and/or the bodhisattva vows—should not take these eight one-day uposadha vows. If you have taken vows for life, and then take these particular one-day prātimokṣa vows, you would be implicitly rejecting, and so losing, your bigger commitment of the life-time vows. In contrast, the eight Mahayana one-day precepts can be taken by people with lifetime vows. This might seem confusing because the number of vows and their content are the same, but they are different in regard to the motivation for taking and keeping them. The Mahayana one-day vows are taken with bodhicitta motivation; the uposadha prātimokṣa vows do not involve bodhicitta. The purpose of the eight-part uposadha prātimokṣa vows is for the practitioner alone to avoid falling to a lower rebirth. Thus, the eight one-day uposadha vows are not the same as the eight Mahayana one-day precepts, however the following explanation of the vows applies to both.

What are the eight one-day lay uposadha prātimokṣa vows?

10. To avoid harming, stealing, engaging in sex, and lying.
     To not drink alcohol or crave food at improper times.
     And to eschew the pleasures of a high seat,
     singing and dancing, and adornments.

The first four precepts are main core of the vows. They are strictures to prevent you from injuring yourself and others. The first vow, to avoid harming, means that you should not kill. You do not injure the life of another being. The second precept is to avoid stealing in any manner. You do not take anything belonging to someone else that is not given to you freely. The third one is to avoid sexual intercourse and any other type of sexual activity. This is a one-day vow of celibacy. (When laypeople take upāsaka vows for life, they vow to give up sexual misconduct, not all sexual activity. This was discussed in the preceding chapter.) Fourth is a vow to not lie. Lying involves cheating others in some way for your own purposes. Indulging in the actions prohibited by these precepts—killing, stealing, sexual activity, and lying—are the most powerful and easily done negative actions of body, speech, and mind. Avoiding these four core types of misconduct keeps many things clear. It is the foundation of a pure body, speech and mind.

You need some help in order to be able to avoid these core negative actions. So, the latter four precepts are minor ones that support the first four. This is analogous to putting up rings of fences to keep thieves and animals out of an orchard. When an outer fence is broken an animal or thief can get closer to the orchard but still not despoil it. In Tibetan, the verse literally says that the first of these secondary precepts is to not drink beer. However, the intent is to avoid any type of intoxicant so that you do not lose the ability to determine right from wrong. Therefore, you promise that for one day you will not partake of anything intoxicating: smoking a drug, taking pills, or drinking even a drop of alcohol. This is the first fence. The next vow is to avoid eating at certain times. Most of us always have our mind on food. All day we think about what we want to eat, shopping for groceries, preparing a meal, eating it, and so forth. This vow provides some limitation on those distractions. The day you take the vows you can eat until noon; after that you don't eat anything until the next day. The third precept is to help you be humble and simple. You avoid sitting on an abnormally big and high seat. People sit on thrones out of pride; their status demands deference. But *high* can also refer to something expensive. For just one day you avoid elegant, high-cost furnishings and sit on a simple seat or bed. The Vinaya rule states that you should avoid a seat higher than a cubit. (A cubit is an ancient measurement equal to the length between your elbow and fingertips.) However, you have to take into account local contemporary customs. In the west it is customary to sit on chairs. An ordinary chair seat may be higher than a cubit. Sitting on an ordinary chair doesn't inflate your pride. It doesn't break your vows to sit in your normal chair or sleep in your usual bed. The vow is to avoid something that is higher, larger, and more expensive. The last minor precept puts a number of things put together. It is a promise to avoid two categories: dancing and singing, and ornamentation. There are exceptions to this rule. If there is a special purpose you can dance, sing, and wear ornaments. For example, moving in a dance-like manner might be necessary to recover from an injury; singing a devotional song; performing a religious dance; or putting on a crown and other jewelry in the course of an initiation. Singing and dancing just for pleasure and enjoyment is what should be avoided for one day. You also dispense with wearing jewelry that is merely for the purpose of ornamentation.

You take the one-day vows early in the morning, just before dawn when you are just about able to see the lines on your palm. You can take the vow in front of your preceptor, or by yourself imagining that you are before the buddhas or the Three Jewels. Then you need to remember to avoid both the major and minor commitments for the next twenty-four hours. There is a great difference between engaging in ethical conduct with or without a vow. It is much more powerful karma to avoid negative actions with a vow. It doesn't create virtuous karma if just by happenstance you don't kill or lie for a day. You haven't created any negative karma, but it is not the same as having the awareness and determination to act morally. A rock doesn't lie, kill, or steal, but it doesn't create any virtue either. Keeping the vows takes effort, so it creates much more virtue.

> 11. When you have taken these eight precepts
>   you are emulating the arhats' moral behavior.
>   Keeping these vows on a sabbath day bestows upon men
>   and women
>   the attractive bodies of the desire-realm gods.

The Buddha recommended that his followers take these eight precepts on special days of the lunar calendar. This is akin to the Judeo-Christian practice of a sabbath; a day during which you eschew ordinary activity and concentrate on spiritual matters. When you take the eight one-day precepts you are practicing in the same way that great arhats and buddhas practiced in the past. Former masters attained their high spiritual level by engaging in pure conduct for many lifetimes over a vast period of time. By keeping their vows pure they had the basis to get rid of their mental afflictions. If you can do so for just one day, you too are engaging in the therapeutic purification called uposadha (Tibetan: *gso sbyong*). To understand this practice it is helpful to understand the etymology of the general Tibetan term, *sojong,* which refers to both a ritual to take or restore vows as well as keeping the eight-part uposadha vows for a particular twenty-four hour period. The first syllable, *so,* means you take and keep vows in order to mend your impure conduct and mind and recuperate to a state of purity. It is a form of therapy. The second syllable, *jong,* means to clean. You clean your impure defiled mind so that it is wholesome. In addition to the eight-part uposadha there are other forms of this therapeutic purification: monks and nuns engage in a practice called *sojong* on the new and full moon every month. The sangha gathers together, performs a special ritual, recites the *Monastic Discipline Sutra,* and individual sangha members purify any vows they have broken in the preceding period through confession. The eight Mahayana one-day precepts are also referred to as *sojong.*

The main result of a karma is a future life. Consciously stopping negative actions is virtuous karma; its main result will be a rebirth in a high realm within the desire realm. As a result of taking and keeping the eight-part uposadha vows you will obtain the body of a desire-realm god. (This practice doesn't result in a rebirth in the corporeal or noncorporeal realms. To be reborn in those upper realms requires additional special training in meditation.) Therefore, to attain a high rebirth in the desire realm, the highest of which is a god, you try to abandon negative actions. If you can't promise to do so for your entire life, at least take the one-day vows as many times as possible.

The eight uposadha vows can be sorted into five functional categories: (1) to avoid harming others, (2) to avoid harming both yourself and others, (3) to preserve your precepts from becoming corrupted, (4) being mindful of the first three core vows, and (5) not losing mindfulness. The first category, not causing others harm, involves the first two core vows: avoiding killing and stealing. The second category, not harming either yourself or others, is to avoid sexual activity. Avoiding sexual contact even with your own partner serves to decrease your sensual desire. You avoid sexual activity with someone else's partner because it can injure another person's mental well-being. The third category, preserving your precepts, pertains to lying. If you have done something that breaks your vows, you should honestly confess your lapse to your guru or the sangha. (Don't confess to just anyone and everyone. That could actually be dangerous.) You confess with strong regret for having done that action and promise not to do it again. People often don't want to admit their negative actions. They stay silent, trying to keep their reputation as being someone good and pure. This silence is lying. You are implicitly saying that you are innocent and have done nothing wrong. Confessing your negative conduct is being truthful. The purpose of confession is to recover and purify and it includes an element of compassion. This particularly pertains to the sangha. The sangha does a confession ceremony twice a month. If a sangha member knows that another sangha member had done something wrong but didn't confess it, they feel compassionate pity knowing the negative consequences that person will experience unless they engage in purification. Therefore, in the ceremony they raise a question, "Is it right or wrong to do such and such a thing?" If the person says, "Oh, that is wrong." Then the response is, "Have you done something like that?" To deny it would be a lie. To confess it allows you to purify. But even laypeople shouldn't lie about their misdeeds. If you don't have someone you can confess to right away, you think that when you have the opportunity you will make a confession.

Three of the four secondary precepts are included in the fourth category, being mindful of the core precepts. In order to be mindful, you avoid music, singing, dancing, wearing perfume and jewelry, sitting on ostentatious high seats, and eating after noon. When you avoid these, you will be quiet and humble, and you will recollect that you are spending the day creating virtue. The fifth category is to not lose your mindfulness. This is the avoidance of intoxicants. You want to avoid losing your ability to determine right from wrong because you don't want slip into negative action.

Thus, there are reasons for each of the vows. The eight-part upoṣadha prātimokṣa vows are for individuals seeking their own emancipation. What is most destructive to the pursuit of individual liberation? Some actions are naturally evil and lead to bad results, for example killing and stealing. Therefore, there are vows specifically prohibiting these actions. To protect yourself from engaging in those actions there are subsidiary vows. These subsidiary vows prohibit actions that are not naturally bad. They are promises to not engage in a particular manner of behavior. If you have taken one of these secondary vows and break it then you must confess it. However, if you haven't taken that vow, you haven't broken the rule if you act in that manner.

Avoiding Wrong Thoughts

Why do we do or say harmful things? Improper actions originate in the mind. The causes of negative physical and verbal karma are the mental afflictions. Laypeople are necessarily involved in worldly activity. In general, these activities are prompted by and further stimulate desire, anger, greed, stinginess, deceptiveness, pride, conceit, and so forth. The mental afflictions are the root cause for rebirth in the bad migrations. Therefore, it is important for laypeople to know how to deal with their mental afflictions. If you understand what the mental afflictions are and their negative consequences, you will try to control them and lessen them. Therefore, Nāgārjuna's third piece of advice to laypeople is to avoid wrong thought.

> 12. See the following as enemies: stinginess, cunning, deceit,
> desire, laziness, conceited pride, lust, hatred,
> and arrogance about the superiority of your race,
> body, learning, beauty, and power.

There are thirteen easy-to-recognize mental afflictions listed here. Stinginess is not wanting to share, even though you have plenty. To be cunning is to try to hide your negative actions and qualities in a deceptive way in order to fool others. Deceit is pretending to have virtues or other qualities—such as wealth, power, ability, knowledge—that you don't really have in order to mislead others. Desire is yearning for possessions.

Lust is sexual desire. Sexual desire is such a strong mental affliction that it is listed separately from desire for possessions. Laziness is to be indolent in regard to doing something wholesome. In other words, laziness is to not think about anything beyond this life. It also causes any positive action that you do to be done in a weak way. In short, laziness prevents you from accumulating merit. Conceited pride is thinking that you have a quality that you don't really have. If you actually have that good quality and rejoice in it, that's fine. But thinking that you are great when you really are not is the mental affliction of haughtiness. Hatred is wanting to harm others for your own benefit. In addition to these eight mental afflictions, there are five forms of arrogance. Arrogance is thinking you are greater and better than others. The first type of arrogance is in regard to yourself; you believe that your heritage and status due to your birth is the best. In India this is caste consciousness; here in the west it is an attitude of racial superiority. Arrogance is also comparative. You believe your physical form and youthful beauty are better than others'. You can also be arrogant regarding your education; you think that no one knows a topic as well as you do. Finally, there is arrogance in regard to your authority and power. Look into your mind to see if any of these mental afflictions are present.

The mental afflictions rise from ignorance. Once the mental afflictions arise, you engage in negative actions. Then you will have no peace and enjoyment. In that sense, the mental afflictions are your enemies. They are not external enemies. It doesn't help to go to war to destroy someone or something outside. The enemy to destroy is inside your mind. The mental afflictions cause you to hurt and deceive others; this ends up harming you in the future. So, you should see the mental afflictions as your real enemy. They need to be controlled and subdued. Eventually you will completely rid them from your mind, but you can't do that right away. For now, you watch and see when one of these enemies is rising up in your thoughts. Then you think, "I don't want to give in to this, I want to conquer it."

In other words, you must be mindful in order to avoid wrong thoughts. This is Nāgārjuna's fourth piece of advice: you should be conscientious. In short, you should be aware of what is going on in your mind and carefully monitor how you are behaving. If you are not mindful, whatever you do, say, or think will be done loosely and wildly. Therefore, you must spy on yourself; you must constantly check to see if you are creating virtue or negativity. We usually spy on others; that selfish concern with others' behavior is bad. In contrast, conscientiousness of what you are doing, saying, and thinking is good because it enables you to control your actions. You can choose to have a good attitude and act in a positive manner; together these are virtue. The mind is the most important element.

BEING CONSCIENTIOUS

Living in the world, having a samsaric life, is as dangerous as walking along a cliff edge. You need to pay attention to where you put your feet. If you look around and get distracted by beautiful things, you could fall off the cliff. If you are attached to temporary sensual pleasure, you likely do many negative actions. Absorbed in the present, you do not see the danger of falling to a lower realm after death. If you are not mindful of your thoughts and conduct you will act in ways that cause you to fall. So, spiritual practitioners are conscientious about their practice.

> 13. Conscientiousness is the source of the nectar of
>   immortality.
>   Therefore, the sage said heedlessness is the source of death.
>   Thus, in order to increase your virtuous deeds
>   please, always be respectfully conscientious.

The Buddha—often referred to as "the sage"—said that serious spiritual practitioners should always be conscientious. The function of conscientiousness, or mindfulness, is to protect your mind from becoming contaminated with incorrect, bad things. From being aware you will avoid evil and develop virtue. This will result in nirvana. Nirvana can be called "the nectar of immortality" because it is everlasting freedom from samsara. There is no more ordinary death, birth, aging, sickness, and so forth caused by karma. The opposite of conscientiousness is to not be mindful. You carelessly let your mind roam. Your actions and speech will then be full of evil. You will let fall a rain of negative karma, the source of impure death and rebirth. This isn't just something that Nāgārjuna made up. A sutra says almost exactly the same thing.

> Conscientiousness is the source of immortality;
> heedlessness is the source of samsaric death.

> The conscientious will not die;
> the heedless die again and again.
> [*Collection of Indicative Verses,* 4.1]

Nāgārjuna's advice to the king, and by extension to us, is to increase our virtues. There are two aspects to increasing virtue. First, you should protect the wholesome actions that you already have done. This means that you do not let the seeds of your prior wholesome actions degenerate and become lost. Second, you should diligently create virtues that you lack at present. Nāgārjuna uses the word *respectfully* to indicate the wisdom that recognizes the value of conscientiousness. If you don't see how important it is to be mindful all the time, you won't respect it and do it.

An entire chapter of the *Introduction to the Practice of Bodhisattvas* is about conscientiousness. There Śāntideva stresses the need for mindfulness because under the power of the mental afflictions we continually do faulty, negative things that harm ourselves and others. According to Buddhism, it is important to know that your continuum of lives, from time without beginning up to now, has occurred due to the power of karma. The realm in which you are born in samsara, and to which you go after you die, is the result of a karmic seed. Therefore, it is very dangerous to live an impure life under the power of the mental afflictions. You have no power to prolong your life; it doesn't matter how much you want happiness, peace, health, and so forth. When you die you will have no freedom or independence about where you will be reborn. Your next rebirth follows from your past karma.

A well-known quotation from the sutras puts this as follows:

> Wherever birds fly in the sky
> Their shadow moves along with them.
> Likewise, a karmic shadow follows
> whatever good or bad actions you have done.
> [*Collection of Indicative Verses* 17.5]

Karmic results follow you after death like a shadow follows a body. We create hundreds of thousands of karmas every day. Each one is unique, and the nature of its results will accord with its cause. The more powerful ones will ripen first. Weaker ones may take longer before they ripen, but there is no escape. If the karmic seed is not purified or hasn't yet fully ripened, it will bring about a result sooner or later. It may take eons. It doesn't matter if the karma was big or little, gross or subtle. The end of a particular karma is only when its result has fully ripened, or it has been completely purified. Impure karma is created because of ignorance, the egoistic view, and the mental afflictions. It results in a rebirth and all the accompanying experiences in samsara.

In contrast, pure or stainless actions are not contaminated by the mental afflictions. The pure actions of bodhisattvas, arhats, and buddhas do not result in samsara. When someone's mind is free from the mental afflictions and is suffused with wisdom, compassion and love, there is no creation of impure karma. Such a person may manifest birth, death, illness, and so forth, but these are illusory. When they die, how they die, where they are reborn, is completely their own choice.

Ordinary beings almost never engage in pure good conduct. Pure conduct necessitates extirpation of the afflictive emotions. Just as clean water clears away dirt, developing pure conduct through being mindful will wash you clean spiritually. Changing your future circumstances isn't something you can do externally; it is the result of internal transformation. Therefore, as long as you are alive you should strive to purify and accumulate virtue. If you are conscientious, you will be aware of what should be done and what should be avoided. Through being conscientious you can make all your actions of body, speech, and mind virtuous.

The next verse responds to a hypothetical question: "Why didn't you tell me this before? If you had told me earlier, I could have done something. Now I've made a mess of things and it is too late!" We so often want to blame others, even our guru or the Buddha, for our shortcomings. However, you can change now. You can realize nirvana even though you did bad things in the past because internally you were overpowered by the mental afflictions and externally you relied upon wicked associates.

> 14. Someone who was heedless earlier,
>   but changes and becomes conscientious,
>   is as lovely as the moon freed from clouds;
>   just like Nanda, Aṅgulimāla, Ajātaśatru, and Udayana.

Even a careless person can meet a spiritual teacher. If they learn what should be done and what should be avoided, they will come to have great regret about what they've done in the past. They will be as remorseful as someone who realizes that they have ingested poison. They will engage in purifying their past negative actions and no longer create new ones. A person who uses the rest of their life that way can attain nirvana or even enlightenment. For example, the moon is sometimes obscured by clouds, but when the clouds drift away the moon shines brightly. The mind can be obscured by the mental afflictions, but the negative afflictions can be made thinner and thinner by wholesome practice. Finally, they will be completely eliminated. Nāgārjuna gives some examples of people like that. The stories about them appear in the sutras. These can be very long, so I'll just summarize them here.

Nanda was the Buddha's younger cousin. He was a handsome young man and was very fond of women. Dominated by the poison of lust, Nanda didn't want to be separated from his attractive wife for even a moment. The Buddha tried to teach him the Dharma. He wanted Nanda to become ordained. This, of course, meant that Nanda would have to leave his wife. Nanda felt he had to do what his elder relative said, but no matter what the Buddha taught and no matter what Nanda did, he couldn't overcome his sensual desire. Finally, the Buddha asked his disciples Śāriputra and Maudgalyāyana to use their miraculous powers and show Nanda the realms of rebirth, from the heavens to the hells. One day they showed him an emanation of the god realm called the Heaven of the Thirty-Three. There he saw lovely pleasure gardens filled with wonderful palaces and hundreds of goddesses far prettier than his wife. The gods told Nanda that if he engaged in virtuous actions, he could be reborn there. Of course, Nanda wanted that rebirth! Then another day they showed him a horrific emanation of a hot hell. Nanda heard a voice explain that if he did nonvirtuous actions he would end up there. This helped Nanda switch his focus from his present life to his future lives. He took ordination as monk. During the rest of his life he studied, meditated, and practiced. He closed the door on all negative actions of body, speech, and mind. He eliminated his desire and eventually became an arhat. The most important aspect of control is control over your mind. The Buddha praised Nanda as the most restrained of all his disciples.

The name Aṅgulimāla means a "having rosary made of human fingers." The man who became known as Aṅgulimāla was a prince during the time of the Buddha. He met an evil teacher who told him that to get emancipation from samsara he must make many sacrificial offerings. In particular, he was told that he needed to kill one thousand people. Aṅgulimāla believed this teacher. To keep count, after he murdered someone he cut off a finger from the corpse and strung it onto a necklace. Eventually he was just one short of the thousand murderous sacrifices he had been told were necessary. People were now so frightened of him that they avoided him completely. When he couldn't find anyone to kill, he decided to go home and murder his mother. He was filthy, covered in gore, and very frightful looking as he went down the road. The Buddha saw that Aṅgulimāla was ready to receive teachings. So, he appeared on the road just ahead of Aṅgulimāla. The Buddha walked with a lovely calm gait; he paced slowly, like a deliberate elephant. Aṅgulimāla chased after him. But no matter how fast Aṅgulimāla ran, even though he pursued the Buddha for miles, Aṅgulimāla couldn't get close enough to catch him. When Aṅgulimāla was about to give up, the Buddha stopped and waited for him. He asked Aṅgulimāla what he wanted. Aṅgulimāla explained his need to kill one more person. The Buddha said, "OK you can kill me. But first let's sit down and talk a bit." Then the Buddha taught him about karma. Aṅgulimāla listened and realized that what he had done was very evil and would result in rebirth in the hells. So instead of killing the Buddha, he bowed to the sage and vowed to follow his teachings. Aṅgulimāla said, "Today I see the shape of my evil actions in the mirror of the Dharma. I feel great remorse and fear my future suffering. From now on I will put all my energy into practicing the Dharma." The poison that had dominated Aṅgulimāla was ignorance. He thought wrong things were right and right things were wrong. But after meeting the Buddha, he practiced conscientiousness every moment for the rest of his life. He learned, studied, practiced and in that life attained nirvana.

Ajātaśatru was also a prince. Through the influence of evil ministers there was contention between the prince and his father, King Bimbisāra. The prince thought his father was doing things that would harm the kingdom, so he had him thrown in jail. Although initially the prince planned to execute his father, he changed his mind and sent a large troop of men to release the king. However, when Bimbisāra heard the men coming, he thought they were coming to kill him, and he died of fright. So, Ajātaśatru caused his death. Killing your father is one of the five most heinous actions. Their result is to immediately take rebirth in hell after death. The story continues differently in Hinayana and Mahayana sutras. Although some sutras say that because Ajātaśatru changed his mind that heinous karma wasn't complete, later in his life when Ajātaśatru became religious and wanted ordination, this became an issue. According to the Hinayana system of Vinaya, someone who has committed one of the five heinous actions cannot obtain the vows. Also, they say that someone who has committed one of the five heinous actions cannot attain either the path of seeing or arhatship in that life. Further, they say that actions of immediate retribution cannot be fully purified. So, for some amount of time, the perpetrator must be born in hell. The Mahayana Vinaya is different. It says that you can purify even the most powerful negative karma though tantric and bodhisattva practices. According to the Mahayana tradition, it was after Ajātaśatru had taken ordination that he realized that his orders had killed his father. When the sangha he had joined learned this, they threw him out. But because he felt great sorrow and guilt, and did a lot of purification, in that life he attained arhatship.

Udayana also lived at the time of the Buddha. At one point, Udayana was having a sexual affair with another man's wife. His mother learned about it and tried to stop him. Udayana got very angry at his mother and killed her. Later he felt great guilt and requested that the Buddha ordain him. He did a tremendous amount of purification, but not quite enough to completely purify the action of immediate retribution, killing his mother. So, after his death he was born in hell, but that life in hell was very short because of the power of his practices of purification, creating merit, and keeping the ordination vows. Just like a ball, he bounced back up from hell to rebirth as a celestial being. During the time of the Buddha, some gods were able to hear the teachings and practice. In Udayana's life as a god he attained the fruit of a stream winner. A stream winner is no longer an ordinary being. They are an ārya because with a direct realization of reality they attain the path of seeing. Although he didn't achieve this status in his human life as Udayana or in his next life in hell, he achieved it in his subsequent life as a god.

These stories show that even the worst negative actions can be purified. No matter how dark and heavy the clouds are in the sky, they can be blown away by the wind. No matter how heavy your negative karma, it can be purified through pure spiritual practice. You can achieve a high spiritual goal if you meet a good teacher and practice the antidotes. At the very least if you are conscientious you can block being reborn into a foul destiny in your next life.

PRACTICING PATIENCE

So many situations in lay life can cause you to get angry and act badly. Endless activities connected to raising children, working, paying taxes, buying and selling, and so forth can be frustrating. Your friends, relatives, food, clothing, shelter, sensual pleasures, and especially sex, can fuel anger. There is so much potential for annoyance and impatience. These emotions can lead you to become very angry. Therefore, the fifth practice Nāgārjuna emphasizes for lay practitioners is patience. Patience is the opposite of anger. If you are patient your mind is calm and loving; you are able to bear aggravating and painful circumstances. Of course, not only laypeople get angry. Monks, nuns, and yogis can get extremely angry too. But the ordained try to live simply; they try to engage only in spiritual activities; they try to strive only for spiritual goals. So, while the practice of patience is important for everyone, given their circumstances it is even more imperative for laypeople. The following verse shows the virtues of patience.

> 15. Because there is no austerity like patience
>   you should not give anger a chance to rise.
>   The Buddha said that by eliminating anger
>   you will obtain the state of being a nonreturner.

Some non-Buddhist religious practitioners practice austerities. Under the guise of religion they deliberately injure themselves. Their religious practice is to endure extreme self-denial. For example, some of them don't eat, or eat only uncooked root vegetables; some sit in fires; others jump into freezing rivers; and some only wear bark clothing. But no great spiritual benefit comes from privation and physical difficulties. They are simply exhausting. It is like boxing: boxers hit each other until one of them is knocked out. Boxers practice a kind of austerity; they are able to bear being pummeled again and again. They patiently endure these beatings because they make a lot of money and the fights make them famous. This may be heroic in a common, worldly sense, but boxing will not result in a better rebirth. So, is there a need to say anything about how it will not result in complete liberation from samsara?

Buddhists don't encourage extreme physical asceticism. They emphasize training the mind. Among the various types of mental training, patience is the most powerful practice. The nature of patience is to be undisturbed no matter what happens. Patience is the antidote and opposite of anger. Stopping anger from arising isn't easy. Some physical exercises might help you calm your mind, but they are not the main cause of patience. You need to develop a specific kind of wisdom so that anger has no opportunity to arise. Your mental training begins with recognizing what fuels your anger and what the negative consequences of anger will be. Then, even if anger arises in your mind, at least you stop holding onto it. If your anger does continue, you try to keep it from getting stronger. You can do this if you try again and again. Eventually, you will not get angry even if someone comes to kill you.

Because patience prevents many negative thoughts and actions, it provides numerous benefits: patience is the real cause of peace and happiness; it is the most noble friend; it is a savior and protector; it beautifies a person; everyone likes someone who is patient; a patient person will have less trouble in this and future lives; a patient person's tendency to create evil actions is lessened; and finally, someone who always practices patience will attain the state of being a nonreturner.

What is a nonreturner? In the Abhidharma the Buddha taught that there are four sequential spiritual fruits: stream winner, once returner, nonreturner, and arhat. A stream winner is someone who has engaged in spiritual practice and become an ārya. Āryas are spiritually superior to ordinary beings because they have a direct realization of ultimate reality. From the Śrāvakayāna perspective this is a direct realization of the four realities for āryas; from the Mahayana perspective this is a direct realization of the emptiness of both the self of persons and phenomena. With that wisdom, they have definitively entered the stream flowing toward emancipation.

The next two types of spiritual results are a bit more complicated to understand. You need a bit of background regarding the structure of samsara. There are three realms in samsara: the desire realm, the form or corporeal realm, and formless or noncorporeal realm. All those living in the three samsaric worlds have desire. But desires in the desire realm are far more powerful and coarse. In the desire realm, your mind is greedy for sights, smells, sounds, tastes, and touch—particularly sexual contact. Your life is dominated by desire to possess things. When you don't get what you want you get angry. Anger and desire work together to keep you in the desire realm. Therefore, it is said that anger is a cause of a rebirth in the desire realm. The upper two realms are celestial. They are subtler both mentally and physically. There is so much less manifest mental affliction in the two upper realms that living there is like being in a trance.

There are nine levels of mental afflictions that cause rebirth in the desire realm. These mental afflictions are gotten rid of sequentially, progressing from the roughest to the subtlest. It is like cleaning an item of clothing so filthy that the dirt is even thicker than the cloth. First you get rid of the heaviest, most obvious dirt on the surface. Then you gradually work down to more and more subtle stains. It takes a lot of spiritual washing to clean nine levels of mental affliction. When a yogi has permanently gotten rid of the first six levels of these mental affliction, they are called a once-returner. That practitioner will take at most one more rebirth in the desire realm. It isn't definite that they will be reborn in the desire realm; in the remainder of their life they could remove the last three levels of desire-realm mental afflictions and not have to take another rebirth in the desire realm at all. But if they are not successful in doing that, they will be born in the desire realm just one more time. During that last life in the desire realm, they will be able to eliminate the final three subtlest levels of desire realm mental affliction. When they are removed, the yogi will never again be reborn in the desire realm due to karma and the mental afflictions. At that point, they are called a nonreturner. This spiritual achievement doesn't mean "nonreturner to samsara"; just to the desire realm. A nonreturner may be reborn in the corporeal or noncorporeal realms.

Actually, there is a benefit to living in the desire realm. It is there that practitioners find the conditions to practice the Dharma and quickly attain complete freedom from samsara. In the desire realm, you can see the problems of samsara in their entirety. From the point of view of physical and mental pleasure, the corporeal or noncorporeal realms are best. But these upper realms are not completely free of mental afflictions; there is attraction and attachment to peaceful concentration. Lives in the corporeal and noncorporeal realms are peaceful for eons. The beings there do not experience any gross mental or physical suffering. When you are born there, it seems like a little nirvana. It can be addictive.

Virtuous karma can cause rebirth in the desire realm or in the upper two realms. However, nonvirtuous karma is the cause of suffering only in the desire realm. Hatred or anger is completely nonvirtuous. If you get rid of anger completely, the rest of the nonvirtues will be eliminated too. The other mental afflictions are purged along with anger because to prevent anger from arising you must destroy your attraction to sensory objects. Thus, eliminating anger frees you from being reborn in the desire realm. For that reason, a sutra says, "Monks, it is like this. You should eliminate anger. If you eliminate anger and hatred, I assure you that you will become a nonreturner."

Therefore, it is worth looking at the anger in a bit more detail. Anger has two negative consequences: visible and invisible. The visible result is how you look and behave when angry. Your physical demeanor changes: your face becomes red and you shake. You say inflammatory words that are meant to cause harm. You lash out physically. Anger steals the wisdom that sees the reality of the object. It is likely that the person with whom you are angry has both good and bad qualities. But when you are angry, all you see is the negative side of others and you want to retaliate. The second consequence of anger is a karmic seed. The karmic seed left by anger will ripen into a lower rebirth. Even if you are born human, past anger causes negative experiences: no one likes you; people see you as ugly; people shun you; accuse you; harm you; and even insects and the elements cause you problems.

Anger is extremely powerful. One moment of hatred toward a bodhisattva can destroy the seeds of virtue created over thousands of years. It functions like a fire that destroys many, many years of forest growth. Candrakīrti wrote,

> There is no negativity like anger, because
> a moment of being angry at the Victor's children
> instantly destroys the virtues created by generosity
> and ethical discipline practiced over the course of a hundred
>   eons.

It creates an ugly countenance and leads to what is low,
it robs you of critical reason distinguishing right from wrong,
and anger swiftly casts you to the lower realms.
Forbearance creates qualities contrary to those just described.
                                    [*Entering the Middle Way*, 3.6–7]

This is why you should practice patience and not give anger the opportunity to arise. Anger is your enemy. It is inextricably mixed with being self-centered and egoistic. You feel you are right, the best, and the most important, so if anyone or anything counters you, you are ready to fight. You get angry for many reasons: when someone points out a fault that you have tried to keep hidden; when someone calls you a bad name like "stupid idiot," "thief," or "liar"; when someone harms you physically; and when someone steals your wealth. You even get angry at the weather if it rains when you want it to be sunny. If anger arises, you will likely feel resentful, and then your anger will get stronger and last longer. Some texts explain that there are nine causes of resentment. Usually when you are really angry with someone you ruminate about three actions that person did in the past, three they are doing now, and three they will do in the future. You think, "He harmed me in the past, he harmed my relatives and friends in the past, he harmed me by supporting my enemy in the past." When you think about the present, you think, "He is still harming me now, he is harming my friends and relatives now, he is helping my enemies." Then, you think of the future, "He will harm me and my relatives in the future. He will help my enemies in the future too." When you think over and over in these ways your anger becomes like a fire burning you inside. It grows into spontaneous hatred. We know this experience well; it is part of samsara.

> 16. "This one criticized me, that one defeated me,
>   this one stole my wealth." Repeating this
>   is holding onto resentment. It produces strife.
>   Those without resentment sleep easily.

An angry person has no peace. They are unhappy and unsettled. Sometimes they can't even sleep. Śāntideva said,

In brief, an angry person never enjoys
happiness and well-being.
> [*Introduction to the Practice of Bodhisattvas*, 6.5cd]

If you don't want to be under the sway of anger, you need to cease concentrating on your resentment. Controlling your resentment closes the door on hatred. Even if you can't think of any good things about the person with whom you are angry, you can start thinking in a very different way about why they harm you. Śāntideva wrote,

> Because in the past I have harmed
> sentient beings in this way,
> it is right that as result
> they are my abuser now.
> [*Introduction to the Practice of Bodhisattvas*, 6.42]

When someone or something hurts you, your usual response is to think something like, "I am innocent. There is no reason for this to happen to me. It is all his fault." You almost never think of your part in causing the situation. However, according to Buddhism you should think that in the past, in some prior life, you must have created the cause for this experience. You must have done to someone the same kind of thing that is harming you now. If you hadn't created the cause and conditions for this kind of unpleasant experience, it could not occur. Things don't happen randomly; there must be a cause. Everyone doesn't harm you; you are not harmed all the time in every situation. Your current situation is specific and has a particular cause. Thinking about causality is how great practitioners bear difficult circumstances. They see that the harm they are enduring is a result of their own prior actions.

There are direct and indirect causes for any particular incident that harms you. The indirect cause is your karma and mental afflictions. The direct or immediate cause is not just the other person who is harming you, it also your own body. If you didn't have a sensitive body, others' weapons, words, or actions wouldn't bother you. Your body is like a big wound or a boil. It is unbearably painful when anything touches it. You are very protective of your open wound of a body. If you must be angry about your situation, you should be angry at both causes: the weapon and your body. Actually, you don't need to be angry at the body itself. You should be angry with the cause of this type of body. The true focus of your anger should your own karma and mental afflictions.

Śāntideva wrote,

> Both the weapon and my body
> are the causes of my suffering.
> He brought the weapon, and I created my body,
> so, with whom should I be angry?
>
> If in blind attraction I cling to
> this suffering abscess of a human body
> that cannot bear to be touched,
> with whom should I be angry when it is hurt?
> [*Introduction to the Practice of Bodhisattvas*, 6.43–44]

If something can be changed, it is right to try to do so. But if something has to be experienced, you must accept it. If you don't like an experience and don't want to experience something similar again, then you need to eliminate the causes for that type of experience. So, a bad experience is like a teacher showing you what you need to purify. Development comes from thinking about what caused your misery and how to get rid of those causes. In other words, patience arises from the wisdom that understands why things happen. If you make a strong effort to conquer your anger, you will have peace and happiness in this life and future lives.

Śāntideva also said,

> Someone who perseveres and overcomes anger
> finds happiness in this and future lives.
> [*Introduction to the Practice of Bodhisattvas*, 6.6cd]

It isn't easy to be patient. Patience is a difficult practice, but it can be done. If you repeatedly contemplate the meaning of these verses, you will want to eliminate anger. If you don't make this effort, when the causes and conditions are present, anger will arise, and you will not be able to turn away from it. However, if you think again and again about the negative results of anger eventually you will be able to be more patient. You will be able engage in positive behavior and avoid the negative actions that harm yourself and others. Therefore, the sixth piece of advice Nāgārjuna offers to laypeople is to avoid negative actions.

Abandoning Negative Actions

Everything that you do, whether good or bad, comes through the three doors of your body, speech, and mind. How do you close these doors to negative actions and open them wide to positive ones? The next three verses provide the answer.

> 17. You should understand that thoughts are like
> drawing figures on water, in earth, or in stone.
> For mental afflictions the first is best.
> For aspiring to the Dharma, the last is the best.

The mind of an ordinary individual is mixed. Sometimes they have virtuous thoughts, but more often they have nonvirtuous thoughts. Some thoughts arise and dissipate quickly; some last a little while; others are firm and long-lasting. Nāgārjuna uses the example of drawing on three different surfaces to illustrate the varied nature of an ordinary person's mind. If you write on water, the letters disappear as soon as you move your finger. If you draw in sand, the letters might last a little while, but not too long. If you inscribe words in stone, they are firm and long-lasting.

Ordinary people can't be perfect from the start. You try bit by bit to make your positive behavior more stable and more frequent. You want to avoid negative behavior, but if it occurs you want it to be limited. It would be best if your deluded, negative mind were like drawing on water. Then the mind afflicted with mental afflictions like desire or anger will not last long.

The ordinary use of the word *dharma* implies holding an identity. Everything that exists has an identity and is therefore called a dharma. Something that doesn't exist, like a rabbit-horn, is not a dharma. Dharma, when used to mean the teachings and practice of Buddhism, also implies a type of holding. The wholesome mind of virtue holds you up so that you don't fall into the lower realms. Therefore, your desire to engage in the spiritual practice of Dharma should be as firm as a stone inscription. To make this desire to practice firm you must develop wisdom.

Wisdom is like a lamp for the mind. It clears away the darkness of ignorance. In the beginning, wisdom arises from learning. You study to learn what is right and what is wrong: you need to know what a deluded mind is and what a mind aspiring to the positive is. This isn't something that you just intuitively know. In fact, many times we have been led to think the wrong way. Therefore, you need to read authoritative texts or listen to teachers who can explain this. Once you know which is which, you try to develop good mental qualities and eliminate bad ones. Then you want to stabilize your positive mind. That is meditation: becoming so familiar with positive qualities your mind gradually transforms from the negative to the positive.

When your wisdom derived from learning is strong it can't be taken from you. You have this knowledge wherever you go. Your inclination for virtue and abhorrence of nonvirtue can never be destroyed by the elements, thieves, animals, and so forth. Your spiritual mind should be as engrained as if it were inscribed on stone.

The next stanza is about verbal actions. Just as thoughts were compared to three types of writing, here we find speech compared to three things.

> 18. The victor said there are three types of ordinary speech:
> pleasing, truthful, and improper. Respectively,
> these three are like honey, a flower, and filth.
> The last type of these should be abandoned.

Words that are as sweet as honey go right to someone's heart. Hearing such words is very enjoyable. Flowers are truly pleasing to see. Words that are truthful and without fault are as beautiful as a flower lauded for its beauty. Disrespectful, cheating, and nasty words are ugly, even disgusting. No one likes hearing these types of words just as no one wants to touch filth. Therefore, you should be mindful of what you are saying. You should use the first two types of speech and try to avoid the last.

The next stanza refers to actions that come through the door of the body. The sutras explain four types of beings based on their conduct.

19. There are four types of beings:
     those who go from light to light,
     from dark to dark, from light to dark,
     and dark to light. Be like the first.

Gods and humans have good lives because of their earlier practice of virtue. Some of them use the positive conditions of their lives in the upper realms to create virtuous karma that will result in another good rebirth. Thus, they are said to go from light to light. The next type of being goes from darkness to darkness. This refers to those in the three lower realms: the hells, hungry ghosts, and animals. They are born there because of prior negative karma. Life in the lower realms is so difficult that they engage in more negative actions and so are born in a bad situation again. This also refers to humans born in poverty, with chronic illnesses, or in horrible places. Through no fault of their own in this life, their entire life is miserable because of negative karma from prior lives. Many people in this type of situation are desperate; they get angry, jealous, frantic, and so forth. They rush around trying to satisfy their needs. The result of acting this way is to be reborn in a lower rebirth, probably something worse than their present life. They have gone from dark to dark. There are those who go from light to dark. They start with a good rebirth, but they don't practice virtue. They use up all the merit they created in past lives and don't accumulate any more good karma. They just enjoy themselves and, in the process, engage in evil actions. As a result, after death there is nowhere for them to go but down. Finally, there are those who go from dark to light. This refers to people born in miserable situations. But they use their minds. They understand that whatever they experience is a result of their own past karma. Because they don't want to endure future suffering, they endeavor to cease blaming others and getting angry. They are patient with people who are cruel or nasty to them. Their experience of misery exhausts the secondary results of their past negative karma. Using up the last of this negative karma allows another, better karma to ripen. So, those who practice virtue despite their miserable situation go from dark to light. This also pertains to some beings in the lower realms who have a better rebirth; but only very rarely will a positive past karma be strong enough to result in a good rebirth in the upper realms from a life in the lower realms.

Nāgārjuna advises us to be the first type of being. Like someone who goes from light to light, we should abandon inferior behavior, the bad conduct that comes through the three doors, and train ourselves in good conduct. Śāntideva provides us with more detail on how to think about our situation in order to be able to do this.

> For the sake of my desires
> I've burned and suffered in hell many times.
> I have not brought benefit to myself
> nor have I benefitted others.

> This present suffering is but a fraction of that
> and it will bring about great benefit.
> It is right to take delight in suffering
> that eliminates the misery of all living beings.
> [*Introduction to the Practice of Bodhisattvas*, 6.74–75]

You have committed many negative actions and as a result you have endured much suffering. You have had thousands of past lives. Sometimes you had a high rebirth, sometimes medium, and sometimes you had the absolute worst experience. All these lives, all that misery, were results of your karma. It has all been a waste. You just endured it without making things better for yourself or others. Now that you've attained a human life, you can really do something about the thousands more lives you will likely have in the future. The pain and difficulties in this life are nothing in comparison to suffering the results of negative karma in the lower realms. Instead of blindly enjoying this life, instead of angrily fighting to get the best for yourself, you can use your current difficulties as a stimulus for purification. You should be glad when you recognize your problems for what they are. You can rejoice when you experience suffering, because a particular karma has now been exhausted. You can be happy because when you identify the causes for your problems, you will know how to act differently.

You may want to change your behavior and decide to abandon negative actions. But there are many circumstances that make this difficult to do. Laypeople live in society. They are influenced by their friends, family, and associates to act in certain ways. Some people lead you into wrong conduct and some people promote good conduct. How do you recognize which is which? Nāgārjuna explains the varying quality of people in the next stanza.

UNDERSTANDING THE CHARACTERISTICS OF THOSE WITH WHOM YOU SHOULD ASSOCIATE

20. Understand that people are like mangos:
     some are unripe but appear to be ripe,
     some are ripe but appear to be unripe,
     some unripe ones appear unripe, some ripe ones appear
        ripe.

Four types of people are introduced here in an analogy. You already know how to choose a piece of fruit. When you choose a mango to eat you want it to be ripe and tasty. You have to be careful because some fruit seems ready on the surface but is not ripe inside. Some fruit is ripe on the inside but superficially seems unready to eat. Some fruit is unripe and appears that way. Other fruit is perfect; it seems ripe, and it is.

The first type of person's actions may appear to be good, but their mind is actually evil or selfish. For example, someone who wants to cheat you or even kill you may lure you in with nice food and gentle manners. This description applies to all actions that seem to be beneficial but are done with a bad motivation. The person's attitude and behavior are not in harmony. The next type of person is the opposite of the first one. This person has a kind and loving heart, but the way that they act and speak seems harsh and cruel. You see this in families sometimes. Parents may want the best for their children; they are lovingly concerned about every aspect of their children's lives. However, to teach their children a lesson they may say harsh words or punish them. If parents only indulge children with gentle and sweet behavior the child might become spoiled. This pertains to relationships between friends too. We also see this in the biographies of some great practitioners. For example, the great Tibetan saint Milarepa's guru Marpa Lotsawa made Milarepa miserable for a long time. The tasks he made Milarepa do looked like cruel punishment, but actually they were all designed to purify Milarepa's earlier bad karma. Eventually

Milarepa was ready to receive the tantric teachings and Marpa lovingly bestowed them. Bodhisattvas and great teachers may seem to act harshly, but their attitude is always good and kind. The third type of person has a selfish, egoistic mind. They have no concern for others and use others badly. Their behavior and attitude are both evil. The final type is someone whose actions and mind are both virtuous and wholesome.

So, which should you be? With whom should you associate? Nāgārjuna's advice is to choose to be with those who will help you better your situation. You should recognize when someone's behavior is in accord with their mental qualities. You should recognize that even if there is a discrepancy, sometimes that is necessary for your development. You can make a decision about your associates when you see that some characteristics are good and that others are not.

Choosing a Proper Spouse

One of the most influential people in your life is your spouse or partner. In the root text of *Letter to a Friend,* before Nāgārjuna explains the characteristics of an appropriate spouse, he teaches how to suppress your desire for another person both temporarily and permanently. In other words, in Nāgārjuna's text, the technique to suppress and completely eliminate desire is the eighth piece of advice primarily for laypeople, and choosing a proper partner is the ninth. However, for contemporary readers it makes more sense to reverse the order of these last two topics. There are a number of reasons I have done this. First, the brief discussion about choosing a partner logically follows the topic of determining what type of people you should associate with. Second, choosing a life partner is something laypeople may do; it is never done by those who have taken ordination. And most important, the elimination of desire is important for both the laity and the ordained. In the root text this topic merits a long discussion in its own right. I think it would be confusing for you if I followed the original order. Therefore, I am ending this chapter with the two verses about choosing a spouse taken from later in the text. But note that I am keeping the original numeration of the verses, so if you have been counting it will look like I am skipping fifteen verses. Don't worry, they will be covered in the next chapter.

This text was written for a king. The king was a layman; it was fine for him to desire a wife. Therefore, Nāgārjuna specifically talks about the characteristics of women who would be suitable. Although the female pronoun is used, these characteristics are equally applicable to men who would be good husbands. Nāgārjuna was a monk, so his advice on this topic is quite concise.

36. Avoid a wife with any of these three qualities:
    a murderess associated with your enemies;
    a tyrant contemptuous of her husband; or
    a thief who steals even the smallest things.

A marriage is a close association for a long period of time. The partner you choose for a long-term intimate friendship should be helpful, beneficial, and kind. You don't want someone who will cheat, steal, be cruel, and so forth. Everyone can understand that those types of partners won't make for a happy life together. For example, a woman who is too closely associated with her husband's enemies might conspire to kill her husband. A man who has no respect for his wife will continually scorn and disparage her. A person who hides even a small amount of money is untrustworthy. These types of spouses, male or female, should be avoided.

Now for the positive qualities you should look for in a partner. Again, this is written with the female pronoun, but is equally applicable to men and women.

37. A strong woman who is as easy-going as your sister,
    as affectionate as a helpful loving friend, and
    as supportive as your mother or a servant,
    should be honored as your family's deity.

Someone with kind and loving characteristics is actually quite powerful. They don't have a wrathful type of power. They are dominant because they are helpful and gentle. The traditional role of a sister is to care for her younger siblings; she plays with them, teaches them, and shows them kindness in many ways. Your friends are dear to your heart; they are affectionate and helpful. A mother always wants to benefit and serve her children. She doesn't lord it over her family; her attitude is that others should be cherished. When people in a relationship have these positive attributes, their life together will be good. Unfortunately, nowadays so many people are egoistic. They want to control their partner. They want some benefit from their partner and think nothing of cheating to get it. They lust for other men or women and wish their spouse was not there. All this can lead to violence, divorce, or even murder. These problems are not the result of a government policy, an economic circumstance, or anything else. They all derive from the selfish attitude, "me, me, me." If the individuals in a relationship have this egoistic attitude there will always be trouble; there will never be peace.

4. The Way to Eliminate Desire

As you well know, as a layperson you are involved with many people in a variety of worldly affairs. Your activities are often focused upon the objects of your senses. You usually don't think this is a problem, but so much turmoil arises from the fact that your senses are wide open. Sensory objects can seem overwhelmingly desirable. Śāntideva wrote about why desire is problematic.

> Desire is the cause of all calamities
> in this world and after death too:
> being killed, imprisoned, or dismembered in this life,
> and in future lives being in the hells, and so forth.
> [*Introduction to the Practice of Bodhisattvas, 8.40*]

There are two types of desire: pure and impure. Pure desire arises from wisdom that knows ultimate reality. This wisdom makes you desire to achieve the goals of perfect peace, happiness, and release from suffering. You should cultivate pure desire. But when you lack wisdom, your desires arise from an incorrect perception of the objects of your senses. This mistaken perception has a number of facets: you see things as pure, but they are actually impure; you grasp things as being permanent, but actually they are changing moment by moment; you perceive things as pleasurable, but actually they are unpleasant; and you identify yourself, the perceiver, as having an absolute nature that owns all kinds of things, but actually there is no such self or soul. You really believe that things truly exist in the way that you have mistakenly perceived them. Then you are attracted to, or feel aversion for, the objects that you have perceived. You want to get things you don't have. You want more and better things. You don't want to lose what you already possess. All three poisons—ignorance, desire, and hatred—make you dissatisfied, unhappy, and without any purposeful goals. That is why Nāgārjuna and Śāntideva warn us about impure desire.

This is the problem. Impure desire naturally brings about mental turmoil. The most intense type of desire for beings in the desire realm is sexual desire. Sexual desire is very difficult to control. It often results in sexual misconduct. The negative effects of sexual misconduct can be great. Therefore, Nāgārjuna's next piece of advice for laypeople is to abandon desire for another person's partner. Adultery is presented as shorthand for all the varieties of sexual misconduct. There are two methods to avoid the desire to be sexually involved with another person's partner: a method to suppress desire temporarily and a method to permanently suppress desire. Permanently eliminating any mental affliction is very difficult, especially in the beginning. For that reason, an antidote that simply suppresses a particular mental affliction is well worth applying. In the next six verses Nāgārjuna presents a three-part method that will significantly reduce your desire for sexual pleasure for the present.

How to Temporarily Suppress Desire

Many Hinayana sutras give instructions on how to do this. They say you should meditate on the impurity, impermanence, and suffering nature of the human body—both your own and others. This is similar to what is taught here. In the *Treasury of Knowledge* Vasubandhu says that mental afflictions do not arise on their own. He explains that there are two primary conditions for the arising of the mental affliction of desire: the person or thing to which you are attracted must be nearby and apparent to you, and you must have an improper perception of the object of your desire. No matter how many lovely objects and people surround an arhat, impure desire will not arise because they no longer have a mistaken perception of things. But, for ordinary laypeople, even those with vows, there are three steps you can take to at least suppress your desire. First, you change your attitude so that you no longer perceive the object of your desire as attractive. When you desire someone, you see them as beautiful and without flaw. You come up with many reasons for why this person is attractive. Your desire intensifies because you think about this person in this way over and over again. Soon you find them overwhelmingly desirable. This is the mistaken perception that we have to change. Second, you guard your mind and restrain your senses. And third, you contemplate the faults of both the desired object and your desirous mind. With these techniques you are just trying to suppress desire. But if you can do that, then you can engage in additional methods that will permanently eliminate desire.

Changing Your Perception

The first thing to do in order to suppress desire is to avoid being near the object of your attraction. If you must be near the object of your desire, at least do not pay attention to them in a sensualized way. The following verse explains how to change your manner of thinking.

> 21. Don't gaze upon another's wife. However,
>   if you do look, think of her as your mother,
>   sister, or daughter, according to her age.
>   If lust arises, contemplate the body's impurity.

Like so many other ancient religious texts, *Letter to a Friend* was written for men. So, it says, "don't gaze upon another man's wife." But these instructions apply to everyone. Relationship customs have significantly changed over time. So, you should understand this line to mean, "don't gaze upon another person's sexual partner." This doesn't literally mean that you should never look at someone else's partner. That certainly would make life difficult! Merely seeing an object isn't a complete cause for the arising of desire. If it were, then even arhats and buddhas would have desire whenever they opened their eyes. However, seeing an object causes ordinary people to experience impure desire because they look at it with a wild mind that is under the power of the mental afflictions. Monks are instructed to keep their eyes downcast because until their mind is trained it is easy for desire to arise when something attractive is perceived. In a sutra Ānanda asked the Buddha, "Reverend One, how should we conduct ourselves toward women?" The Buddha replied, "Ananda, do not gaze upon them." He didn't mean that his disciples should close their eyes and go about blindly. The Buddha was giving a warning about the danger of desire. Therefore, he advised his followers to avoid looking at women, or men, with a mind predisposed to find them attractive, sexy, and so on. Looking at others that way causes disturbing thoughts and feelings to arise. These thoughts and emotions lead you to act improperly. This karma results in misery. In short, this advice is to avoid situations that can lead you to engage in problematic behavior.

But let's say you do see another person and lust arises. How do you stop feeling sexual desire? Nāgārjuna says you should stop thinking about that person as a possible sexual partner. Instead, if it is a woman, think of her as if she were your mother if she is older than you. Think of her as if she were your sister if you are around the same age. Think of her as if she were your daughter if she is younger. Again, this also applies to those looking at men as their objects of sexual desire; you think of them as your father, brother, or son. Thinking this way will help you focus on something other than your desire. The person who is the object of your desire may be there in front of you, but your desire will not be there.

Because lust is a very powerful mental affliction, that method might not work. If it doesn't, think about the unattractiveness or impurity of the object. We become entranced with people and things because we think they are lovely. But the reality is that bodies are not pure and are not really attractive. The meditation on impurity will be explained in more detail later in the text, but briefly it is a technique to help you see the reality of the body of the person to whom you are attracted. The reality is that person's body has nine orifices: two eyes, two nostrils, two ears, mouth, anus, and urinary aperture. Does anything nice come out of these? Think about mucous, spittle, urine, and excrement. What is beneath their skin? Think about muscles, bones, intestines, and so forth. Your mind doesn't want to go in this direction. But if you think about someone's body this way it will reduce your lust for it.

However, even this may not work. Even if you have concentrated on the impurity of that person's body, you may still feel lust. If the person to whom you are attracted still appears to be lovely, you employ the second part of the method to temporarily suppress desire: guarding your mind and restraining your senses.

Guarding Your Mind and Restraining Your Senses

22. Protect your wavering mind as if it were
your education, child, treasure, or life.
Renounce sensory pleasures for they are like
poisonous snakes, weapons, enemies, and fire.

How do you protect your mind? Either you stay away from situations that are conducive to mental afflictions arising or you keep your mind from going toward objects that are harmonious with the production of a mental affliction. To understand the nature of a protective attitude, Nāgārjuna gives a variety of examples of things that ordinary people feel they should shield from harm. When you want to master a subject, you want to protect your learning. You review the subject matter again and again so that you don't forget it. Another example of something to be protected is a beloved child. A parent always tries to guard their child from harm. They worry and do so much to keep the child safe. Wealth is also something that people usually see as worthy of protection. Someone rich employs protective measures to keep their valuables from being stolen or ruined in some way. Of course, you see your life as something that should be cherished. It is the most important thing that you have. You are willing to try almost anything to protect it and maintain it. But your mind is in even more need of protection than any of these four things.

If your mind is not controlled, it is not protected. The final two lines of the verse contain analogies for the danger of an uncontrolled mind's pursuit of sensory pleasure. You should turn away from attractive sense objects as if they were poisonous snakes. Weapons can cause pain and injury if they are used against you, so you should stay away from them too. An enemy who wants your life or property should obviously be avoided. Fires are also dangerous.

"But," you may say, "I like seeing nice things, hearing beautiful sounds, eating tasty food, and indulging in sexual pleasure. Why shouldn't I enjoy these things? Why should I have to give all this up? Wouldn't it be foolish to avoid this pleasure when I have the opportunity to enjoy it?" The seventh-century Buddhist lay scholar Ācārya Candragomin answers those questions.

Those living in the world desire pleasure
like an elephant that craves a few mouthfuls
of grass growing deep inside the walls of a well.
The elephant falls into the cavernous hole without getting any.

[Letter to a Disciple, 77]

This verse gives another example for the dangerous nature of your desire for pleasure. Elephants enjoy eating fresh greenery. If an elephant sees some fresh grass growing down on the interior wall of a deep well, it will reach further and further into the well to get it. The elephant will fall in; it can't get out and doesn't even get the pleasure of eating the grass. This is similar to your continual reaching for the enjoyment of sensual, worldly pleasure. You strive throughout your life to gain wealth, fame, praise, and sexual pleasure. When you don't get what you want, you get angry and jealous. To get what you want you engage in so much negative karma. Looking for pleasure you lie, cheat, and harm others. You think that you have to act in these risky ways to get these desirable things. Without knowing it you create the negative karma that is the cause for you to suffer in the future.

You have the capacity to free yourself from misery and attain the highest level of peace. But this ability is blocked when you leave your senses open and unprotected. If you do not guard your senses, your mind will lock onto all sorts of sensory objects. To restrain your senses is to close the door of your sense organs. You can reverse your pattern of thinking and behavior. Instead of letting your senses control your mind, your mind can control your senses. A wild elephant can be tamed; your mind can be tamed too. You can make your actions positive and beneficial to yourself and others. The next two verses in Nāgārjuna's text makes this point.

23.   The Buddha said that objects of the senses lead to ruin
and should be discarded like kimpāka fruit.
Their iron chains bind those in the world
to the prison of cyclic existence.

The reason you have to turn away from sense objects is that attraction and attachment to the pleasure of using them leads to disaster. You may get some temporary enjoyment from sensory objects, but it is deceptive. Nāgārjuna says that they are like kimpāka fruit. A kimpāka fruit tastes sweet, but its flesh is poisonous. Similarly, sense objects seem sweet on the surface, but their nature is to produce suffering. For example, eating when you are hungry is pleasurable. But food doesn't have the nature of pure pleasure; if you eat too much you will feel ill, and if you eat the wrong thing perhaps you will die. Craving sensory objects is like wanting to lick the honey on a razor blade. Every object of sensory desire can give you a kind of joy initially, but in the end, they bring suffering. These desired objects are like chains that have tightly tied your mind to samsaric misery from time without beginning. What makes these chains so tight? Attraction or desire. So, this is the answer to the question of why you shouldn't enjoy these sensory objects. Using them looks like it will provide pleasure, but really, they are like poisonous fruit—tasty but deadly. You renounce desire because you no longer want to be tied to this prison of cyclic existence.

Some people are able to bear the difficulties that arise when pursuing a goal. They control themselves from becoming distracted by attractive objects. Other people don't have any mental strength. They are swayed from their initial purpose whenever they come in contact with an attractive object. Their goal is always changing because they are attracted to one thing after another. They reach for different desirable things all the time. If something seems pleasant, they are happy. The smallest difficulty is unbearable to them. In contrast, someone who has tamed their senses and controlled their mind is more courageous and brave than a military hero.

> 24. When the wise compare those who conquer
>   the six unstable and constantly wavering senses
>   with those who triumph over enemy hosts in battle,
>   they see that the former are the great heroes.

What makes someone a hero? Is it defeating external enemies or masterful control of your internal enemies—a wild mind and unrestrained senses? Society may acclaim someone who has killed many enemy combatants in battle. But your real enemy is your uncontrolled mind that chases after sensory objects. This is what truly harms you and others.

Think about what this inner enemy does. Great yogis and bodhisattvas have done the difficult work of gaining control over their senses. Wise people see those who have fought to control their senses as more heroic than ordinary soldiers.

Contemplating the Faults of the Object of Your Desire

The third part of the method to subdue desire is to contemplate the negative features of the desired object and the mind that desires that object. The technique here is to think about the negative side of both the subject—the mind—and the object. Earlier I alluded to the impurity of the body that is the object of desire. Now I will go into more detail on how to think along these lines. Even though this is an effective way to reduce sexual desire, we don't like to think this way. Remember, you can substitute a man's body for the woman's body in any of these verses. It certainly isn't the case that a woman's body is dirty while a man's body is pure. This instruction is for any practitioner who wants to subdue their sexual desire. Everyone should think this way about regardless of the gender of their object of sexual desire. Sexual desire is very difficult to control; to subdue it you must do this meditation repeatedly and intensely.

> 25. Look at a youthful woman's body
> without any attractive embellishment.
> It has a foul odor; filth is emitted from nine orifices;
> It is like a pot full of garbage; it is hard to fill; and it is
> covered with skin.

Usually when you see a young person's body you think it is attractive. But you should perceive it in the opposite way. A body is like a plastered and painted vessel. The surface looks nice, but things inside aren't so pleasant. The bones, intestines, organs, and so on that make up your insides are not very appealing. A body is like a sack filled with all kinds of disgusting things: urine, excrement, digesting food, blood, phlegm, etc. If you had a pot filled from a cesspool or a garbage can full of rotting refuse you wouldn't think it was attractive. Human bodies are even worse than that. Nothing nice comes out of any of the body's orifices. Nāgārjuna also says this body is difficult to fill. You eat three or more times every day trying to fill it up. But it is never enough. You have to eat again tomorrow.

So, you may think to yourself, "OK, the interior of a body isn't something to lust after, but the exterior is different. It is beautiful because of perfumes, jewelry, clothing, and so forth." However, those things aren't a person's body. The smell of perfume isn't the odor of the body. The pretty jewels aren't the body. So why should you be attracted to someone's body because of them? Śāntideva said,

> Perfumes applied to the body
> are only sandalwood and so forth,
> Why are you lustful when the scent
> is the fragrance of something else?
> [*Introduction to the Practice of Bodhisattvas*, 8.65]

Now we move on to examine the defects of the subject—the desirous mind. What are the faults from this perspective?

> 26. Know that someone desiring sense objects
>   is like a leper tormented by maggots.
>   He resorts to using fire to find comfort,
>   but there is no relief to be found.

In ancient India many people suffered from leprosy. There was a folk tradition that if a leprous wound became maggot infested, it would feel better if the maggots were burnt out. Although heat may have made the wound feel better initially, a burn just made the suffering worse.

From the spiritual point of view, ordinary beings are like children. Children don't see beyond the surface. They go after whatever looks like it will be pleasurable. They do not consider what is beneficial, what is dangerous, what is good for them, or what is bad in the long run. Out of desire for sensual pleasure, ordinary beings act in this childish way. They are always looking for sensory—particularly sexual—gratification. They don't see what the results of their actions will be. Partaking of sensory pleasures may seem pleasant, but it is not real happiness or peace. The enjoyment that comes from eating, drinking, and sexual intercourse is never completely fulfilling. Indulging in these things brings on greater desire for another such experience. Sensual enjoyment is only a small fleeting pleasure. Subsequent to that moment there will be an increase of misery.

In another work Nāgārjuna wrote:

> There may be pleasure in scratching mangy sores,
> but it is more pleasurable to be without mange.
> Likewise, there may be pleasure in world of desire,
> but it is more pleasurable is to be without desire.
> [*Precious Garland,* 2.69]

Ordinary people deceive themselves by thinking that life is pleasurable. They are willing to sacrifice so much for the worldly concerns of wealth, praise, fame, and pleasure. To gain even a small amount of these things, they lie, deceive, cheat, and so forth. Even in this life there are consequences to such actions: you may lose your dignity, your reputation, your wealth, be put in jail, etc. Therefore, applying the methods to temporarily subdue desire is very useful. You should think along those lines even to protect yourself in this life.

HOW TO PERMANENTLY ELIMINATE DESIRE

Desire is like a poisonous tree. If you cut back the branches and chop the trunk down to the ground the tree will be gone for a while. But it will grow back if you don't cut it out from the root. Desire is similar. You can temporarily suppress desire with the above methods. But what kind of meditation should you do to become permanently and completely free of both your current desire and the potential for desire to arise again? Śāntideva said that to completely eliminate desire you need to realize the ultimate nature of reality.

> A mind focused on objects other than emptiness
> can be stopped but will arise again
> like a nonconceptual meditative absorption.
> Therefore, you must meditate on emptiness.
> [*Introduction to the Practice of Bodhisattvas,* 9.48]

A meditative absorption that is without thought can be attained by practicing the mundane path. First you achieve śamatha. Then you combine that with wisdom that understands the disadvantages of the desire realm and the advantages of the first level of the corporeal realm. In this way, you temporarily abandon the mental afflictions that belong to the desire realm and attain the first level of the corporeal realm. Then you do the same process again: with single-pointed concentration you develop wisdom seeing the disadvantages of the first level of the corporeal realm and the advantages of the second level. In that way you suppress the mental afflictions associated with the first level and attain the second level of the corporeal realm. You do this successively for each level of the corporeal and noncorporeal realms to attain the next higher level. Finally, you attain the subtlest level of mind in samsara. At the highest absorption of the noncorporeal realm there are no sensory or conceptual functions; all gross thought has stopped. The mind is even more subtle than when you faint or fall into a deep sleep. Some people maintain this nonconceptual mental absorption for a very long time. Although thought and the mental afflictions have ceased, this isn't a true cessation. It is merely temporary. The mental afflictions have not been completely removed. At some point they will arise again.

In order to eliminate any mental affliction, particularly desire, totally and permanently you need to extirpate its root cause. The root of desire is ignorance. Ignorance is the egoistic view. In other words, it is believing in a real and absolute personal identity. Thus, ignorance is more than simply not knowing the nature of reality. It is an active misconception; it is perceiving things as having inherent and independent existence. Ignorance pertains to both subject and the object: both perceived objects and the perceiving person seem to have a true nature that exists as it appears. We uncritically hold this absolute existence to be the case without any examination or education. This is the ignorance that is the root of our problems.

To actually eliminate ignorance, you must have a direct realization of emptiness. Emptiness is the fact that everything lacks—or in other words, is empty of—intrinsic objective existence. Although from the perspective of ignorance things appear to exist that way, nothing exists in the way that it appears to ignorance. At the same time, you must understand that things are not totally nonexistent. They are dependent on causes, conditions, parts, and the mind perceiving them. Therefore, we say that things exist relatively. To remove the root of the mental afflictions you have to eliminate the ignorance that misapprehends the perceiving self and other phenomena as being really existent—that is, existing in the way that they appear—and simultaneously not deny conventional contingent existence. Thus, the actual method to become free from desire is to develop the wisdom that understands the ultimate nature of phenomena. This is the highest wisdom.

Removing desire along with its root cause is a long and difficult process. First you have to conceptually understand ultimate reality. But just seeing the ultimate once isn't enough for it to be an effective weapon to use against the obstacles. You have to reinforce your realization over and over again. You gradually develop your understanding through contemplation. Eventually it becomes a direct perception of the ultimate nature of reality.

> 27. In order to directly see ultimate reality
> properly condition your mind to all things.
> There is no other Dharma
> with greater good qualities than this.

What is ultimate reality? It is the nature of all existing things. It is emptiness. Well, that probably doesn't clarify much, does it? So here I will go into a bit more detail.

Ultimate Reality

Previously I mentioned that there are 84,000 mental afflictions—which is a way of saying there are a truly enormous number of afflictions. All of these stem from the three poisons: desire, hatred, and ignorance. If you want to eliminate any of the mental afflictions you must eliminate the most basic root of them all: ignorance. Ignorance is incorrectly apprehending that a subject—an *I*—exists as an independent, substantive, real thing. In addition, it is the same incorrect apprehension of objects, thinking that they are substantially real when in truth they are not. On that basis desire and aversion arise. If a thing looks attractive, you run after it; if it is ugly, you run away. You don't see the reality of the object or the subject. To correct your mistaken apprehensions, you need to examine how things exist and how things do not exist. You must analyze the self—the subject side, and external things—the object side.

How do things exist? There are two realities: phenomenal or conventional reality, and ultimate reality. Ultimate reality is emptiness: things do not exist in the way that they appear to ordinary people; things appear to be intrinsically existent, but they are not. However, things exist, just not in the way that we ordinarily think that they do. Phenomenal things exist dependent on causes, parts, and designation. Conventionally existent things are determined to exist when they meet three criteria: (1) they are commonly established for people, (2) they are not contradicted by a conventional avenue of knowledge, and (3) they are not contradicted by reasoning that investigates the final nature of things. So, there are two aspects of reality to understand: dependent origination and emptiness. When you see both of these in every phenomenon you remove the mental afflictions. Without this wisdom you can't get rid of karma and its resultant impure lives in samsara.

This is a deep and difficult teaching. It is hard to express in a way that is easily understood. When the Buddha first taught about emptiness people thought he was crazy. They thought, "How could it be that things are like illusions because they arise from causes and conditions?" Buddha's contemporaries, and many today, used the logic of dependent origination to come to the opposite conclusion of the Buddha. They thought that causality proves that things are real and intrinsically existent. They thought that the Buddha was espousing nihilism. He was not; he said that because things are dependent upon conditions they exist, but they are not intrinsically and independently real. Dependent origination is in fact the primary reason for saying that everything is empty; dependent origination shows that nothing exists independently, that everything is empty of independent existence. The profundity of this point makes it necessary to study books and listen to teachings. Only then can you come to understand it.

Instead of properly analyzing the way things exist, many people want to sit in meditation. But what can you meditate on if you haven't learned anything? Nothing. And emptiness isn't nothingness. Meditation is the process of becoming accustomed to something. There are two kinds of meditation: analytical meditation and stabilization meditation. In analytical meditation you critically examine something. In stabilization meditation you work to develop the flexibility and control of meditative concentration in order to focus your mind on a single object for as long as you wish. Later, when you are more advanced, you combine these two forms of meditation, but initially they are separate practices. Meditation on emptiness is solely analytical until you can employ śamatha along with it. You examine phenomena and try to logically understand what exists, how things exist, and what does not exist. You repeat this analytical process again and again. When you add śamatha to your analytical meditation your understanding will eventually become spontaneous and vividly clear. You will attain insight, a direct realization beyond ordinary thought.

The process of meditation is the same as athletic training. First an athlete has to learn the techniques involved in their sport. Then they practice those skills again and again. Eventually the skills become totally natural, spontaneous, and require no effort. This is how meditation works in both the sutra and tantra forms of practice. First you study so that you understand what is going on. Then you repeat your analysis many, many times. Just thinking about something once may give you a vague understanding, but it is only through repetition and the powerful focus of meditative concentration that you can develop your intellectual understanding into a direct realization. Think about the ancient method of using a fire drill to create a fire. A fire drill is a wooden spindle and baseboard. If you just rotate the tip of the spindle on the baseboard once or twice, you don't create enough heat to start a fire. You need to grind the spindle again, and again, and again, and finally you produce enough heat to create an ember.

This is how great yogis develop the wisdom understanding ultimate reality. It is an active process. It is like learning to walk on a high wire. At first it is very difficult. But acrobats practice until it is very easy to do. Once they are accustomed to it, they no longer need to think or pay attention to their feet. Yogis habituate themselves to emptiness and attain a direct realization by going through a gradual and laborious process of training their mind. Once they have successfully obtained a direct realization of ultimate reality, they don't need to apply the same reasoning process to every single thing that exists. When they understand emptiness in regard to one meditation object, they recognize that it applies to everything else too. However, they still continue to meditate on emptiness so that it becomes spontaneous. So, the first thing to do is examine both the perceiving subject and perceived objects. The teachings provide you with the logical framework for this examination. After you understand ultimate reality, you have to make your mind accustomed to it until a direct realization arises spontaneously. That is what it means to meditate.

No other meditation can compare to the meditation on emptiness. There are many other meditations that are powerful, important, and necessary. But nothing but this meditation on ultimate reality can directly cut the chains of samsara. When you look at how a logger cuts down a tree, you see that there are many parts involved. The engine of a chainsaw, the handle, the fuel, the man holding the saw, and so forth, all combine so the tree can be cut. But it is the blade of the chainsaw that does the actual cutting. The rest of the parts are supports; they are necessary, but they don't directly cut the tree. No matter how sharp and powerful the blade is, it couldn't cut the tree without the other supporting elements. And it doesn't matter if you have all the supports; if the blade is weak and dull it won't cut the tree either. The sharp blade is analogous to the highest wisdom that comprehends the ultimate; it is that wisdom that is the direct antidote of the mental afflictions. It cuts the chains that bind you to samsara.

Tsongkhapa said,

> You may meditate on renunciation and bodhicitta,
> but without the wisdom that understands the way things exist
> you cannot cut the root of worldly existence.
> Therefore, strive in the means to understand dependent
>   origination
> [The Three Principal Aspects of the Path, 9]

"Worldly existence" is samsara: the condition of being born again and again into impure lives under the power of karma and the mental afflictions. Someone under the power of the mental afflictions has no control over where they go after death, no control over experiences in their life, and no control over how long a life will last. Samsara is to live in a cycle: sometimes high, sometimes low, sometimes intermediate. Being free from samsara doesn't mean nonexistence or that you become nothing. It is existence of the highest purity because of the elimination of impure karma, ignorance, and the mental afflictions.

Until you have a realization of the nature of reality you live in confusion. You think that you have some kind of immutable substantial existence. You feel like *you* possess your body and mind. It seems like you have an identity that is separate from your body and mind. You make a similar mistake in regard to objects. Things appear to exist independently and autonomously. Because of this confusion, mental afflictions arise and you create all kinds of karma.

The first step is to try to suppress or reduce the mental afflictions by practicing the appropriate antidote. A spiritual antidote is to think in a way that is the opposite of a mental affliction. For example, the antidote to anger is patience; the antidote to desire for samsaric pleasure is to meditate on the negative qualities of things in samsara. The latter antidote is the way to develop renunciation. Renunciation is turning away from samsara because you see samsara clearly with all its faults. You are so disgusted by the misery of samsara that you no longer want any part of it. You want to be free from it completely. All day and all night you want to obtain liberation. Bodhicitta is the extension of renunciation from yourself to all others. You see that others are suffering in samsara too. Just as you do not want to be in the misery of samsara any longer, neither do they. Therefore, you take responsibility to free others from their suffering. However, you recognize that until you achieve enlightenment yourself you cannot complete that task. So purely for the benefit of all sentient beings, not for your own pleasure, you want to attain enlightenment.

With some work you can become so familiar with the steps to produce the attitudes of renunciation and bodhicitta that they arise spontaneously. That is wonderful. But even with them, if you don't see the true nature of phenomena, you cannot cut the root of samsara. Therefore, you should try to understand dependent arising. Why? Because emptiness means that things do not exist in the way they appear. However, they do exist. They exist in dependence upon causality. Nothing is independent and singular; nothing is free from dependence on something else. Every single thing exists dependently, relatively, conventionally.

Ultimate reality is true for everything. This does not mean that there is one big emptiness that pervades everything. It is simply that every single thing is empty of intrinsic existence. Because everything lacks intrinsic existence, we say that emptiness pervades everything. So, what is ultimate reality? What does *ultimate* mean? How do you analyze it? How do you meditate on it properly? Nāgārjuna describes the ultimate as follows:

> The definition of actual reality
> is not understood from others, it is peace,

> indescribable by verbal expression,
> nonconceptual, and undifferentiated.
> [*Fundamental Verses on the Middle Way*, 18.9]

This verse is meant to help you understand ultimate reality, but the verse itself isn't easy to understand! Roughly, Nāgārjuna is saying that the way things really exist—in other words, actual reality, ultimate reality, or suchness—is emptiness. This is the reality of all existing things. Emptiness doesn't appear to ordinary beings. Things look like they are substantively real to them. For example, an illusion of an elephant created by a magician appears to be an elephant. As an object it looks like an elephant. But it isn't. It depends upon the magician, a basis, a viewer, and a magic trick of some sort. It is empty of being an elephant even though it appears to be one. All conventional things are like this. When a yogi directly sees emptiness, emptiness appears exactly as it is. There is no other interpretation.

So, what do the different qualities listed in the above verse mean? The first one, "not understood from others," seems odd because initially you do learn about ultimate reality from others. You depend upon your teachers and books. Even though their words are only indicative, and not ultimate reality itself, without them you can't come to understand reality. Through study you gain an inferential understanding and think, "Oh, it must be like this." But a general conceptual understanding isn't enough. You use logic to understand things roughly but then you have to put your correct understanding into meditation. Eventually through repeated meditation you have an insight that doesn't rely on conceptions or images. So, your actual insight comes from purifying your mind through meditation; it isn't directly produced by your teacher's instructions or the words in books. So, this phrase is pointing out that you must go beyond the inferential understanding that you gain from other sources and work on your own to familiarize your mind. It doesn't mean that you shouldn't rely upon others at any time.

Ultimate reality is the object of ultimate wisdom. Emptiness is the only object of a yogic direct realization; only that wisdom sees emptiness. Thought doesn't apprehend its object directly. (But remember, this doesn't mean that thought isn't a necessary step along the way to developing a direct realization through meditation.) A direct realization is knowledge that doesn't depend on other thoughts or concepts that are separate from it. A very rough analogy is that it is like seeing a fresh, shiny olive on the palm of your hand. You see it directly; the color and shape are clear and obvious. You don't need someone to tell you about it; you don't need to think about it; you don't need to describe it to yourself in words.

The Heart Sutra says that the object of perfect wisdom is beyond thought and words. It is not born nor does something else create it. It cannot cease; it cannot be destroyed like a physical thing. It is the essential nature of everything. In a way, emptiness is like space. Space is a mere lack of obstruction. It is there all the time, but, like emptiness, it is defined by its absence. It isn't produced by causes and conditions and it can't be destroyed. However, without space you couldn't build a house. If that house burns down, the space is still there. Empty space is not nonexistent. Similarly, emptiness is not a conceptual thing, like a rabbit horn, that does not exist. It isn't like an ordinary thing can be described verbally with expressions such as, "it exists as one," or, "it doesn't exist," and so forth. It cannot be completely understood on the conceptual level. Thought differentiates subject and object. Emptiness is not an object that can be dualistically conceptualized. Why? Because emptiness is not something different from the thing that is empty. This is very important. Emptiness is merely the negation of that thing's intrinsic existence. It is the mere lack of that thing existing as it appears. It isn't a separate object. For example, the emptiness of a table isn't something other than a table. A table seems to be something solid; it seems to exist intrinsically on its own as a table. Yet a table is actually a combination of parts, colors, and atoms. It exists as a result of various causes and it is changing, imperceptibly, moment by moment. We give this concatenation the name *table*. When you look at it this way, a table only dependently and contingently exists. That is its phenomenal reality. It is there, certainly, but it is empty of absolute, intrinsic, and autonomous existence. The table's emptiness is the nature of the table, not something else. The table and its emptiness exist at the same time. They are not different.

Thus, emptiness doesn't exist independently of dependently arisen things. You can't find emptiness somewhere else. So, in regard to a table, for example, you have to understand both phenomenal and ultimate realities. There is a table on the conventional, phenomenal, level, but from the ultimate perspective there is no intrinsically existent table. In terms of ultimate reality the table is empty; but conventionally it is a table. The phenomenal reality of the table can be understood conceptually. In contrast, when you realize emptiness directly, your mind is completely merged with emptiness, like water poured into water. Emptiness is the object of the highest gnosis. It is only perfectly known in a direct realization. When you get up from that meditation you can recollect what you understood, but that recollection is already conceptual.

So, it is a mistake to look for ultimate reality somewhere other than within dependently arisen phenomena. In other words, do not try to realize an absolute that is something other than dependently arisen things. It is wrong to leave conventional things aside and look for ultimate reality somewhere else. The very things you see, subject and object, are what you should investigate. Your body, your house, and your very self are all the same on an ultimate level—they all lack independent existence in the same way. You can softly identify a combination of causes, conditions, parts, labels, and so forth as a phenomenal thing. It is like a reflection of a face in the mirror. It looks like a real face is there, but a reflection is a product of various conditions: light, a shiny surface, an object to reflect, and so on. There isn't a real face in the mirror. Nonetheless, a reflection of your face is useful when you are shaving or washing up. You need to look at everything in the world this way. Things have a way of appearing that isn't real. A proper understanding of phenomenal reality goes beyond accepting that things exist if they are commonly established and not contradicted either by a conventional avenue of knowledge or reasoning that investigates the ultimate nature of things; it is knowledge of dependent origination. A proper understanding of the actual nature of things, how they ultimately exist, is knowing that they are empty of having an intrinsic identity. You combine these two understandings: on the conventional phenomenal level things dependently exist, but their ultimate nature is empty. Nothing has intrinsic existence; everything merely conventionally exists. This is what you must look into. This is an important point.

Ignorance

Looking for some reality other than a mere dependent nature will not lead to freedom from samsara. Sometimes people think that if they understood something real, absolute, and permanent then they will be freed from the cause of suffering. They believe that all mental afflictions will vanish when they know this absolute. For example, most ancient Indian religious traditions believed that beings trapped in samsara could achieve liberation through coming to know the nature of absolute reality. In this very general way they are like Buddhists. However, these traditions differ from Buddhism regarding the nature of the reality that must be realized for the attainment of emancipation. They were looking for a separate ultimate reality that truly, intrinsically exists.

Let's look at one important example that existed at the time of the Buddha: the Sāṃkhya. An brief overview of their ontology is necessary if you want to understand their view of the ultimate knowledge needed for liberation. They were dualists; they distinguished matter—which includes consciousness—from the soul. They established twenty-four types of matter and one thing—the soul— that is not matter. Some types of matter are causes, some are effects, some are both a cause and an effect. The first and most important type of matter is a cause called the universal principal. It creates all other types of matter including consciousness. The universal principal is the invisible, permanent, intrinsically existent, singular, and uncaused nature within everything. Everything, all the manifold differences in the world and the conscious mind, arises from this one universal principle. It is the only cause. It is pervasive; it has no parts. It is not caused itself; in other words, it isn't the effect of some other cause. It is a form of subtle matter, not mind. So, some Sāṃkhyas said there is no god. Others asserted that there must be some god or intelligence, along with the universal principal for creation to occur. But even this god or intelligence is understood to be permanent, partless, intrinsically existent, and so forth. Coming from this first cause are seven categories of matter that are simultaneously causes and effects. Then there are sixteen forms of matter that are purely effects; they don't cause anything else in turn. Totally separate from these twenty-four forms of matter is the soul. The soul is neither a cause nor an effect. There is a permanent indivisible soul within every living being. This soul has been free from the beginning of samsara, it is partless, it has no qualities in and of itself, it has no function, it is pure. From the Buddhist perspective, the Sāṃkhyas are saying that the object of the egoistic view is real; there is a soul. This soul is permanent; it exists intrinsically; it is pervasive; uncaused; and is invisible and hidden. According to the Sāṃkhya, because the soul gets involved with matter it becomes confused, attached, angry, etc. Living beings will be trapped in samsara until they realize that the soul is distinct from even the subtlest matter, that it is more than the empirical ego, that it is a real, permanent, personal identity. Once this is understood, the universal principle will not create anything anymore and everything that already exists will dissolve back into the universal principle. Samsara will cease to exist for that person. All there will be is the soul. This isolation is freedom.

Buddhism rejects this; Buddhism says that apprehending and believing in a real intrinsic identity, whether of a person or phenomena, is ignorance. It is never the case that someone who has meditated on some universal principle, or god, or the soul has attained liberation. Why? The problem with the Sāṃkhya view is that it takes the self and the universal principle to be permanent and absolute. How can the cause of change in the world be permanent and independent? If something is permanent it can never change. If something is absolutely independent, it cannot cause change in other things. If you couldn't change, there would be no possibility of emancipation. This is a complicated subject and I have given just a very brief summary. Although the Sāṃkhya system may not be perfectly clear to you, I wanted to present it as one common type of belief that cannot lead to liberation. In this regard, Nāgārjuna wrote,

As long as you hold that the aggregates are real
you will believe in a real personal identity.
From this belief in the self, you create karma.
From karma, you will cycle in rebirth again.

These three paths mutually cause each other;
they are like a rapidly whirling torch that creates
a circle without a beginning, middle or end.
This is what it is to cycle in samsara.

[*Precious Garland*, 1.35–36]

Three things are necessary for samsara to exist: ignorance, karma, and rebirth. The traditional way to say this was that there are "three paths." These paths have to converge for there to be an uncontrolled cycle of rebirths. First there must be mental afflictions that are based on ignorance. From the mistaken belief that things really exist as they appear along with its corollary mental afflictions, you create impure karma. The path of the mental afflictions and the path of karma are like parents; their union creates a baby, the path of rebirth. Whenever and wherever you are born, you are deluded and create more karma. So, you go round and round. You cannot point to a beginning of this cycle. It is similar to the glowing wheel created when you whirl a torch or sparkler around quickly. You can't see a beginning, middle, or end of that circle of light. Similarly, ignorance, karma and rebirth produce each other one after the other. This is the meaning of the phrase, "to cycle in samsara."

It is only through understanding the dependent nature of phenomena that you can become free. For example, if you think that a coiled rope over in the corner is a poisonous snake, you get scared and emotional. This fear arises because you are ignorant of the fact that there is no poisonous snake over there. How do you become free from your anxiety about this "snake"? You have to recognize that a piece of rope, a condition of light, and your perception combined so that it seems like a snake is there. You will not be free of your fear until you have a deep understanding that the rope is empty of being a snake.

Śāntideva said,

> If every sort of adversity, fear, and suffering
> that there is in this world arises
> from apprehending a real personal identity,
> what use is this great devil to me?
> [*Introduction to the Practice of Bodhisattvas*, 8.134]

Every living creature in samsara has their own life experiences. They exist differently and experience things differently. Nevertheless, wherever they are born they have misery. Humans too have their own unique physical and mental experiences. Although similar in being human, each individual's fear, pain, suffering, and happiness are the result of their own past actions. You, like everyone else, want peace, happiness, and enjoyment. To get what you want you did things that are harmful to yourself and others. Why did you act this way? It is because of your powerful ignorance. You don't know how things really exist. Because you do not know the actual nature of yourself and phenomena, you misperceive them and believe that your misperception is true. Based on this ignorance, desire, jealousy, and so forth arise. Your mind is blind to reality and reacts. This leads you to do all sorts of actions.

This ignorance is particularly connected to your feeling about yourself. We call this concept of ego, the *I* or the *self*. Closely related to the *I* is your possessiveness, the strong belief that things are mine. Even animals have this attachment to I and mine. Candrakīrti said,

> First thinking, I, they cling to a self,
> then thinking, mine, they become attached to things.
> [*Entering the Middle Way,* 1.3ab]

When you believe that things exist as they appear to you, your mind is occluded by ignorance. That is the problem in a nutshell. The subjective side of ignorance is the egoistic view: apprehending a real personal identity. You perceive yourself incorrectly; you don't know how a perceiving subject actually exists. You see yourself as being substantive, permanent, and independent. Based on that egoistic view all of the other mental afflictions arise. Also, based on the egoistic view is your belief that objects are intrinsically real.

The most essential thing that the Buddha taught is that everything is empty of intrinsic existence, and every sort of undesirable experience in the world arises from not knowing that reality. Wisdom is the opposite of ignorance; it sees reality, that the self and all phenomena are empty of an intrinsic inherent nature. When through meditation you come to understand that everything, both the personal self and all phenomena, lack inherent existence, you simultaneously see how everything exists conventionally and relatively. All phenomenal things—subjects and objects—are seen to be without an intrinsically real nature. You see that the nature of things is like a reflection in a mirror or a magical illusion. They appear due to causes and conditions. They are dependent on other things. Not a single thing is independent of causes, conditions, parts, designation, and so forth, therefore they exist relatively.

Freedom means that your mind is liberated from ignorance and the mental afflictions. A result of freeing your mind is to become free from deluded actions. Therefore, we call ultimate reality—emptiness—a holy object because realization of it leads to peace, enjoyment, and all spiritual goals including enlightenment.

Sometimes people think that you are a buddha as soon as you have a direct realization of emptiness. You are not. A direct realization of the ultimate makes you an ārya. An ārya is superior to an ordinary being; their way of seeing, perceiving, and understanding reality is different from what is usual in the world. When they are meditating on the ultimate, āryas see things as they really are. They directly see emptiness, and only emptiness. Nothing appears to intrinsically exist. Conventional things do not appear during their direct perception of emptiness. But when an ārya arises from meditation, conventional things appear to them again. However, they no longer strongly cling to the idea that things exist as they appear; they understand that phenomena are like illusions. They know from their meditation experience that things have a relative nature and don't exist intrinsically or objectively. So many analogies are used to explain to ordinary people what this understanding is like. It is said that everything is like a mirage, a reflection of the moon on water, a magical illusion, or an echo. For ordinary people things don't seem to exist this way. Ordinary people believe that things exist as they appear. Āryas are mindful of their meditative experience and how things appear subsequent to their meditation. They work on their meditation more and more and gradually ignorance is completely uprooted. Then there is no longer room in their mind for desire, hatred, or any other mental affliction created by ignorance.

Why are we stuck in samsara? Why do we cause ourselves to suffer over and over? It is because we don't realize that all phenomenal things are relative and dependent. We don't know that these things lack an inherent intrinsic nature. In other words, we don't understand the two realities: the phenomenal and the ultimate. Those who do not realize the nature of reality are like children attached to their toys. Adults see those toys differently and are not attached to them. Similarly, what binds us to samsara is our own ignorance and karma. We mistake the nature of internal and external reality; we misapprehend things to be real and believe that they exist objectively in their own right just as they appear. If a thing looks beautiful, we believe it is objectively beautiful; if it looks ugly, we believe it is objectively, really ugly. We are stuck in our thinking; our minds hold things and ourselves as having a real and absolute true nature. From this comes many other incorrect thoughts. Therefore, we act wrongly and that ties us to rebirth in samsara. Thus, ignorance is the primary cause of suffering. If you were not deluded about the nature of reality, you wouldn't create karma. As long as you create karma, you suffer. As you develop wisdom, the opposite of the mental afflictions, the bondage gradually loosens. Eventually your wisdom will be perfect, and you will be completely free from bondage.

Rejection of the Extremes of Nihilism and Eternalism

So how do you get out of samsara? How do you get off this wheel of uncontrolled rebirth? In the following verse from the *Precious Garland,* Nāgārjuna explains that all mental afflictions, wrong conceptions, and confusion are gotten rid of by understanding emptiness. Having abandoned these completely you will be liberated.

> Belief in the self is quashed when you see
> that samsara does not arise from itself,
> from something else, from both, or in the three times.
> Due to that karma and rebirth cease too.
>
> [*Precious Garland,* 1.37]

There has never been a time, nor will there be a time, that things arise absolutely or intrinsically. Never in the past, the present, or the future—the three times—has anything had independent, substantive existence. When you search for things and how they come to be, you will realize things do not intrinsically arise from themselves, from other things, from both themselves and other things, or without a cause. This wisdom eliminates all belief that you—the I—and phenomenal things have an intrinsic identity. Because you understand that the emptiness of intrinsic existence is the true nature of yourself and phenomena, you will not create any more impure karma. And no longer will there be any conditions that would allow previous karma to ripen. If karma ceases there will be no more rebirth in samsara.

This understanding destroys the wrong views of nihilism and eternalism. Because the extremes of absolute existence and nonexistence are obliterated, a correct view of emptiness is called the "middle way," or in Sanskrit, Madhyamaka. *Middle* means that this view is free of both extreme ontological positions. Only the Buddha taught the middle way. Worldly gods, like the ancient Indian deities Vishnu, Īśvara, Indra, and so on did not teach this view. Because they did not teach emptiness, they did not provide their disciples with the means to achieve freedom. Sometimes buddhas are given the epithet Īśvara. This appellation doesn't mean that a

Buddha is Īśvara—a supreme being or God—it simply indicates that buddhas are the most powerful. In short, if you understand emptiness, you will attain liberation; if you do not understand it, you will not. To clarify this point, Āryadeva, the primary disciple of Nāgārjuna, said,

> No-self is said to be
> the sole doorway to peace,
> the destroyer of all wrong views,
> and the main subject of buddhas' teachings.
> [*Four Hundred Stanzas,* 12.13]

Later Madhyamaka masters may have differences regarding some philosophical points, but they all accept that Nāgārjuna and Āryadeva were the greatest Madhyamaka masters. It doesn't matter what term you use for the ultimate nature of reality; you can call it śūnyatā, emptiness, selflessness, anātman, or no-self. Whatever you call it, it is the principal thing that you have to know if you want freedom from samsara. There is no other method to attain liberation than understanding it. All buddhas directly realized it in order to attain their enlightenment.

You must understand emptiness in relation to all phenomena: your body, mind, senses, and sensory objects. As an ordinary person, your mind holds things to be real and absolute. You mentally project permanence and absolute reality onto dependent, changing things. You see beauty, ugliness, and other qualities as truly real. You think things objectively exist with their own identity in the manner that they appear. But in reality, everything is dependent upon causes and conditions, and upon parts, or atomic particles. For example, let's look at a tree. It looks like a tree is really just outside your window. Something with the nature of *treeness* seems to be absolutely there. But what is the reality of the tree? It has many parts: roots, bark, leaves, branches, and a trunk. If you clear these away one by one, looking for the real identity of the tree, you find that there is no such thing. The tree is a mere designation dependent upon many parts. Everything is like this. Your body, others' bodies, houses, and so forth, are dependent. This is their true nature. Things arise merely based on conditions. There is nothing that stands by itself alone.

If you don't understand this, you fall to one of the two extremes, either nihilism or eternalism. Nihilism is going too far towards nonexistence.

You have annihilated every possible form of existence until there is nothing left. If you have a nihilistic view, you think that causality, karma and its results, do not exist. You think that it is untrue that bad actions bring bad results and good actions bring positive results. Then you have no reason to act in a positive way. You have annihilated the possibility of practices leading to enlightenment. The other extreme wrong view, eternalism, is to believe that things exist as they appear—stable, enduring, and substantively real. Negative emotions arise from holding that whatever appears to you is real. And then you create impure karma.

The right view, the view that is without these two wrong views, is difficult to understand. The Buddha explained it in many ways at many places in the sutras. For example, the *Question of the Nāga King Anavatapta Sutra* says,

> Whatever arises due to conditions is unarisen;
> it doesn't originate due to an intrinsic nature.
> Whatever is contingent upon conditions is said to be empty.
> Whoever knows emptiness is conscientious.

On the surface it seems contradictory to say that whatever arises due to conditions doesn't arise. But the second line clarifies this statement. It says that there is no absolute arising; there is no intrinsic arising; and nothing arises independently. Emptiness means that things are without their own independent nature; in other words, they are contingent upon something else. Things that are dependent upon conditions lack independence. To be conscientious here means that you have the knowledge that the self and phenomena, subject and object, are empty. If you understand that this is the reality for everything, then you have knowledge necessary for the attainment of liberation.

Nāgārjuna says something very similar in another text:

> There are no things whatsoever
> that do not arise in dependence.
> Therefore, there are no things
> that are not empty.
>
> [*Fundamental Verses on the Middle Way,* 24.19]

Nāgārjuna wrote six texts to logically prove that everything is empty and only relatively existent. "But," you may ask, "how can things like causes and effects be empty? We see all around us that a particular cause yields a specific result: for example, an apple seed causes an apple tree, and a human sperm and egg cause a human birth. Thus, things do arise from causes and conditions. This is the way things really come to be. So, how can you reject the production of things from causes and conditions?" The Buddhist response is that you have to understand what it means to say dependent origination. An understanding of how things arise is closely connected to an understanding of emptiness. In other words, you have to understand how to reject intrinsic arising or production.

There are only four possible ways that things could absolutely and intrinsically arise: (1) they could arise from themselves, (2) they could arise from something else, (3) they could arise from both themselves and something else, or (4) they could arise without any cause. There is no other way that things could be produced. The Madhyamaka texts reject each of these possibilities of intrinsic arising. Each one of them is an extreme and leads to illogical consequences.

Let's look a little more at the problems with each possible means of intrinsic production. First, there were some Indian philosophical schools, like the Sāṃkhya, who said that things do arise from themselves. According to them, if things didn't already exist within the principal cause, they could never become manifest. Their view is that the universal cause, and everything within it, absolutely and intrinsically exists. This is logically inconsistent. If things did exist and arise that way, then every single thing would be the creator of itself. If a thing already exists, there is no need for it to produce itself. That makes the very idea of production meaningless. If things intrinsically arise from themselves, there would also be the problems of infinite regression and infinite progression: they would have arisen forever and never stop arising.

The second possibility, arising from other, is the hard one to understand. We are so sure that things arise from causes other than themselves. Even some Buddhist philosophical schools accepted arising from other. You have to be clear about what is being rejected in the refutation of arising from other. The extreme is that things arise from a cause that is *intrinsically different* from the result. In other words, this is a rejection of a real, absolutely existent cause producing a real intrinsically existent result.

The notion that things that exist as autonomous, substantive realities with their own intrinsic identity can be a cause or an effect is rejected. If a cause and its result were intrinsically existent, the cause and its effect would be totally unconnected and absolutely independent of each other. There can be no relationship between intrinsically different things. Without some connection a cause cannot produce an effect. If it were the case that an intrinsically different thing could cause something else, then everything and anything could arise from anything else: a cow could give birth to a horse; a rice seed could produce corn; or a fire could produce darkness. This is obviously unacceptable. But this illogical consequence becomes possible if there is no relationship between a cause and its effect.

The third possibility is that things arise from both self and other. Since we have already seen that neither means of production is possible on its own, the combination doesn't work either. If things arise from both, all the faults of either possibility would be incurred. So, it is easy to reject arising from both.

The last possibility is that things simply arise without any cause. That was the position of the ancient Indian Cārvāka school. They said that the roundness of a pea is just its nature. Nobody creates it that way. There is no cause for the sharpness of a thorn. No one makes it so. A peacock feather's lovely color and pattern were not made by anyone. They just spontaneously arise. Water flowing down and flames going up also just happen. They denied any form of causation, be it a god, a universal principal, or karma. The problem with their position is that if things arise without needing a cause, then things would always be existent or would never exist. If something does not exist now, then it could never come to exist because there is no cause for it. There would be no reason for it to exist. If something does exist now, it would be permanent because it isn't contingent upon causes and conditions. So, positing that things exist without causes leads you to fall into one or the other of two extremes: if things arise without a cause they would always arise or never arise. Because of these assertions, the Cārvāka were often called nihilists. Further, if things occur without a cause, there would be no purpose in doing something hoping for a result. We put great effort into creating the causes for the results we want. But if things arise without a cause this effort is senseless.

Nāgārjuna praised the Buddha for teaching that none of these four extreme means of production exist.

Sophists have imagined that suffering
arises from itself, or from something other,
or arises from both, or without a cause.
You taught that it arises in dependence.
> [*Praise of the Supramundane, 19*]

All philosophers and religious teachers try to explain to their followers why there is so much suffering in the world. They have come up with various answers to explain the nature of reality. Unfortunately, all of them, except the Buddha, have held one of the four extreme views of production. Their views are not a reflection of reality; they are merely imagined theories about how suffering comes to be. In contrast, the Buddha taught that suffering arises from causes and conditions. It doesn't arise by itself intrinsically, or arise intrinsically from something else, or intrinsically arise without a cause. This is amazing.

Earlier in the same text Nāgārjuna wrote,

A sprout does not come into being
from a seed that has perished, or one that has not perished.
You have taught that everything that arises
is like the arising of a magical illusion.
> [*Praise of the Supramundane, 16*]

A seed and sprout do not intrinsically exist simultaneously, as the Sāṃkhya would say. We can see that the moment a seed germinates the original seed itself is gone, it doesn't maintain its existence. But a sprout doesn't arise from a seed that has completely disappeared either. If an intrinsically existent seed was absolutely destroyed before the intrinsically existent sprout arose, where did the seed connect with the sprout? A sprout doesn't arise from a seed that has both ceased and not ceased to be. So, you have to conclude that things do not rise from any of those four extremes.

So then, what is arising? The answer is that everything arises from causes and conditions. The Buddha used the example of a seed and sprout to teach about dependent origination in the *Rice Seedling Sutra*. This sutra was given its name because in the course of his teaching, the Buddha held up a rice sprout and talked about how it came to exist. A rice plant depends on many causes. There must be a rice seed, earth, water, the warmth of the sun, and many other things. A seed alone cannot yield a plant. A seed on dry ground cannot yield a plant. If certain causes and conditions are met with, certain things arise. If those causes and conditions are not there, then the specific result doesn't arise. The Buddha said, "because this happened, that occurred; because that occurred before, this happened." There are no real absolute intrinsically existent things that continuously go from one thing to another. Everything is impermanent, dependent, and changeable. There is no intrinsic, absolute, truly existent thing in the cause, the result, or the causal function. It is all relative.

The Buddha taught that arising is like a magical illusion. Let's look again at the example of a magician's creation of an illusion of an elephant. It appears; it seems as if an elephant is objectively there. It seems like it exists due to its own nature. But that is not true. It exists for your mind only because of certain conditions of light, a background environment, a magician, and a means of projecting colors and shapes. Based on all these conditions you might be afraid of the elephant, or you might be attracted to it. Either way, that elephant doesn't exist in its own right. The fact that everything arises dependently upon causes and conditions is what is meant when it is said that things are like an illusion.

We can take this further. Dependence means to not be absolutely separate and independent. So, because everything has a dependent existence, everything lacks an independent, inherent, intrinsic identity. Another way of saying this is, because things do not arise independently, they are empty of intrinsic existence. These empty things do exist; they are not totally nonexistent. Everything is designated or labeled as having an identity based on a dependent concatenation of causes, conditions, your mind, and other factors. That is to say, existence is contingently designated. Things nominally exist, but we imagine that they exist in a real substantial way.

Nāgārjuna said,

> Whatever is dependently originated
> is what we call emptiness;
> that is dependent designation;
> that is the middle way.
>
> [*Fundamental Verses on the Middle Way,* 24.18]

Things appear to be real, but they are a product of various causes and conditions. Seeing that everything relatively exists and nothing intrinsically exists is the path between the two extremes of eternalism and nihilism. Because everything is relative and dependent, your impure mind can be made pure. The imperfect can be made perfect. Samsara can be changed to nirvana. By changing the causes and conditions the result can be changed. This is a very positive perspective! Understanding that everything dependently exists and so is empty of intrinsically existing is the right view. Realization of dependent origination is the highest view; there is no view higher than the realization of emptiness.

This right view removes all wrong views. You must accustom your mind to these ideas over a long period of time. You can't just sit down, close your eyes, and understand emptiness. Remember, to meditate is to become mentally accustomed to something by reflecting upon it over and over again. Before you can meditate on something, you have to logically understand it. If you haven't understood something, you cannot meditate upon it.

The first stanza of Nāgārjuna's *Sixty Stanzas on Reasoning* says,

> Those whose intelligence is not fixated anywhere—
> having gone beyond existence and nonexistence—
> ascertain the profound reality devoid of objectification
> in the sense of conditionality.
>
> *[Sixty Stanzas on Reasoning,* 1]

In this stanza, the words "existence" and "nonexistence" are used to indicate the two extremes of eternalism and nihilism. If you believe that things are more than they are, that they have an intrinsic identity, you are holding on to too much. That is the extreme of eternalism. If you think that emptiness means that things do not exist at all, that is going too far in the other direction. That is the extreme of nihilism. Those whose wisdom goes beyond those two extremes are able to know the profound reality of the middle way.

In contrast, there are some people who believe that to meditate on emptiness is to empty the mind of all thought. They contend that any type of thought—whether good or bad—should be blocked. There is some purpose to calming the thoughts that arise in your mind. Sometimes your mind may run so uncontrollably that you cannot work on your mental development. So, at the beginning, but just for a while, you need to block thought. But having a blank mind and remaining in that state is not a meditation on emptiness. Empty doesn't mean "empty your mind of all thoughts and conceptions." It does not mean you should make your mind completely blank. If you do that kind of misguided meditation, you will lack the wisdom that comprehends the dependent nature of phenomena. If you sit in meditation with a blank mind, you will not learn anything from your meditation. When you arise from your meditation you will have no antidote to the mental afflictions.

So, after you quiet your mind, you need to meditate on a correct understanding of the nature of reality. But often people go too far in their analysis and fall into eternalism or nihilism. They may concentrate on things as having a real intrinsic identity. They think that something that they perceive as attractive is really, truly attractive. Or something that they perceive as unattractive is really, truly bad. This type of meditation invites the afflictions of desire and hatred into your mind. Or people convince themselves that things are completely nonexistent. They do not understand that the emptiness of intrinsic existence means that things exist relatively and dependently.

So, what is the perfect meditation on emptiness? It is to produce the wisdom that understands the dependent nature of phenomena. When you completely understand dependent arising you will know that nothing intrinsically exists. This is what you meditate on. That is a proper meditation on emptiness. We say that this is the highest form of meditation because it sees ultimate reality. It is beyond ordinary thought. This kind of meditation on emptiness is called perfect wisdom, in Sanskrit *prajñāpāramitā*. Any type of sutra that has this wisdom as its subject matter is called a prajñāpāramitā sutra, or perfection of wisdom sutra.

For wisdom to be powerful enough to cut the mental afflictions you need some additional qualities. Now we will move on to a discussion of what must accompany wisdom in order to make it strong enough to reach your spiritual goals.

5. The Qualities That Accompany Wisdom

THE WISDOM UNDERSTANDING the ultimate is like a chainsaw that cuts through ignorance. But a chainsaw is useless unless you also have a power source, a person to wield the saw, and so forth. Nāgārjuna presents six qualities that assist you to develop wisdom, maintain wisdom, and eliminate conditions that oppose wisdom. First, wisdom must be accompanied by pure ethical conduct. Second, to practice pure ethical conduct—in other words to engage in morality—you turn away from worldly things. Third, not only do you turn away from worldly things, you should also possess the superior qualities of the āryas. Fourth, in order to develop the seven riches of an ārya practice, you avoid creating conditions that promote their opposite. Fifth, to be harmonious with these ārya qualities you must be satisfied. And finally, sixth, you should choose an appropriate spouse or partner. In this chapter I will talk about the first five qualities. Remember that we covered the sixth one—choosing the right spouse—in chapter 3.

THE QUALITY OF PURE ETHICAL CONDUCT

The wisdom that understands ultimate reality cannot arise unless it is preceded by the ability to control your mind. You have to be able to keep your mind focused single-pointedly on its object to gain a direct realization. In order to develop the meditative concentration of śamatha you need pure ethical conduct. Engaging in ethical conduct allows you to start to control your mind. If you lack pure conduct, you cannot develop concentration and then the wisdom that is the antidote to the mental afflictions. In short, wisdom must be accompanied by pure morality.

Someone who has both wisdom and pure ethical conduct is worthy of respect and praise.

> 28. A person may come from a high family, be learned, and
>   attractive,
>   but if they lack wisdom and morality, they are not worthy
>   of respect.
>   In this regard, if they have these two good qualities vener-
>   ate them
>   even if they lack other positive attributes.

It is appropriate to put your faith in someone holy. What makes someone a holy being? Wisdom and ethical discipline. Here Nāgārjuna is specifically talking about the ethical conduct of body and speech: this is avoidance of three types of physical misconduct and four types of verbal misconduct.[26] The precepts to protect yourself from the three modes of mental misconduct, and the higher precepts for bodhisattvas and tantric yogis are not the issue here. If a person lacks this most basic form of moral conduct and the wisdom understanding the ultimate, they are not worthy of your respect. If someone has pure ethical discipline and high wisdom, then it doesn't matter if they come from a low background, are physically ugly, or poor. They are worthy of honor. Why? Because someone possessing pure ethical conduct will not engage in nonvirtues. When a person with ethical discipline also has the wisdom understanding ultimate reality, they will engage in pure virtuous activity.

You practice ethical discipline in order to reach the ārya path—a direct realization of ultimate reality. You begin to remove mental afflictions from their root only when your realization of emptiness is unmediated by conceptuality. An ārya is considered a superior being because they have merged onto the highway to emancipation. Before you become an ārya, you are an ordinary being traveling on a small side road.

THE QUALITY OF TURNING AWAY
FROM WORLDLY THINGS

What else should you do in order to get onto this superior path? What obstacles should you avoid in order to gain entry to this superior path? You should turn away from worldly concerns that are solely related to obtaining pleasure and avoiding discomfort in this life. When your primary focus is temporary sensual gratification, you cannot enter the ārya path. Nāgārjuna lists the eight common worldly concerns that you should turn away from. These eight are in four pairs: the first member of each pair is something that ordinary beings crave; the second member is the opposite of the first—something that ordinary beings strive to avoid.

> 29. The eight worldly concerns are: gain and loss,
>   pleasure and pain, praise and blame, fame and disrepute.
>   The knower of the world says you should be indifferent
>   to them and not let them occupy your mind.

Śākyamuni Buddha—here called "the knower of the world" due to his omniscience—taught that because of the egoistic view of a personal self your mind is dominated by eight worldly concerns. The first two are the pair of gain and loss. Gaining and having wealth and losing it so that you fall into poverty in and of themselves are not a problem. An advanced practitioner can be rich or poor; either way it doesn't affect them. It is the mental attitude that ordinary beings have in relation to gain and loss that creates the problem. The problem is our dissatisfaction, not the presence or absence of money and possessions. We ordinary beings are always looking for food, clothes, shelter, and money. No matter how much we have, we crave more and more. No matter what we have, we want something better. When we are wealthy, we indulge in the pleasant feelings but underneath we are uncomfortably afraid of losing what we have. If we lose a bit of our wealth, we are unhappy. When we lack things, we find it very unpleasant. When what we have isn't perfect, we are unhappy. Dissatisfaction is the problem with the remaining pairs of worldly concerns too; we are never satisfied with who we are and what we have. The next pair of worldly concerns is physical and mental pain and pleasure. The third pair is praise and blame. When people directly praise us, we are happy whether we actually have that quality or not. If someone criticizes or disparages us, we get angry and are unhappy whether we have that fault or not. Sometimes people can't even sleep when they hear certain things about themselves. Not only do we react to direct praise and criticism, we also crave fame from far away. If a bit of our fame becomes tarnished, we get upset. We don't want a bad reputation. Praise and fame are empty words, but we think that they are absolute causes of happiness or misery.

Usually, these eight are our primary objectives. We work throughout our life to gain these things. We assume that our actions in pursuit of these concerns will bring us happiness. Whatever we do we are trying to gain wealth, sensual pleasure, praise, and a good reputation. We are trying to block their opposites: we don't want to lose our wealth, or experience pain, criticism, or disrepute. We are continually involved in wanting and enjoying the positive side or pushing away the negative in anger. But we can't always get the positive side or avoid the negative and so we vary between giddy happiness and unhappiness.

If you are under the power of desire for these worldly concerns, you have no opportunity to become a superior being. Someone influenced by these goals has just ordinary mental qualities. Ordinary people don't think about the results their actions will produce in future lives, much less think about higher spiritual goals. They just think about enjoyment, peace, and pleasure for themselves in this life. We habitually think of ourselves as being the best and want the finest things for ourselves. We don't want the undesirable things for ourselves; we try to throw that discomfort onto others. From the religious point of view, we waste our lives pursuing these eight worldly concerns. Under the sway of the egoistic view and desire we cause so much misery for ourselves in this and future lives. If an ordinary person engages in some virtuous practice, their motivation is often under the influence of these eight worldly concerns. Then there is no real Dharma.

Nāgārjuna isn't saying that gaining wealth, praise, fame, and pleasure are things that have to be given up. You don't have to get rid of all your possessions and your livelihood. That would be crazy. What is to be abandoned is the attitude you have in relation to these objects. Wealth can be useful if you have a positive attitude; you can help so many people by using it well. But if you are mentally attached to your wealth, it is a problem. Your primary endeavor shouldn't be pursuit of wealth, but if it comes to you, it isn't necessarily a problem. Thus, when Nāgārjuna says that you should be indifferent to these worldly concerns he is saying that you need to control your mind. To cease your overwhelming desire for them, you have to understand the nature of these worldly things. When you recognize the fleeting and dissatisfactory nature of these goals, you see that they are not really important. You think about this over and over again. This practice equalizes or neutralizes your desire. In other words, you no longer become unhappy when you are poor and no longer become elated when you are rich. You see both situations as equal. This is how you can create happiness and peace for yourself in this and future lives.

You might think that someone with a high position in society or heavy family and business responsibilities wouldn't have time or ability to practice Dharma. However, Nāgārjuna says that wealth, position, and responsibilities are not necessarily obstacles to religious practice. If you change your attitude, you can successfully practice the Dharma. It is the choices you make. Your attitude can be harmonious with a spiritual practice or a hindrance to it. If everything you do is about seeking pleasure, wealth, praise, and fame and avoiding their opposites, then your attitude is a block to religious practice. Being happy and content with simple things leads to a peaceful mind.

In connection with this advice about worldly concerns, Nāgārjuna further explains a misconception that some ordinary people have about actions. Some people think that even very unwholesome actions are positive if they are done for the purpose of religion, or for great gurus, or other revered objects. For example, they think that if you kill someone in order to protect your religion it isn't a negative action. Or they may think that animal sacrifices to please a god is a good thing to do. This is simply confusion.

> 30. Do not commit any evil actions for the sake of
>   brahmins, monks and nuns, deities, your guests,
>   your parents, or even your queen and retinue.
>   They will not share the resulting experience in hell!

This verse is clearly addressed to a king in ancient India. Kings then had numerous queens, large retinues, and monks and brahmins in their court. Nāgārjuna says that the king shouldn't do any unwholesome actions to please any of them. For example, usually when guests came to visit, a king might have ordered a sheep be killed for a feast. You might think that this passage is not be applicable to you today because you do not have a court and retinue. However, the general advice not to do anything negative for anyone else, no matter who they are, applies to you too. The reason you shouldn't do any negative actions is because their main result is misery and suffering. If you create a karma—an action—you alone have to experience the karmic result. No one else will share the results of your karma. You may say, "I did this for you, so you should share in the result." But no one will show up to take some of the resultant suffering.

Remember that according to Buddhism hell isn't permanent or absolute in the way it is described by some other religions. Hell, in the Buddhist worldview, is impermanent; but that doesn't necessarily mean it is short-lived! You may experience hell for an eon or more; a length of time so long that it seems to last forever. But eventually when that karma's power runs out that experience will end. In other words, when the karma that caused that birth is finished, that life will end, and another karmic seed will come to fruition as a new rebirth. Hell beings are like us. They too have the potential to achieve the ārya path, liberation, or enlightenment. Temporarily they are stuck in hell. We feel superior to hell beings because we have a human life right now. But there is the possibility that we will go down to hell in our next rebirth. The mind is impermanent and changeable. The sequence of rebirths goes up or down based on your actions.

Karma functions in the same manner as a seed planted in your garden. A flower seed is the main material cause. However, it will not germinate and sprout unless there is soil, moisture, sunlight, and so forth. A seed may remain dormant for years, but it will sprout when the right conditions are present. Further, the result can be far greater than the cause. If you plant an apple seed, eventually you will get hundreds of apples from a tree, and along the way there will be leaves, branches, buds, etc. This multiplicative feature is even more true for karma. When a karmic seed ripens, your future experience will be far more negative or far more positive than its cause. The maturation of the most negative actions results in a rebirth in hell. You haven't seen the hells or the hungry ghost realm so you may think you can ignore them. You may think that type of result will not occur. But if the karma for them is created, it will bring its result. Karma is like a body and its shadow. Wherever you go your shadow follows. The key point here is that a karma's primary maturation is a type of life in samsara.

A karmic seed isn't physical; it is a predisposition in your mind. When you have done something, whether positive or negative, it leaves a seed or potential in your mind. In that sense, your mind is like a field. The physical or verbal action is done and then it is over. Although the action is finished, the karmic seed of that action is now planted in your mind. It may not ripen right away, but it is there and when the right conditions arise it will come to fruition. An aspect of your mind carries all your karmic seeds from life to life. When you die from this life the karma you created is carried on in your mind.

Because spiritual practitioners understand this, they are very careful about their actions. It doesn't matter if no one sees what they do, they know that the results will occur. However, you can get rid of a karmic seed before it ripens, just like you can destroy a physical seed so that it can never sprout. The process to destroy a karmic seed is called purification.[27] Even if you have created a huge number of very heavy negative karmas, if you apply the purification methods then those karmas will never be able to bring about their results. However, if you have not done any purification, then that karma will ripen when the necessary conditions are present. This is definite; a karmic seed is never wasted. A karma doesn't become ineffective or ruined on its own. At some point, even eons later, your karmic seeds will ripen unless you act to purify them.

Usually, we think that the consequences of our actions will occur right away. If there are no immediate repercussions, we think that we have gotten away with something. But that is not the case. From the point of view of the time of ripening, there are three different types of karmic results. Certain karmas bring about their result in this very life. We call these *visible* or *manifest karmas* because you can actually see their results in a few days, a few months, or even many years later. Sometimes an action is so powerful that some of its consequences are experienced in this life, but its main result will still be a future rebirth. A second type of karma definitely will be experienced in the very next life. Finally, some karmas will not be experienced in either this life or the next life. Their results will come to fruition in the life after next, or some lifetime beyond that in the future. Even eons later these karmic seeds may ripen.

There are a number of stories from the Jātaka tales, the stories about the former lives of the historical Buddha, that illustrate these three types of karma. One ancient story that illustrates visible karma is about a man who was born without a penis. At one time another man came by his house leading 500 bulls on the way to get them castrated. The man without a penis thought, "In my previous lives I must have castrated many animals and so I was born this way. I probably have been born this way many times. This man is going to create the karma to undergo misery for many lives in the same way that I have." Feeling compassion for both the animals and the owner, he bought all the bulls. The owner was happy with the money and saved from creating the negative karma. The animals remained whole. As a result of this, later in his life the hermaphrodite suddenly grew a penis. That was the result in the same lifetime. Then for many future lifetimes he was a complete man.

The karmas that will definitely bring about a result in the immediate next life are the five most heinous actions: killing your father, killing your mother, killing an arhat, injuring a buddha, and causing a schism in the sangha. Out of ignorance and anger people might do these things and then right after their death they will suffer terrible results. There is almost no intermediate state, or bardo; you are reborn after just an instant. The suffering in the next rebirth is terrible and long-lasting. After doing such actions they will suffer even in the current life. What makes these such powerful karma? They are powerful due to the object of the action, the manner of thought precipitating the action, and how the action is done. Buddhas, arhats, your parents, and the sangha are special high fields of action. The actions you do in relation to them are very strong. In terms of Buddhism, killing any being is not good, but killing your parents or an arhat is much worse. The next verse is about this second type of karma.

> 31. Doing an evil deed will not instantly
>   cut you as if slashed by a sword;
>   the result of your evil deeds
>   will become apparent at the time of death.

According to the sutras, if you have done one of the powerful negative karmas that will throw you directly to hell, a sign of that will appear at the time of your death. Just before you die, as if you were dreaming, you might see beings like the torturers in the hells. It seems like they are ready to harm you. This isn't a vision of an external being who will chop you up, burn you, or throw you in the freezing cold. This is your own karma manifesting as a punisher. You may be overwhelmed by regret for your previous negative actions. But your unpleasant feelings and visions are simply a sign of what is to come. Śāntideva also expresses this:

> Tormented by grief your face becomes swollen
> while tears trickle from your red eyes.
> You gaze upon your relatives without hope
> and see the faces of the servants of the Lord of Death.
>
> Tortured by recollection of your evil deeds
> you will hear the sounds of hell.
> Crazed with fear you will lose control of your bowels.
> And then what can you possibly do?
> [*Introduction to the Practice of Bodhisattvas*, 7.9–10]

When you are dying it is too late for regret. At that point there is nothing you can do. Nāgārjuna's advice is, first of all, to try to avoid engaging in negative actions. If you have done negative actions, you probably will not see the results of your evil deeds immediately. However, that is not a reason to rest easy; you must purify those negative actions before you die. If you do not do any purification, then at the time of your death you will recall what you've done and feel great regret. But at that point you will not be able to do anything about it.

All of the above is about avoiding desire for worldly concerns. If you abandon those worldly concerns, what should you strive to possess instead? The answer is the riches of the āryas.

THE SUPERIOR QUALITIES OF THE ĀRYAS

Unlike ordinary wealth, which can cause you to create negative karma while trying to gain and protect it, the riches of the āryas always bring about positive results. What type of wealth is particular to those who have a direct realization of emptiness? It isn't ordinary possessions, money, or property. The sutras say there are seven types of wealth cherished by the āryas. Nāgārjuna lists them in the next verse.

> 32. The Buddha taught that there are seven riches:
> pure faith, conduct, generosity, learning,
> a flawless sense of modesty, decorum, and wisdom.
> Know that other common types of wealth are worthless.

These seven are real wealth. These are what āryas pursue, develop, and maintain. You should too. So, what are these? Faith is the foundation. (There is an extensive explanation of faith in chapter 2, so I'll not repeat it here). In short, every spiritual practice requires faith. Faith means that you trust the goal and the method to get there. Without faith you will not be happy and comfortable undertaking a practice. Faith is like a mother of a baby. In order for humans to be born, they have to have a mother. Once a baby is born, a mother protects and nourishes her child physically, mentally, and socially. Spiritual growth can't begin without the mother, faith. Faith brings forth spiritual results. Faith leads to firm refuge. Another analogy for faith is the attitude you have when you invite a valued, special guest to your home. When you are expecting this type of visitor, the first thing you do is clean your house. If your house is dirty and disorganized, even a tasty spread of food wouldn't be very nice. So first you clean, arrange things in a lovely way, and then prepare some delicious food. In the case of faith, you are inviting wisdom and the path that leads to enlightenment for yourself and others. The preparations you make are of two types: clearing away mental hindrances and creating merit to be able to practice the path. These are encapsulated in the superior wealth of the āryas.

The second of the seven riches is ethical conduct. (This topic was also covered in detail in chapter 2 under the heading of Karma.) Just to briefly review, pure moral conduct is to avoid or abandon negative physical, verbal, and mental actions. There are many aspects of pure conduct, but in the beginning you focus on abandoning the ten nonvirtuous actions and taking up their opposite, the ten virtuous actions. Of primary concern are the three mental actions. From the negative side, you try to avoid the three poisons: desire, hatred, and ignorance. From the positive perspective, you want to develop equanimity, compassionate love, and wisdom.

Mental actions are the source for verbal and physical actions. Controlling your verbal and physical actions with awareness is virtue. Simply not doing something isn't virtuous. For example, rocks don't commit murder, but that isn't virtuous. Mental development is built on the foundation of pure behavior. It is the foundation for all virtuous qualities. This includes both a higher rebirth within samsara as well as the definite and permanent results of nirvana and enlightenment.

The third of the seven riches is generosity, which was also discussed in chapter 2. Generosity is to give gifts. The most important gift you can give is spiritual instruction regarding the path. This will greatly benefit the recipient in both this and future lives. You give material charity according to what recipients need. Your generosity develops step by step. You start by giving what you can while feeling comfortable. You don't want to give and then feel regret and discomfort. That doesn't create much merit. So, perhaps you begin by giving someone a little bit of food, maybe just a vegetable. As you feel good about doing that, you are able to give a bit more. Even though we have good human rebirths as a result of our former practice of ethical conduct, we are still caught up in the eight worldly concerns and that makes pure generosity difficult.

Śāntideva explained that the perfection of generosity doesn't mean that all the poverty in the world is eliminated. If the elimination of poverty were the perfection of generosity, then the Buddha would have not perfected it because there are still poor and destitute people, animals, and hungry ghosts. So, what is the perfection of generosity? It is having no stinginess whatsoever when giving.

> The perfection of generosity is said to be
> the thought to give everything to all beings,
> along with the result of such a thought.
> Hence it is only a state of mind.
> [*A Guide to the Bodhisattva Way of life*, 5.10]

When you give a little bit and see that it made others happy, it will make you even happier. The happiness you feel when your generosity makes others joyful is not ordinary happiness. This kind of joy can't be bought with money.

Je Tsongkhapa said,

Generosity is the wish-fulfilling jewel that protects migrating
    beings;
it is the supreme weapon for cutting the knot of miserliness;
it is a bodhisattva practice that gives rise to unfailing courage;
it is the basis for your fame to spread throughout the ten
    directions.

Knowing this, the wise rely upon the profound path
of giving away their body, wealth, and accumulated merit.
I, a yogi, have practiced in this way;
you who seek liberation should do the same.
    [*Condensed Points of the Stages of the Path*, 23–24]

If you practice ethical conduct and generosity, you will have a good
rebirth. In that life you will have wealth, friends, and a good environment
without having to do too much to get them. This will make your practice
of the path much easier. Looked at this way, ethical conduct and generosity have a beneficial temporary result on the way toward complete
liberation.

The fourth of the riches is learning, or you could say education. The
traditional word used here literally means "hearing." In ancient times the
way you learned something was by listening to someone's instruction.
Nowadays we can learn from books and the internet as well as teachers.
But without any study at all, you won't know how to do anything, not
even a worldly skill like cooking. You need an education to open your
mind. In order to reach a spiritual goal, you need to study extensively and
intensely. The perfection of spiritual study is wisdom. We have a saying,
"Studying is like a lamp that dispels ignorance. Learning is real wealth." If
a room is dark, you can't see what is there. But when you turn on a lamp,
you can see colors, what is attractive, and what is ugly. Ordinary possessions can be stolen by thieves or ruined by fire or water. But your education cannot be taken from you; your knowledge cannot be destroyed. In
that sense too, it is supreme wealth. Also, education is like a weapon that
destroys your enemies. An external person isn't your real enemy; someone
who kills this sort of enemy isn't really a hero. That enemy will die anyway.
A real hero or heroine is someone who overcomes ignorance, particularly
of spiritual matters.

We all know the value of education. There is a great deal of emphasis on education in the West. Every one strives to send their children to school to learn things so that they can live well in the world. Knowledge of how to live, how to create wealth, and how to get along in society all require a worldly education. A spiritual education involves learning how to become free from suffering and attain enlightenment. To that end you strive to gain knowledge of phenomenal as well as ultimate reality. If you know how things exist, you will know what to do and what to avoid. Then even if you face difficulties, your education serves as a good friend who helps you to handle those situations. Thus, you don't leave what you have learned on a shelf somewhere. The real purpose of study is to put into practice what you have learned. There are many colloquial sayings in the Indo-Tibetan tradition about the importance of study. For example:

> The essential goal of practice follows from learning;
> with that you will be easily freed from the prison of rebirth.

Someone who desires to attain a spiritual goal begins by studying the spiritual teachings. If you do not learn these, you will not know what to practice. If you don't practice properly, no matter how many austerities you undertake you will not reach your goal. If you do practice properly you will be liberated from samsara with ease.

Another saying is:

> Through study you will know good from bad.
> Education helps you abandon senseless things.
> Studying turns you away from evil activity.

And also:

> How can someone be a great meditator without education?

Real practice can only follow from study. It is only from study that you can know the goal, the obstacles, the proper path, and the methods to purify your body, speech and mind. It is from learning that you will know what to do and the purpose for doing it. You know what to fight against and what to foster.

Nāgārjuna says the first four riches—faith, ethical conduct, generosity, and learning— should be practiced purely. What does it mean to say that an action is pure or impure? When your motivation is one of the eight worldly concerns, your action is impure. In other words, impure or flawed actions are done in order to obtain temporary goals for yourself and those you care about in this life. For example, studying and reading hundreds of books over a course of many years in order to get a religious education may look like Dharma practice, but if you do this for fame, praise, or money, there is really nothing of spiritual value there. Stainless, or pure, learning is engaging in study so that you will know how to free yourself and other sentient beings from suffering and attain the real happiness of liberation and enlightenment. Any hardships you endure when your motivation is pure are not wasted.

The fifth and sixth riches are shame and modesty. Having a sense of shame is positive. It is a feeling that you have when what you are doing is improper. Shame is thinking, "This kind of activity is not right to do; it is contrary to the Dharma; and, if I do it, I will not be a good person." Your rationale for avoiding the action is based on your feelings about yourself. Modesty is similar; it is thinking that you would be very embarrassed if others knew that you had done a particular action. In addition to your concern about what others think about you, modesty's rationale for avoiding an action is that it will displease the buddhas, bodhisattvas, your teachers, great beings, and others. Both shame and modesty keep you from engaging in negative actions. Someone who is shameless and free from embarrassment will do many negative actions. That will land them in a bad situation. Thus, you should always have a sense of shame and modesty. These qualities don't come easily. You need to study and consider your own and others' feelings.

The last of the riches is wisdom. In a general sense, wisdom is the ability to distinguish details. It is the opposite of ignorance that just lumps everything together. There are many levels of wisdom: from the mundane worldly sense to the supramundane. Without wisdom you cannot do even common ordinary things properly. In every situation, no matter what you are doing, wisdom is vitally important. If you work hard but without any wisdom, you will not get the results you desire. Even farmers need wisdom to succeed: they must know when to plant, the best seed to plant, how to nourish the seedlings, and so on. When your diligence is accompanied by wisdom, your hard work will bring forth significant results. Thus, even in a worldly sense you need wisdom.

Wisdom from the spiritual perspective is even more important. Even if you engage in the practices of the first five perfections—generosity, ethical conduct, patience, perseverance, and meditative stabilization—they won't be great practices unless you conjoin them with wisdom. Without wisdom, you are practicing blind. Imagine being blind and walking along a road; you don't know what is around you; you don't know what dangers are there; you don't know the right way to go. For example, without wisdom you may be patient in the wrong situation, or your generosity may be wasted. That is why in the perfection of wisdom sutras, wisdom is likened to having the ability to see. There will be more about wisdom later; here Nāgārjuna simply tells the king that he needs wisdom regarding understanding the conventional nature of things. And, he needs ultimate wisdom that knows the ultimate nature of reality because without that he will never attain freedom from samsara or enlightenment.

According to Nāgārjuna, the Buddha said that the seven riches of the āryas are the cause of uncontaminated bliss and happiness. Thus, they comprise superior wealth. Ordinary people think that having a lot of money and possessions is wealth. From the spiritual point of view, common wealth is purposeless because it cannot pacify your mental afflictions. What will a lot of money bring you? Some kinds of pleasure, but along with those it will bring a lot of mental turmoil. Because it is combined with the mental afflictions and impure karma, your temporary pleasure becomes the cause of more anger, desire, jealousy and so forth. Ordinary wealth is like the husk of grain. A husk is the cover for what is really essential. It isn't the essence itself. Or think of ordinary wealth as the outer bark of sugar cane. It only has the slightest hint of sweetness. It isn't the essence of the real sweetness inside. You should compare these two types of wealth, common and superior, and determine to pursue the latter.

THE QUALITY OF AVOIDING THE CREATION OF CONDITIONS THAT HINDER YOUR ATTAINMENT OF SUPERIOR WEALTH

The next verse lists six things to avoid because they prevent you from obtaining and maintaining superior wealth.

33. Gambling, joining crowds to see shows,
     laziness, relying on evil companions,
     liquor, and roving at night lead to lower realms
     and a loss of reputation. So, give up these six!

When you are trying to practice the Dharma, your motivation is important, but so are external influences. Many things you ordinarily enjoy can cause you problems. Gambling here means any type of gaming or maneuvering that you do to try to gain ordinary wealth. When given the choice of meditating for an hour or going to the movies, we usually chose the movie. But seeing a movie doesn't produce anything positive. Your mind is influenced by the illusions; later in your dreams you may experience anger, desire, jealousy, and so on. In general, laziness is not doing something even though you know it is a good thing to do. There are three types of laziness. First, desire for pleasure leads you to not bother to do good actions. Second, even though you may want to do positive things, you procrastinate. And third, you think these positive actions are not for you because you are not good enough, smart enough, or skilled enough. You may like your friends, but it is not good if they always lead you to do negative actions. Say, for example, you have a friend who often shoplifts. They may be a nice person, but if you associate with them over time, you will naturally join them when they are stealing. They lead you downward. The opposite is also true. When you associate with a superior spiritual friend, they will lead you to become better. As we've discussed, if you take intoxicants, you lose your inhibitions. You become unaware of what you are doing. You can hurt yourself and others. We know this even in ordinary worldly situations. That is why there are laws concerning intoxicants and organizations to help people with substance abuse problems. The last thing to avoid is going out at night to run around town. This doesn't mean that you shouldn't go to temple at night!

If you engage in any of these then you won't have real spiritual wealth. Not only will your virtuous practices degenerate, but you will lose your good reputation and your material wealth, and perhaps put your life in danger. Śāntideva gives similar advice about avoiding certain external situations and activities.

> A wounded person will carefully protect their injury
> when they are in the midst of a boisterous uncontrolled crowd.
> Similarly, you should always protect your wounded mind
> when in the midst of a crowd of evil people.
> [*Introduction to the Practice of Bodhisattvas,* 5.19]

If you have a large wound on your arm, you have to be very careful when you go out in public. You can't enjoy the activities around you because the slightest touch to your arm is very painful. When your mind is agitated by anger, desire, or ignorance we say that it is injured or wounded. Your mind is sensitive and easily influenced by other people and situations. A disturbed mind is more serious and more painful than a physical wound. A physical sore is temporary. But, if your mind is wounded by ignorance, desire, and so on, the injury lasts longer than just the present. It will affect your future lives. The unwholesome karma you create now will cause an unpleasant future life. What makes an action wholesome or unwholesome? It isn't something external. It depends on your mind. When your motivation is compassionate and merged with wisdom, then your actions are good karma and will bring about a good life. If your mind is disturbed and out of control due to strong desire or hatred you will create bad karma.

At present mental afflictions are always with you. They may be dormant for a minute, but they are ready to arise. You are easily disturbed by the slightest things. If you see something or someone attractive, desire arises. If someone says something a little bit critical, you immediately get angry and frustrated. If you are with a rowdy group of friends, you follow along. Look around, there is no safe place if your mind is not trained. Whatever peace and happiness you have is the result of spiritual training. Your wounded mind will be healed when you reduce desire, hatred, ignorance, and all the other mental afflictions, and replace them with the highest wisdom, great kindness and love. Until then, you need to protect your wounded mind.

So, how do you protect your mind? Although you can't completely protect it with weapons or walls, you can safeguard it a bit if you are careful about your external circumstances. This will not eliminate your mental afflictions, but they don't arise as strongly without certain objects and conditions being present. In the beginning of your mental training you work to control your senses as they interact with the external environment. As you gain control of some aspects of your senses it will help you train your mind. That is why the fifth compatible condition for the development of wisdom is to be satisfied or content.

THE QUALITY OF SATISFACTION

34. "Contentment is the best type of wealth,"
     taught the Teacher of gods and humans.
     So always be content. If you are satisfied
     you are wealthy even if you lack material riches.

Usually, no matter how much money and how many houses, cars, and so forth you have it is never enough. You are always dissatisfied. No matter how much you own, you are poor, because you always crave more and more. If you are not content, you are extremely possessive of your material wealth: you worry about losing it; or that your things are getting old; or that someone might steal them. You are fixated on the fact that you had better things in the past. And you are always strategizing how to get more in the future. But if you are satisfied with something simple, you can be happy. If a person living on the streets with filthy clothes and simple food feels that he has enough, he possesses true wealth. Satisfaction with what you have is the opposite of craving. When you are content you do not obsess over things that you had, but lost, in the past; you do not desire to have more things for the future; and you are not attached to what you have now nor do you covet others' possessions. In short, when you are satisfied, you don't have too much desire. Satisfaction keeps you from engaging in negative actions like gambling, drinking, and so on. Thus, the best type of wealth is knowing how to be satisfied with what you have.

The *Question of Surata Sutra* says,

Those who see things properly explain
that someone without even a morsel of food
yet is always generous nevertheless,
has the greatest wealth in the world.

The nature of your body is suffering, but really, just some simple food and shelter can satisfy your needs. The reason you and others want to accumulate wealth is so that you will feel safe and satisfied. Until you are satisfied, you want to accumulate more and more. Even if you have a mountain of food, you want more, a different type, or fresher and better choices. If you are satisfied, then even if you have just a little you feel rich enough to share. In other words, if you are content with what you have, then you are wealthy. This type of satisfaction is not easy to get. But it can be done. When you are satisfied, all your energy can go toward spiritual pursuits. Satisfaction is a positive quality.

The next verse talks about the faults of not being content.

35. O faithful one! To have many possessions is misery.
    Those with few desires are not like that.
    Nāga kings have as many headaches
    as they have heads.

This verse alludes to legends about nāgas—intelligent and powerful part-snake part-human semidivine creatures who often control the natural environment. Every nāga king is said to have a different number of heads. Each one of those heads could experience emotional and physical pain. So, the more heads, the more suffering. We can analogize this to having lots of jewelry. If you try to wear it all at once, it can be uncomfortable. Not only that, whenever you wear it, you worry about losing it. Śāntideva said,

You should understand that wealth is an endless misfortune
because of the misery of gaining it, protecting it, and losing it.
[*Introduction to the Practice of Bodhisattvas*, 8.79 ab]

This concludes Nāgārjuna's general advice on how to suppress desire and develop wisdom. Much of this advice pertains to the ordained and the laity. But he also gave specific instructions on how to live as a layperson: you care for your parents, your partner, and your children. Even if you don't meditate, you are engaging in religious activity when you help others. When your focus is upon helping others, you are loosening up your egoistic, selfish attitude. Putting your energy into benefitting others is a Mahayana spiritual practice. In many prayers we say, "May all mother sentient beings be free from misery and have happiness." Maybe you can't include all sentient beings right now, but you can start with your family and friends. Gradually you extend your love from your own family to another family. Eventually you will reach the level of a bodhisattva who includes all sentient beings. Then there will be peace in the world.

6. *Advice for People Who Desire Spiritual Goals*

THE FOLLOWING ADVICE is for anyone who wishes to practice the Dharma in order to attain a high rebirth and/or liberation from samsara. A high rebirth within samsara is a temporary goal. It doesn't last long, but it is necessary platform for doing the work to attain the ever-lasting goals of both complete personal liberation and enlightenment in order to benefit others. To attain liberation from samsara you need to create a lot of merit and eliminate your mental afflictions. It is a gradual process. It takes a long time to completely remove the mental afflictions from your mind; for most people it takes far longer than just one life. So, your first spiritual goal is to have another good rebirth. You need one good life after another so that you can continue to engage in the practices that will eventually free you from samsara.

Within samsara there are many types of rebirths. Some are good and some are quite awful. A high rebirth is better than a low rebirth, but it is still within samsara. There is no certainty that your future after you die will be pleasurable. Even the highest samsaric gods can be reborn into a lower realm. Rebirth is uncertain: sometimes high, sometimes low, sometimes in the middle. It is like riding a Ferris wheel. The wheel takes you to the highest point, the middle, and then down again to the very bottom. You go around and around, stopping briefly wherever the machine takes you. You have no control; you just go around in that circle. The word *samsara* is defined as cyclic rebirth under the power of karma and the mental afflictions. Your mental afflictions impel you to create karma. Depending upon the karma you have created, you go up or down. You have been revolving in this way continuously, from time without beginning.

How do you get out of this cycle? If you are on an ordinary mechanical ferris wheel, you get off when the machine stops your seat at the landing. In contrast, the machine causing you to cycle in samsara is internal; it is comprised of your ignorance and mental afflictions. The only way to get out of samsara is to eliminate ignorance and its derivative mental afflictions. As long as you have mental afflictions in your mind you will cycle in samsara. While you have a high rebirth in samsara you can develop your mind and engage in higher practices that will eliminate ignorance. The type of body, mind, and the external conditions you have right now are the essential basis for working to achieve any spiritual goal in the future. You have intelligence, health, the teachings are available, there are those who can help you practice, and so forth. Although a human body may be fragile, it is very powerful from the point of view of the mind's ability to engage in spiritual practice.

Śāntideva spoke a great deal about the value of a human life:

> If I do not train my mind to practice virtue
> after I have obtained a fortunate life like this,
> there is no greater way to deceive myself;
> there is no stupidity greater than this.
>   [*Introduction to the Practice of Bodhisattvas,* 4.23]

Working toward a high rebirth within samsara is better than merely working for the enjoyment of this life. With a high rebirth you can work to attain permanent peace—the final goals of liberation from samsara or complete enlightenment. As explained in more detail above, to achieve either of these goals you must create the accordant causes and clear away the obstacles. You need a human life that has both external and internal qualities that allow you to practice. Externally you need conditions that allow you to live easily and the presence of teachers and the doctrine. Internally you need the mental capacity to study and understand. A life like this is like a wish-granting jewel. If you have a precious jewel in your hands, it would be a shameful waste to toss it away like a pebble. But even a wish-granting jewel can't give you freedom from samsara. However, a human life can grant you your highest wish. If you use your life properly it is like a powerful machine that can prevent you from falling into a lower rebirth and guarantee another high rebirth. There is no greater way to deceive yourself than to deliberately not take advantage of the opportunity you have. It is the height of stupidity to work hard just for the temporary pleasure and enjoyment of this life.

Many of the recommendations that we have already discussed are applicable to both laypeople and those with ordination. But for the most part, that advice was primarily directed to laypeople leading ordinary lives. Now we will look at advice that is applicable for both laypeople and the ordained who aspire to spiritual goals. There are many practices taught for attaining a high rebirth and emancipation. Some are a common foundation for both goals. Some are specific only to the goals of permanent liberation. We start with those practices common to the attainment of both a higher rebirth within samsara as well as a permanent goal of complete liberation from samsara. Nāgārjuna lists six important common practices: (1) regulating your consumption of food, (2) regulating sleep, (3) the four limitless thoughts, (4) the four dhyānas, (5) understanding karma, and (6) avoiding the five obstacles. You need to engage in these common practices to prepare yourself to be able to accomplish the special, more unique practices.

Regulating Consumption of Food

The first thing Nāgārjuna advises you to do is to regulate how much you eat and sleep. It is one thing to say that your human life is so meaningful you shouldn't waste a minute, however, you can't meditate or study all the time. You need to take care of yourself. A human body isn't stable and strong; it has to be protected and nourished. If you don't take care of your body, your mind will be unable to do anything. Therefore, the advice on eating and sleeping is to nourish your body so that you can practice. You don't want to eat so much that you get sleepy or sick, nor do you want to starve. You also need sleep; without sleep you cannot survive. But you don't want to sleep so much that you waste all your time.

> 38. Recognize that food is like medicine.
>   Eat without desire or anger;
>   do not eat out of vanity, hatred, or egoism.
>   You should eat only to maintain your body.

Traditionally it was said that there are four types of nourishment: (1) ordinary food, drink, and sleep; (2) a healthy mental attitude that nourishes the body; (3) contact between the five senses and their objects that causes a feeling of pleasure; and (4) yogis' meditative equipoise that causes physical and mental health and ease. The first type of nourishment is what we normally consider to be food. The second points to the fact that you need a healthy attitude toward what you eat. The third is about creating a balance between your mental reactions to the sensations that occur when your senses contact their respective objects. This isn't just a spiritual matter; it is also true in the worldly sense. Even medical doctors talk about moderation of food and drink.

Food is medicine for your body. You need to treat it like a prescription drug. Even if a medicine tastes sweet, you don't eat as much as you want. It has to be measured out so that you don't take too much. Even if a medication is bitter and unpleasant to consume, you don't want to take too little. You need the right amount for it to be effective. You should eat in the same way that you take a precise dose of medication. In other words, don't eat simply because you enjoy the taste of something. Nor should you eat out of anger, jealousy, or vanity. The Tibetan word I am translating as "vanity" literally means "to get fat." In traditional cultures if you were fat, it signified that you were rich. So, to eat only to get fat and show off would be a form of vanity. In modern times this would also apply to the vanity of being so thin that you starve yourself. Further, you shouldn't eat simply for the purpose of body building. The purpose of consumption isn't to get strong enough to conquer your enemies or look a certain way. You eat to make your body strong enough to accomplish a spiritual goal.

Eating looks like a common worldly activity. We think about food and eating a lot. We spend a lot of time and energy on food. We scrabble to get the money to buy food, we go shopping, cook, store our food, and we eat. If you do all this simply for your enjoyment or to triumph over your adversaries in some way, then your actions are inferior, or even evil. However, eating isn't necessarily a nonvirtuous activity. With the right motivation any action can be meritorious. Even going out to buy food, preparing food, and eating can be a practice of virtue if your motivation includes recollecting your goal—being able to truly benefit others. The same is true for sleeping, walking, or sitting. You want to nourish your body with food, sleep, and exercise so that you can become a great practitioner. If your motivation before going to sleep, going for a walk, or listening to music is that you are doing this action to refresh your body so that you can practice the Dharma, then the action becomes positive. Therefore, when you finish that activity, you should dedicate the merit created.

When you look at things this way you don't lack the opportunity to practice the Dharma. Dharma practice isn't just sitting in a cave and meditating. When you have a good motivation and use your body and mind positively, then you are practicing Dharma. The indication that an action is virtuous is that your motivation is to benefit, respect, and honor others. It doesn't matter if anyone else knows this. It is a question of what is in your mind. That is why Śāntideva said,

> Without the discipline of guarding my mind
> what use are the many other religious trainings?
> [*Introduction to the Practice of Bodhisattvas*, 5.18cd]

REGULATING SLEEP

Sleep is also one of our main activities. Nāgārjuna says to the king:

> 39. Virtuous Lord! Properly use your entire day
> and the first and last periods of the night.
> Sleep with mindfulness between these two,
> and then even your time of repose will not be fruitless.

The night can be divided into three sections. You should engage in virtuous activities during the first and last sections. Only during the middle of the night should you sleep. This will give you the right amount of sleep. Then when you are refreshed you can engage in the practice of merit once again. Your sleep will be virtuous if your motivation for going to sleep is, "I am going to sleep in order to strengthen my body and mind so that I will be able to generate bodhicitta." Don't go to sleep without this type of motivation. You should also monitor your sleep with mindfulness and introspection. Mindfulness is recollecting that you will get up again soon to use your life in a meaningful way. Introspection is carefully examining whether you are acting correctly or incorrectly. With these two you will get up at the right time and know what you are doing.

Some activities, like faith, are naturally virtuous. Other activities are not virtuous in and of themselves, but the power of the correct motivation can make them meritorious. Sleep is one of the latter. Therefore, in a Vinaya teaching the Buddha gave detailed instructions on sleep. He said that during the first part of the night you should sit down and do some practices. If you get sleepy you should get up and walk a bit to clear your mind. Then in the middle section of the night he said that you should go outside the temple and wash your feet before going to your room to sleep. Remember, this advice was for monks and nuns in ancient India. It was a dusty place, so the Buddha instructed his followers to wash up before going to bed. Then, when you get in bed, he suggested that you recline on your right side with your left leg on top of right. This posture is good for the internal winds and channels of the body. At the same time, you should generate mindfulness and introspection. Together, this physical posture and mental activity is called the sleeping-lion pose. It is given this name because the lion is the king of beasts. A lion has no fear of any other animal. He can lie down without fear. This is how the Buddha lay down right before his body expired and he entered parinirvāṇa. When you attain enlightenment, you have completely eliminated all the mental afflictions and have no fear.

Just like a machine has to be tuned and oiled to work properly, you have to make your body and mind ready to work. Once they are readied through judicious eating and sleeping, you can move on to slightly more complex meditation practices.

The Four Limitless Thoughts

There are many types of meditation. But all of them depend on a basic level of concentration. In this context, the preparatory practice for attaining concentration is to meditate on the four limitless thoughts, often called the four immeasurables.

> 40. Constantly and perfectly cultivate love,
>   compassion, joy, and equanimity.
>   Even if you do not attain the highest goal
>   you will obtain the bliss of the Brahma realms.

The practices of love, compassion, joy, and equanimity are called "immeasurable" or "limitless thoughts" for two reasons. First, these attitudes extend to every single living being, and the number of living beings cannot be calculated. They are also limitless from the point of view of the merit created; their value for the attainment of your spiritual goals cannot be measured. If you practice the four immeasurable thoughts you can attain permanent emancipation from samsara. Even if you do not achieve the high goals of enlightenment or nirvana, through this practice you will be reborn in a higher realm and have temporary enjoyment. "Brahma realms" refer to the four dhyānas, or levels of meditative stabilization, of the corporeal realm.

The first two limitless thoughts are love and compassion. You work on developing these at the same time. They arise almost simultaneously. The difference between them is their affect. Love is the desire that all beings have happiness. Compassion is the desire that all beings be free from every type of misery. So, love looks at the positive side; it is a wish that every living creature would have happiness. Compassion focuses on the negative side: it is a wish that every living being would not have suffering. Your mind right now is dominated by deluded partiality. If someone is your friend or a beloved family member, you feel pleased if they have some happiness. You are displeased if someone you do not like has some happiness. If your enemies suffer you feel happy. If your friends suffer you feel sad. You naturally and spontaneously have these desires for yourself too: you want to be happy and don't want to suffer. You don't need to meditate to have love and compassion for yourself and those you love. There are special meditations to develop these attitudes for all sentient beings without a single exception.

Immeasurable joy is to feel delight when all sentient beings have peace and happiness. Thus, love and compassion are directly related to joy. When parents see that their darling child is happy, they are happy too. If your love and compassion are only for a few people, then your joy is limited. We usually divide others into three categories: some are our friends, some are our enemies, and some are neutral. When our loved ones are successful and happy, we are happy. When our enemies have success and happiness, we are jealous and unhappy. We don't care one way or the other about those who seem neutral to us. This partiality causes our joy to be biased and incomplete. In contrast, if our love and compassion are limitless, then our joy is immeasurable and impartial.

The last of the immeasurable thoughts is equanimity. Equanimity is a wish that all beings live in harmony; in other words, that they do not have the bias of hatred for some and attraction to others. So, this is a wish that all sentient beings—the objects of your thought—have equanimity in their minds. Sometimes students are confused about equanimity because in some ritual prayers, the words are something like, "May all sentient beings be equal." This is a very good wish. It is out of love that you wish all beings experience the same happiness and freedom. But in reality, until all beings attain enlightenment, they will not be equal. You can't make everyone equal, but you can change your mind so that you don't hate some and love others. The most important form of equanimity is in the mind. Thus, in addition to wishing that all sentient beings have equanimity in their minds, there is also subjective equanimity—you have equanimity in your mind towards others. In other words, your own attitude to all others is impartial; you have good thoughts toward all. When you have equanimity, you do not discriminate between those you like and those you dislike. If you have equanimity for all living beings, the other three immeasurable thoughts naturally arise. Equanimity is the basis for the other limitless thoughts because if you have an impartial attitude, you feel joy when you see someone is happy, no matter who they are. When you see anyone suffering, you feel a compassionate wish that they be free from misery and a loving wish that they experience happiness.

The four limitless thoughts are not easy to produce; these attitudes do not arise naturally. However, you can develop them. There are detailed, step by step instructions for how to develop these in the stages of the path, or *lamrim,* literature. Let's take love, for example. How do you develop love for all sentient beings? In the beginning you may aspire to love all beings, but your love isn't sincere. You can say the words, but your mind and emotions don't follow. You start to expand your love by using the three categories that you already discriminate in your mind: your friends, your enemies, and those you feel neutral about. These are people you know. You imagine in front of you actual people whom you love, whom you hate, and those who are strangers. It is easiest to develop love for those you already hold dear. You start with one such person and gradually expand your attitude toward everyone you consider a friend. You wish that they all have every desirable thing. Then, you move on to the category of beings in the middle. Picture a stranger who you pass in the street every day. You can identify them, but they are a stranger to you. You do not feel either love or hatred for that person. Following the reasoning in the lamrim literature, you gradually change your lack of care into love for that person. Then you expand your love to all those for whom you feel neutral. Finally, you move on to meditate on someone who you dislike. You already know that when circumstances change someone whom you hated in the past becomes a friend. If they say something nice or do something helpful, you think, "Oh, he's not so bad after all." Eventually you might really like them. It can work the other way too. Someone you love now may become your worst enemy. In both cases the object didn't change, but your mind did. Considering this, you expand your love to all those whom you currently dislike. Once you have done this with all three categories, then you expand to all sentient beings.

You have the kernel of love and compassion now. But it is partial. When you succeed in expanding your love and compassion to all living beings, those attitudes are limitless. The mark of your successful development of the immeasurable thoughts is when the mental division between your friends and enemies dissolves. You no longer separate categories of beings. When you visualize someone whom you previously categorized as an enemy, you feel the same love, compassion, joy, and equanimity as you do for someone you had categorized as a friend. You sincerely wish all those you put in either category have peace and happiness and are free from suffering, and so forth.

The process to develop the other limitless thoughts is the same as the one that you use to develop love. The only difference is that when you are trying to develop immeasurable equanimity, you start with those beings you put in the neutral category, and following that concentrate on friends, and finally enemies.

The four immeasurable thoughts are not solely a Mahayana practice. They are common to many religious traditions: they are developed on the Hinayana path; they are practiced by ārya practitioners and practitioners who have not yet had a direct realization of emptiness; they are practiced by some non-Buddhists too. The description above are the common immeasurable practices. In the common immeasurable practices your attitude is, "How nice it would be if all sentient beings had happiness and the causes of happiness," and so forth. In the Abhidharma system for the Śrāvaka and Pratyekabuddha path these attitudes are primarily directed to beings in the desire realm, not the two upper realms. In other words, the objects of the four immeasurable thoughts developed on the Śrāvaka path are only the beings living in the six realms of the desire realm. Those in the corporeal and noncorporeal realms are excluded. Not because they don't deserve it, but because the beings living in the corporeal and non-corporeal realms do not have manifest desire, anger, jealousy, and so forth. The immeasurables are the antidote of these manifest afflictions so they are not applicable to those without manifest afflictions.

The bodhisattva practice of the four immeasurable thoughts is different. In the Mahayana practice you take on the responsibility to make all sentient beings, in every realm of samsara, have happiness and so forth. The Mahayana attitude of immeasurable love is more than a mere wish that all others have happiness; it is to feel that it is your job to make that happen. No matter how difficult it is for you, you take on the burden of making all sentient beings free from misery and to have true happiness. You vow that you will do it yourself; you will be in the service of all other sentient beings. You believe that you have no other purpose in life. Everything a bodhisattva does is for the benefit of other sentient beings. Every Mahayana practice begins with the motivation of these four limitless thoughts.

Each of the immeasurable thoughts has three levels of refinement based upon your understanding of the object. Taking compassion as our example, the three are: compassion focusing on sentient beings; compassion focusing on phenomena; and compassion focusing without concepts. The first type, compassion focusing on sentient beings, is a meditation on compassion for beings as they ordinarily appear to you. You don't need to think about the fact that they are impermanent and dependent to see that they are in misery and to wish for them to be free from it. This kind of compassion can be developed while still believing that sentient beings are substantively real and exist independently. The next two types of immeasurable compassion are based on a more in-depth look at why sentient beings are suffering. They suffer because of their ignorance. Ignorance causes them to create the karma that results in suffering. Knowing that ignorance and karma cause them to suffer, you wish that they had the wisdom that comprehends the nature of reality, because when they develop that understanding they will break the bonds of suffering.

Although the second type of immeasurable compassion is given the name "compassion focusing on phenomena," in this context it refers specifically to compassion focusing on the ultimate nature of the self of persons. This form of compassion is based on the understanding that your nature, and the nature of all beings, is impermanent and without an independent, substantial, inherent essence. The person is just a label imputed upon the five mental and physical aggregates. Your compassion now incorporates the wish that all other sentient beings would understand their own ultimate nature: the selflessness of persons. Until now they have ignorantly thought that they existed as they appeared. But when they directly realize the emptiness of the self of persons, i.e., that they have no intrinsically real independent identity, they will destroy ignorance. Your compassion is focusing on the wisdom that they must have in order to be free from suffering. In short, your wish is that all beings be free from suffering and the cause of suffering. The third type of immeasurable compassion is even more subtle than the second. It is immeasurable compassion mixed with an understanding that all things—subjects, objects, and actions—are empty of inherent existence and exist only in dependence. It is called compassion focusing without concepts because it is based on the understanding that all phenomena, not just the self of persons, lack an intrinsic identity—everything is empty. So, this type of compassion includes the wish that all beings no longer have the ignorance that apprehends a self of phenomena. Compassion itself doesn't understand emptiness. Compassion is based upon first having an understanding of emptiness. All of the immeasurable thoughts have these three graduated levels of subtlety.

In some schools of Buddhism, the second and third levels of immeasurable compassion are not explained this way. It depends whether or not they accept that śrāvakas and pratyekabuddhas must realize the selflessness of phenomena. All Buddhists agree that ordinary beings, who have not yet directly realized the four realities for āryas or emptiness, can practice compassion focusing on sentient beings. Ordinary beings may have an inferential knowledge of ultimate reality, but they are not āryas. Their compassion is based on seeing others' misery as it appears. The second type of compassion, compassion focusing on phenomena, is developed by all Hinayana āryas, both śrāvakas and pratyekabuddhas, and Mahayana āryas too. According to the lower schools, a direct realization of selflessness of persons is the key to attaining nirvana. Therefore, all Hinayana practitioners meditate to eliminate the ignorance that holds that the self of persons is ultimately real. However, they do not meditate on the selflessness of all phenomena. Only āryas practicing the Mahayana path develop compassion focusing without concepts. Mahayana practitioners develop compassion based on the recognition that nothing exists as it appears, things only exist relatively and dependently, like a magical illusion. They do this type of meditation because they do not want freedom from samsara just for themselves. They want to help all sentient beings become liberated from samsara. To do that they need the highest type of wisdom, compassion, love, and other abilities. So, they work to get rid of the subtle knowledge obstacles to omniscience. Hinayana practitioners who reach nirvana have gotten rid of their mental afflictions from the root, but they do not remove the knowledge obstacles. This makes a huge difference in the results of the path: the individual peace of nirvana versus complete buddhahood. The difference is as great as the amount of water in the footprint of an elephant and the amount in the ocean.

There are two different Madhyamaka schools: Prāsaṅgika and Svātantrika. According to the Prāsaṅgika, all āryas—whether they are śrāvakas, pratyekabuddhas, or bodhisattvas—must have a direct realization of both the selflessness of persons and the selflessness of phenomena. They say that you can't attain nirvana without the realization of both types of emptiness. Therefore, all āryas will develop the three types of compassion.

The types of compassion are from the point of view of your focus upon an attribute of the object. We are all familiar with giving different names to a single thing depending upon what we are trying to highlight. For example, in Sanskrit and Tibetan the moon has ten different names. The moon is a single object, but the various names point out different attributes. Sometimes it is called "the one with cooling light" because when a cool night breeze arose, it seemed to people in ancient times that the moonlight itself was cool. Sometimes it is called "the possessor of the rabbit" because when people look at the full moon they see the shadows of the craters in the form of a rabbit. Sometimes it is just called "the moon." Whatever name you use, you understand that attribute but also the general concept of the moon. In that sense, for advanced practitioners all three types of compassion can be encompassed in a single moment.

What is the result of successfully practicing the four immeasurable thoughts? The final result is to become an arhat or a buddha. When you see the misery of sentient beings and feel compassion and love based on an understanding of the ultimate nature of sentient beings then your meditations are conjoined with the wisdom understanding emptiness. In that way they become the antidote to ignorance and act as the cause to become completely free from samsara. If your compassion based on the wisdom understanding the emptiness of phenomena is motivated by bodhicitta, it becomes the cause for attaining the highest enlightenment.

If you are not able to do that right away, meditation on the four limitless thoughts, done with a different special technique, will lead you to be reborn in the corporeal, or form, realm, as discussed in the next section.

The Four Levels of the Corporeal Realm: the Dhyānas

The Sanskrit word dhyāna has two connotations: focused meditative stability in general and a more specific reference to the four levels of meditative stabilization of the corporeal realm. Nāgārjuna explains that to attain the temporary goal of a rebirth in the four dhyānas of the corporeal realm or the absorptions of the noncorporeal realm, and to attain the permanent goals of nirvana and enlightenment, you need śamatha. Śamatha is a form of meditative concentration. It is the ability of the mind to remain focused on an object of observation with complete freedom from distraction and mental laxity for as long as desired. This effortless mental flexibility and control is accompanied by physical and mental pliancy and bliss. So first let's look at this necessary tool for attaining temporary and permanent spiritual results.

Śamatha, is a meditation technique common to many traditions, not just Buddhism. Right now, it is hard for you to hold an object vividly in your mind for even a few moments. Your body sits in meditation, but your mind travels widely. You are thinking a bit about your object and at the same time halfway somewhere else. Śamatha is the ability to control your mind so that you can hold your focus; you can keep your mind on whatever object you wish for as long as you want without any distraction. Not only are you not distracted, but your mind doesn't get sleepy or dull either. Distraction and sinking into dullness are the two opposites of śamatha. True śamatha is spontaneous; it doesn't require constant effort. When practitioners attain śamatha they have physical and mental dexterity as well as physical and mental subtle pleasure. This isn't a rough or ordinary form of pleasure that would disturb your concentration.

When you achieve śamatha you will have a powerful mental instrument. You can apply it to any object of meditation. In his explication of the six perfections, Śāntideva makes it clear that training in meditative concentration is crucial.

> A clear and concentrated mind results
> in being reborn as Brahmā, and so forth.
> Physical and verbal actions done with
> weak concentration do not have that sort of result.

> The omniscient one said that
> recitations and the practice of austerities,
> even if done for a long time,
> are pointless if done with a distracted mind.
> [*Introduction to the Practice of Bodhisattvas*, 5.15–16]

A mind trained in single-pointed concentration is clear, vivid, and stable. No matter what spiritual goal you are trying to reach, it is most important to have a concentrated mind. Śāntideva alludes to this in the verse above by his use of the word *brahmā*. In the common worldly sense, it refers to the god Brahmā, a being of the first dhyāna of the corporeal realm. The second sense of brahmā is "perfect highest result," in other words, it is buddhahood that is completely free of obstacles and in possession of all perfect qualities. For a higher rebirth in the corporeal or noncorporeal realms you need to add the mental training of śamatha to the practice of virtue. The practice of virtue without śamatha results in a good rebirth in the desire realm. Śamatha is also needed for attainment of the highest permanent spiritual result. Enlightenment is the result of the practice of wisdom understanding ultimate reality in conjunction with śamatha.

Traditionally śamatha is introduced in the context of the four dhyānas of the corporeal realm, which is one of the three realms of Buddhist cosmology. To be born into the corporeal realm you have to perfect śamatha and apply it to a specific type of wisdom. If you do that, even while you are still alive—in your human body in the desire realm—your mind moves beyond the desire realm and is on the first dhyāna. Then when you die and are reborn it will be in the first dhyāna of the corporeal realm. The next verse in Nāgārjuna's text is an extremely concise description of the meditation done in order to attain the first dhyāna—the lowest level of the corporeal realm—then how to progress through the successive levels of the corporeal and noncorporeal realms.

> 41. The four dhyānas are total abandonment
> of sensory experience, joy, pleasure, and discomfort.
> Through them you obtain the same good fortune as the
> god realms
> of Brahmā, Ābhāsvara, Śubhakṛtsna, and Bṛhatphala.

The inhabitants of the four levels of the corporeal realm are a type of deity. They live a long peaceful life that is the result of prior mental training. They don't have bodies with sexual organs like beings in the desire realm. Their bodies are very subtle, with a nature like light. They don't have to eat or eliminate waste. They do not crave sex. They have mental enjoyment rather than sensual enjoyment. Their subtle mental happiness is akin to the feeling you have in the deep meditation of śamatha. These deities do not have ordinary physical or mental suffering for as long as they live. In technical terms, in the context of the three types of suffering—ordinary suffering, the suffering of transformation, and the suffering of being created by causes and conditions—they do not have ordinary gross suffering. However, they do have the suffering of transformation and the suffering of being created by causes and conditions. No part of this realm is permanent. Their life is conditioned. They are born there as the result of powerful meditation practices and merit. But when that karma is used up, they are reborn somewhere else. Although deities in the corporeal realm do not have anger or gross manifest desire, they still have subtle desire. They are subject to suffering in that they are under the power of karma. They are not completely free.

There is a lot of technical detail regarding progression through the four dhyānas of the corporeal realm. I'll give you a broad overview to help you understand it. To be born in the first dhyāna, you join śamatha with a specific meditation on the wisdom side in order to temporarily remove the mental afflictions that belong to the desire realm. There are three categories of desire realm mental afflictions: gross, medium, and subtle. Each of these categories is further divided into three levels of big, medium, and small. There are specific meditations to remove each section. You start with the three types of gross mental afflictions, going from the biggest to the smallest ones. Then you work on the medium ones, from biggest to smallest. Last you work on the subtlest ones. When you have removed all nine levels of the mental afflictions of the desire realm you reach the first dhyāna. The first dhyāna is named after the god Brahmā. The successively higher dhyānas of the corporeal realm are named after the prominent gods of that level. They are listed in final line of the verse above. (See also appendix 3.)

The wisdom side of practice that when done with śamatha will temporarily remove the dominant mental afflictions of the desire realm is an analysis that contrasts the coarseness of the desire realm and the subtlety of the first dhyāna. First you think about all the negative aspects of life in the desire realm: a short life, an ugly body, physical and mental pain throughout life, and so forth. In this context you don't consider the positive aspects of having a human life; the purpose of this meditation is solely to develop an attitude of disgust for the entire desire realm. Then you meditate on the wonderful qualities of life on the first dhyāna: life there is long, there is no pain or suffering, the body is light, peaceful, beautiful, and so on. You do both a general conceptual meditation and a detailed analysis: sometimes you focus on the coarse aspects of the desire realm, sometimes you focus on the peaceful aspects of the first dhyāna, and sometimes you compare the two. Your attachment to the desire realm will diminish as you come to recognize the repulsiveness of a desire realm life. Meditation on the positive qualities of the first dhyāna will make you desire to have that kind of life. This is actually a common psychological technique. If you think about the value and desirability of an object over and over, you want it more and more. If you think about the negative qualities of an object over and over, you become less enamored of it.

There are two aspects to the first, and each successive, dhyāna: the preparatory stage and the actual stage. The preparatory stage refers to the period during which you are removing the mental afflictions that are the obstacles to the actual stage. When that work is complete and those particular mental afflictions are all removed, you reach the actual stage of that dhyāna. For example, in your current human life you can do this meditation practice to eliminate your desire for the desire realm and develop a longing for the first dhyāna. If you succeed in that practice, you have entered the preparatory stage of the first dhyana. After you die, your rebirth in the first dhyāna is the actual stage.

The first dhyāna has three divisions that are the result of great, medium, and small preparatory meditations. These divisions are due to the differences in the intensity and duration of the preparatory meditations. The small meditation refers to people who don't work enthusiastically and don't continue for a long time. In the middle, people may have one or the other characteristics: some people enthusiastically work really hard but for just a few days, or they keep at it for a long time but without much enthusiasm. The third type, the great, has both enthusiasm and continuity.

The same meditation process and types of result apply to moving up to the second, third, and fourth dhyānas. You compare the coarseness and problems of the first dhyāna to the better situation on the second dhyāna. The second dhyāna also has three levels based on the preparatory meditations. Then to reach the third dhyāna you compare the second dhyāna's drawbacks to the third dhyāna's subtlety. The third dhyāna also has three levels. The same goes to reach the fourth dhyāna. The actual fourth dhyāna has eight levels, five of which are pure abodes. So, in all there are seventeen levels of the corporeal realm.

Overall, this comparative meditation technique can be described as having three general sections: the actual direct antidote, the benefits of applying the antidote, and the base. The first two sections are each further divided into two, making a total of five parts. The two parts of the direct antidote are a meditation using general concepts and a more detailed analytical meditation. Although these two meditations differ in detail and subtlety, they both focus on the same object. The two together are the direct antidote. The results, or benefits, of applying the direct antidote are also two-fold: a special form of mental joy and peaceful physical pleasure. The base or foundation is śamatha itself. It is the basis for both the two aspects of the antidote and the two results that arise from applying the antidotes.

This type of meditation is a mundane path. It is called a path because it is a meditation technique to reach a goal. But this is a mundane path because it only temporarily removes the mental afflictions. It is a common path because it is common to both Buddhist and non-Buddhist traditions.

UNDERSTANDING KARMA

In addition to śamatha conjoined with a form of wisdom, you must engage in the practice of ethical conduct in order to attain a higher rebirth or permanent emancipation from samsara. How do you do perform virtuous actions and avoid nonvirtuous actions? In short, you need to watch your mind. It is difficult in the beginning to monitor every single action you do. Eventually you will be able to control all your actions, but beginners cannot do that. So, the best way to take up the practice of engaging in virtue and steering clear of negative actions is to focus your effort on the most powerful virtues and nonvirtues. You begin to change your behavior by learning which actions will have the weightiest results. In this regard, Nāgārjuna said,

> 42.   Five attributes determine the strength of good or evil
> deeds:
> those done constantly, with a strong motivation, lacking an
> antidote,
> and in relation to the two bases of the highest good
> qualities.
> Therefore, strive to engage in the practice of virtue.

The factors influencing the power of your action were discussed in chapter 2 in a slightly different way. Here Nāgārjuna introduces five attributes that determine the power of your actions. Whether your actions are positive or negative, these five qualities govern the strength of the result. What are these attributes? First, is the frequency of the action, which, in this context, is given the technical name *preparation*. Second, your motivation; it matters whether you do something accidently or carefully consider how you will do it. Third is whether you engage in an antidote. You can purify even a very negative action, but if you don't have an antidote, even a small negative action becomes very powerful. The fourth and fifth attributes are in regard to the basis, or object, of your action. The basis is divided into two and counted as two different attributes. It depends upon whether the object of your action is an ordinary sentient being or a superior being such as a buddha, a bodhisattva.

Preparation, the first attribute, is the regularity with which you do an action. It may be a minor action, but if you do it constantly it makes it much heavier. Think of a slowly dripping faucet: drop by small drop it will fill a bucket. Your motivation—the second attribute—is the thought or attitude behind your action. If you are motivated by anger or other mental afflictions, your actions are negative and nonvirtuous. If you are motivated by faith or enthusiasm for helping others, then your action is virtuous. If you do something very good, but your positive motivation is weak, it is still a weak action. The reverse is also true: a small action done with a very strong motivation is a powerful action. The third attribute is the application or nonapplication of an antidote. You may have done something quite negative, but later you recognize that it was a bad thing to do, you regret having done it, and want to purify it. A desire to purify your action will weaken that karma. In contrast, even a small negative action becomes a heavy karma if you are happy about what you have done and have no wish to apply the antidote. The opposite holds true for virtue. If you regret having done something virtuous it weakens that virtuous action. We have a traditional example for this. A foolish ignorant person who doesn't apply the antidotes to their negative actions is like someone who throws a small metal pellet into a pool of water and lets it sink to the bottom. A careful wise person may have much bigger piece of metal, but they flatten it carefully so it can float on top of the water.

The next attribute listed in the verse, "the two bases of highest good qualities," is a combination of the fourth and fifth attributes. The basis is the object of your action, meaning the sentient being who is affected by the action. It is the field of your activity. Regardless of the first three attributes, the beings who are the object of your actions affect the heaviness of your karma. The higher field of action has two parts: ordinary beings who have benefited you in a conventional way and those with excellent qualities of their own who have benefited you in a spiritual way. An example of the first field of action is your parents. They gave you life; nourished you when you were an infant; sincerely promoted your welfare over the course of your life; sacrificed their own happiness and health for you, and so forth. Even when they scolded or disciplined you, they had those attitudes. The second type of higher field is an even more powerful object. Those with good qualities who have benefitted you in a spiritual way are, for example, your spiritual teachers, bodhisattvas, buddhas, the Sangha, and so forth. They have only love for you; they always want you to become free from misery and suffering; they have no other interest than to help you and other sentient beings. If you recognize this and do good things for the objects in these fields, your actions are powerful. If you do something negative toward these objects it becomes a very powerful negative action. When we talk of a field of action it is analogous to a farmer's field. The quality of a field itself makes a difference in the harvest. A field with good soil and few rocks will yield a good harvest. A sandy, rocky, dry field will naturally yield less. From a societal perspective we already understand that the object of an action affects the repercussions of that action. For example, it is not treated as simple crime if someone tries to harm the president of the United States. The president represents the entire country, so harming them is a powerful action.

In his great work, the *Treasury of Knowledge*, Vasubandhu said that the higher field includes both enlightened beings, those who are āryas, and also those who are not:

> Even if they are not āryas, if you act well toward
> your parents, those who are ill, a Dharma teacher,
> or a bodhisattva in his last life as a sentient being,
> the merit you create is measureless.
>
> [*Treasury of Knowledge*, 4.118]

It is important know how the strength of a karma is affected by these attributes. This knowledge gives you a framework for creating great virtue and avoiding great nonvirtue. You will be able to monitor your motivation, your actions, and the objects of your action. Furthermore, with this knowledge you can choose to increase the power of your virtue and decrease your nonvirtue by applying the antidotes. Nāgārjuna illustrates this point with a pithy example.

> 43.   A pinch of salt can change the taste
>   of a little water, but not the entire Ganges River.
>   You should know that the same applies to
>   minor negative actions and vast roots of virtue.

AVOIDING THE FIVE OBSTACLES

Now that you know the basic structure of how karma works, you need to be aware of the obstacles to training your mind. What is it that keeps you from watching your mind, creating virtue, and avoiding nonvirtue? In general, Nāgārjuna says, the obstacles are your mental afflictions. At present, even while you are trying to do positive actions, your mind is full of mental afflictions. Whenever an attractive object appears to your senses, you desire it. Whenever you perceive something unattractive, you hate it. Desire is like an underground river constantly flowing in your mind. Hatred can erupt like a destructive wildfire.

Śāntideva likened the mental afflictions to a band of thieves.

> My mental afflictions are a host of thieves
> searching for a good opportunity.
> Finding it, they steal my virtues
> and destroy my future in a happy rebirth.
> [*Introduction to the Practice of Bodhisattvas,* 5.28]

The mental afflictions lurk deep in your mind. As soon as they find an opportunity, anger, desire, and all the other mental afflictions sneak out and damage your wholesome mind. When your virtuous mind is damaged, your positive actions are demolished too. Thus, your practice of virtue is ruined and the possibility of attaining a high rebirth destroyed.

Nāgārjuna specifically warns us about five primary obstacles to the practice of virtue.

> 44. Recognize that excitement and regret, malice,
> sluggishness and sleepiness, yearning sensory desire,
> and doubt are the five obstacles
> that steal the riches of virtue.

The first obstacle has two aspects: excitement and regret in relation to desire. When you are attracted to a desirable sensory object, your mind becomes excited and completely distracted. Desire for food, clothing, shelter, and sexual pleasure can easily overwhelm your mind. Your mind rushes to those objects and you cannot keep it focused where you want it to stay. Regret has a specific context here too. You are unhappy or uncomfortable at some point every day because you do not have the things or experiences that you desire. You feel that something is wrong, and you regret that you didn't act in a way to get what you want. "Why did I give that away?" "Why did I say that?" "Why did I eat that?" "Why didn't I do this to get that?" "Why didn't I attack and destroy that?" Even a simple thing like why you didn't hang a picture at a different place on the wall can upset you. You regret all your seeming mistakes, whether they were actually wrong or not. This robs you of your peace of mind; sometimes you cannot sleep due to your regret. Obviously, this is a very different type of regret than that explained in the context of the four opponent powers for purification. In that context regret is conjoined with wisdom that recognizes you have done something that will bring you terrible negative consequences. That is a useful type of regret because it helps you avoid similar actions in the future.

The second obstacle is malice. Out of anger and hatred you have ill will toward those you consider your enemies. You wish to harm those you feel have done you wrong. Your mind is riled up with negative thoughts. The strength of your animosity is based on how much you engage in a type of thought process. The stages of the path literature divides this process of rationalization into nine: you think about how someone has acted toward you, your friends and relatives, and your enemies in the past, present, and future. You think, "This person did this harmful thing to me in the past, he is doing that to me now, and he will do it in the future." You think, "This person did that horrible thing to my friends and family in the past, he is doing it to my loved ones now, and he will do it again in the future." You think, "This person did helpful things for my enemy in the past, he is benefitting my enemies now, and he will do that again in the future." When you think this way, your anger becomes stronger and stronger. Eventually it becomes so firm that it takes complete control over your mind. You see the person as completely horrible and vile. You want to hurt them and destroy them. It doesn't matter if they have some other good qualities. Your mind is so disturbed that you physically change: your face turns red, you can't sit still, and you may lash out and hit a wall.

The third obstacle is also divided into two: sluggishness and sleepiness. Sluggishness is mental dullness. When your mind is dull you become discouraged. What you want to do is unclear and you feel you cannot function properly, either physically or mentally. When you are sluggish you aren't asleep, but your body and mind are unsuitable for the practice of virtue. You know this well; think about how you feel if you eat way too much Thanksgiving dinner. The second aspect of this obstacle is to actually fall asleep. Getting too sleepy while you are trying to do something completely steals away the power of your action. You don't need an extensive explanation about sleep. In short, as you fall asleep the power of your mind is drawn inward; it ceases to focus on doing something.

The fourth obstacle is desire itself. This is desire for the objects of your five physical senses. When you perceive a desirable object, it is as if your mind is magnetically pulled to it and then glued there. The fifth obstacle is doubt or uncertainty in relation to virtue. If you are uncertain whether emancipation exists, or doubt whether following the path of the spiritual teachings will lead you to freedom, then you will not practice seriously.

Vasubandhu concisely outlined how these five obstacles are categorized.

> The hindrances exist in the desire realm.
> Two are counted as one because they have
> the same opposite, fuel, and function.
>
> [*Treasury of Knowledge,* 5.59]

We have seen that excitement and regret are counted as one because they are similar in opposing meditative concentration. They both arise from desire. They both function to distract the mind. In the Abhidharma they are referred to as causes that lead the mind away from concentration; in that sense, they are a type of food or sustenance for distraction. In a similar way sleepiness and dullness are caused by similar things. They function in the same way; they make your mind lose its energy so that you can't study or meditate. Sleep and sluggishness are the opposite of concentration because they destroy the bright vividness of the mind.

Why are only these five obstacles mentioned when the teachings say there are 84,000 mental afflictions? It is because these five are particularly detrimental to the three higher trainings of ethical conduct, meditative concentration, and wisdom. You need to master all three higher trainings in order to attain any spiritual goal. Only on the basis of pure moral conduct can you develop stable mental concentration. This mental ability is necessary for wisdom—a direct realization of the four realities for āryas and emptiness.

Desire, and its corollary anger, are the main obstacle to the superior training of ethical conduct. They prevent you from wanting to take religious vows. Vows are a form of self-control. They demand conduct that is the opposite of how you normally act when you have a strong desire for sensual pleasure. Sluggishness and sleepiness interrupt the superior training of concentration. Sleepiness and dullness can seem close to śamatha because they too are internalized. But they are not like vivid calm control of śamatha in any other respect. Excitement and regret are obstacles to the superior training in wisdom. Wisdom is understanding reality, whether ultimate or phenomenal. First you analyze the subject, then when you have firm understanding you hold it firmly in your mind. Excitement and regret disturb the development of wisdom because they distract you toward external things.

The last obstacle is doubt. It is a mental affliction that harms both higher concentration and higher wisdom. Why? Because if you are uncertain about what you are doing you cannot remain in the state of equipoise that is the union of these two higher trainings. The union of the two higher trainings is when you can fix your mind on an object for as long as you wish, when you understand the subtlety of the object clearly (but not necessarily directly), and when your body and mind are pliant and blissful. The practice of śamatha is the same whether applied to the wisdom of the mundane or supramundane paths. In this chapter we focused on the wisdom practice of the mundane path; ultimate wisdom was discussed briefly in chapter 4 and will be further elaborated in chapter 7.

The five obstacles can be understood more specifically in a narrower context: the development of śamatha. In *Ornament for the Mahayana Sutras,* Maitreya explained that you face five obstacles when attempting to develop śamatha. The first and most powerful obstacle is laziness. Laziness prevents you from even starting to try to develop śamatha. The second of the five obstacles also precedes engaging in practice: you are motivated to try to develop śamatha but you forget the instructions on how to do it. The latter three obstacles occur during your meditation practice: the third obstacle is mental laxity and its opposite, excitement; the fourth is failing to apply the remedies to laxity and excitement when they are needed; and the fifth is an unnecessary application of the antidotes when your meditation is perfect.

To remove those obstacles Maitreya prescribed eight antidotes. The first four antidotes are methods to eradicate laziness. There is one antidote each for the remaining four obstacles. The four antidotes to laziness are: (1) faith, (2) admiration, (3) diligence, and (4) flexibility. The first two antidotes combat the first type of laziness – not wanting to even try to develop śamatha. Faith leads you to have an interest and a desire to practice. Faith in combination with admiration makes you diligent; diligence opposes both the laziness that is procrastination and the laziness of self-denigration. When you are diligent, you put a lot of effort into your practice. The first three antidotes together lead to a suppleness or flexibility and dexterity of your body and mind. Whatever you want to do becomes easy; your perseverance becomes spontaneous. The fifth antidote is to recollect the instructions; this counteracts forgetting what you should do. The sixth antidote is introspection so that you are aware when your mind becomes excited and flighty or sleepy and dull. The seventh antidote is to apply the appropriate countermeasures for excitement and dullness. The eighth antidote is to cease applying the countermeasures when they are no longer needed. The chart in appendix 2 summarizes these obstacles and antidotes.

In the beginning concentration and wisdom are different practices. Śamatha practice is learning to single-pointedly focus on an object; the practice of wisdom is to analyze a subject to gain understanding of it. So, one is a stabilization meditation and the other is an analytical meditation. But later, the two are joined together. They have the same object; they function in union. We had an example for this in Tibet. If someone had some fresh butter and wanted to use it for a meal in a few hours, they didn't want it to melt or to freeze. They wanted to keep the butter soft and smooth so they could spread it on their toast. So, they put it in some cool water and put the basin out in the sun. The water kept the butter cool; the sun warmed it enough to use. The power of śamatha keeps the mind from being distracted by analysis; the power of wisdom keeps the mind from being frozen. Another analogy for the union of concentration and wisdom is putting a small fish in a big tank of water. The fish can swim all around without disturbing the main body of water. The union of concentration and wisdom is similar. The mind stays on the object and understands it; it is in equanimity, not too much of one or the other.

This concludes the presentation of practices that form the basis for the attainment of both a high rebirth and complete liberation from samsara. The next topic is the practices that are specifically focused on the attainment of complete emancipation from rebirth due to ignorance, the mental afflictions, and karma.

7. The Practices to Attain Spiritual Goals

So FAR, we have looked at the practices that are the foundation for both the attainment of a higher rebirth and permanent liberation from samsara. These practices are common to all Buddhist practitioners, whether their goal is temporary—a high rebirth—or the permanent goals of nirvana or complete enlightenment. Now we move on to the practices that are specifically devoted to the attainment of permanent liberation from samsara: nirvana, which is the goal of the śrāvaka path, and perfect enlightenment, which is the goal of the bodhisattva path. These practices presume that a practitioner, whether lay or ordained, has worked on all the earlier practices that are the common basis for both the temporary and permanent spiritual goals. The goals of personal liberation (nirvana) and complete enlightenment are superior to the enjoyment of a good rebirth. Although a good rebirth is a spiritual goal beyond this life, it will not last forever. You will die and take rebirth. When you attain either nirvana or enlightenment you have cut the root of rebirth in samsara. In both cases, it is definite that you will never fall under the power of karma and the mental afflictions again. What is the key method to attain these definite, permanently good goals? Nāgārjuna explains three intertwined topics: (1) becoming familiar with the five powers and five strengths, (2) eliminating the detrimental condition of conceit, and (3) developing the right view.

THE FIVE POWERS AND THE FIVE STRENGTHS

Whether talking about the Hinayana or Mahayana, there are five successive paths that are followed to reach your final goal. (This discussion about the five paths is not applicable to the mundane path leading to the goal of a temporary rebirth in the upper realms.) The word *path* isn't a reference to a road outside; it is about a method of gradual internal development. So, it might seem like there are fifteen different paths: five paths to become a śrāvaka arhat; five to become a pratyekabuddha arhat; and five paths to attain complete buddhahood. However, each set of five has many commonalities and they share the same names: (1) the path of accumulation (2) the path of preparation, (3) the path of seeing, (4) the path of meditative cultivation, and (5) the path of no further training.[28] The path of accumulation is the beginning. The path of preparation is given that name because it is readying you to enter the next path, the path of seeing. On the third path you directly see reality. In the Hinayana system this is a direct perception of the four realities for āryas; in the Mahayana it is a direct realization of the emptiness of the person and phenomena. On the first two paths you can subdue the mental afflictions, but they are not removed from the root. It is only with a direct realization of ultimate reality that you can permanently remove the mental afflictions. But directly seeing ultimate reality on the first moment of the path of seeing is not enough. You must use your wisdom to remove all the mental afflictions step by step. That is what you do on the path of meditative cultivation, sometimes called the path of meditation. You have already had a direct realization of reality but now you are using that to sequentially cut out different levels of the mental afflictions. The fifth path, the path of no further training, is the final goal. You have gotten rid of the mental afflictions that are the cause of suffering, suffering itself, and so forth. Your mind is fully imbued with positive qualities and all negative aspects are gone. You don't need to do anything further to gain something or get rid of anything.

There are many, many teachings about what you do on each step of these five paths. At the beginning, on the path of accumulation, you are very vague about the qualities of the final goal, the method to get to the goal, and the conditions required to practice the method. To remedy this, you need to accumulate merit. Merit can be created physically or mentally, but here the emphasis is on the mental side. Since at the beginning you don't really know very much, you start by studying with those who have more advanced knowledge. You don't just accept what you are told; you must examine and analyze the subject matter yourself. It is your personal investigation that gives you some understanding. To improve that understanding you meditate. The point of meditation is to make your understanding clearer and deeper. Therefore, the process is to develop śamatha first and then use that stable single-pointed concentration to develop wisdom. Thus, on the path of accumulation you have two main things to do: studying and developing śamatha.

Let's look at an example. On the Mahayana path of accumulation, you start your study of emptiness, the ultimate nature of reality. You may come to understand it logically, but you don't clearly see it directly. Your mind will be wandering a lot too, so you learn to practice śamatha. As your śamatha meditation becomes stronger, you gradually add subtle wisdom to your practice. Eventually your concentration and wisdom will be in union. In other words, the main part of your mind remains without moving on the topic of emptiness, but a subtle part of your mind is engaged in investigating the details of emptiness. Neither aspect of the mind, the stability and the wisdom, disturbs the other. They help each other. When you accomplish this union of śamatha and wisdom you have reached the path of preparation.

You gain a special kind of mental power when you seamlessly join the meditation techniques of concentration and wisdom. This is the tool you need to further develop in order to attain a direct realization. While you are practicing on the path of preparation you are still an ordinary individual. You are not ordinary in the common sense because you have this strong mental power, but you are ordinary in that you have not yet attained a direct realization of ultimate reality.

So, what do you actually do on the path of preparation? First of all, you become familiar with what are called the five strengths and the five powers.

> 45. The five supreme dharmas are: faith, perseverance,
> recollection, meditative concentration, and wisdom.
> Strive in earnest for these. They are called
> the strengths, the powers, and what takes you to the peak.

We have already talked about these five practices in general, both in the context of a general practice of virtue and as a common basis for attaining a high rebirth and liberation. Remember, faith is a special trust in reality. On the Mahayana path, ultimate reality, or the truth, refers to emptiness, and on the Hinayana path it refers to the four realities for āryas. Your faith gives you the confidence to diligently persevere in your practice. The *Ornament for the Mahayana Sutras* says that perseverance is to take delight in the practice of virtue. This feeling of joy itself is diligence. Recollection, or mindfulness, is to remember the object. When you have these first three, you add meditative concentration and wisdom that understands the subtlety of the detail of the true nature of reality. Now the advice to practice these five is more specifically directed to the practice of the path that leads to liberation from samsara.

These five mental competencies are called powers or strengths in the context of the path system. In the lower Abhidharma, as outlined in Vasubandhu's *Treasury of Knowledge,* they are called powers when practiced on the path of accumulation. They are called strengths when practiced on the path of preparation. In the higher Abhidharma system, as explained in Maitreya's *Ornament for the Mahayana Sutras* and accepted by Nāgārjuna, both the powers and strengths are practiced on the path of preparation. The five practices keep their individual names on each successive level, but we change the name of their category, from power to strength, in order to indicate their increasing efficacy. This gets a bit technical. As your practice of these five becomes stronger and stronger, your ability to conquer obstacles becomes greater. Based on the removal of certain manifest mental afflictions, the path of preparation is divided into four levels: heat, summit, forbearance, and supreme worldly dharma. As you progress through the levels of the path of preparation you are doing the same practices, but your ability and their power increase. So, according to the higher Abhidharma, you practice the powers on the lower two levels of the path of preparation and the strengths on the higher two levels.

The first level of the path of preparation is called heat because it is like a spark starting a fire or the sun coming up. At first there is just the slightest bit of heat and light, but these are signs that it will get warmer and brighter. When your practice on the heat level becomes stronger, you enter the second stage, called the summit. As noted above, according to the Mahayana, during these first two stages, these five practices are called powers because they give you a kind of positive capability. On the next two levels of the path of preparation—forbearance, or patience, and supreme worldly dharma—they are called strengths because you cannot be affected by their opposites. Your practice is firm and strong. In this context, the word *patience* refers to your understanding of ultimate reality. We are not talking about patience or impatience in terms of emotions here. This is patience in the sense of forbearance—being able to bear an understanding of ultimate reality. When we are impatient, we are uncomfortable, often because there is something we don't know. But by this level of practice you have the mental strength of wisdom; this has reduced your discomfort with reality. As your practice gets stronger yet, you come so close to the third path, the path of seeing, that the level is called the highest peak, or supreme worldly dharma. This is the last moment of being an ordinary individual; once you have attained the path of seeing you become an ārya.

CONCEIT

When you are close to reaching the path of seeing, but are still on the path of preparation, a detrimental condition may arise in your mind: conceit. Arrogance or conceit is to be puffed up about your own importance or abilities. It is a form of deluded pride. It is a powerful negative condition. In order to eliminate conceit, you concentrate on the reasons why it is unwarranted.

> 46. Conceit will not arise if the antidote
>   is considered again and again. Think,
>   "I am not exempt from sickness, aging, death,
>   separation from my loved ones, and subjugation to my
>   karma."

You may be able to practice śamatha in union with wisdom. You may be getting close to the path of seeing. But that is no reason to be full of yourself. Think about your nature. You can still become sick. You age every moment, with every breath, until the moment you stop breathing and die. There is no possibility of avoiding death. It could happen at any time. Not only that, you also have so many problems in your life. You are always facing the possible loss of those you love. You don't want to separate from your friends and relatives, but you will have to at some point. You don't want any connection with those you do not like, but those situations fall upon you like rain. You want happiness. You don't want misery. But neither of these depend upon your wishes. You have to experience the results of whatever karma you have created in the past. There is no way to get out of that. This is your nature. When you think this way, there is no basis for conceit to arise.

Conceit is also negative in an ordinary sense. We have a Tibetan saying, "Conceit is like a balloon." If you tie off the end of an air-filled balloon, no matter how much water you pour over it not a drop will get in. It all runs off. Conceit is like a mental balloon. If you are conceited, you never remember to practice the Dharma. When you are conceited not even a drop of good quality will get into you. A bodhisattva works to open their heart to universal love and compassion. A conceited mind cannot develop these things.

THE RIGHT VIEW

Having warned of the dangers of conceit, Nāgārjuna then advises the king to adopt the right attitude towards spiritual practice. You need to develop the right view because all your past, current, and future problems start with its opposite: the mental afflictions. The mental afflictions are the enemy of your peace and happiness. You can't fight this enemy with a weapon; the only way to conquer the mental afflictions is to develop wisdom, in other words, the right view. The right view, sometimes called the correct view, or perfect view, has two aspects: one is in regard to conventional phenomena, the other is in regard to the ultimate object. In other words, one is the right view of phenomenal reality, the other is the right view of ultimate reality. Whether you want liberation from samsara or complete enlightenment you need the right view of the two realities.

47. If you desire a high rebirth or liberation
     you must become familiar with the right view.
     Someone with the wrong view may do good deeds
     but they will experience horrific results.

The right view of phenomenal reality is a proper understanding of causality. More specifically, it is a correct understanding of karma and its effects. For example, it is knowing that evil actions will only bring a miserable suffering result and wholesome karma will result in only peace and happiness. It is most important to understand that there is a definite relationship between causes and their effects. You have to consider this over and over again until you are irreversibly convinced that everything and every experience fits into this framework. Only then will you see that you can remove the possibility of taking future samsaric rebirths by removing the cause for them. Only then can you put this into practice. Because you know which actions result in negative experiences, you avoid them; because you know which actions bring happiness, you develop them. This keeps you from falling into a lower rebirth. According to the Mahayana, the right view of ultimate reality is a realization of emptiness. This is what will remove the root of suffering forever. This will free you from all rebirths.

What is the wrong view then? Sometimes you will hear that the worst wrong view is the opposite of the ultimate right view, the correct understanding of emptiness. Because the ultimate right view is that everything lacks inherent existence, the wrong view opposite to that is eternalism, thinking that things intrinsically exist. But for beginners the opposite of the ultimate right view isn't really the worst wrong view. For practitioners at the outset of the path, the most ruinous wrong view is nihilism, the opposite of the phenomenal right view. Nihilism is a denial of causality: it denies the connection between actions and resultant experiences, including the world, the environment, sentient beings, enlightenment, and nirvana. It is believing that only the body is real, and that the mind is simply a quality of the body, and that when the body dies that is the end. So, nihilists conclude there is no need to practice the Dharma. They think we should just enjoy this life. Nihilists can and do engage in good actions. However, if a positive action is accompanied by or motivated by nihilism, the strength of the merit created is greatly reduced. The result of that good action will come fruition in samsara; in other words, it will have the nature of suffering. That is why Nāgārjuna says that if you have the wrong view, even your positive actions result in misery.

Buddhists say that denial of the possibility of future lives is very destructive. It throws away the opportunity to attain emancipation and enlightenment. To counter that assertion, nihilists give three examples to show that mind is a function of the body. First, they say that the body-mind relationship is similar to a flame and the light it gives off; when the flame goes out the light is gone. Another example of this relationship is wine and its ability to intoxicate. The power to intoxicate is in the wine; if the wine is not consumed, you don't get drunk. Further, the mind depends upon the body in the same way that a mural depends on a wall. If you paint a mural on a wall, and the wall is demolished, the mural is destroyed too. Similarly, nihilists claim, the body is a product of the four major elements of earth, water, air, and fire, and that at death, the body along with the mind decomposes into the elements.

The phenomenal correct view is extremely important. Sometimes people think that the phenomenal right view is less important than the ultimate right view because having the right view of the ultimate nature of reality is necessary to cut the root of samsara. In this sense the ultimate right view is in fact the most important. However trying to understand emptiness without understanding karma will not work. It is only by having irreversible faith in causality that you can begin to understand the cause of samsara.

Because the right view is difficult to understand, Nāgārjuna next gives a more detailed explanation of it by presenting five topics: (1) how to meditate on the four aspects of mindfulness, (2) recollecting selflessness, (3) giving up the three shackles, (4) practicing the three higher trainings, and (5) recollecting the body.

Mindfulness

Traditionally *mindfulness* means to actively turn your attention to a particular object or topic, as in keeping something in mind. This is slightly different than contemporary uses of the word to mean self-awareness of the present moment. There are four types of mindfulness: (1) mindfulness of the body, (2) mindfulness of sensations and feelings, (3) mindfulness of mind, and (4) mindfulness of all phenomena. These are common to the both the Hinayana and Mahayana. The first three, mindfulness of body, sensations and feelings, and mind are covered in the next verse. The last one will be covered separately because it requires a discussion of emptiness.

48. Understand that in fact humans are
    suffering, impermanent, without a self, and impure.

> Those who have not established these four recollections
> adhere to the four wrong views and fall to ruin.

According to Buddhism samsaric life has four qualities: it is (1) suffering, (2) impermanent, (3) lacks a self, and (4) impure. If you do not recollect these four consistently you will always see things in the opposite way. You will perceive things through ignorance. In other words, you will have four wrong views: you will think that your body, feelings, and mind are pleasurable when actually they have the nature of misery; you will think that impermanent things are permanent; you will have the egoistic view, thinking that there truly are real subjects and objects when really nothing has such a self; and you will think that your impure body and possessions are attractive and lovely. Due to these perverse ways of thinking you will fall under the power of desire, hatred, and the other mental afflictions. Then you create karma and continue to suffer in samsara. The essence of being mindful is to recollect that the four objects of mindfulness—body, feelings, mind, and phenomena—all have the nature of suffering, impermanence, selflessness, and impurity. This is wisdom. It is called mindfulness because you are remembering these facts. If you do these meditations properly you eventually will have a realization of the true nature of the body and so forth. That will lead to liberation.

The first wrong view is attraction and attachment to your ordinary life. You think that your life is so good and pleasant that you are loath to lose it. The antidote to that is to see the suffering nature of life in samsara. In this regard, you consider that you are enduring three types of suffering: ordinary suffering, the suffering of transformation, and the suffering of being created by causes and conditions. The first type of suffering is the nature of your body and mind: physical and mental misery. Your body is delicate; it is like an open wound that hurts at the lightest touch. Tiny things, a mosquito bite or a pebble in your shoe, can be incredibly painful. Sickness, pain, and so forth are the nature of life. The second type of suffering is the suffering of transformation or change. Nothing, neither your body nor your possessions and friends, last for even a moment without changing. The third type of suffering is that everything experienced in samsara is created by impure karma and the mental afflictions. You suffer from the reality that have no control over what happens in life.

The next wrong view is thinking that things are permanent. The remedy to this is to recollect impermanence. Each moment is gone by the time the next moment arises. Things change no matter how much you want them to stay the same. The third wrong view is believing there is some special I or me that intrinsically exists. This feeling of I, me, mine is strong; even animals have it. The antidote to this is to remember that the object of that feeling does not exist as it appears. There is no independent subject that is in control and has power over everything. This egoism is a comfortable illusion, but when you look for that self you will find that it isn't there. The final wrong view is feeling that you are clean, pure, and perfect. You are convinced that is the nature of your body. You don't see that actually there is nothing clean and pure in your body. When you look with wisdom at your bones, skin, muscles, blood, and so forth you see they are the opposite. All the components of your body are impure and unattractive. You should be mindful that your body is just a collection of filthy things.

All four wrong views pertain to each of the four objects of mindfulness meditation: the body, feeling, mind, and phenomena. Mindfulness is to recollect each of these objects' general characteristics of suffering, impermanence, selflessness, and impurity. The method to do this is to first examine the particular characteristics that comprise the identity of each object and then meditate on the four general characteristics. Although all the objects have all four general characteristics, you concentrate more on one quality particular to each object. For example, when yogis examine the nature of their body, they first look at the particular features of the body. They see that the body is a combination of various things: bones, muscles, skin, and so forth. After that they look at the four general characteristics of the body; they consider that the body is suffering, impermanent, selfless, and impure. Here they put particular emphasis on the impurity of the body. When feelings are their object, they deconstruct them in a similar way. First, they look at the features particular to feelings: there are physical feelings, emotional feelings, sometimes feelings are pleasant, sometimes unpleasant, and sometimes neutral. Then after that they contemplate how feelings are suffering, impermanent, selfless, and impure. Here the emphasis is to meditate on feelings having the nature of the three types of suffering. You use the same method when contemplating the mind. In that meditation, you emphasize the general characteristic of impermanence. You all know about death, but nevertheless feel that something about your mind will never change. To counter this feeling of permanence you first examine the particular characteristics of your mind. It is constantly running and changing, moment by moment flickering between sensory objects. Then you recollect impermanence by thinking about past and future lives.

Selflessness

The last object of mindfulness meditation is all phenomena. The quality emphasized in the context of this meditation is selflessness. *Selfless* here means that there is no independent real subject. You mistakenly think that everything, whether internal or external, has some kind of special governing subject or owner. You think in terms of me and mine: my house, my body, my possessions. You feel that you have ownership, even when considering the entire universe. How do you meditate on the selflessness of houses, and so forth? No one thinks a house, a rock, or tree has an ego. But you do feel as if these things have some kind of substantive, singular identity. But when you realize that there is no single, independent, overall thing, you realize these are selfless.

Nāgārjuna delves more deeply into the mindfulness of all phenomena because the characteristic you focus on here—selflessness—is harder to understand than the characteristics of suffering, impermanence, and impurity. Questions about selflessness arise for many of us. How can things lack a self? It certainly seems like there is a soul, or self, that goes from life to life. There must be something that lasts: a part of me that creates karma, carries the seeds of that karma to future lives, and experiences the results of that karma later. If the self or soul is impermanent who creates karma? Who experiences it? Who carries the seed of karma? If the self is impermanent, then the person who creates the karma is gone by the time of the experience of the result. Humans have developed all kinds of ideas in attempt to answer these questions. Many traditions have concluded that karma cannot work unless the soul is permanent and goes on after the body dies. Buddhists say that is incorrect; they concluded that there is no permanent, intrinsically existent soul. In other words, the right view of the nature of the self of persons is selflessness.

To understand the right view of selflessness, we begin by looking a bit further into the wrong view and the problems that result from it. Dharmakīrti said,

If you have a strong notion of I, you differentiate others.
Then attachment to yourself and aversion toward others arises.
All the other faults of the mental afflictions and karma arise
in those bound by these two afflictions.
[*Commentary on Valid Cognition*, 2.219c–220b]

The wrong view of the self of persons and phenomena is the root of all faults because self-cherishing and the other mental afflictions arise from it. When you have the egoistic view, you feel that anything other than yourself has little value. This deluded mind compels you to act, and all life experiences are the result. This is the reality of the cause of suffering: the problems you experience in samsara are the result of the mental afflictions, and the mental afflictions arise from the egoistic view. This is true for everyone, not just you. Therefore, the primary target of Buddhist practice is to get rid of ignorance. So, how do you get rid of ignorance? You don't have to go somewhere to find the three poisons of ignorance, desire, and hatred. They are operating within your mind. The opposite of ignorance is wisdom that comprehends the way that the self and phenomena actually exist. You need to understand that there are no intrinsically existent phenomena, neither subjects nor objects. That understanding must be developed and become spontaneous and nonconceptual. Eventually it becomes a powerful antidote that will remove the root of samsara. Candrakīrti put it this way:

Seeing that all the mental afflictions and faults
stem from the mistaken view of the transitory composite,
and realizing that the self is the object of this view,
a yogi will engage in negation of this self.
[*Entering the Middle Way*, 6.120]

A more literal translation of what I am calling the egoistic view would be "the mistaken view of the perishable aggregates," or "the view of the transitory composite." Your five aggregates, in Sanskrit *skandhas*, are the basis of your idea of I and me. These five are physicality, feeling, perception, karmic formations, and consciousness. Each of these aggregates are impermanent. They perish moment by moment. They are transitory. Their nature is to change. In addition, each aggregate is dependent on the others. Further, each one is made up of many things, hence they are called an aggregation or composite. They are not singular, independent, unique things. But we don't see them that way. We think, "This is me; this is my identity." We believe that there is some real, independent, and absolute *me*. This is the self-centered egoistic view: it is a wrong view about the collection of transitory aggregates.

Wisdom means understanding that you have no real, ultimate, independent, or singular identity; it is to understand that the self of persons as you usually conceive it does not exist. This is the realization of *anātma*—the Sanskrit word we translate as "selflessness" or "no-self." It is an aspect of the understanding of emptiness, in Sanskrit, *śūnyatā*: the understanding that the self and the aggregates lack an inherent intrinsic nature. When you understand that, you see that the object of the egoistic view does not exist as it appears. What does it mean to say, the object doesn't exist as it appears? You have to divide the object into two: one is the object that is the basis of what you are perceiving; the other is something that you have incorrectly superimposed upon that basis. In other words, the latter is the way you hold the basis. For example, let's take a table as our object. The physical table itself is the basis of the perceived object. The second aspect would be an implicit belief that the table is permanent. The table does conventionally exist, but its permanence does not exist; on the ultimate level it is empty of self-nature. Thus, our perception of the table is a mixture of two things: the phenomenally existing table and the substantive, independent, and long-lasting nature of the table that doesn't exist at all.

To analyze the self of persons, you take the five aggregates as the object of your investigation. The five aggregates exist conventionally. We don't deny that this base is there. The problem is that the wrong view doesn't recognize the aggregates as transitory composites. The egoistic view sees the basis as a permanent and singular thing with an independent identity. Take the example of just the aggregate of physical materiality. Even though you know that your body is made of many parts—fingers, toes, arms, bones, and so forth—you think of it as a single unified body. You also feel that your body has continuity through time. That is why it is called the mistaken view of the transitory composite. It is important to not negate the conventional object that is the base. But the way you hold that referent object, as a real, an inherently existent I or me, is incorrect.

The object of this incorrect thought, an intrinsically existing I, is what should be rejected.

The egoistic view has two aspects: the innate and the philosophically imagined. Everyone has the innate wrong view. It is a feeling that naturally arises; our minds, because of samsaric conditioning, are set up so that it is always there. The philosophically imagined, or dogmatic, wrong view comes from learning the ideas of various incorrect philosophical and religious schools. For example, the idea that there is an absolute substantial soul that is different from your aggregates is something that you learn. Nevertheless, the dogmatic wrong views are important because you start to learn the right view through an analysis of the various ways people have tried to rationalize the existence of a permanent self or soul. The Buddhist scriptures say that there are twenty different wrong views of the transitory composite. We get this number by looking at each of the five aggregates in four ways. Take, for example, the physical aggregate. The four incorrect ways to think of the self in relation to the physical aggregate are: the self is the same as your physical body, the self possesses your physical form, the self is dependent upon physical things, and physical things are dependent upon the self. You can substitute each of the other aggregates into this format. These twenty are dogmatic ideas that are aspects of the created egoistic view. Some sutras analogize these twenty views as tall mountains surrounding you. There is no clear pass to get out. Although you are shadowed in the ignorance of these mountains, they can be destroyed by the diamond weapon of wisdom. A diamond can destroy any other stone; but no other stone can destroy a diamond. These dogmatic views are like ordinary stone; the realization of ultimate reality is like a diamond.

Nāgārjuna paraphrases this idea from the prajñāpāramitā sutras to outline a counter to these wrong views:

49. It was taught that physical things are not the self,
    the self does not possess physical things,
    the self does not dwell in physical things, nor do physical
        things dwell in the self.
    Understand that the four remaining aggregates are similarly
        empty.

The Buddha taught this, but how do you know for sure that it's true? How can you prove this? The Buddha himself said, "Don't rely upon my words. You should examine what I say with wisdom, just as an assayer tests gold before accepting it." Traditionally an assayer would employ three tests to determine whether a lump of metal was gold. First, they would put the gold into a fire to test the external color. Next, they would cut the metal to see if the inside was the same as the outside. Finally, they would rub it with special compounds to test for impurities. If no problems were found, the assayer would accept the gold. You should examine the Buddha's teachings in a similar manner. You shouldn't just accept his words out of respect for him. You need to use your analytical wisdom to assess what you hear and read.

Nāgārjuna said,

> Wisdom is the root of understanding
> all the qualities of perceptible and imperceptible things.
> Therefore, it is taught that perfect wisdom is necessary
> to accomplish both of the two realities.
> [*One Hundred Stanzas on Wisdom,* 1]

There are three sources of valid knowledge: (1) perception, (2) inference via logic, and (3) reliance upon the valid words of someone with supranormal mental powers. In relation to the three types of knowledge there are three objects of knowledge. First, with your senses you can examine things that are directly perceptible. You don't need logic to understand them; they are obvious. You use inference via logic to examine slightly hidden objects; these are things that you can't understand with ordinary perception. Slightly hidden objects are not perceptible to your senses alone; you need to think about them. Logical inference can give you knowledge whether they are true or false. The simplest example is that you can infer that there is a fire on the next mountain because you see smoke. Other examples of slightly hidden objects are things like time, space, impermanence, and enlightenment. You may not see these directly, but you can prove that they exist with logic. For example, you can infer that certain causes and conditions will have a certain result. If that weren't the case, farmers wouldn't bother to plant their fields because they couldn't expect a harvest. Buddhists put past and future lives into this category. They can't be seen, but there are logical proofs that establish them.

Very hidden objects are the last type of object of knowledge. These can neither be perceived by the senses nor proved by logic. Very hidden objects are only known by those who are omniscient. To establish the existence of this type of object, ordinary people must rely on scripture or the valid speech of someone utterly reliable. An example of a very hidden object is exactly how a specific past karma created by one being was experienced in a future lifetime when specific conditions came together. There are many instances in the sutras where people asked the Buddha why a certain type of result had occurred. You can understand the general characteristics of karma with logic; in general, you can say that virtue results in pleasant experiences and nonvirtue results in suffering. In that sense karma is a slightly hidden object. But in terms of the specifics of action, circumstances, and results, you have to trust what the Buddha said. People don't like to simply trust. But at the same time, you can't simply dismiss the existence of things that you or others like you haven't directly perceived or logically proven. There are things beyond your ordinary comprehension. However, if you put your trust in someone's words, you have to be sure that the speaker is completely reliable and has no faults.

Selflessness is a slightly hidden object. It can be proved via inference. It can be known. The words in the verse aren't the proof. There are reasons behind the words. So, let's expand upon these reasons. The basic question is whether there is a permanent, substantive self that has ownership and control over the components that make up the person. There are only two possible ways that such a permanent, substantive soul could exist: it either has the same nature as the aggregates, or it exists independently and outside of the aggregates. Another way to phrase this is that there are only two types of relationships: identity and dependency.

We start by examining whether the self is of the same nature as the aggregates. In other words, is there an identity relationship between the self and the aggregates. I will use the first aggregate, physicality, in this discussion, but remember that the same logic pertains to the self having an identity relationship with the aggregates of feeling, perception, karmic formations, and consciousness. You first test whether the intrinsically existent self has the same nature as the physical aggregate. In other words, you investigate if you are identical to your body. This cannot be correct. If they were the same, then the self would be impermanent. The self would change as your body grows and ages. In addition, your body has many parts: hands, arms, legs, torso, and hundreds of hairs. If the soul, or self, were identical to the body, you would have to accept that the self is a multiple too. The qualities of impermanence and multiplicity directly contradict our wrong view that the self of persons has a unitary, independent, unchanging, intrinsically existent nature.

Candrakīrti said,

> If the aggregates are the self,
> since they are numerous, the self will be multiple too.
> And the self would be substantially real; and viewing it thus
> would not be erroneous for it relates to something substantially
> real.
>
> [*Entering the Middle Way*, 6.127]

The last two lines of Candrakīrti's verse bring up another problem with the self having the same nature as the physical aggregate. The body is a substantial, material thing. If the self is the same as the physical aggregate, it would be substantial too. If that were actually the case, there would be no problem with thinking the soul or self is substantially existent. But no one believes that the soul is matter. People who believe in a soul think that it is invisible and immaterial. In summary, the self must be different than your physical form.

What is wrong with thinking that the self is something intrinsically different from the aggregates? If the self, the I, were different from the aggregates, several other questions arise. First, is there a relationship of possession between the self and the aggregates? Does the self possess the aggregates? Imagine a person named Devadatta who owns a lot of cows. Devadatta possesses the cows; he is a different entity than his cows. Is the soul a completely unique entity that possesses the body in that way? There are two refutations to this position: it is contradicted in the scriptures, and it is illogical. You can read many scriptures that say the self does not possess the body or the other aggregates. The logical reason is a matter of control. Devadatta controls his cows: he can keep them in one place; he can make them move to another pasture. The cows have to do whatever Devadatta wants them to do. But the self has no control over the body.

The self cannot keep the body from changing. The body ages, gets sick, changes color, all without permission from the self. The body will decline and die even though the self doesn't want it to end. If the self had power over the body, the body would do whatever the self commanded. This is not the case. Nor is it the case for any of the other aggregates.

Another possible type of dependency relationship between the self and the aggregates is that the aggregates and the self are related in the way that Devadatta's body wears clothing, or the way Devadatta dwells in a house. Again, we can quote scriptures that say this isn't the case. The logical reason is that this is a dependency relationship. In a conventional sense, Devadatta can change his clothes or move to another dwelling. His body doesn't change when he changes his clothes or moves to another house. The clothes and houses are not part of his body. But we are not talking about a conventional case of dependence here; the topic here is the nature of the relationship between an alleged absolute, intrinsically existent self and the aggregates. The self does not exist dwelling in dependence upon the physical aggregate because the body is impermanent. If the self were dependent upon the support of physical aggregate, it too would be impermanent. As the body changed, the soul would have to change.

"Well," you might wonder, "are the aggregates related to the inherently existent self in the same way that creeping vines depend upon a tree? More specifically, does the physical aggregate rely on the self the same way that a plant relies upon the ground?" This too describes a dependency relationship. This is not the case either. If the aggregates, which we know are transitory, relied upon a permanent, absolute, intrinsically existent self, then the aggregates could never change or die either. Something that is intrinsically existent is independent and absolute. This means it isn't dependent upon causes and conditions. If the cause of something never changes, there is no reason for the thing to change. So, if the body were dependent upon a permanent self, it too would necessarily be permanent. The body could never change; it could never be destroyed. Also, if external physical things were intrinsically dependent upon a permanent self, there could be no arising and ceasing. From observation of external material objects, we know that they undergo destruction without reliance upon a permanent self. After you apply this analysis to the other four aggregates, you recognize that the aggregates are empty of depending upon an intrinsically existent self.

Most people don't examine the I, but they have a strong feeling about it. They may not profess any of the dogmatic, philosophically created views, but they do have the innate wrong view. When you think about yourself, you see someone respectable and worth cherishing. If someone sees you differently you think that they are wrong. Everyone has this egoistic view. It arises naturally all the time. It doesn't require you to learn any philosophy or believe in a religion. You don't put this feeling into words, but if you did you would say, "I am intrinsically existent." This creates attachment to things that are yours.

Candrakīrti explained how the innate egoistic view arises in the introduction to *Entering the Middle Way:*

First thinking, "I," they cling to a self.
Then thinking, "mine," they become attached to things.
Like buckets on a waterwheel they revolve without control.
Entering the Middle Way, 1.3a–c]

This wrong view is the true target of your spiritual practice. With the mindfulness of phenomena, you develop the wisdom that destroys this process. Mindfulness of phenomena includes both conventional wisdom that properly understands causality and ultimate wisdom that properly understands emptiness. This is what yogis work on. They employ many reasons to come to understand that there is no intrinsically real I or me. They don't negate the conventional, relative I. What they reject is the wrong conception that clings to that which does not exist.

We talk about the self in relation to its base, the aggregates. In this regard, emptiness is the lack of an intrinsically existent self on the basis of the aggregates. Therefore, Nāgārjuna proceeds to further discuss the aggregates in terms of causality. Some philosophical traditions say that things, including the aggregates, occur without any cause at all. Others believe that things are created by a God or some other absolute unified causal substance. We know that results are always concordant with their causes, so if a cause is unchanging and permanent, then the resultant effect would always exist. And, if something changes there must be a temporal, impermanent cause for that to have happened. Even if you don't see the cause, it must be there. If there were no cause for happiness, why would you bother practicing virtue?

Dharmakīrti said,

> Suffering is the samsaric aggregates;
> it arises in accordance with transient causes.
> [*Commentary on Valid Cognition*, 2.147ab]

How do you prove that suffering has a cause? The answer is that suffering is caused because it is temporary. It arises sometimes in some places and sometimes it goes away. When the conditions are right, suffering arises. When conditions are lacking, suffering does not arise. All impermanent things are caused. An impermanent thing only exists when its causes and conditions exist. If the cause never existed, then the effect would never arise. If the cause were permanently present, the effect would also be permanent. If a thing was not temporary, once it existed it would always exist. It is easiest to understand these points in an analogy to a material thing like corn. If you plant the seeds and provide the conditions of good earth, water, sunshine, fertilizer and so forth, corn will grow. Corn will not grow if you don't have the primary cause—the seeds—or lack some of the other conditions. If the conditions are present but faulty, you may get corn, but it will poor quality. If a corn seed, sunlight, moisture, and so forth, were permanent, then they would always exist simultaneously in an unchanging manner: since the causes are unchanging, they cannot transform into the resultant corn harvest. Expanding on this example, we can see that suffering, and the aggregates, are dependent, relative, and temporary. The aggregates look like they are permanent and independent, but they are not because they are caused by causes and conditions. They do not exist intrinsically in an absolute way. The way they appear to exist isn't true.

To help us get rid of the wrong views that the aggregates arise from incompatible causes or arise from no cause at all, Nāgārjuna says,

50. The aggregates do not arise randomly, nor do they arise
     from time.
     They do not arise from a primordial nature, nor from their
     own essence.
     They do not arise from God, nor do they arise without a
     cause.
     Know that they arise from ignorance, karma, and craving.

In this verse Nāgārjuna rejects a number of incorrect concepts about the cause of the aggregates. After he's done that, he asserts his own view: the aggregates arise from appropriate causes and conditions. Let's look at the reasons he rejects these other positions. The first incorrect view is that the aggregates arise through their own nature, on their own whim, without depending on causes and conditions. This is not correct because there is no independent self-arising. If things arose randomly then they could arise anywhere, anytime, and without any reason. However, even a blade of grass depends on specific material causes and conditions. When they are there, the grass can grow; when they are not, the grass won't grow. Further, there is not just one cause and condition for all the aggregates. Each aggregate is completely dependent upon its own special causes and conditions.

There was a school of thought in ancient India that posited that the aggregates, and everything else in the universe, arose from time. They believed that time was always present, that it was permanent. This school of thought argued that whatever occurs happens because of time. In other words, time was the cause of everything. They said seasons happen due to time; our life is due to time, and when the time comes, we die. Even going to sleep and waking up, they said, are caused by time. For them, time was like God. The rejection of this position is that time is an incompatible cause for transitory things. If time was absolute, real, and permanent, where is it? We posit time based on functional things. We use language to describe something in the past or future based on events occurring and things changing. Time does not exist independent of that. There is nothing called *time* out there in the world. It only exists relatively and phenomenally as a construct of language and thought. Also, if permanent time were the cause of everything, you would have the same logical contradictions as before: if a permanent thing is the cause, nothing would ever change, and, there would be just one permanent cause so everything would always simultaneously exist forever. You couldn't have some things arise sometimes and other things that arise at other times. All the results would always have to be present.

A different ancient school of thought that we have discussed before, was the Sāṃkhya, which means "the enumerator." They were called this because they posited that everything in the universe could be divided into twenty-five categories. They further claimed that all twenty-five are manifestations of one absolute, unified, material substance that is the primal cause. This primal cause, they argued, is ultimate, permanent, absolute, and intrinsically existent, and not the result of anything else. They believed it is indivisible and that it pervades every individual thing. It never transforms yet it manifests as phenomenal things because of different amounts of the attributes of purity, passion, and impurity. They argued that although cows, trees, and rocks look like they are different, they all have the same absolute nature. The Sāṃkhyas also posited that the self or soul is not caused, that it didn't cause anything, and that it is totally separate from all twenty-five categories. According to them, samsara is caused by being confused about the absolute nature of the soul and engaging with the various categories derived from prākṛti. When the separate nature of the soul is seen, along with a recognition that everything else is a product of the primal cause, they believed that the categories would dissolve into the primal cause and the yogi would become free from samsara, leaving only the permanent self. This is the goal of Sāṃkhya practitioners.

There are contradictions in the Sāṃkhya argument. If the primal substance and all manifest things have the same nature, then both are either permanent or they are impermanent. The Sāṃkhya claim that a permanent cause results in impermanent phenomena is refuted with the logic outlined above. Buddhists say that if something transforms it is impermanent by definition. So, if the primal cause has the same nature as the phenomena it causes, it is impermanent too. This contradicts their theory. If they fall back to say that manifest things and the primal cause have different natures, they contradict their own tenet that everything is pervaded by and caused by the absolute substance.

The next position Nāgārjuna rejects is that things arise from their own essence. By definition, something that arises from its own nature does not depend upon any other causes and conditions. This was the position of the Cārvāka school. The examples they give to prove that things arise naturally from themselves are the eye on a peacock feather, the roundness of a pea, the sharpness of a thorn, and the facts that water always runs downhill, fires blaze upward, and the sun rises in the east. If their position were correct—that things arise from themselves without any other causes and conditions— then corn should grow without a field, or without someone planting seeds, water, sun, and so forth. We know this is not the case; many causes and conditions are necessary for a crop of corn.

Another incorrect view of causality is that all things are caused by an omniscient God. Adherents of this position claim that God is indescribable, extremely subtle, and invisible. God is eternal, in other words, permanent. God is the creator; God pervades everything and everywhere like space. They say that an ordinary mind cannot conceive of God, but yogis with high levels of practice can perceive it. And, that practitioners who want peace and happiness should concentrate on God. But the position that everything arises from an eternal, unchanging, all-pervasive God is also incorrect. Why? As we have seen above, if there is just one everlasting cause without any other necessary causes and conditions, everything should arise together at once or never arise at all. These believers may reply, "God's will causes things to arise sequentially or at different times." This contradicts their own position because now they are asserting an additional cause: God's intentions. God's will is different than the singular nature of God. Is God's will independent and absolute like God itself? Different intentions do not arise simultaneously so they must depend upon something else. So, does one wish depend upon another wish, which depends on yet another wish. You end up with an infinite regress.

Faced with the argument that there can be no relationship between a singular permanent cause and the multiplicity of impermanent results, some people have concluded that things arise with no cause at all. But this too is incorrect. If there is no cause, why should things ever arise? There is no reason for them to arise. Or things would always be in existence.

So where do all the phenomena of samsara come from? Nāgārjuna says they arise from ignorance, karma, and craving. How does this work? It is like planting a seed to get a plant. The cause—the seed—requires many conditions to germinate into a sprout. Karmic causation works in a similar way. Karma is the actions of body, speech, and mind. Your actions are like seeds because they have the potential for a future result. Karmic seeds are planted in the ground of ignorance and watered with desire and the other mental afflictions. This combination of the karma and the mental afflictions results in future impure rebirths. You might say, "Well, buddhas do things, so why are they free from rebirth?" Although buddhas engage in activity, they do not plant them in the ground of ignorance and fertilize them with the mental afflictions.

The Three Shackles

If you desire to be free from rebirth in samsara you need to have the positive conditions described above: ethical conduct, meditative concentration, and wisdom. In addition, you have to avoid obstacles that prevent liberation. What keeps you from abandoning the causes of rebirth? There are three things that tie you to samsara and keep you from getting out. These are listed in the next verse.

51.	Know that the three shackles binding you to samsara
	and blocking the gate to the city of liberation are:
	clinging to asceticism as a superior practice,
	having a perverted view of yourself, and doubt.

The first shackle is believing that an incorrect ethical system is the prescription for proper behavior. This is thinking that engaging in ascetic practices that have no moral purpose is the correct way to practice ethical conduct. For example, some religious practitioners think they should starve themselves, self-flagellate, sit in the hot sun surrounded by fires, or wear no clothes. There are so many strange forms of religious conduct. People do these things because they don't understand the causal relationship between their behavior and what will result. Some of those actions are actually harmful, but they believe they are the best kinds of behavior. What are the sources for wrong views about right conduct? People may rely on scriptures or one of the supranormal knowledges attained with a worldly form of śamatha, for example clairvoyance, clairaudience, telepathy, and the ability to discern—in a limited way—the prior or future life of an individual. This last power is why someone might think they should act in a strange manner. If someone with this kind of supranormal knowledge sees that someone who engaged in extreme asceticism was reborn as a god, they might conclude that they should act in the same way to get that kind of rebirth. The second shackle is a perverse view of the transitory composite. This is the egoistic view that was discussed at length above. And the third fetter is doubt about the correct path to emancipation. You are unsure whether liberation is possible and what the path to liberation might be.

There are so many obstacles to liberation. So why are these three singled out for abandonment? In the *Treasury of Knowledge* Vasubandhu provides an analogy. He says that although there are many obstacles that can keep you from getting to a particular destination, there are three that are primary. The first obstacle is not wanting to go. Second, even though you want to go, you erroneously take a route that leads somewhere else. Third, even though you want to go and have been shown the correct road, you dither and hesitate thinking, "maybe this isn't the right way to go." The first one, not wanting to go, is analogous to the egoistic view. If your self-cherishing attitude is strong, you are involved in enjoyment of temporal pleasures. You want to continue to revel in your experiences. Therefore, the very idea that you have no self is abhorrent. You don't even want to consider that your idea of yourself is incorrect; you have no interest in investigating selflessness. This is how the mistaken view of the transitory composite blocks a desire to try to become liberated.

When you want freedom from samsara, you will look for a method to gain emancipation. There are so many religious traditions out there; many of them seem attractive. You may think you have found a good path, but it may not be the cause of higher rebirth and emancipation. So, you may have a right conceptual view of the transitory composite, but your understanding of the method is wrong. A wrong path will lead you the wrong way. The third problem is doubt. Even though you have the right view and the right method, you are not completely sure that you do. Uncertainty makes you hesitate; it interrupts your practice. It really holds you back; it makes your progress much slower. Many other obstacles arise from these three, particularly from the mistaken view of the transitory composite. The Buddha didn't list all of them; that would be overwhelming. Instead, he gave us the main three that include all the others.

Until you reach the path of seeing and have a direct realization of ultimate reality, these three are your primary obstacles. After you reach the path of seeing they will no longer be problems for you. But until then, holding wrong conduct to be superior will lead you to a lower rebirth. Holding a wrong view of the transitory collection that is constructed based on a religious system or philosophy will block you from attaining the path of seeing. When you do not have a realization of reality, having doubts will weaken your practice.

The Three Higher Trainings

Now that we've looked at what prevents you from progressing to freedom, we move on to the necessary conditions for the attainment of liberation. These are the three higher trainings: (1) pure conduct, (2) pure meditative concentration, and (3) pure wisdom. These are nothing other than ways of training your mind. Nothing external, whether environmental or a person, is as important as your mind. Wisdom that understands ultimate reality is what you concentrate on with śamatha to attain liberation. This combination can only be developed on the basis of pure ethical conduct.

> 52. Emancipation depends upon you alone;
> no one else can do anything to help.
> So, endeavor to pursue the four realities for āryas
> through learning, morality, and concentration.

"Emancipation" is freedom from rebirth in samsara caused by ignorance, the mental afflictions, and karma. Samsara is the mind bound in ignorance and the mental afflictions and their resultant suffering. When these bonds are broken you are liberated from samsara. Emancipation isn't a perfect place or heaven; it is simply removing ignorance and the mental afflictions from your mind. So, obtaining emancipation is dependent upon purifying and developing your mind. Nobody else can liberate you. You will never find someone who can lift you out of samsara, no matter how much you beg and plead. This doesn't mean that no one else can help you at all. The Buddha gave teachings that lead to liberation, spiritual teachers give you personal advice, and there are others who help you in an ordinary sense. But no matter how many buddhas, teachers, and scriptures there may be, you still have to train your own mind. Teachers can show you the method, but you have to employ it yourself. Of course, there are some religions that say you as an individual have no power; freedom or heaven depends upon some external mighty God who chooses to liberate you. Buddhism isn't like that.

If, as the Buddha said, you have to do it yourself, what is the method to employ? Nāgārjuna says first you have to learn about the three higher trainings. Then you practice them: you engage in pure ethical behavior and employ the techniques of meditation to develop the wisdom that understands the four realities for āryas. Vasubandhu outlines this in the

Treasury of Knowledge. First, he says, your behavior must be moral. In other words, with the attitude of renunciation you keep whichever of the vows—lay vows, novice vows, or vows of complete ordination—that you have taken. "Renunciation" is to be so repulsed by the problems of samsara that you want to be totally free from them. You turn away from samsara. With that attitude, you take and maintain vows in order to prevent yourself from engaging in negative actions and to foster pure actions. This is the foundation that makes it possible to develop your mind. When your senses are wild and uncontrolled, your mind is distracted. It has no place to settle and work toward emancipation. But with the vows, you control your senses, and this leads to control of your body and speech. This restraint lets you develop your mind by studying. From your studies you come to know what is right, what is wrong, the goal, the obstacles to your goal, the antidotes to your problems, and how to apply the antidotes. Your study is like a lamp that illuminates the darkness of ignorance. There is a lot to learn!

Even when your conduct isn't absolutely perfect, you learn how to develop meditative concentration and wisdom. Meditative concentration is the ability to focus on a topic for as long as you wish without distraction or sleepiness. The combination of wisdom and meditative concentration is the tool that cuts the bonds to samsara. So, what is wisdom in the context of the three higher trainings? It is understanding the four realities for āryas and relating them to your own mind. You will recall that the four realities for āryas are the reality of suffering, the reality of the cause of suffering, the reality of the cessation of suffering, and the reality of the path to cessation of suffering. Suffering is the effect; the cause of suffering is karma and the mental afflictions. The cause isn't someone else's karma and mental afflictions. It is your own karma and mental afflictions that cause you to endure the misery of birth, aging, sickness, and death. You should make an effort to get rid of suffering and its cause. You should try to attain permanent cessation. The way to do that is to practice the path. The path is the antidote to the mental afflictions.

Each of the four realities can be understood on two levels: the phenomenal and the ultimate. The conventional or phenomenal nature of the four realities is explained as the sixteen aspects of the four realities for āryas: four for each one of the realities. This is a framework to look more in depth at the meaning of each of the four realities and counter the wrong views associated with them. The ultimate nature of the four realities is emptiness free of the extreme of conceptual elaboration. Conceptual elaborations are ideas such as abiding, destruction, impermanence, color, shape, and so forth. On a conventional level, impermanence is the nature of the body. But it is incorrect to believe that impermanence is absolute and intrinsically existent. Everything, all sixteen conventional aspects of the four realities for āryas, are empty of intrinsic existence. In this respect, there is no difference between them; they are equal in being empty of intrinsic existence. When you meditate on their emptiness you are meditating on ultimate reality. You have to be accustomed to both of the realities: the phenomenal and the ultimate. If you just meditate on just one or the other, you will fall to an extreme view.

No additional practices are necessary for the attainment of liberation. All the topics, methods, and instructions in the hundreds of volumes of Buddhist teachings are included in the three higher trainings. That is why Nāgārjuna tells us to practice in this way.

53. Always train in higher ethical conduct,
      higher wisdom, and higher concentration.
      There are more than 250 precepts for the ordained;
      all are included in these three higher trainings.

There is ordinary ethical conduct, wisdom, and meditation and there is higher ethical conduct, wisdom, and meditation. Here we are talking about the superior forms of the three higher trainings. What does it mean to say higher ethical conduct? It is a matter of motivation. Ethical conduct done with a common worldly motivation is ordinary. A worldly motivation might be to take vows because you are afraid of your parents, fear the government, or think it is an easy way to get food or some other samsaric pleasure. In contrast, when you take precepts with the motivation of renunciation, it becomes higher ethical conduct. Renunciation has two aspects: to free just yourself from samsara, and to free yourself and all others from samsara. You will have renunciation when you understand that the nature of samsara is suffering. This is the first reality for āryas. The difference between ordinary meditative concentration and wisdom and higher meditation and wisdom is similar. If you practice meditation and wisdom for the purpose of having a good life now, it is ordinary; training in meditation and wisdom is higher when it is dedicated to the purpose of either attaining individual emancipation or enlightenment in order to emancipate both yourself and others. The practices of meditation and wisdom done out of desire for a rebirth in the corporeal and noncorporeal realms are not considered to be higher trainings. We have talked about the worldly path and practice of meditation in order to be reborn in the dhyānas of the corporeal realm. Practicing that way is ordinary. However, one reason to develop the mind of the dhyānas is to join the heightened power of that meditative stabilization to wisdom. You join your concentration and wisdom in order to achieve the path of seeing. That makes it a higher practice. In short, a higher training is motivated by the desire for your own emancipation or bodhicitta. You dedicate your practice to that end as well.

The three higher trainings include everything you need to attain emancipation. There is nothing left out. They are complete in the sense that every practice in the sutras and tantras is included. For example, the twelve volumes of the Vinaya explain what actions laypeople, novices, and the fully ordained should try to avoid, the reasons to avoid those actions, how to keep the vows, the situations where a bodhisattva should break a vow, and if you do break a vow how to purify it. In our tradition, fully ordained monks have 253 vows and fully ordained nuns have around 311. No matter how you count them, and different traditions come up with different numbers, they all fit into the training of ethical conduct. *Complete* also connotes that you need all three higher trainings. Just one or two of them is not sufficient to become free from samsara. You need all three, and they must be correctly practiced. Since they are complete in both senses of the word, the three higher trainings are considered to be the reality of the path.

The path of a person who is seeking emancipation has two aspects: ripening and liberating. Think of ripening as preparation. When you prepare a field for planting: you want the ground to be fertile, moist, and free from stones. Similarly, ripening makes your rough and wild mind suitable for practicing the liberating path. Actual liberation is by attained by direct realizations, but you can't practice wisdom properly until your mind is controlled and tamed with morality. Thus, all practice of ethical conduct is part of the ripening path. Some of the concentration practices are for ripening; you suppress successive mental afflictions on the dhyānas. These levels of concentration do not free you completely, they are a temporary form of control. Sometimes it is easier to suppress the mental afflictions and on that basis work to remove them from the root. The part of concentration that is conjoined with the wisdom seeing ultimate reality is on the liberating path. Wisdom is the liberating path.

Recollecting the Body

In order to successfully practice the three higher trainings, Nāgārjuna says to his friend, the king, that he should practice mindfulness of the body. The earlier discussion of mindfulness of the body, in Verse 48, was in the context of removing the misconceptions about your body and coming to realize that it has the nature of suffering, impermanence, selflessness, and impurity. Here the emphasis is to recollect the import of what you are doing with your body. The body doesn't engage in wholesome or negative actions on its own; physical actions are motivated by your mind.

> 54. My lord, the Buddha taught that mindfulness
>   of the body is the one path to follow.
>   Hold it and guard it tightly.
>   Losing mindfulness destroys all Dharma.

What is mindfulness of the body? In this context it is not simply being aware of your body itself; it is to be aware of what your body is doing. You do so many things physically: sit, stand, walk, eat, read, and so forth. Mindfulness is to be cognizant of everything your body does in every situation. You should examine what you are doing. You must apply your wisdom to determine whether this is something you should or should not be doing. The Buddha said that this type of mindfulness is the one path to follow because it leads to the attainment of emancipation and enlightenment. This mindfulness is practiced on the Hinayana, and the Mahayana, and within the Mahayana on both the Sutrayana and Tantrayana paths. Without it you cannot progress on any of these paths. Mahāmati's commentary on *Letter to a Friend* summarizes a long sutra passage as follows:

> O monks it is like this: the path that purifies living beings, that
> takes them beyond suffering and sadness, that produces an

understanding of the correct Dharma, and that makes nirvana
manifest, is mindfulness of the body's activities.

Mindfulness of what you are doing is important for successful completion of ordinary activities too. If you are not mindful, you get distracted
and don't complete your task properly. So, what need is there to say that
for important things, like going beyond sorrow, mindfulness is critical?
Because it is the one route to reaching a direct experience of liberation,
you should try to be mindful and introspective all the time. You should
examine what you have done, what you are doing, and what you are about
to do. If your mindfulness degenerates, all the virtuous karmas you have
done may be destroyed. A mindless state leads you to do all kinds of nonvirtuous actions.

Mindfulness can simply mean self-awareness. But not here. In this
form of mindfulness, you add to your self-awareness a recollection of what
is right and wrong and the results of right and wrong actions. If you don't
do this, then you will stray from the right path. A dharma practitioner
needs to know the right conditions that will help them, and the negative
conditions that will hinder them. That is the only way to keep yourself
on the positive side and create the necessary conditions. You need to be
mindful of all you have learned to do this. Merely being aware of doing
something won't help much.

Śāntideva said,

> The lack of introspection that follows
> the loss of mindfulness is a thief who steals
> all the merit you have accumulated.
> You will have to go to a bad rebirth.
> [*Introduction to the Practice of Bodhisattvas,* 5.27]

Thus, when training in mindfulness you need two mental techniques:
introspection and recollection. Introspection is looking at how your mind
is operating; where it is going; and what it is doing. I've often called this a
mental spy. It is an aspect of your mind that acts like a watchful gatekeeper.
Without introspection you will not be aware of what your mind is doing;
it will wander about in every direction without you knowing it. Recollection is to recall what should be done and what should be avoided. You

studied and learned these topics; and now you need to remember what to do and what not to do. Introspection and recollection together are the most useful tools for the practice of Dharma.

Even as you try to do something virtuous, the mental afflictions and ignorance are in your mind. If you let them arise, they will steal and destroy your opportunity for a high rebirth and liberation. You will be left with just powerful negative karmas. And so, you will have to go to a lower rebirth. It is introspection and recollection that hold ignorance and the mental afflictions at bay. Śāntideva provides a vivid analogy for this:

> Once it gets into your bloodstream
> poison is carried throughout your body.
> Similarly, if given the opportunity
> a fault will pervade your mind.
> [*Introduction to the Practice of Bodhisattvas*, 7.69]

Therefore, you want your mindfulness—with both introspection and recollection—to be continuous. You must be diligent. You don't want to practice one day, and forget about it the next day, and then next week you try to do it again. That is not the way to practice. The proper way to practice is to be vigilant.

> A practitioner should be as careful
> as a frightened man carrying a jar
> full of mustard oil who is threatened
> with death by the sword if he spills a drop.
> [*Introduction to the Practice of Bodhisattvas*, 7.70]

8. Using Your Human Life

You have the foundation to engage in the practices necessary to obtain either a higher rebirth or complete liberation from samsara. If you were in one of the lower realms your mind would be so overwhelmed by ignorance and your body so consumed with suffering that you couldn't practice. If you were born as god you would have such extreme pleasure that you wouldn't feel any need to practice the Dharma. It is as if the gods are drunk with pleasure. So, the best basis for practice is a human life. A human life is a high rebirth, but at the same time humans can be aware of sickness, aging, death, and the rain of unfortunate and undesirable experiences they face in life. A human mind can understand the causality underlying these experiences.

But even though you have this valuable opportunity, the normal human tendency is to live without purpose. Whether you are a layperson or have taken ordination, you need to use your life in a constructive way. Before you die you should use what you have. You have so much potential and so many possibilities. You can create many virtues and engage in wholesome spiritual practice. You can ensure another high rebirth, work toward your own emancipation from samsara, or strive for complete enlightenment in order to benefit all living beings. You have all the fortunate conditions that you need to attain these goals.

Śāntideva said you should be heroic in this endeavor rather than wasting your life in common worldly pursuits.

Discounting all suffering,
a true hero conquers
the enemy—hatred and so forth.
It is not heroic to kill a corpse.
    [*Introduction to the Practice of Bodhisattvas,* 6.20]

The people you see as your enemies will die sooner or later no matter what you do. They are alive for a while but are soon to be corpses. If you create powerful negative karma by killing them, you are not doing anything heroic. A true hero conquers the enemy of their own mental afflictions. How do you do this? There are many practices of purification and meditation. All these practices require a human body and mind to do them. So, what you have is something very special. Śāntideva says you should think of it as a boat.

Think of this body as a boat to be used
as a vehicle for going and coming.
In order to accomplish the goals of sentient beings
transform it into a body that grants wishes.
    [*Introduction to the Practice of Bodhisattvas,* 5.70]

All sentient beings are travelers. You have traveled throughout samsara from time without beginning up until now. Sometimes you went up, sometimes down, but always within samsara. Now you have a human life. Your body isn't something that you need to hold on to forever. It is like a boat used for crossing the river between a past life and your next life. You use a boat when you need it. When you reach the other side of a river you journey onward leaving the boat behind. Your desired destination is permanent peace and happiness—the other side of the ocean of samsara. You need a human life to cross that ocean, but when you attain liberation, it is no longer necessary. There are quite a few sutras where we find a human body and life analogized as a boat for traveling beyond samsara, for example:

Those who have been nonvirtuous and done no virtuous actions
are far from the Dharma and always get the results of nonvirtue.
Like those traveling a turbulent ocean in a leaky boat,
those with evil karma will be very afraid of death.

Those who have not been nonvirtuous and have been virtuous
have utilized their life in the manner of holy beings.
By doing that, those beings will never be afraid of death;
They are like someone traveling to the far shore on a strong, safe
 boat.

> [*Collection of Indicative Verses* 28.39–40]

The above verse from *Introduction to the Practice of Bodhisattvas* also likens your body to a wish-granting jewel. Other sentient beings have the same goal that you do: they too want to have true peace and happiness. They need help to achieve this ultimate goal. And they need assistance even to achieve the temporary goal of a good samsaric life with spiritual teachers and the opportunity to train on the path to liberation. Think, "At the least, everyone should have a good rebirth, and better yet complete liberation from samsara. I will take responsibility for that to happen. I will become a wish-granting jewel for them." To do this you need to become a buddha yourself. An enlightened mind and body has the capability to save others. In that sense it is a very special wish-granting jewel. It is much better than an ordinary wish-granting jewel that only can provide nice things in samsara.

You have the ability to change. You can change in a negative way or a positive way. It isn't easy to evoke positive changes. Now in your ordinary life you experience pain and problems. But you can treat these difficulties as an opportunity. Be like a soldier who sees his wounds as a spur to fighting his enemy. Sometimes people who are scarred with battle wounds, treat their scars as if they were a medal for heroism: "Look at me. I fought the enemy!" These people endured the pain and suffering of fighting and are proud of it. But really their scars are just a sign that they have created negative karma in fighting others out of hatred. Their actions were purposeless in terms of beneficial results for themselves or others in the future. In that sense, a war wound is senseless. But the hardships and difficulties you may endure in order to accomplish the great purpose of attaining enlightenment to free others from suffering are very meaningful. Śāntideva put this very succinctly.

Scars inflicted by an enemy are pointless,
yet people wear them as if they are ornaments.

Why I am I bothered when suffering hardships
that come from pursuit of a very meaningful goal?
[*Introduction to the Practice of Bodhisattvas,* 4.39]

A verse in the *Guru Pūjā* by the fourth Panchen Losang Chökyi Gyaltsen echoes the sentiment that as a great practitioner you will be able to endure many hardships.

Inspire me to complete the perfection of diligent effort
and strive for supreme enlightenment with compassion,
even if I must remain in the fires of Avīci Hell
for an ocean of eons for the sake of each sentient being.
[*Guru Pūjā,* 104]

A bodhisattva's attitude is one of self-sacrifice. They are willing to fall into hell for a long time even to help just one sentient being. Even in that situation they will not lose their compassion. They may endure physical pain and suffering, but they feel joy if they see that it benefits others. This is the bodhisattva's perfection of diligence. You haven't gotten that far yet. Even a little unpleasantness for a few hours causes you much suffering. However, sometimes to achieve an ordinary goal, to lose weight or to build up your muscles, for example, you happily put yourself through a great deal of suffering. So why is the difficulty of doing something that has a spiritual purpose seen as so onerous? Actually, these difficulties should give you the strength to practice. Your problems in the course of your Dharma practice are like uncomfortable medical treatments that will cure a terrible illness. They may be painful for a time, but the result is something to be happy about. You shouldn't think, "I can't take this." You should engage in spiritual practices even if they cause you to have some difficulties, because you can turn your body and life into something like a wish-granting jewel.

How do you transform your thinking so that you can use your life properly? Nāgārjuna says there are three things to do. First, you need to eliminate attachment to your body by thinking about its impermanence and lack of essence. Next, you contemplate the difficulty of attaining again a life of opportunity like the one that you have now. And finally, you meditate on the favorable conditions that you have—in particular,

having a spiritual friend—and the unfavorable conditions that you wish
to avoid.

THE IMPERMANENCE OF LIFE

Why do you find yourself unable to use the opportunity that you have?
The problem is your attachment to your life and your body, and desire for
things that seem necessary for your life. You put a lot of effort into obtaining wealth, shelter, food, and so forth. Desires for such things are a great
obstacle to spiritual practice. You need to diminish your attachment to
this life. The way to do that is to meditate on your body's impermanence
and lack of essence. Normally you don't think that your body is not going
to last for a long time. You may never actually say, "it will last forever," but
you think it will remain for many, many more decades. You don't think
about the actual nature of your body; you imagine that it is something
lovely and something solid. However,

> 55. Your life is tenuous due to many harmful things;
>   it is as unstable as a bubble tossed by the wind.
>   Why, it is quite amazing that you breathe
>   in and out when you wake from sleep!

Is there any reason that you will not die? No, there really isn't. Other
people, animals, insects, weather, and microbes can be destructive. Not
just obviously harmful things can kill you; the very conditions for your
survival can be conditions for your death. Food can nourish you, but it
can be poisonous. Clothing is necessary, but if you fall in a river wearing
heavy clothes, they will drag you down until you drown. The same goes
for your house, your associates, and so forth. Any little thing can destroy
your life as easily as the wind pops a water bubble. In short, your life is
impermanent.

A breath is all that separates you from your next life. If you don't
breathe in, you may not wake up from sleep. Think of how amazing it is
that you have woken up today. What do you think about when you wake
up? Do you think about making money, eating tasty food, or doing something else for enjoyment? Religious practitioners start every day thinking
about impermanence. That leads them to think about how short their

life may be and how they should prepare for their next life. You have no assurance that you will wake up tomorrow, so you should not procrastinate practicing the Dharma. Starting the day with a short meditation on impermanence will induce you use each day in a meaningful way. Then you will have no regret when you go to sleep at night. Monks, nuns, and laypeople can all practice this way.

Nāgārjuna said,

> There are so many causes for death.
> There are few conditions for survival,
> and even those can be the cause of death.
> Therefore, you should always practice the Dharma.
>
>   [*Precious Garland*, 3.78]

There are many poetic passages in the sutras about impermanence. A very famous one in the *Extensive Sport Sutra* is:

> The three realms are as ephemeral as an autumn cloud.
> The birth and death of living beings should be watched like a
>   drama.
> A person's life is but a flash of lightning in the sky;
> it goes by as quickly as a mountain waterfall.
>
>   [*Extensive Sport Sutra*, 13.70]

There is no way of knowing how long you will live. You could die before tomorrow. The desire, corporeal, and noncorporeal realms may look permanent, but because every life in those realms is dependent upon karmic causes and conditions, they are as transitory as clouds in the sky. In a play, an actor can look like a king in the first act and then be a peasant or a demon in the second act. Someone enlightened looks at ordinary beings' lives that way. They see how beings are born due to karma, how they change during their life, then die, and are reborn in a different body due to other karmas. Nothing is permanent. In the grand scheme of things, a human life is very short. It is like a flash of lightning or water rushing down a steep mountain.

Śāntideva said,

> The untrustworthy lord of death
> doesn't wait for incomplete tasks to be done.
> It doesn't matter at all if you are sick or healthy;
> this fleeting lifespan is unreliable.
> *[Introduction to the Practice of Bodhisattvas 2.33]*

If someone asks you to go somewhere, you can ask them to wait a bit until you finish what you are doing. But the death never waits. Death comes suddenly, unexpectedly. You can't determine exactly when you will die. You can't assume that because you are healthy and doing something important you won't die right away.

Śāntideva said,

> Today, right now, I am without sickness.
> I am well-nourished and not afflicted.
> But this life is momentary and deceptive;
> this body is like something borrowed just this once.
> *[Introduction to the Practice of Bodhisattvas, 4.16]*

You can say that you have a good life if you are healthy, have everything you need, and not undergoing any particular tribulation. In these circumstances you don't pay attention to the fact that your life will end quickly, so you engage in all kinds of activities to keep it going. At the time of death, your mind-stream will continue to another life, but not even an atom of your body goes with you. Nevertheless, you spend all your time serving, protecting, saving, worrying, and caring for your body. You think, "this is me." You feel that you are never separate from your body. However, your body is like something you borrowed to use for a short time. If you borrow a dress for a special occasion, you give it back after the event when you are finished with it. In past lives you didn't have this body; after death you will not have this body. Consider that your body arose from the sperm and egg of your parents; so, in a way you've borrowed this body from your parents.

The body is nothing in and of itself, but you can derive benefit from it. With this borrowed body in combination with a wholesome virtuous mind you can accumulate virtuous karma. It is like having a wish-granting jewel or a powerful machine that can better your future. This combination of a human body and mind is most unusual; it has the ability to do enormous good but also enormous evil. You need to use it like a serious yogi. Because yogis realize the impermanence of life, they don't act out of desire thinking, "my body," or, "my possessions." They are not egoistically trying to maintain their position in society, obtain and keep possessions, and satisfy their body's senses. They view their human mind and body as a tool that can help them attain their objective—everlasting peace and happiness for themselves and others. Someone who realizes this is a great practitioner.

Sometimes when people recognize the impermanence of their life they become afraid. Ordinary people are afraid to die. But mere fear of death is senseless. Everyone has to die; there is no question about it. So, death is not a unique or frightful thing. But, according to Buddhism, you should be afraid about where you will be reborn. Whether you go up or down depends upon your karma. If you have purified yourself of evil karma and accumulated virtuous karma, then you will definitely be born in a higher rebirth. If you have not done that, you will definitely go down. You may be stuck there for eons and experience great physical suffering and stupidity. You are right to be afraid of this. Fear about what will come next spurs you to prepare for your next life now while you have the opportunity in this life. Therefore, you should be mindful of the impermanence of life.

If nothing other than material disintegration occurred after death, then you would only need to be concerned with this life. You wouldn't need to worry about the impermanence of this life and what happens after you die. However, not only is life impermanent, the body also has no essence that makes it something worth being attached to.

> 56. This body will end up as ashes, dry dust, or putrid filth.
>   You should understand that this body has no essence;
>   it is destroyed, it dissolves,
>   it decomposes, and disintegrates into pieces.

When someone dies, what happens to their body? Here in the West, you may embalm a corpse to make it look clean and lifelike. You place it in a pretty and expensive box. Then you bury it deep in the ground to keep it safe. On top of the grave, you put a stone with the name of the dead person and plant a few flowers. Some people even go to the cemetery to talk to the dead person. This was not the custom in other parts of the world in ancient times, and in many places even today. After the body and mind separated at death, some cultures burned the corpse in a fire until it became ash. Some left the body, either whole or chopped in pieces, in a desolate uninhabited place. In that kind of cemetery, the corpse would rot, or desiccate, or animals would consume it. These cemeteries were frightening places as the corpses disintegrated. Yogis would go there to remind themselves that their bodies were no different than the corpses they saw there.

In Tibet, traditionally a few days after someone died and all the prayers were completed, the family would call in a professional for disposal of the body. This person would fold the body up and tightly tie it into a small bundle. Then he would carry the bundle up the mountain to some huge flat rocks. There he would chop the body up into pieces. He would hide the head, but the rest of the flesh would be left for the vultures. The vultures know what time to come to eat. After the vultures ate, the man would crush the bones into tiny pieces. Then he'd retrieve the head and mix the brains with the crushed bones for the vultures' dessert. Everything would be completely gone; only a greasy flat rock would remain. This was a way that the dead person could make a final offering of their own body to the birds. This was done unless the person died in a contagious disease epidemic. In that case, the corpse was buried in the ground.

People think that many things in the world are stable and are indestructible. The earth, oceans, and mountains seem very firm. They look permanent. But all these things too are destroyed in the end. So, what need is there to talk about a fragile human body.

> 57. The earth, Mount Meru, and the oceans
>   will be incinerated by seven suns.
>   Not even dust will remain from the environment,
>   So, what needs to be said about weak, puny humans?

In traditional Indian Buddhist cosmology, at the end of every eon the universe is destroyed by an element: either fire, water, or wind. After destruction it regenerates, only to be destroyed again. Seven consecutive eons end when blazing suns burn up the entire desire realm all the way to the first dhyāna of the corporeal realm. At the end of the eon after that, the universe will be destroyed by water. Water destroys the entire desire realm and the first dhyāna. The second dhyāna and above remain. After the set of seven fires and one water, there will be seven eons that end in destruction by wind. Wind destroys the desire realm and the first three dhyānas. The beings in the fourth dhyāna of the corporeal realm and those in the noncorporeal realm are not destroyed by the elements. If you have supernatural knowledge, you can see the universe coming to be, existing, and then being destroyed over and over again. The universe comes and goes like clouds in the sky.

The present eon will be destroyed by fire. Fire destroyed the preceding eon too. The Abhidharma explains the process of destruction by fire. As an eon progresses, the environment degenerates and the human lifespan decreases. The sun becomes hotter and hotter. Finally, over the course of seven days the entire universe, the central world axis, and all the surrounding inner and outer oceans and continents will be destroyed. On the first day the sun will burn up all vegetation; every plant will die. On the second day, the sun will dry up all smaller waterways, streams, rivers and so forth. The third day's sun will dry up the great rivers and huge lakes. The sun that rises on the fourth and fifth days will dry up all the oceans. The sun on the sixth day evaporates any moisture that may be left. The earth itself is now so desiccated and hot it is ready to burst into flame. On the seventh day, the sun causes everything remaining to explode into a huge ball of fire. Everything is completely destroyed so that not even ashes remain. If that happens to things like the globe of the earth, do we need to say anything about what happens to a human body?

Now that Nāgārjuna has shown that life is impermanent and that the body has no essential nature, in the following verse he urges the king, and other readers of the text, to develop renunciation.

> 58. Since everything is impermanent and without a self,
> there is no protection, savior, or resting place.
> Therefore, O great one, turn your mind away from samsara
> for it is like a banana tree; it has no essential core.

Every external physical thing is impermanent. Your body and mind are also impermanent. Not one single thing has an independent self-identity. It looks like there is a subjective self behind the aggregation of body and mind that makes up this life. Ordinarily you perceive a subject that owns and controls all the aggregates. But that is not the case. There is no real, permanent, absolute subject as you perceive it. Also, nothing owned by the self exists objectively as it appears. So, none of these things can protect you from suffering. Nothing can save you from future suffering. There is no place or occasion that is peaceful and without difficulty. You have no independent freedom; everything changes all the time due to causes and conditions.

Given that everything in samsara—both external and internal phenomena—have no real essence, what is there that is desirable or attractive? When you look deeply at anything, you find it is as hollow as a banana or plantain tree. Those types of trees look nice and strong. But when you look inside the trunk there are many layers but no real core. Therefore, Nāgārjuna exhorts you to renounce samsara. In other words, you should turn away from being born in samsara due to the forces of karma and the mental afflictions and put your energy toward attaining liberation. When you realize what samsara is really like, you will see that it is the worst kind of prison. Then your attitude will be, "How can I escape? I must get out of here! I want permanent peace and liberation." The sign that you have actually developed renunciation is when that kind of thought arises spontaneously. It is a constant feeling that being in samsara is something to be sad about.

In summary, how do you make this life, whose nature is hollow, into something meaningful? The first step is to think about how you spend your time. You are born with attachment to your body. You work your entire life as a servant to your body. You worry about how to protect, maintain, beautify, and strengthen your body. You fret about how to attract others and how to conquer those who obstruct your desires. You have no time to think about doing anything else. To counter this habitual way of thinking and acting you have to think about your body's impermanence and lack of essence. This is the method to reverse your attachment to your body and life. You can't stop your desire without repeatedly meditating on these attributes. Only then can you switch things around and make the body your servant who works for a higher spiritual purpose.

THE DIFFICULTY OF OBTAINING A HUMAN REBIRTH

Now we switch our focus to how difficult it is to obtain this useful kind of life. You have a human life now, but can you get another one like it again? Often people think that contemplating the difficulty of attaining a human rebirth is a low level of teachings and practice. They are not very interested in meditating on this topic. But without a solid beginning based on a lack of attachment to your current life and a firm interest in your future lives, there is no way to engage in the higher practices. Even if you have some understanding about how you could use your life, you procrastinate. Your assumption is likely, "Well, right now I'm enjoying my life, I'll work harder on religious practice in my next life." The beginning of the spiritual path is to strongly believe that the appearances of this life are not important and the sacrifices you might endure for the benefit of your future lives are well worth it.

Three modes of thought make you engage in practice right away and every day: (1) appreciating the value of this life because it can be used to obtain permanent spiritual goals, (2) thinking that your life is impermanent and you could lose it at any time, and (3) understanding that if you procrastinate and don't practice now you might not obtain a human life again for many eons. These three contemplations are your inner teacher. Your own wisdom will propel you to practice.

So how difficult is it to obtain another wish-granting jewel of a human life? Nāgārjuna paraphrases the *Great Sutra on the Final Nirvana* to illustrate the difficulty:

> 59. It is more difficult for an animal to be reborn as a human
>   than for a sea turtle to find a single yoke
>   floating on an ocean. So, O mighty king,
>   practice the Dharma to make this life bear fruit.

Imagine that the entire universe is a huge ocean. A blind sea turtle lives in the ocean. She mostly stays on the bottom of the ocean, only once in every hundred years does she come up to the surface. Floating on the surface of the ocean is a golden board with a hole in the middle. This yoke is constantly pushed hither and yon by the wind and the waves. Do you think it is easy for the blind turtle to put her neck through the yoke?

Of course not. You could say it is possible; but it is almost impossible. If the turtle could see there might be a possibility. Or, if she came up to the surface often it might be more possible. Or, if the yoke was stationery, she might find it. If the ocean were a small pond, it would be easier. But put it all together, catching the yoke on her neck is almost impossible.

A human life is like this golden yoke. It isn't out of samsara, but it is not on the bottom of the samsaric ocean. Most of the time we are in the lower realms of samsara. We cycle in the three lower realms because to be reborn as a human requires merit. It is almost impossible to create virtue in the lower realms. Regarding this, Śāntideva said,

> If I don't create merit when I am capable
> and have a fortunate life,
> what can I possibly do
> when stupefied by the suffering of the lower realms?
> [*Introduction to the Practice of Bodhisattvas*, 4.18]

Look at what you are doing with your body, speech, and mind. You may find that not many of your actions are geared toward a high rebirth or emancipation. If everything you do is for temporary pleasure and selfish enjoyment, you will see that you have primarily created negative karma. If that is the case, it will be difficult to find a high rebirth in your future. Āryaśūra said,

> Someone rich with virtues becomes human;
> to create enough virtue for that can take eons.
> A human life is like a treasury full of merit;
> but out of ignorance we do not use it.
> So, after death we will enter an abode of inexhaustible suffering.
> We are like a merchant who reaches a place full of jewels
> but returns home empty handed.
> [*Tale that Is a Jewel Casket of Good Advice*]

You are someone rich with virtue; your past virtuous karma resulted in your life here. Even among humans your situation is excellent. This ideal situation doesn't happen accidentally. It may take eons to create enough merit to be reborn human. If you waste this precious opportunity, you are like a merchant who has traveled long and far to trade for precious items. You finally reach an island of jewels, but you don't purchase any and leave empty handed. If you don't use your life to create merit, when you die, the only way to go is down. No one puts you in the lower realms. You do it to yourself. Once you are born in the lower realms you will be in a far worse state than you are at present. There the only experience is suffering. You are ignorant in every possible way. When born as an animal, hungry ghost, or hell-being, all you will do is attempt to find food, comfort, and shelter, fight your enemies, and so forth. Trying to preserve your own life, you will only do sinful things. You will not have the opportunity to create virtue. Śāntideva summarized the situation this way:

> If you do not create any virtue
> and just continually accumulate evil karma,
> you will not hear the words "high rebirth,"
> for hundreds and hundreds of eons.
> [*Introduction to the Practice of Bodhisattvas,* 4.19]

You can prevent that from happening. You have in your hands the opportunity to practice. This is how to remind yourself to not procrastinate practicing the Dharma.

A LIFE OF OPPORTUNITY

Not every human life has the fortune and leisure that you have now. If you recognize that and still waste your precious life, you are the most stupid person imaginable.

> 60. Someone who has taken a human rebirth
>   and performs evil deeds is more stupid than
>   someone who has a bejeweled golden vessel
>   and fills it up with vomit.

Imagine that one day a very poor beggar finds a precious vessel made of pure gold and encrusted with jeweled ornaments. How unusual it is for a beggar to obtain something so precious! However, this beggar is so impoverished that he doesn't recognize the value of this priceless vessel.

If he knew what he'd found he could sell it for a lot of money and ease his poverty. But because he is ignorant of what he has found, he uses it as a garbage can. It is laughable that a person would be so foolish. But even more stupid is someone who is born human but spends their entire life doing sinful activity. Wasting this human life that is so difficult to obtain is hundreds of times more idiotic than using a golden vessel as a trash can. In fact, it is quite disgraceful to fill your human life with filthy karma that will bring you much future suffering.

Now Nāgārjuna speaks directly to the king. He tells him that someone born into royalty has obtained a particularly precious life that can support practice of the Dharma. When you think about it, you have the same opportune conditions that the king had.

> 61. You reside in a place that is conducive,
>   you rely upon holy individuals, you are devout,
>   and you have previously accumulated merit.
>   You are in possession of these four great wheels.

A wheel is something mechanical. Four free-rolling wheels enable a car to travel quickly. Gear wheels in machines make them very powerful. Here the conditions that enable you to practice are analogous to the four wheels of a vehicle. The first wheel is that you live in a place favorable for practice. All the conditions necessary for practicing the path of the āryas are present. There is nothing in the environment that will hinder you from attaining the path of seeing. While the first wheel is the quality of the place where you live, the second wheel is your associates. You could associate with bad company who lead you into doing negative actions, but you don't. You trust and rely upon spiritual guides and proper practitioners who show you the right way to live. The third wheel is that you aspire to attain emancipation and enlightenment. Without this inclination, even a good environment with many teachers is as useless as a broken wheel. So, the third wheel is a strong wish to attain freedom from samsara for yourself or to attain perfect buddhahood in order to help all suffering beings. Finally, the fourth wheel is that you have practiced virtue in previous lives. To expand on this, the fourth wheel is being driven in a virtuous direction by the force of your previous karma. For example, think of a family with three children. One child naturally gravitates to religious practice; one may want to hurt others; and the third is indifferent. The parents don't try to make any of their children negative or careless. The children's dispositions come from previously accumulated karma. Likewise, your inclination towards virtue comes from your previously accumulated karma.

Not everyone has this good situation and these qualities, but you do. When you see that you have these wheels you can decide how to use your potent life. If you have a powerful machine but don't use it, the machine is just a lump of metal. You have the potential to do good things with great power. So now you have to drive the vehicle with these four wheels along the road to the highest spiritual goals. Examine what kind of wheels you have. Is one more powerful than another? You can work to build up the weaker ones.

The most important of these wheels is reliance upon a spiritual friend. A spiritual teacher is a holy being, ideally someone who has a direct realization of ultimate reality. In order obtain enlightenment you have to traverse the higher, superior paths. This by definition means cultivation of a direct realization of emptiness. If you want to produce this path yourself, the most important thing to do is to rely upon spiritual teachers who can give you the information and advice you need. Your spiritual teacher must have practiced this path themselves, have this knowledge, and have the ability to lead others.

> 62. The Buddha said that reliance on a spiritual friend
>   is the way to completely fulfil a virtuous life.
>   Many who relied on the victorious one obtained peace.
>   Therefore, rely upon holy beings.

In a sutra the Buddha told Ananda that relying on a spiritual teacher is the main cause for the attainment of enlightenment. Why? Because you are ignorant of the means to break free from samsara. You need someone to show you how to become free. To do the virtuous practices that lead to enlightenment you need to find a good spiritual teacher and follow their instructions. Therefore, finding and relying upon a teacher is the first step on the spiritual path. Taking someone's advice means that you put it into practice; you don't just put the teachings on a shelf. By engaging in the practices you were taught, you will achieve the perfect, highest goal. It is through the help of your teacher that you can attain complete enlightenment. Reliance on a spiritual teacher is important in the beginning, middle, and end of your practice of the path. All good qualities arise from reliance on a holy person. You can see how a close association with someone is influential even in a worldly sense. People who succeed have associated with powerful and knowledgeable people who mentor and assist them. Others associate with bad friends who kill, lie, steal, drink, and so forth. They too are influenced by their companions but are led astray.

Many beings, who were once just like you, have obtained the permanent peace of nirvana and enlightenment. How did they attain those perfected states? They relied on spiritual teachers. We often say there are two types of spiritual friends: external and internal. You need both to attain enlightenment. An external spiritual friend is another being who can teach you. From their teachings you develop realizations within yourself. Your own development is your internal spiritual teacher. Your internal spiritual friend urges you to practice. By relying on these spiritual teachers even beings like us can attain freedom from impure birth and death.

What qualities should a spiritual guide have? You can find a lot of detail on this topic in the stages of the path literature. Here is just a summary from the *Ornament for the Mahayana Sutras*:

> Rely on a spiritual friend who is disciplined, calm, peaceful,
> in possession of superior qualities, energetic, rich in scriptural
>   knowledge,
> who understands reality and is skilled in explaining it,
> who is compassionate by nature, and never tires.
> [*Ornament for the Mahayana Sutras*, 17.10]

You should look for a teacher with these ten characteristics. This general description pertains to teachers of both sutra and tantra. (For a teacher of tantra there are additional qualities you should look for.) The first three qualities—disciplined, calm, and peaceful—refer to the three higher trainings: pure ethical conduct, pure meditative concentration, and pure wisdom. Someone who is disciplined possesses pure morality; they have tamed their body, speech, and mind with ethical conduct. Based on their ethical conduct, they have calmed their mind with meditative concentration. Being peaceful refers to śamatha joined to wisdom that understands ultimate reality. This wisdom pacifies, in other words eliminates, all the mental afflictions, especially ignorance. The fourth quality is that a teacher should possess qualities that are superior to their students. Students want to learn from a teacher, so the teacher should be better than the students. Fifth, a teacher should be diligent when helping his disciples; their effort should never slacken. Sixth, a teacher should have mastered the scriptures of the Tripiṭaka: the Vinaya, the Sutras, and the Abhidharma. Seventh, a teacher should have a realization of ultimate reality. Eighth, a teacher should be skillful in teaching his students about the nature of reality. Ninth, a teacher should be as compassionate toward their students as a mother is toward her only child. Because of that strong compassion, the last quality is that a teacher should have given up feeling fatigue and disillusionment with teaching. In other words, a teacher should be tireless in teaching their students.

It is wonderful if you find a teacher with all ten of these qualities. They are perfect. But at least, they should have a quarter of them. If someone has less than that, you should not take them as your spiritual teacher. How should you rely upon such a teacher once you have found one? This is extensively explained in the stages of the path literature. Here, suffice it to say that you have to generate complete trust in your teacher by developing the idea that your teacher is a manifestation of the Buddha. Buddhas have promised to liberate all sentient beings. They don't stay in solitary enjoyment of their own liberation. They take action; they come to help sentient beings. Ordinary sentient beings cannot perceive a buddha directly. So, buddhas manifest as ordinary beings that ordinary people can relate to. There are many places in the scriptures that explain that buddhas take the form of spiritual teachers, parents, rulers, and so forth.

What does your teacher help you to do? A perfect teacher helps you to practice the path that leads to emancipation. You likely will not be able to accomplish the path in one lifetime. So, you need to practice in a way that will result in special human lives one after another. This is what you need to try to do first. You need to ensure that you will have the proper type of vehicle to traverse the ocean of samsara to the far shore of definite freedom.

We traditionally talk about a perfect human life as possessing leisure and fortune. On the one hand, you are free from various negative circumstances; on the other hand, you have the necessary positive conditions.

Leisure means that you have the freedom to do something; fortune means you have all the necessary conditions to do that. In the following verses Nāgārjuna lists the eight states that lack freedom of opportunity. His point is that you should work to attain the opposite of these states.

> 63. To be born as someone holding wrong views,
> as an animal, a hungry ghost, or in the hells,
> or where there are no teachings of the Buddha,
> as a barbarian in a remote place, or as someone unintelli-
> gent and dense,

> 64. or as a long-life god; any rebirth of this sort
> is one of the eight defective states lacking opportunity.
> You must find the leisure that is free of these;
> strive to turn away from rebirth.

There are eight aspects of leisure. Four of these pertain to being free from nonhuman states that lack the opportunity to practice. If you are born in any of the three lower realms—as an animal, hungry ghost, or in the hells—you have no opportunity. You lack every single one of the four wheels. The fourth nonhuman state lacking leisure is to be born as a long-life god in the fourth dhyāna of the corporeal realm. At the first moment of a birth in that dhyāna there may be consciousness, but the remainder of that long life is unconscious. You remain for eons in nonconceptual peace. Although you don't suffer in that life, it is a waste of time and lacks opportunity. When the karma for that life is finished, you wake up. But then there is nothing you can do. Your next rebirth will likely be way down. This type of life is feared by spiritual practitioners who want to attain enlightenment quickly.

There are another four aspects of leisure from the perspective of the human realm. You will have no opportunity to practice if there are no spiritual teachings, particularly the words of the Buddha, in the place where you are born. According to Buddhist cosmology, there are some eons and some places where a buddha never appears and a buddha's teachings never exist. The second problem is that even if a buddha had appeared and the teachings and teachers were available in some places, you may take birth in a remote area where you cannot meet them. This is sometimes referred to as taking rebirth as a barbarian in a savage environment. The last two human states lacking opportunity refer to people born where Buddhist teachers and the teachings exist, but their own internal qualities make taking advantage of that impossible. Some people are unintelligent, their minds are dull, and they cannot understand anything. Other people may not be unintelligent, but they hold wrong views. So even though buddhas, teachers, and teachings are right there in front of them, their own nihilistic or materialistic views block them from taking advantage of this opportunity.

The eight states that lack leisure are karmic results. You should not create the karma to be born in those states. The ten nonvirtues are the causes to be reborn in states lacking the opportunity to practice. Avoiding these, and practicing pure conduct of body, speech, and mind, are the causes for a good samsaric rebirth having all the necessary conditions for practice.

You can also look at your life from a positive perspective. You are fortunate because you are a human, your faculties are complete, your mind is functional, you are in a place where the doctrine has appeared, the teachings and teachers are still available, and so on. Everything is available to you. You have no excuse for not practicing because something is lacking. You simply don't recognize the value of what you have. Some people feel that their lives are so irredeemably miserable that they kill themselves. But if you really think about the value of what you have you will want to use it. You won't want to waste it. You will fear that if you don't take this opportunity, it may be eons before you have this type of life again.

Now that you understand what a good rebirth is, you understand why it is valuable, and you know the practices necessary to attain a life like that again, we move on to developing renunciation for all of samsara. In other words, we will be discussing additional practices for the attainment of a permanently good goal—liberation or enlightenment—rather than the temporary goal of a good rebirth.

9. Developing Aversion to Samsara

To renounce is to reject or turn away. In Buddhist terms, renunciation isn't an ordinary feeling of repugnance like when you are tired of a specific place or your family. That is just wanting to go off alone to a more pleasant situation. You are still attached to samsara; you are repulsed by a certain situation but feel that somewhere else will be very enjoyable. It is selfish renunciation. Spiritually there can be a certain amount of selfishness. In the Hinayana tradition, you want liberation from samsara for yourself alone. You develop renunciation of samsara in order to achieve that goal. But even the Hinayana form of renunciation is not ordinary selfish renunciation.

To develop a real desire to turn away from all of samsara, you need to understand the defects of samsaric rebirth. If you don't feel disgust about being in samsara you will not want to become free from it. This disgust is not the same as anger. Anger is a corollary of desire. You get angry when someone or something blocks you from getting what you want, takes something from you, or thwarts your desires in some way. The attitude of renunciation is not based on desire for your own pleasure. It is based on understanding the nature of samsara. It is analogous to understanding that the nature of fire is hot. There is no point in being angry at a fire because it burned your hand. If you don't want to be burned, you don't create the cause to be burned; you don't put your hand in the hot flames. In other words, disgust with suffering is not enough, you have to want to get rid of what causes you to be re born in samsara.

Tsongkhapa said in the condensed lamrim:

If you do not strive to contemplate the defects of the reality of
　　suffering,
a genuine aspiration for liberation will not arise.
If you do not contemplate the causal process of the origin of
　　suffering,
you will fail to understand how to cut the root of cyclic
　　existence.
[Condensed Points of the Stages of the Path, 19]

In short, you must counter your desire for samsaric pleasure in order to develop a strong motivation to gain liberation. You strengthen your motivation by reviewing the dissatisfactory nature of samsara over and over again.

The following verse is in a prayer written by Tsongkhapa:

Even excellent sensual pleasures are never satisfactory;
they are the cause of misery and they are unreliable.
Please bless me to see these disadvantages
and to strive to attain the happiness of liberation.
[The Foundation of Good Qualities, 5]

The General Nature of Suffering in Samsara

The faults of samsara are unlimited. Therefore, Nāgārjuna tells the king that he can't explain all of them. But it is very important to pay attention to at least some of them because this is the only way to develop sincere renunciation. To show that samsara is completely dissatisfactory, in the next verse Nāgārjuna points out some of its general problematic characteristics. In subsequent verses he will go into more detail.

65.　My Lord, to become disgusted
　　　with samsara, the source of so much suffering,
　　　pay heed to some of its faults: frustrated desires,
　　　death, sickness, aging, and so forth.

The first general defect of samsara is a result of desire. We want beautiful things to see, tasty things to eat, lovely sounds to hear, soft garments and sexual partners to touch us, enticing odors to smell, and so forth. There are almost unlimited sensory objects, and ordinary beings are dominated by desire for them almost all the time. These objects in and of themselves don't make you suffer. Buddhas and arhats interact with these objects but because they do not have desire for them, they do not engage in impure actions and endure suffering as a result. In contrast, ordinary beings perceive these objects through their egoistic view and therefore strong desire arises. When you don't get what you want, you feel impoverished and desperate. You spend your entire life doing all kinds of actions to get these things. When you get them, you want to improve them and keep them. You get angry if someone or something obstructs you from enjoying these objects. Sooner or later, you will die. And when you die, all those things you worked so hard to obtain have to be left behind.

Before death, while you are struggling to get what you want, you experience sickness. Ancient traditional medical systems explain that your body is made up of elements. If the elements are not in balance, you fall ill. Imbalances can be caused by external or internal factors. So many things can make you sick. Like sickness, aging is also not under your control. No matter how much you say, "I don't want to get old," as soon as you are born you begin to age. Each breath is one step further toward death. Your body changes, getting older and uglier every moment. Sometimes it gets to a point where people don't like their own body.

These four defects—frustrated desires, sickness, aging, and death—are from a list of eight types of general samsaric suffering found in many sutras. Nāgārjuna indicates the additional four—birth, encountering unpleasant circumstances, separating from pleasant experiences, and the five appropriated aggregates—by the words "and so forth." A detailed explanation of all eight is found in Tsongkhapa's *Great Treatise on the Stages of the Path*. In short, if you are in samsara, you will experience these eight types of misery. Since samsara is the source of this misery, you should be disgusted with it rather than desire it. When you have that attitude you will want to be free from samsara.

RENUNCIATION

Without renunciation you cannot genuinely desire emancipation. Āryadeva said,

> How can esteem for peace arise
> if you aren't disgusted with samsara?
> Like leaving home, it is also hard
> to leave samsaric existence behind.
>
> [*Four Hundred Stanzas,* 187]

Someone incarcerated in prison sees its disadvantages. They really want to get out of jail. But you won't want to get out if you think, "Jail isn't too bad. Someone brings me food. There is a bed. I don't need to do anything. It is actually a nice home." It is the same for those of us in samsara. If you don't see the problems and misery of being in samsara you will not turn away from it. You need to really feel that all of samsara, not just the three lower realms, is misery. This will make you deeply sad. You don't want to be in that situation. If you don't see this clearly, how could you desire liberation? If you are strongly attached to your home, you only see its good qualities and none of if its faults. Even though your perception may be inaccurate, you see your home as attractive. You don't want to leave it. You want to live there for a long time and develop it into the best house possible. If someone tries to ruin it, you get angry. If someone has something better, you get jealous. In the same way, your desire for things in samsara keeps you from working for the future beyond this life. When you are attached to your present life, you won't be sincerely interested even if you hear teachings and try to practice. Your prayers and dedications are mere words. They don't reflect a real desire for liberation or enlightenment. Your focus is to satisfy your desires in this life.

So, the problem is attachment to this life. From the point of spiritual development, you have an improper way of thinking. As discussed in chapter 7 in regard to Verse 48, your mind is dominated by four incorrect manners of perception: (1) you see impermanent things as permanent, (2) you see miserable things as pleasurable, (3) you see impure things as pure, and (4) you see selfless things as having a self. These four misperceptions are the way that the innate mind operates. Your actions follow those patterns of thought. You make many comparative judgments, but they are all based on these misperceptions. Ordinarily you don't worry about where you may be reborn in your next life. You simply don't think about that. You only think about this life. Therefore, it is hard to break your desire for the seeming good qualities of this life, and even more difficult to want to attain liberation from all of samsara.

Renunciation has two levels. First, you develop renunciation that turns away from this life to care about your future lives in samsara. Complete renunciation is to turn away from all of samsara with the sole motivation of desiring to attain liberation. How do you know if you have renunciation or not? How do you know if your renunciation is sincere or not? Do you have a little? Or a lot? The mark of having renunciation is when you have a spontaneous desire to attain permanent cessation of samsara, all the time, day or night. This desire has to arise continuously without any effort. True renunciation isn't just getting goosebumps when you deliberately think about the defects of samsara at a certain time.

No matter where you are born in samsara, high or low, your life is under the power of karma and the mental afflictions. When you see samsara this way it is like a big prison camp. To be clear, samsara is not an external place. The thought of renunciation isn't, "I reject this place, this town, and this country." No matter what external place you try to escape, running from one country to another, it will not help if your mental afflictions are not under control. Buddhas can come to various places to help other beings. They manifest, but they are not in samsara. Samsara is each individual cycling life after life, without their own control, under the power of impure karma and the three poisons. Existing this way is samsara. Each individual has existed this way from time without beginning. Each one builds their own samsara out of desire, hatred, ignorance and so forth. The thought of renunciation is a strong, spontaneous, and continuous desire to no longer exist in this cycle caused by karma and the mental afflictions.

The only way to get out of samsara is to get rid of ignorance and the mental afflictions. Therefore, purification of your mind is the main practice of the path. To begin to practice you must develop the thought of renunciation. Therefore, you need to think about the various problems that are concomitant with life in samsara. You don't just meditate on the suffering. You need to think about the causes of suffering and how to eliminate those causes. But you start by contemplating the faults of samsara.

Therefore, the next few verses go into more detail about seven types of samsaric defects: (1) there is no certainty, (2) there is no satisfaction, (3) you die and lose your body repeatedly, (4) you are reborn again and again, (5) you continually cycle up and down, (6) you have no companions, and (7) the specific types of suffering in each of the various realms. Many of you will have heard these verses before. Tsongkhapa often quoted *Letter to a Friend* in his *Great Treatise on the Stages of the Path* when he explained these topics.

A Lack of Certainty

The first problem is that there is no certainty in samsara. *Certainty* means that people and things fall into definite and stable categories. But that is not the case in reality.

> 66. Your father becomes your son, your mother becomes your
>   wife,
>   people who are your enemies become your friends,
>   and the reverse occurs as well. Therefore,
>   in samsara there is no certainty.

You think your friends and relatives are on your side and so you are fond of them. Other people are the opposite; they are your enemies. These categories seem definite. But when your father dies, he may be reborn as your son. Your mother in this life may be reborn as your daughter. Even in this life categories are not definite. You cannot be certain that someone is definitely your friend or definitely your enemy. There are some people whom you really don't like; you are sure that they are your enemies. But you know that there have been times when your adversaries became your dear friends. Or someone who was your friend became your enemy. It is your own mind that makes someone a friend or enemy. A little thing can make you change your mind; your friend could criticize you; your enemy could give you a meal. Because there is no absolute friend or enemy, you shouldn't be attached to any particular relationship in samsara. They all occur because of karma. Your attraction to some people and hatred for others cause you to create terrible karma that will ripen in the future. Therefore, these biases should be avoided. Purifying your mind of desire and hatred is what you need to do.

In this regard, there is a story in the sutras that you may have heard. Śāriputra had supranormal knowledge; he could see some past and future lives. He saw a family consisting of parents and their adult son and his wife. They lived together in a house with a fishpond behind it. The family had a terrible enemy and there was a blood feud between the two families. The patriarch of the family died. He had been very attached to eating the fish from the pond and was reborn there as a fish. The matriarch was very attached to her house. After she died, she was reborn as a house dog. When their enemy died, he was born as the child of the adult son and his wife. One day the family was having dinner. They were enjoying eating a big fish—actually the rebirth of the father. The dog was begging for food at the table, so they kicked it. The dog was the rebirth of the man's mother. They petted and loved the baby on their laps; the infant was their former enemy. Seeing all this Śāriputra said,

> He is eating his father's flesh,
> beating his mother, and,
> holding his enemy on his lap.
> How laughable is the nature of samsara!
> [*Sutra on the Distinctions of Karma*]

There is No Satisfaction

The second general fault is that you can never be satisfied in samsara. You are always unsatisfied and want more and more. You eat breakfast, but by lunchtime you want to eat again. You drink some beer, but one isn't enough, you want a second, a third, and so on. It is never the case that if you eat or drink enough you won't want to do so again. Nāgārjuna gives an example that extends beyond just this life:

> 67. Every being has drunk more milk
> than the four great oceans could contain.
> More than that is still yet to be drunk
> in the subsequent samsaric rebirths of ordinary people.

You have been born in samsara from time without beginning. Each time you were born, whether as an animal, human, hell being, and so forth, you had parents. Every other being has been your mother countless times. They have been your father countless times. You have been their mother and father countless times. Each time you were an infant you drank milk from your mother's breast. How much milk have you suckled from one single sentient being's breast in all these lifetimes? If you put it all together it would be more than the amount of water in the four oceans on earth. This is just considering one sentient being! The amount of milk is even more inconceivable when you think that this is the case for every sentient being.

How much more are you going to drink if you don't attain freedom from samsara? It will be even more than you have consumed before.

Repeated Death and Birth

The third and fourth defects are that you have to die and be reborn. You might think that if you were born in a nice place in samsara and could stay there forever it would be all right. Or, if you did not have to be reborn under the power of karma and the mental afflictions it might be all right. But that's not how it is. You have to die; and then you are reborn. This happens again and again. If you piled up the bones from all the bodies you have had, it would be a mountain larger than Mount Meru—the mountain that is the central axis of the universe.

> 68.　The pile of bones from each individual's lives
> 　　　equals or surpasses the height of Mount Meru.
> 　　　There is not enough soil on earth to make enough
> 　　　juniper berry-sized pellets to count those in your maternal
> 　　　　　line.

Ordinary beings not only suffer death, but under the power of karma and the mental afflictions they have had to take birth again and again. This has been the case from time without beginning. When you are born you have a mother. Your mother had a mother. Your grandmother had a mother. There is no end. You might try to count everyone in your matrilineal lineage using counters of little pellets of earth the size of a juniper berry. But you couldn't make enough pellets even if you used every bit of soil on earth. There is yet another way to look at this. You can consider how through your beginningless chain of births, every sentient being has been your mother countless times. Either way there is no counting the number of sentient beings you have been related to. If you could have exhausted the need for further rebirths just by taking rebirth, as though there was a finite number of births you had to take, you would have done it by now. Because rebirth is caused by karma and the mental afflictions you will continue to take rebirth until you remove those causes.

The Uncertainty of Cycling Up and Down

The fifth problem with samsara is that you continually go up and down. This is another type of uncertainty. Sometimes you are born in the lowest hell realm, sometimes you take rebirth in an upper realm of the gods. Even in the human realm, your social and economic situation fluctuates. Sometimes you may be rich and powerful, but then you can fall into destitution. You don't want this to happen, but change occurs as a result of past karma. You have no certainty.

> 69. Indra, who is revered throughout the world,
>   falls to earth through the force of karma.
>   A monarch of the entire universe
>   will become a low servant in samsara.

Indra is the king of the desire realm gods in the Heaven of the Thirty-Three. He has tremendous power and enjoyment. All the gods in that heaven—and many humans too—pay homage and worship him. But Indra has not achieved permanent peace and happiness. His wonderful environment and personal circumstances are the result of his past karma. When that karma is used up, he will die and be reborn. You and everyone else have been born as Indra many, many times. Then in your next life you may have been reborn in hell or fallen to earth and reborn as an ordinary human. In your life as Indra, you had so much wealth, and then in the next life you could be an impoverished human.

According to traditional Buddhist cosmology, at the beginning of the current eon human beings had a much longer lifespan. Certain kings at that time had much more power than present day rulers. Through the power of their karma, they ruled an entire continent or even more than one continent. They didn't need to conquer these areas militarily; their control was due to the power of their merit. No one would contend with them. The literal term for such a universal monarch is a "wheel-wielding king." There were four graded types of these "wheels," and the level of a universal monarch was determined by which type he possessed. All of the wheels, even the lowest sort, enabled their owner to fly from place to place. Only a universal monarch had that kind of power. But again, this incredibly high level of samsara is temporary. You experience it for a little while as a result of your karma. If a universal monarch continues to create powerful merit, he might be reborn as a universal monarch again. But if he just enjoys that state, when that karma is finished other karmas will bring about their result. So, he may be reborn as a servant of a servant. This is how samsara is always changing.

The next verse illustrates that the amount of happiness that you experience in samsara also vacillates. Pleasure is unreliable, it goes up and down.

> 70. After blissfully caressing the breasts and hips
>   of celestial maidens for a long time,
>   once again you are stroked by machines in hell
>   that crush, slash, and tear you unbearably.

There is some pleasure in the desire realm. Not much in the three lower realms, but humans and desire-realm gods experience some kinds of ordinary pleasure. The two lowest god realms, the Four Guardians and the Heaven of the Thirty-Three, are similar to the human realm in some respects, but far more pleasurable. The highest form of enjoyment in the human realm and these two god realms is sexual pleasure. (In the higher levels of the desire realm gods, a physical sexual partner is not necessary for experiencing pleasure. Those gods experience sensual pleasure in more and more subtle ways—just by holding hands, smiling, or merely seeing another god.) Much of the time the gods in the Heaven of the Thirty-Three and the Four Guardians realm enjoy many gorgeous sexual partners in lovely palaces and gardens. Only occasionally do they get angry and fight the jealous demigods. For the most part they have no incentive to create virtue because they are so comfortable and happy. They don't worry about future lives because they are drunk on the pleasure of the present. But no matter how long their life lasts, it eventually ends, and they experience the misery of death.

Various types of rebirth are the result of evil karma. Different negative actions result in different types of experience. The hells are the result of the worst kinds of karma. In the hells you may be crushed between huge mountains; mechanical devices may grind up your body like hamburger meat; or your body may be pulled apart the way vultures or wild dogs attack carrion. Details about these experiences and other hells are explained in the sutras and stages of the path literature. As horrible as those conditions are, they too are impermanent. The hells do not last forever; a life there is not absolute. Its duration is determined by the power of the karma that led to rebirth there. When the karmic result has been fully experienced, the hell being will die and be reborn under the power of a different karma.

Many Western people don't like to hear about the hells. But we are going through Nāgārjuna's text, so we can't skip over it. Here the point is to make a comparison. One life may have tremendous pleasure; the next life may have hellish torment. If you think about how and why things change, you will really fear suffering like this. You will want to make a correction before you die. If you don't want to hear about this, or think, "Well, I don't see the hells, so they don't exist," or if you think this just pertains to someone else, you won't take this personally. You won't consider how this could happen to you. You won't experience fear and as a result will not change the type of causes you are creating; you will just continue doing what you have done before. You won't take refuge or seriously practice. Fear of samsara and faith in the Three Jewels are the causes of taking refuge. And taking refuge is the starting point for all spiritual practice. Therefore, you must think about the nature of samsara, how it applies to you, and who and what can help you.

There are many types of uncertainty. Even in the course of one human life the pleasure you experience is indeterminate. Things can start off well, but then deteriorate. Circumstances can start off being very bad but change into a wonderful state. It always changes; it isn't trustworthy. The next three verses elucidate the uncertainty of places by contrasting extreme environments: the two lowest levels of the desire realm gods and various hells.

71. Consider that after living for a long time on Mount Meru's
        summit
     and enjoying the ground softly yielding to your feet,
     once again you will be struck by the unbearable suffering
     of the Firepit and Swamp of Filth hells.

In one life you may be in a god realm. The environment is beautiful
there. The ground is soft and pliable; it depresses slightly when you step
down and then springs up helping to lift your foot. But eventually you will
die and may be reborn in a place that is many thousands of square miles
of terribly hot ashes or scalding mud filled with voracious worms. No one
builds these places. They are a result of your unique karma. When you
realize how uncertain pleasure and comfort are in samsara you will want
to obtain the permanent peace of liberation. Without understanding the
uncertainty of pleasure in samsara you cannot change your mind.

Humans and gods try to make beautiful places that they can enjoy. We
build parks with gardens and swimming pools. But these pleasures too are
not trustworthy.

72. After going to play in lovely parks,
     enjoying and escorting divine women,
     you will arrive in the forest with leaves of swords
     and your legs, arms, nose, and ears will be cut off.

A celestial garden is not like one of our gardens. There are spectacu-
lar flowers, there are no mosquitos, and no burning sun. Handsome gods
and beautiful goddesses experience great pleasure there for a long time.
Their enjoyment is the result of virtuous samsaric karma. But after they
die, most of them are born in the hells. They have used up their virtuous
karma; they only have the seeds of the negative karma they have created
in the past. The opposite of these celestial gardens are forests in hell. From
a distance you see a grove with huge trees. But when you get there, you
see that the trees don't have ordinary leaves; the leaves are sharp weapons.
The sword-leaves fall and this rain of weapons chops you up. There is no
pleasure there.

You may think that you haven't created this kind of negative karma so
when you die you will have a good rebirth. But you have probably killed

many bugs and felt happy about it. That karma builds up to where it is like having killed thousands of people. The heavens and the hells are unmixed experiences. In the heavens you don't feel pain or misery; in the hells you don't have any pleasure, only misery. While you are in the hells the ripening of your virtuous karma is blocked; while you are in the god realms your negative karma doesn't ripen. This is different from the human realm where you have mixed karmic experiences. In a human life both your good karma and bad karma can ripen, leading to various pleasant and unpleasant experiences.

The next verse also illustrates that you cannot be sure that you will always live in a pleasant environment.

> 73. After living in the realm called Gently Flowing Stream
> where there are goddesses with lovely faces, and golden
>   lotuses grow,
> you will once again fall into the caustic boiling water
> of the hell called River Without a Ford.

In another part of the lower god realms there are lovely rivers of crystal-clear water. The rivers form delightful pools for swimming. Golden lotuses flower there but they don't grow from muck. There is no mud or dirt. The environment is completely enjoyable. But a god in this place will die eventually and in their very next life they may be reborn in a hell called River Without a Ford. The water of this huge river is extremely hot and dirty. The water scalds your flesh as soon as you touch it. If you are born here, you sink down in the river and your flesh is burned off. Then you rise up to the surface, your flesh regenerates, and then you sink into the burning water again. You want to escape, but the river is miles and miles wide and there are no shallows that would enable you to cross it. This is an unbearably miserable place.

So far, the verses have illustrated how the pleasures in the two lower levels of the desire realm gods can switch quickly into the suffering of the hells. The next verse shows that pleasure is also unreliable in the upper levels of the desire realm gods and in the corporeal and noncorporeal realms. The higher four levels of the desire realm gods, the seventeen levels of the corporeal realm gods, and the four levels of noncorporeal realm gods do not have the same kind of sensual enjoyment experienced by the lower levels of gods in the desire realm. In comparison to these higher levels, the lower-level gods are in misery! These higher gods of the desire realm and corporeal realm have bodies, but they are not physical bodies of gross matter. The corporeal realm gods, from the first to the fourth dhyāna, don't need or take pleasure in the senses. They do have senses, but primarily they are mental. The gods of the noncorporeal realm are purely mental in nature. We say they are "formless" or "noncorporeal," but they do have a form that is a very, very subtle combination of vital wind and mind. The name, "noncorporeal," is given from a negative perspective. It is like saying someone with a tiny nose has no nose.

As discussed above, all these higher levels of gods are still in samsara. The highest level of samsara is the highest level of the noncorporeal realm. You are born in those realms as a result of virtuous karma and different levels of meditative concentration. For as long as you are there, you experience peace and happiness far beyond anything experienced by humans and the two lowest levels of the desire realm gods. From the point of view of samsara this is as good as it possibly can be. But still, it isn't reliable or certain. When you die from these realms, you can fall way down.

> 74. After having the great pleasure of being a desire realm god
> and having Brahmā's bliss free of all gross desire,
> you again endure unceasing suffering
> as kindling in the fires of the Avīci hell.

"Brahmā's bliss" refers to the pleasure of the gods in the first dhyāna, the lowest level of the corporeal realm. According to the Abhidharma, beings in the corporeal realm are free of the mental afflictions of desire and hatred. This doesn't mean they have eliminated desire from the root; it means that desire, jealousy, hatred and the other mental afflictions are temporarily absent. They still have previously created karmic potential that can ripen as the worst type of life in hell. This bad karma can't ripen until a life of eons of enjoyment in the corporeal realm ends. But that karma is there and will ripen when the good karma is used up. The worst of the eight hot hells is called Avīci—unremitting misery. There your entire body—even your bones—is on fire. From the outside no one can see a body there; it just looks like a fire. You burn for eons without cease. You can't know for sure whether or not you have created the kind of karma to be born in this hell. But you have had innumerable past lives in which you created karma. So even if you take a rebirth in the corporeal or noncorporeal realms, you can't be sure that you will not fall again into extreme physical suffering.

Nāgārjuna wrote this text for a king who had high status, wealth, and so forth. The king had the best human experience, but it didn't compare to the pleasure of the gods. Nāgārjuna warns the king that when his life ends another karma will ripen and it most likely will be bad. And, even more important, this advice pertains to you too. You should be aware that although you are enjoying the result of virtuous karma now, you have created other karmas that will ripen as future rebirths. Therefore, while you can, you should create powerful virtuous karma and nullify prior negative karma. By creating powerful virtuous karma that will ripen in the very next life, you push back negative karmas from ripening into a bad rebirth. Then in the life after that you do the same thing. You eventually rid your mind of mental afflictions enough so that the countless bad previous karmas will never have the opportunity to ripen.

The next verse uses the sun and moon as an example of the unreliability of samsara. This can be explained from the mythic perspective where the sun and moon are deities, or from the point of view of light.

> 75. When you have obtained the state of being the Sun or
>   Moon
>   the light of your body illumines the entire world.
>   But once again you can return to enveloping darkness
>   so thick you cannot see your outstretched hand.

In traditional Indian cosmology, you can be born as a Sun or Moon deity. There is no distinction made between the basis—the physical orb—and the living being inhabiting that basis. During that life you have a body that sends out light to the entire world. We now know through science how illumination occurs. But in ancient times people believed that divine beings caused the light. They thought that the moon was a block of crystal that sent out cooling light and the sun was a type of fire that sent out hot light. You don't need to take this literally to understand Nāgārjuna's analogy. Here think about how some beings are born with beautiful bodies that are decorated so wonderfully that other people see them as shining. These glittering beings are experiencing a specific type of karma. But there are some places where the sun never shines, for example below the earth or in some of the lower realms. In such darkness you cannot even see your own hand in front of your face. One being can be born consecutively in each of these places, sometimes so bright and glowing sometimes so unbearably dark.

You create so much karma without thinking about the results your actions will bring about. You have done so many things that you should regret. Finding yourself all alone in overwhelming darkness is a result of your own actions of body, speech, and mind.

Lacking Companions

Being without any friendly companions is the sixth type of general samsaric defect.

> 76. Three types of virtue are the lamplight that dispels
> the causes for suffering that you have created.
> Take these up or you will be alone in darkness
> so deep it is not affected by the sun or moon.

Just as a lamp enables you to see in the dark, three types of virtuous actions will bring light in your future lives. The three virtuous actions are pure ethical conduct, generosity, and meditation. Pure conduct will result in a human or other high rebirth. Generosity prevents poverty and causes you to have enough of every necessity in that rebirth. These are the two most important forms of merit for ordinary people. Together they bring the type of future life that you want. The main purpose of meditation is training and purifying your mind. The result of meditation is to become so familiar with compassion, love, and wisdom that they are spontaneous and constant. It is familiarity with a direct realization of ultimate reality that will permanently clear away the darkness of samsara.

A second way to understand the three types of virtuous action is as study, analysis, and meditation. These are the three progressive ways to develop wisdom. Yet another way to count three types of virtuous actions is that they are the wholesome actions of body, speech, and mind. All activity comes through one of these three doors. Whichever way you understand it, each of these different sets of three virtuous activities are like a bright lamp that clears away the darkness. From now on you should develop these so that that you will not be alone in the dark. The *Extensive Sport Sutra* also expresses this idea:

> The virtuous actions that you have done
> are the only friends that follow and accompany you.
> There is no other companion in causally created existence.
> There is no other savior, family, friend, or helpful retinue.

Only your karma follows you after death. Virtuous karma will help you; nonvirtuous karma will harm you. If you are looking for a friend who can assist you wherever you go after you die, you must create merit. Ordinary friends and helpers are of no help at the time of and after your death. Your only friend is your virtuous karma. It leaves in your mind the potential for good experiences.

The Specific Suffering in Each Realm

So far, we have looked at the general faults of samsara. Now we will look at the specific forms of misery endured in each type of rebirth in the desire realm. Each part of the desire realm is caused by specific karmas and has its own type of suffering experience. Nāgārjuna divides the desire realm into five categories: (1) hells, (2) hungry ghosts, (3) animals, (4) humans, and (5) the gods. You may be more familiar with a description of six parts of the desire realm. The difference is whether the gods and demigods are counted together as one realm or considered to be two distinct realms. However you count them, the purpose of meditating on each type of suffering is to develop a serious and sincere desire to block those miserable experiences.

As Śāntideva said,

> Furthermore, suffering has some good qualities:
> by despairing of it your arrogance is dispelled,
> compassion arises for those in cyclic existence,
> evil is shunned, and joy is found in virtue.
> [*Introduction to the Practice of Bodhisattvas,* 6.21]

In and of itself, suffering has no good qualities. But by thinking about the suffering of the various realms in samsara you come to fear that misery.

You feel despair when you consider that you will experience it. Despair pops the balloon of your conceit. Right now, you are puffed up with vanity regarding your good situation and you have a misplaced confidence in your future. From understanding the nature of samsaric experiences and the causes for those experiences you will develop a desire to block them and attain true happiness. For example, by meditating on the suffering of the hells you realize that you really do not want to endure them in the future. You realize that you don't want to create those causes for that type of rebirth and you want to make impotent any such causes that you have already created. Not only do you become concerned for yourself, you consider all the other beings in samsara and feel compassion for them. But merely wishing for freedom from suffering won't do. Fear of suffering and despair about having to experience it, should make you avoid creating evil karma of even the smallest type. And finally, doing even the slightest type of wholesome action should give you great joy.

The Three Lower Realms

Nāgārjuna starts by listing the hells. His description of each hell realm is based on various sutras. We generally say there are sixteen great hells: eight hot hells and eight cold hells. The sutras list even more. Here we will just go over a few examples. I don't want to make you stop smiling, but to develop the real thought of renunciation you need to reduce your attraction to and desire for samsara. You need to stop seeing any part of samsara as pleasant and attractive. Without renunciation of samsara, you cannot develop bodhicitta. You can't want to help other beings get out of samsara if you don't want to get out yourself. And without bodhicitta you will not be motivated to search out an understanding of ultimate reality. That is why you meditate on the faults and misery of every realm in samsara.

> 77. For beings who engage in evil deeds
> there will be unrelenting misery in these hells:
> Reviving, Black-line, Intense Heat,
> Crushing, Screaming, Incessant, and so forth.

The verse lists the names of only seven great hot hells. To get to eight, divide the Screaming Hell into two: Screaming Hell and the even more miserable Howling Hell. Or another way to get to a total of eight is to divide the Intense Heat Hell into two: Intense Heat Hell and the Extremely Intense Heat Hell. There is only suffering in these great hells. None of them occur without a cause. You are born there as a result of your own very evil karma.

The suffering in the hot hells is even more severe than the suffering in the cold hells. The misery there is unrelenting. The Reviving Hell is the lightest of the eight great hot hells. The others are progressively worse. When you are born in the Reviving Hell, you perceive other hell-beings and become very frightened. You don't see anyone as a friend or helper. Instead, you are so terrified of attack from your perceived enemies that you feel you must strike first. So, you pick up all sorts of weapons: spears, knives, axes, and any other sharp thing. The types of weapons you find are a result of your own karma. Then, you hack others to death and you are hacked to death too. The pain these weapons can inflict is far worse than any kind of pain experienced in the human realm. But unlike in the human realm, you don't really die. You revive and repeat the process again. This happens repeatedly for eons.

The Black-line Hell is an even worse experience than what you endure in the Reviving Hell. To be born there you must have created the karma of torturing or executing other living beings. You have a huge body when born in this hell. But your body is fragile and easy to injure. In this hell you perceive very frightening guards who seize you and haul you away. The guards draw black lines all over your body—sometimes four, sometimes eight, and sometimes more. Then they use various types of saws to cut along the lines. This torture can go on for eons.

In the Crushing Hell there are huge mountains in every direction. The appearance of the mountains depends upon the karma of the person who is born there. They are in the form of whatever type of creature that person had killed in the past. So, depending upon your karma, the mountains look like cows, sheep, or humans, and so forth. Remember, even a tiny cause can eventually have great results. You should be wary of even slapping mosquitos! Once you are born there, the mountains come closer and closer. You try to escape, but you can't. Finally, you are smashed and crushed between the mountains. This doesn't kill you though. You are still terrified and in pieces. Each piece feels pain. Then you recover and a huge meat-grinding machine appears. Your body is ground up like hamburger. As before, this happens repeatedly for a very long time. The sutras describe

many other ways you can be crushed in this hell. Nāgārjuna alludes to two
of these in the next verse.

> 78. Some are crushed like sesame seeds,
>   others are ground as fine as flour.
>   Some are cut to pieces with blazing saws,
>   others are hewn with unbearably sharp axes.

Some beings are put into an oil-press and squeezed until there is nothing solid left. Others are caught in between blazing hot iron millstones
and ground up. The last two lines are about the misery of the Black-Line
Hell.

Sometimes people cry out in pain when they experience suffering. The
next hell, Screaming, is named after that. When you are born here you
seek safety. You find a metal house. But once you enter it, you cannot get
out. It is as if you are in a pot with a fire underneath it. You feel heat from
every direction. Imagine you are like a live lobster thrown into boiling
water, or a live chicken having its feathers singed off. Once you are in this
situation, you voice your misery by screaming. In the next hell, Incessant,
your screams escalate into howls. This hell is similar to the preceding one,
but the suffering is even worse. The metal house is doubled: one house
inside another. The karmic result is different depending upon the cause.
You may be in a cauldron of molten metal or pounded with red hot ham-
mers on a blazing metal plate.

In the next two hells, Intense Heat and Extremely Intense Heat, you
are skewered from bottom to top by red-hot spikes. The only difference
is that there are more points on the spikes and spears in the Extremely
Intense Heat hell. Fire comes out of the holes in your body made by these
spikes. Sometimes your burning flesh is stretched out and nailed down
with flaming metal stakes on a red-hot base.

> 79. Likewise, others are forced
>   to swallow liquid molten metal.
>   Some are completely impaled upon
>   blazing hot barbed iron spears.

The last hell is the worst of all the hells. It is called Avīci—unremitting misery—because here there is no temporary revival or resuscitation after what looks like death in the earlier hells. Huge fires are in each of the four directions. Imagine a huge forest fire approaching your house from every side. The heat of a forest fire is miniscule compared to these infernos. The fires of hell come closer and finally reach you. Your body becomes a wick for these flames. You cannot escape. There is no interruption, not even for a moment, to this misery that lasts for eons.

There are other hells surrounding and adjacent to these eight great hot hells. They are like the suburbs surrounding a city. In each of the four cardinal directions outside each of the eight great hells there are four surrounding hells. Thus, there are sixteen surrounding hells for each great hell. The *Treasury of Knowledge* says,

> There are sixteen for each of the eight:
> Firepit, Swamp of Filth, Trees
> with Sword-leaves, and River Without a Ford.
> [Treasury of Knowledge, 3.58–9]

Even if you become free from the great hell after eons of misery, you are then caught in these surrounding or ancillary hells. There are rings of these hells going outward. The four surrounding hells are called Firepit, Swamp of Filth, Trees with Sword-leaves, and River Without a Ford. Nāgārjuna mentioned these earlier in verses 71–73, where he contrasted the pleasures of the desire realm gods to the misery of the surrounding hells in the context of the uncertainty of the environment where you can be reborn. Now we focus on the misery of these surrounding hells more particularly.

In the first, the Firepit, there are mountains for miles around you. The surface of the ground looks like ash, but this light ash covers red hot coals. Each time your foot goes down you sink in to your knees and your flesh and bones are incinerated. When you lift up your leg, your body regrows and is then burned again. No matter how far you go trying to escape, you will not get out until your karma is exhausted.

The second ancillary hell, Swamp of Filth, is very hot foul-smelling mud. The mud sucks your feet and you fall over. It burns your flesh and bones. In this hot mud there are worms with sharp beaks that attack your body to eat your flesh. Some insects get inside your body, others eat at you from the outside. This mud extends great distances. If you manage to get out of this swamp, you see a beautiful garden with groves of trees in a distance. You struggle to get there. But when you get there, and go into the shade of these trees, you find that each leaf on every tree is a sharp weapon that falls and cuts you up. Then dogs attack the pieces of your body. This is the hell called Trees with Sword-Leaves. Near this place, but counted as part of the same surrounding hell, there are some trees that seem as tall as mountains. You hear your closest friend or lover's voice coming from the top of a tree. You desire to see this dear friend, so you climb up the tree. As you climb up, the razor-sharp leaves on the trees point down and slash your face and body. When you get to the top no one is there. Then you hear that beloved person's voice from down below saying, "Why are you up there, come down to me!" So, you start to climb down; now all the razor leaves point upward and you are sliced to shreds. This happens repeatedly. As this is happening huge birds flock to the trees looking for something to eat. They tear at you, plucking out your eyes, and so forth.

> 80. Some throw their hands toward the sky
>   as vicious iron-fanged dogs tear at them.
>   Others are helpless while pecked by crows
>   with sharp iron beaks and terrible claws.

> 81. Some writhe on the ground and wail
>   as thousands of worms, beetles, deer-flies,
>   and black bees bite into them
>   leaving huge wounds that are agonizing when touched.

The fourth surrounding hell is the River Without a Ford. There are no shallows in this river; it is deep throughout. The water of the river is boiling hot. Huge guards with weapons force you to stay in the river. If you do manage to get out of the river, the guards will tie you flat on a burning hot surface and pour molten metal into your mouth.

> 82. Some are immersed in blazing hot mud
>   and constantly burned with their mouths agape.
>   Some are dumped headfirst into iron cauldrons
>   and boiled like dumplings bobbing up and down.

In the eight cold hells beings have to endure freezing temperatures. In general, the cold hells are miles and miles of frozen mountains. In between the mountains there is water with floating icebergs: it is half ice and half water. There is no sun or any light whatsoever. It is totally dark and cold. There is no escape from this circle of mountains. Within this general environment each being experiences their own unique karmic effect. As you sink deeper and deeper down into the freezing water the experiences are worse and worse. The first cold hell, the lightest one, is called Goosebumps, because when you are touched by a very cold wind you shiver and your skin pimples up. In the next lower cold hell, these pustules pop. The next three hells are named for the sounds the hell beings make as they are tormented by the cold: Tham-tham-pa, Kyi-hu, and Ah-chu. In the next one your body turns a bluish color, and it splits open into five or six sections like a simple lotus. After that there is a hell that is even more painful; your skin changes from blue to reddish in color and splits into ten or more sections like a more complex lotus. In the deepest cold hell, your body turns even brighter red and splits into one hundred or more sections.

In addition to the hot hells, cold hells, and surrounding hells there are hells called occasional or partial hells. These partial hells sometimes can be perceived here on earth. Someone can look human but actually be experiencing the results of very, very bad karma. The main result of that karma may have already been experienced as a birth in a great hell, but some of that karma might remain and be experienced in a partial hell. The sutras contain descriptions of some these hells. One story tells of a man who wanted to go to the ocean to find jewels and wealth. But he went down the wrong road and ended up in a very strange place. There he saw a man who would enjoy great pleasure in a celestial palace every night. But as soon as the sun rose, the celestial mansion and all the sensory pleasures disappeared. He would fall to the ground and huge fearsome wild beasts would attack and eat his flesh. After a full day of this misery, when the sun set he would recover and experience heavenly enjoyment. The traveler asked, "Why is this happening to you?" The man replied, "When I was a human, I did many evil things during the day. But at night I would maintain pure ethical conduct. So, I created the causes for both good results and bad results." The lost traveler saw another man who experienced pleasure during the day, but at night would be eaten by ogresses from his head down to his toes. In a former life this man had kept pure ethical conduct during the day but at night engaged in in sexual misconduct.

To deny the existence of the hells because you don't see them is very foolish. It is good to be afraid after hearing about the intense and unrelenting suffering of the hells. Being frightened isn't pleasant, but fear of the consequences of your karma is a good thing. It will make you serious about using your life in a productive way. It will make you regret what you have done and vow never to do anything like that again, even at the cost of your life. This is just a brief explanation of the hells. Nāgārjuna says we should be afraid of creating the causes that result in this type of horrible experience.

People who have created many heavy negative actions and haven't purified them are called evildoers. They have created no virtue and they possess only negative karma. The only thing keeping them from experiencing the result of this karma is that they are breathing out and in. To breathe is to be alive. If you breathe out, but don't breathe in, you have died. Usually after you die and before the next rebirth, there is an intermediate state called the bardo. But here in the next verse Nāgārjuna says that some evildoers go right to hell from the life during which they created heavy negative karma. Their negative karma is so powerful that the intermediate state is extremely short; it lasts just an instant. There is no long journey in terms of time or distance between this life and the next life in hell—it is just a matter of breathing out and not breathing in.

> 83.　As soon as an evildoer ceases to breathe
> 　　　he will instantly experience the hells.
> 　　　Someone who hears of this immeasurable suffering
> 　　　and isn't afraid has a diamond-hard nature.

Most people don't think about their death or what will happen to them after they die. But you don't know what the future will bring. You don't even know what will happen tomorrow. You can't deny that there will be a tomorrow, but maybe not for you in this human life! Every individual has their own experiences because of their own karma. It looks like we share circumstances with others, but really the situations are unique. There is some common karma that results in the shared aspects of experience, but for the most part karma is individual. For example, in a family with five children, each child has a completely different experience despite growing up with the same parents, living in the same house, and so forth. One child may always be blamed despite doing nothing wrong; another may be well liked by everyone. All this is a result of each child's unique past karma. We never want to blame ourselves when things go wrong. We think we are honorable, respectable, and innocent. When negative things happen, we want to blame other people, the weather, God, or something else. We rarely think that our unpleasant experiences are the result of our own karma.

If you can hear about the horrific results of bad karma and have no fear at all, you must have an incredibly tough and hard mind. To be fearless in this way is extremely stupid. That is why it is said that someone without fear has a diamond-hard blockhead.

> 84. If it is terrifying to see pictures of the hells,
>   or to hear, recollect, read about, or encounter statues of
>   them,
>   what need is there to say anything
>   about actually experiencing that maturation of your karma?

If even just hearing about the hells is unpleasant or scary, think about how awful it must be to experience the hells. Pictures and stories aren't real, but they can frighten you. Think about whether you have created the causes to actually be born in hell. Even if you haven't created those causes in this life, you should be frightened because you don't know what you have done in prior lives.

Śāntideva said that we have all had many rebirths in hell, but all those eons of suffering had no purpose. We suffered, but that misery doesn't prevent future suffering. It didn't help us to reach our own goal, much less the goals of others.

> For the sake of satisfying my desires
> I have burned in hell many times.
> My actions did not fulfill my own goals
> Nor did they benefit others.
>
> [*Introduction to the Practice of Bodhisattvas,* 6.74]

Those who have created the causes to be born in hell and haven't done much purification should be afraid. Once your karma has ripened and you are born in hell there isn't anything you can do about it. So now that you are afraid because you have thought about the causes you have created and their effects, you should do something to prevent those results from occurring. Remember that there are methods you can employ to avert rebirth in the hells. Sometimes that practice will cause a negative karma to ripen in this life in a more minor way. The experience of human misery is much less than the suffering in the hells.

Śāntideva said,

> Isn't it fortunate for a man who is condemned to death
> to be freed with just his hand having been amputated?
> Isn't it fortunate that by experiencing human suffering
> a person avoids suffering in hell?
> [*Introduction to the Practice of Bodhisattvas*, 6.72]

So, fear of the hells and doing something about it is a cause for rejoicing. On the other hand, it is very dangerous if you are without fear at all and just sit around and smile.

Are the miseries and pleasures of samsara all equal to each other? No. There are differences in the intensity of experience between even the eight great hot or cold hells.

> 85. Among all the types of pleasure,
>   the extinction of craving is the highest bliss.
>   Similarly, among all the types of suffering,
>   the suffering of Avīci is the worst.

Ignorance is the source of desire and hatred. Hatred and anger are closely related to desire. You get angry because you do not have, or you lose something that you desire. Hatred may come up only occasionally, but craving or desire is virtually continuous for beings in the desire realm. Desire is as much a part of desire realm beings' minds as an oil stain is indelibly embedded on paper. When desire, hatred, and ignorance are completely eliminated you achieve nirvana. Ordinary pleasures within samsara come and go. No matter how high your rebirth, sometimes you have happiness and sometimes you don't. When you achieve emancipation, you will have permanent peace and happiness. There is nothing better. In the same way, there is nothing worse than the suffering in the Avīci Hell. There isn't even an adequate analogy for what it is like to be in that hell.

> 86. The pain of being violently stabbed three hundred times
>   by sharp spears in a single day during this life
>   doesn't equal or even approach a fraction
>   of the smallest of the miseries in the hells.

Even the worst type of human suffering you can imagine doesn't compare in the slightest to the misery of Avīci. No matter how much you say about human misery, it is minor compared to any of the suffering in the hells.

As far as the length of a life in the hells, the *Treasury of Knowledge* says,

> A day in the six hells, the Reviving, and so forth
> is as long as the life of a desire realm god.
> A lifespan in each of these hells corresponds
> respectively to the lifespans of the desire realm gods.
>   [*Treasury of Knowledge,* 3.82–3]

In general, the number of days in a life in each of the hells corresponds to the number of days in the life of the six levels of the desire realm gods. As you go up higher in the god realms the lifespan doubles. Similarly, as you go lower in the hells, the length of life is double what it is in the previous level. However, a life in hell lasts much, much longer than a god's life because one day in hell is as long as the entire lifespan of the corresponding desire realm god. Let's get a little more specific. In a human year there are 365 days that are 24 hours long. One day in the lowest of the desire realm gods, the gods of the Four Guardians realm, lasts 50 human years. These gods live 500 of their own years. So, they live 500 years of 365 days where each day is 50 human years long. In the first hell, the Reviving Hell, one day lasts as long as the entire lifespan of a god in the Four Guardians realm. This first hell being's length of life is 500 years composed of days that long. In the Extremely Hot Hell a life span is half of the shortest form of eon. In the worst hell, Avīci, a lifespan is the full length of an interme-diate eon. This is a very, very long time.

The types of torture in the hells would kill a human very quickly. As a human you don't want to die. But in the hells you wish you could die and be reborn somewhere better. But you can't die and leave that realm until the power of the karmic cause for that rebirth is completely used up. It is like a fire: it will continue to burn until the fuel is used up.

> 87. Even if you experience for a billion years
>   this extremely unbearable misery,
>   you will not be freed from that life
>   until those negative deeds are exhausted.

A rebirth is the fruit of a karmic seed. Karmic seeds are potentials deposited in the mind by an action of body, speech, or mind. The fruit that ripens from the seeds of nonvirtuous actions are extremely unpleas-ant experiences. Once you have planted these seeds they will ripen when they meet the right circumstances. That is, they will ripen unless you purify your mind. But most people don't do purification practices. They don't recognize that they have planted the seeds for suffering. And they let one little seed expand and multiply over time until it is very big and pow-erful. Therefore, you should resolve to not create even the smallest type of nonvirtuous karma. You need to shut the doors of your body, speech, and mind to negative actions. You need to open those doors to wholesome virtue.

> 88. The seeds of these fruits of nonvirtue
>   are negative actions of body, speech, and mind.
>   Therefore, you must skillfully make an effort
>   to never engage in the slightest wrongdoing.

Most people, even if they believe in rebirth, think, "I'm human, so in my next life I'll be a human." They don't think they'll be reborn as animals, in the hells, or somewhere else. According to Buddhism we are all subject to karma: we will be reborn higher or lower based on our actions. Even if you do an incredible number of good actions but your motivation isn't the wish to be free from samsara, then that karma will be the cause of rebirth in samsara. Yes, these virtues will result in a good rebirth, but still in samsara.

In the stages of the path teaching tradition the three lower realms are usually explained in the order of their misery, starting from the most intense suffering. So, the order is the hells, the hungry ghosts, and the animals. Here Nāgārjuna reverses the order of the latter two. The reason is that some hungry ghosts have sharper intelligence than animals. Of course, the hungry ghosts endure formidable suffering, but some of them have the potential to be receptive to Dharma teachings. So, because hungry ghosts can be closer to understanding the path, animals are considered to be worse off than hungry ghosts.

So next we look at the general misery of the situation of being born as an animal.

89. When you take rebirth as an animal,
        you endure various kinds of misery: being killed, bound,
        and beaten. The unbearable experience of eating each other
        awaits those who have abandoned the virtue that brings
             peace.

No matter how pleasant an animal's rebirth seems to be, they are still subject to being killed by a bigger animal. Even tigers and lions, who look so strong and powerful, are subject to fear of being attacked and killed. Big animals eat small ones. Small animals eat even smaller ones. In addition to animals preying upon each other, humans target animals for their hides or meat. In the past, most physical labor was done by animals. Humans would treat beasts of burden terribly: tying them up, whipping, and beating them.

Why do animals suffer so? It is because in the past they did not create any virtue that was the cause of the cessation of suffering. And, during their lives as animals, they do not create the causes for liberation. They act to protect themselves or their offspring. They act to get shelter, food, and safety. In contrast, even if humans are in miserable circumstances, they can turn their situation into a field for meritorious action. Animals cannot do that. From that point of view, they have abandoned virtue. This is actually a technical point. As discussed in chapter 7, the first two of the five paths—the paths of accumulation and preparation—involve creating a tremendous amount of merit and the practice of alternating meditations of higher wisdom and śamatha in preparation for the path of seeing. It is on the path of seeing that you first understand reality directly, unmediated by thought. Some animals may be able to create some merit on the path of accumulation; but no animal is a suitable vessel for the practices of the path of preparation. It doesn't mean that they will never be able to do it in any future lifetime. But in their lifetime as an animal, they have no opportunity to do these practices.

The next verse gets more specific. In order to have the fear that leads to renunciation, you consider the suffering of animals in a more personal way. What would it be like to born as an animal? Thousands of oysters are killed for pearls. Elephants and rhinoceros are killed for their tusks and horns. Tigers, lions, and cows are killed for their skins. Animals have no freedom. People use horses, donkeys, elephants, and buffalos to do heavy labor. Many are not given proper food or shelter. Have you created the causes to be born as an animal?

> 90. Some are killed because people want
>   their pearls, wool, bones, flesh, or skin.
>   These helpless beings are forced to work
>   by being beaten, kicked, whipped, and goaded.

The problems we see are just examples of the vastness of the misery in the animal realm. There are many more animals that are not visible to us. We don't see the creatures in the depth of the ocean or the tiny organisms that live in our own bodies. If you don't want to be like them, you have to avoid creating the causes that lead to that result and you must disable the causes that you created in the past.

Next, we are introduced to the general type of suffering endured by hungry ghosts.

> 91. The hungry ghosts endure incessant misery
>   caused by their unfulfilled desires.
>   They undergo terrible suffering
>   of hunger, thirst, cold, heat, exhaustion, and fear.

Desire itself is suffering. Misery never ceases because you always lack something that you desire. No matter how much you try to obtain things you never get them all. In the realm of the hungry ghosts, the karma of prior desire and stinginess results in the suffering of hunger, thirst, freezing as if it were winter, or being in a desert so hot you are almost ready to burst into flame. What kind of fear do they experience? They may see something like water or food in the distance, so they run toward it. But when they get there, they find a terrifying situation, perhaps beings with weapons who are ready to attack them.

> 92. Some with mouths like the eye of a needle
>   and stomachs like mountains suffer hunger.
>   They do not have the ability to eat
>   even the tiniest scraps of discarded filth.

Hungry ghosts are always in search of relief from this misery. They have a body with a huge belly but a tiny neck and small hands and legs. So, just moving is exhausting. Sometimes they run for miles in hot sandy deserts looking for something to eat or drink. But everything they find is filthy and rotten. The only food they find is as disgusting as what we eliminate in the toilet. There is no way to clean this "food." Even if they do find something to eat, their mouths are so tiny that it is hard to fill their huge bellies. Their mouths are as small as the eye of a needle; their stomachs are huge, the size of mountains.

> 93. Some are naked, their bodies are just skin and bones,
>   and as dried out as the top of palm tree.
>   Some have mouths from which flames blaze at night.
>   Sand falls into their burning mouths as food.

All hungry ghosts are born as a result of evil karma. But they experience different internal and external difficulties due to their individual karma. There are almost limitless types of misery in this realm. Nāgārjuna just mentions a few of them. Some hungry ghosts have virtually no flesh; they are just skin and bones, as bare as the top of a dead palm tree after all its bark and fronds have fallen off. Actually, other hungry ghosts experience even worse misery. Inside their body cavity there is a lot of air; this bursts into flame and fire comes out of their mouth. Another explanation for these flames is that if a hungry ghost does eat something, it causes their insides to burst into flame. Some people can see these flames at night. They don't see the hungry ghost itself, but they do see the flames. Hot sand, or bits of dirt, are their only food.

The lowest type of hungry ghost cannot find even pus, excrement, or blood to eat. So, what needs to be said about them finding anything palatable?

> 94. The lowest types of ghosts cannot find
> even filth like pus, blood, or excrement.
> They attack each other and eat the pus
> discharged from festering wounds on their throats.

These lowest types of hungry ghosts are so tormented by hunger that anger and hatred naturally arise when they see each other. On sight they begin to fight. The wounds they inflict upon each other get infected and secrete pus. This is all these ghosts can find to eat.

> 95. For them, the summer moonlight feels hot
> and the winter sunlight feels cold;
> trees are completely empty of fruit;
> just their gaze makes rivers go dry.

In hot places like India, the sun can be brutally hot in spring. There is no rain nor are there any clouds in the sky. People say that if you put an egg outside it will cook. In contrast, at night, the light of moon seems cool. But for the hungry ghosts even moonlight is severely hot. For us, a bright sunny day in winter can be warming. But the hungry ghosts freeze even when taking a sun bath. Sometimes they see beautiful trees heavy with fruit. They run towards the orchard, but when they get there, the trees are totally barren and dry. Other hungry ghosts may not even find a tree when they arrive. Hot sun causes mirages of water, so the ghosts struggle to get to that water to drink. But when they get there, there is not even a drop of water. External things are not intrinsically existent. Humans can eat the fruit from the tree; but hungry ghosts see no fruit. Humans may bathe in a river; but for hungry ghosts the river is just a mirage. This is a result of their karma. A traditional example of karma determining experience is a bowl of liquid. A hungry ghost, a god, and a human come at the same time, but they see the liquid in the bowl differently. Humans and animals see it as water; the gods see it as nectar; the hungry ghosts see it as undrinkable, filthy pus. Is it pus? Is it water? Is it nectar? Who is wrong? Who is right? Some scholars explain that all three are there: each type of being experiences it as something commonly known to the beings of their realm. You can't judge the way things really exist just based on the fact that you see them in a particular way or don't see them at all.

How long do hungry ghosts experience this misery? How do we measure their lifespan?

> 96. They experience unrelenting misery.
> Their bodies are tightly bound by
> the karmic noose of evil deeds.
> Some do not die for five or ten thousand years.

Hungry ghosts live much longer than humans. Once they are born, they experience suffering continuously without any interruption. Like animals trapped in a snare, their karma holds them and doesn't let them escape. They cannot stop the experience of this suffering until their karma is exhausted. If we calculate their lifespan in human years, some of the hungry ghosts live 5,000 years. Others may live 10,000 years. For all those years, no matter how much they run searching for food and clothes, they never find them, but they cannot die.

Now, what is the cause for this kind of misery? Life as a hungry ghost is the result of being miserly or stingy. Nāgārjuna summarizes some sutras to prove this point.

> 97. Why do hungry ghosts experience various
> types of misery that have but one taste?
> The cause is taking delight in stinginess.
> The Buddha said miserliness is ignoble.

The traditional way to express that two things are similar is to say that they have one taste. The analogy is to a piece of hard candy that has the same sweet taste as long as it is in your mouth. The Buddha taught that all the varied painful experiences in the hungry ghost realm—hunger, thirst, heat, exhaustion—are similar in that they are caused by miserliness.

> The miserly will be reborn in the hungry ghost realm.
> Or if reborn human they will be in poverty.
> [*Condensed Perfection of Wisdom*]

Stinginess or miserliness is a powerful nonvirtue. It is characterized by not wanting to share anything, no matter how much you have. You may have hundreds of things that you don't need, don't enjoy, and can't even use, but you don't want to give even one to someone who needs it. Not only do you not want to share your possessions, you also want to have others' possessions for yourself.

Śāntideva said,

> If I give this away, what will I have to use later?
> That selfish attitude is demonic.
> [*Introduction to the Practice of Bodhisattvas,* 8.125ab]

We all want worldly pleasure and material things. But if you are stingy, even if you are not born as a hungry ghost, your next human life will be similar to theirs. You will be in poverty; your environment, food, and material situation will never be good no matter how much you strive. You will always worry, struggle, and run around, but nothing will ever work out. If you do not want to be reborn like that then you must eliminate your selfish attitude. There is no external cause that makes you become a hungry ghost. It is simply your own egoistic selfishness.

Śāntideva concludes the above verse by showing the opposite attitude:

> If I use everything for myself, what can I give to others?
> The attitude of caring for others is divine.
> [*Introduction to the Practice of Bodhisattvas,* 8.125cd]

Generosity is to be able to give without stinginess. Generosity isn't giving a lot of things or money; it is your attitude. The perfection of generosity doesn't mean that all the poverty in the world has to be eliminated. If that were the case the many buddhas of the past would not have perfected generosity. Generosity is training your mind so that you want to give. Śāntideva summarizes this:

> If the perfection of generosity
> were the elimination of all poverty,
> how did past buddhas perfect it
> since there are still starving beings now?
>
> The perfection of generosity is said to be
> the idea of giving to all beings all your wealth,
> and the results that will arise from that thought.
> Thus, it is simply a state of mind.
> [*Introduction to the Practice of Bodhisattvas*, 5.9–10]

The Three Upper Realms

Even a life in the higher realms of the gods, demigods, or humans, is still not perfect. It is better than being in the lower realms, but there are still lots of problems and suffering. Earlier in the text Nāgārjuna covered the various types of suffering in the human realm. Now he introduces the suffering inherent in the god and demigod realms.

The gods experience terrible suffering as their death approaches. For seven days, which are much, much longer than human days, they see signs of their imminent death. Their lovely bodies start to sweat and smell, their clothes and flower ornaments deteriorate, and the other gods don't want to associate with them. These things cause them incredible suffering because they had so much pleasure before.

> 98. In the higher realms, the suffering of death
> is greater than the vast pleasures enjoyed there.
> Thinking this way, upright people
> do not crave the transitory higher realms.

> 99. The complexion of their bodies becomes unattractive,
> their seats become uncomfortable, their flower garlands
> wilt,

> their clothing develops an unpleasant odor,
> and their bodies sweat as they never had before.

> 100. These are the five signs of imminent death in the god
>   realms.
>   They arise for the gods who live in the heavens
>   similar to the way signs of impending death
>   arise for humans who reside on earth.

Further, these signs indicate that the good karma that resulted in birth in the god realms is just about used up. Just before their death some of the gods can see where they will be reborn. They see that the seeds of their prior negative actions will result in their next birth being lower, perhaps even in hell. This causes them extreme mental anguish.

> 101. If those who are transmigrating from the god realms
>   have no remaining store of merit,
>   then without any control they will become
>   either a hell being, a hungry ghost, or an animal.

The demigods are a very low-level type of god. They are unbearably jealous of the greater wealth and pleasure experienced by the desire realm gods. Their envy impels them to attack the gods in order to steal their superior sources of enjoyment. The demigods can never win these battles. They suffer physical and mental torment again and again. Because of their strong covetousness and greed, even the most intelligent of the demigods cannot attain a direct realization of ultimate reality. In other words, even if they met a buddha and heard his teachings they could not attain the path of seeing.

> 102. The demigods naturally resent the gods' splendor.
>   This causes them great mental anguish.
>   They are intelligent, but these beings' obscurations
>   prevent them from seeing reality.

In conclusion, any rebirth taken under the power of the mental afflictions and karma is the source of much suffering. You may have some pleasant experiences in samsara due to good karma, but actually there are problems and misery in every realm, whether high or low. Every involuntary rebirth is characterized by misery. So long as you live under the power of karma and the mental afflictions you have no freedom and no control. You don't know what will happen after you die, so right now you should make an effort to not have any kind of samsaric rebirth.

103. Because samsara is like this,
          there is no such thing as a pleasant rebirth.
          Whether it be as a god, human, hell-being, ghost, or
              animal,
          you should know birth is a crucible of great harm.

10. Aspects of the Path Common to All Vehicles

WHAT DO YOU HAVE to do to attain liberation? That is the subject of this chapter: the method to progress along the spiritual path to attain nirvana. Nirvana isn't a physical place; it isn't a pure land that exists somewhere else. Nirvana is the transformation of your mind. So, the path to nirvana isn't a physical thing either. It is a system of gradual mental development. You perfect your mental nature and eliminate your mental afflictions in stages. Right now, you have an impure, disturbed, and wild mind. But it can be purified. Just as dirt can be removed from muddy water and the water is naturally good to drink, the mind is naturally pure but temporarily afflicted.

There are two aspects to the path of practice: common and uncommon. Everyone who wants emancipation—whether it be just personal liberation or completely omniscient buddhahood—must practice the common path. In other words, the common path is followed by both Hinayana and the Mahayana practitioners. By mastering just the practices on the common path, Hinayana practitioners achieve their own emancipation, the state of nirvana. Someone who has reached that state is an arhat. From the perspective of the Mahayana, individual liberation is a lower nirvana. Mahayana practitioners also do the practices on the common path, but they add other practices because their goal is to attain complete buddhahood or enlightenment. Because these additional practices are not shared with the Hinayana, the Mahayana is called the uncommon path and the goal of that path is sometimes called the higher nirvana. (To avoid confusion I will refer to the result of the Hinayana path as *nirvana,* and the result of the Mahayana path as *buddhahood* or *enlightenment*.) In short, the objective of the common path is to attain permanent freedom from samsara—nirvana. Bodhisattvas add the practices of the uncommon path to the common path because they want more than just their own freedom from samsara; they are seeking complete enlightenment in order to be able to benefit all other living beings.

The Buddha taught a wide variety of audiences over a period of forty years. To meet the needs, interests, and abilities of his listeners he described the path to liberation in various ways. In every case, the explication of the path was complete: practitioners need to create all the requisite causes for nirvana. Further, these different iterations of the common path are not distinct paths of practice, nor are they methods to be practiced sequentially. The different descriptions simply highlight particular methods at particular stages along the complete path that leads to nirvana. They focus in depth on particular points while leaving other parts of the path implicit. In this chapter, after a brief introduction in which Nāgārjuna reiterates that all Buddhists must develop renunciation and diligence, he presents six ways to discuss the path: (1) the seven branches of the path to enlightenment, (2) the union of śamatha and vipaśyanā, (3) giving up consideration of purposeless topics, (4) the twelve links of dependent origination, (5) the eightfold path of the āryas, and (6) the four realities for āryas. In addition to the traditional explanation of these topics as ways to discuss the common path, I will add some material to make some of these iterations applicable to the uncommon Mahayana path.

THE COMMON BASIS

At the very beginning of his teaching career, the Buddha taught the reality of suffering. He wanted his followers to understand the nature of existence in the world. The Buddha didn't teach this because he wanted his students to worry and become even more unhappy. He taught it because there are benefits to meditating on suffering. First of all, without having meditated on suffering, everything may seem to be fine. If you feel that things are actually OK, you won't desire liberation from samsara for yourself or others. But when you understand the pervasive nature of suffering, you will want it to cease permanently. Second, without renunciation—a feeling of revulsion for all involuntary rebirth—any spiritual practice will be shallow and ineffective. Meditation on suffering doesn't mean just repeating the word, "suffering, suffering, suffering." Meditating on suffering means to examine and analyze the situation you are in. You contemplate how pain, impermanence, impurity, birth, aging, sickness, death, undesirable things happening, and losing or not getting desirable things all fall down on you like rain. When this becomes clear to you, you will want to know how to eliminate suffering.

Śāntideva said,

> The cause of happiness is rare, and
> there are so many causes of suffering.
> Without suffering, renunciation will never arise.
> Therefore, you mind, be steadfast!
> [*Introduction to the Practice of Bodhisattvas, 6.12*]

A human life is short, and most people think selfishly every moment of it. Because of their mental afflictions people do so many things thinking they are working for happiness. However, their human intelligence makes them experts at acting in an evil way. Even actions that seem wholesome can be the causes of misery. You need to investigate what causes your problems. When you feel disgust for suffering and its causes, you will be motivated to begin to engage in the practices that result in your attainment of a spiritual goal. You are truly seeking a spiritual goal only after you develop renunciation that is spontaneous and arises constantly day and night.

How important is it to make an effort to practice? It is more urgent than putting out a fire. If your hair suddenly caught fire, you would immediately try to put it out, wouldn't you? When there is a fire in your house, you would try to put it out so that it doesn't destroy your possessions. If you don't act quickly in these situations there is the danger that you and your belongings may be badly burned. Everyone understands this. The majority of spiritual practitioners immediately stop what they are doing to put out a fire. But the most skillful yogis know that the faults of samsara are far more dangerous than a fire in the present. They know that the time of their death is uncertain, and they understand what could happen after this life. They recognize that they are powerless before the force of karma and the mental afflictions; they see the danger of falling into the lower realms, the suffering even in the higher realms, and so on. Someone who really wants to achieve liberation would not interrupt their spiritual practice even to put out a fire. They view putting out the fire that is the cause of samsara to be more urgent and important. Their effort is entirely devoted to preventing rebirth in samsara due to karma and the mental afflictions. They work as hard as they can on this before they die. They are not attached to present temporary pleasures and happiness; they do not forget that their goal is everlasting freedom. Nāgārjuna tells us that we should make a similar resolve for there is no greater goal than that.

> 104. If your hair or clothing were to suddenly catch fire
> you would try to put it out immediately. But give that up
> and make an effort to end rebirth in samsara due to karma.
> There is no greater purpose than this.

It may seem foolish to advise people to not try to put out a fire. When we look at some of the great yogis of the past it looks like what they did was crazy. But from their perspective what we do is crazy. Śāntideva spoke pithily about your situation and what you should do about it.

> When you have produced diligence
> you should stabilize your mind in meditation.
> The person whose mind is always distracted
> lives between the fanged jaws of the mental afflictions.
> [*Introduction to the Practice of Bodhisattvas,* 8.1]

You are in a very dangerous spot if a predator has caught you in his fangs and is ready to clamp his jaws shut! The mental afflictions are like fanged jaws. Desire, pride, hatred, ignorance, jealousy, and so on are always ready to rise in your mind. They eat away at any mental strength that you might have and crush your positive resolve. The consequence is that you create samsaric karma. And, that karma results in all kinds of miserable experiences. Therefore, Śāntideva says you should always strive to "stabilize your mind in meditation."

In this context "meditation" doesn't mean just meditative concentration. It indicates being alert and mindful so that you don't fall under the power of the mental afflictions. In other words, meditation is to watch your mind. So, in order to meditate you don't have to sit on a cushion, unmoving, with your eyes closed. You still have to eat, sleep, and go to the toilet. The combination of your body and mind are like a boat that can take you across the ocean of samsara. You have to keep this boat in good repair for it to be useful. Your body requires protection from temperature variations; it needs food and drink; you need companions for assistance; and so forth. You care for your body so that you stay healthy and can practice. But in every situation, wherever you go, whatever you are doing, you should be aware of what your mind is doing. Is anger arising? Is desire arising? You should be aware of what you are about to say or do. This is the most powerful type of good practice. Being aware of your mind all the time is the way to begin gaining control of your samsaric rebirths.

Freedom from suffering only comes from the complete cessation of uncontrolled rebirth due to karma and the mental afflictions. We call this permanent cessation of samsara *nirvana*. In order to desire nirvana, in addition to seeing the defects of samsara you have to appreciate the benefits of your own liberation from it. So, what is nirvana like? Nāgārjuna says,

> 105. Pure ethical conduct, wisdom, and meditative stabilization
> lead to nirvana—immaculate peace and control.
> This state is ageless, deathless, eternal, and separate
> from earth, water, fire, air, and the sun and moon.

What makes nirvana something worth attaining? Nirvana means to have passed beyond sorrow or sadness permanently. It is naturally peaceful. This peace has two aspects: nirvana with remainder and nirvana without remainder. The first is the peace that you attain when you have completely gotten rid of all the mental afflictions through your practices of morality, meditation, and wisdom. You are still alive; you have the living breathing body you had while practicing. Your body is still an ordinary, impure, and physical phenomenon. But your mind is pure and free from karma and the mental afflictions; you have become an arhat. This is called nirvana with remainder. The "remainder" is your body that resulted from previous karma. Until you die you will have the contaminated aggregate of the body even though your mental aggregates were purified. After your death, you have both mental and physical purity; it is peace that is the complete stoppage of the contaminated aggregates. Rebirth is completely finished. This is nirvana without remainder.

The second quality of nirvana is that you are tamed, or you could say disciplined or controlled. Even before an arhat dies, when they are in nirvana with remainder, their sensory organs are under control. They still have physical and mental sensory perception, but they do not react the way that ordinary people do. They see, hear, eat, and so forth, but without any desire, hatred, jealousy, or other mental affliction. All their senses are calm and peaceful. Both nirvana with remainder and without remainder are without stains. They are like clean, clear water from which all muddy residues have been removed. Even those in nirvana with remainder have removed the stains of the mental afflictions. They have no desire, hatred, and so forth. They are not stirred up by ignorance, etc. Having removed the stains, they are immaculate.

When you achieve nirvana without remainder the verse states there will be no aging and death due to the power of karma and the mental afflictions. Nirvana's peace is inexhaustible and lasts forever. In other words, there is no going back to impure rebirth. Nirvana is the complete and permanent cessation of ignorance and the mental afflictions. In other words, nirvana is a cessation, not a physical state. You are free of the elements; you don't need sunlight or moonlight. Our ordinary world is reliant upon the elements, the sun, and the moon. We have an earthly body and senses. Our karma and mental afflictions toss us around and when the elements are out of balance we suffer. In contrast, emancipation is pure perfected wisdom. There is no potential for anything other than this perfect mind. This is the case for those who attain the final result of the Hinayana path—nirvana without remainder—as well as Mahayana practitioners who have attained buddhahood.

So you may wonder, how does a buddha help ordinary sentient beings? The enlightened mind has the ability to manifest into something physical in order to help others. Buddhas manifest in accord with the mental capacity of those they are trying to help. So sometimes they manifest as high bodhisattvas, sometimes as a human, and sometimes in other forms. Their bodies can look ordinary, but they are actually completely free from any ordinariness. They are not killed by disease, accidents, or any other polluted cause. There is a story about Asaṅga that illustrates this.

Around 900 years after the time of the Buddha, the Mahayana had almost disappeared from India. A widow, Asaṅga's mother, wanted the Mahayana teachings to survive. In ancient India it was traditional for a boy to take up the same profession as his father. But when the young Asaṅga asked his mother what his father's profession had been, she replied, "I didn't give birth to you so that you could take up your father's job. Your job is to study pure Mahayana Buddhism. Then you will spread it throughout the world." As he grew older Asaṅga wondered, "How can I do that? It is a huge job." He thought, "Maybe I could do it if I were to have a vision of the future buddha, the great bodhisattva Maitreya. He could give me all the Mahayana teachings."

Therefore, Asaṅga decided to do a lot of purification, preparatory practices, and ritual recitations in order to have a vision of Maitreya. He went off to an isolated place and did a three-year retreat. But after three years nothing had happened. All his hard work hadn't resulted in anything. He left his retreat, and on the road back to town he saw an old man holding the two ends of a cotton string. He was rubbing the string back and forth across a rock. Asaṅga asked, "What are you doing, old man?" "Oh," he said, "I'm trying to cut the rock." Asaṅga thought, "This old man has the courage to do something that seems impossible. How can he cut a rock with cotton string? I lack such courage. I shouldn't give up after three years. I should go back in to retreat."

This gave Asaṅga the courage to practice for three more years. But still nothing happened. So once again he left his retreat place. He saw water slowly dripping, drop by drop, from a cleft in a cliff face. Years of this slow drip had created a large hole in a boulder below. Asaṅga thought, "This water is dripping slowly and gently. It feels soft on my hand. But it has eroded a huge hole in the hard rock. I should try in the same way to gain a vision of Maitreya. I should go back."

He went back into retreat and did three more years of practices. So now it was nine years in all. But still nothing happened. He again left his mountain retreat. In a crack between some rocks, he saw a bird's nest. There was a bird coming in and out to feed her chicks. He noticed that the slabs of rock around the nest were smooth and shiny. He realized that the soft feathers of the bird's wings had smoothed the roughness of the rock. This too gave him courage. So, he went back into retreat for another three years.

Now, after twelve years of practice Asaṅga was completely exhausted. He came out of his retreat place. He saw an old female dog on the road.

Her rear legs had been badly injured, and the wounds were filled with maggots and worms. The dog was begging for food. When he saw this Asaṅga felt great compassion and love for the dog. He wanted to save her. He thought, "First I should remove the maggots and worms. But it wouldn't be good to kill the insects in order to save the dog." In order to give the maggots and worms something to eat so that they wouldn't die, he cut a piece of flesh out of his thigh. Now he had to move the worms and maggots to it. But they were so delicate, and his fingers were so rough. If he tried to pick up the worms and maggots with his fingers, he would crush them to death. He decided that only his tongue was soft enough to do the work of moving them from the dog to his piece of flesh. So, he stuck out his tongue, closed his eyes so he wouldn't see this disgusting sight, and leaned forward. But his tongue hit the ground. There was no dog. Maitreya was standing right there.

Asaṅga was a bit upset. He'd been working so hard for twelve years, and in frustration he said, "Your kindness is rather limited." Maitreya replied, "No, no. I was with you all the time, but your obstacles prevented you from seeing me directly." The old man with the string, the dripping water, the birds' wings, and the dog were all manifestations of Maitreya's wisdom and compassion. When, out of love and compassion, Asaṅga tried to help the dog, he created a tremendous amount of merit. This merit purified all the remaining obstacles that had prevented him from seeing the future buddha. Then Asaṅga was able to go to Tuṣita heaven and receive all the teachings. He realized the four realities for āryas. He had complete disgust with samsara. He saw how to free all sentient beings from samsara by fighting the causes of uncontrolled rebirth. When he returned to earth from Tuṣita he brought with him five scriptures that are known as the five books of Maitreya and taught them. He wrote commentaries on them and other books in order to teach others how to attain liberation.

Now that we have an idea about the value of nirvana, we look at the various descriptions of the means to attain it.

The Seven Branches of the Path to Enlightenment

The path to liberation comprises the techniques you employ in your spiritual battle against your enemy, the 84,000 mental afflictions. As I've explained, the Buddhist path system is divided into five sequential levels: the paths of accumulation, preparation, seeing, meditative cultivation, and no further training. On these five paths you progressively develop and refine the three types of higher spiritual training: pure ethical conduct, meditative concentration, and wisdom. These comprise the common path, the causes for liberation from samsara. The additional practices for the Mahayana path are incorporated into these five paths.

The first description of the path presented by Nāgārjuna—the seven branches of practice to attain enlightenment—is specific to the path of seeing. Why is a focus on this level of the path so important? Because it is on the path of seeing that a practitioner first has a direct realization of the true nature of reality. It is only upon attaining the path of seeing that a practitioner begins to remove the gross mental afflictions from the root. So, in one sense the practices on the path of seeing are the real cause for spiritual attainment. However, you can't jump to this level of practice, you need the foundation of the earlier paths, as described in earlier chapters of this book. Before the path of seeing, on the paths of accumulation and preparation, you reduce the mental afflictions by making them grow weaker and weaker until they are temporarily subdued. This is important and necessary. Although the techniques practiced on the first two paths do not permanently extirpate the mental afflictions, they are necessary precursors to a direct realization of ultimate reality. An initial realization of ultimate reality doesn't remove all the mental afflictions and ignorance simultaneously and instantly. Even after you attain the path of seeing, the mental afflictions are removed gradually, first the roughest mental afflictions and then, progressively, more and more subtle ones. A common analogy to this process is washing a particularly filthy item of clothing. You sequentially use different types of soap, water temperature, and so forth to clear away the surface layers of dirt so that you can remove the stains. In the context of the spiritual path, you first must subdue the mental afflictions, create merit, and prepare your mind. Then a direct realization of ultimate reality can begin removing the mental afflictions.

The essence of the path of seeing is wisdom seeing the nature of reality. However, the path of seeing is not just wisdom knowing reality; this alone is not enough. The seven branches are concomitant practices that reinforce wisdom. They are part of the cause that results in nirvana. They are called "the branches of enlightenment" because they accompany a realization of ultimate reality on the path of seeing. The seven branches have the same names as some of the practices that you do on the first two paths, the paths of accumulation and preparation. However, because the practices on the earlier paths only subdue the mental afflictions temporarily they are not considered to be part of the seven branches of the path to enlightenment. The seven branches of enlightenment are practiced with a direct realization of ultimate reality. Practiced this way they actually remove obstacles to nirvana and replace them with positive qualities. What are they?

> 106.	There are seven branches of the path to enlightenment:
> mindfulness, ascertainment of phenomena, diligence,
> joy, great agility, meditative concentration, and equanimity.
> These amass the merit needed to attain nirvana.

I will first explain these seven aspects of practice briefly to give you the context for a more in depth discussion of each one. (See chart in appendix 4.) Mindfulness is to continuously remember an object. The object here is the true nature of reality. Until you are on the path of seeing you remember your object one moment, and then you forget again. Second, ascertainment of phenomena is the wisdom that knows that the way phenomena appear is not the way that they really exist. This wisdom clearly distinguishes the difference between appearances and the reality of emptiness. Third, diligence is delight in engaging in virtuous actions. From the Buddhist perspective diligence only pertains to the pursuit of wholesome actions; it doesn't refer to the assiduous pursuit of evil activities. Fourth is joy. This is a pleasant mental feeling due to deep focus on the practice of virtue. It brings a feeling of pleasure to the body too. Fifth, agility is the flexibility of your mind and body so that you can use them to practice for as long as you wish—an hour, a day, or a week. Sixth, meditative concentration is single-pointed mental focus that is without distraction or falling into dullness for as long as you wish. The seventh branch is equanimity. This is not neutrality in terms of feeling happy or unhappy, or between desire and hatred, or between virtue and nonvirtue. Here equanimity pertains to the amount of effort needed to meditate. In this type of equanimity, you are neither too tight, energetic, and distracted, nor are you too loose, sleepy, and dull. Prior to attaining equanimity, you must make an effort to apply the appropriate antidote when either of the extremes arises. But when you are in equanimity you are free of the extremes of distraction and dullness; you can stay in meditation without any effort. You have the ability to just let your mind meditate.

Now we begin a more detailed discussion of each branch. Maitreya explains each of the limbs in *Ornament of the Mahayana Sutras*. First, he divides the seven limbs into five categories:

> The essential branch, the supportive branch,
> the branch of departure,
> the branch that is the benefit, and,
> the other three branches that are not mental afflictions.
> [*Ornament of the Mahayana Sutras*, 18.63]

Because mindfulness is the special quality of remembering and never forgetting the object, it is the "supportive branch." It is the cause, or source of all other meritorious virtues because it enables you to keep in your mind whatever you have learned. It is from this basis that you maintain your practice of virtue. Mindfulness keeps your mind precisely in place; you do not forget what you should be doing. Not only does it keep you from losing what you have, it also enables you to master what you have not yet learned and understood. Mindfulness is the basis of religious practice; it is recognizing what your mind is doing, no matter where you are, day or night, in a group or on your own. Is your mind going in a negative direction? If so, knock that down. If it is going in a positive way, cultivate that.

Śāntideva said,

> Someone making an effort to practice meditation
> should not mentally wander for even a moment.
> They should examine their mind,
> asking themselves, "What is my mind doing?"
> [*Introduction to the Practice of Bodhisattvas*, 5.41]

When you are practicing Dharma, you are primarily interested in controlling your mind, not in managing external situations. No matter how much you fight your external foes, you cannot win. Nevertheless, Śāntideva compared ordinary combat to using mindfulness as a weapon in your spiritual battle against the mental afflictions:

Just as an experienced warrior enters
a sword fight with his enemy,
I should protect myself from the mental afflictions' weapons
and skillfully control the enemy, the mental afflictions.
[*Introduction to the Practice of Bodhisattvas,* 7.67]

An experienced warrior has two tasks in battle: protecting himself
and killing his enemy. He doesn't just concentrate on killing his enemy.
If he did that he could be wounded and then not be able to do anything.
This is an analogy for Dharma practice. You are in a battle against the
inner enemy—your mental afflictions. Here you concentrate on both not
letting your mind be wounded by the mental afflictions and also in completely destroying them. Until you have controlled your mind, external
situations can disturb you and cause mental afflictions to arise. You need
to maintain your mindfulness, otherwise a small thing easily makes you
angry or desirous. This wounds your mind. You then engage in negative
actions. When your mind is stable, and you have mindfulness, you are
properly protecting yourself.

Maitreya said that mindfulness is critical for spiritual progress:

In order to master subjects not yet mastered
you must always engage in mindfulness.
[*Ornament of the Mahayana Sutras,* 18.58]

Maitreya compares each of the seven branches of practice to one of
the symbolic possessions of a universal emperor. He says that mindfulness
is like a universal emperor's precious wheel. A universal ruler's wheel is
not an ordinary man-made wheel. This wheel naturally arises from the
emperor's merit; the ruler could fly anywhere on this wheel and extend his
rule without opposition. Mindfulness is like this magical wheel because
by remembering the antidotes you can be victorious over any and all the
mental afflictions. This is extraordinary; without the wheel of mindfulness, you couldn't do this. It is the wheel of mindfulness that enables
you to conquer the mental afflictions and travel to liberation. The eight-
spoked wheel symbol is also used to represent the entirety of Buddha's
teaching, not just mindfulness as it does in the current context.

The second branch of practice, discernment of phenomena, is wisdom.

Wisdom is the "essential branch." It is wisdom that cuts out the mental afflictions; in that sense, wisdom is the principal and essential cause of liberation. From the perspective of functionality, wisdom is like a great elephant, another possession of a universal emperor. Ancient kings treasured elephants because they are very powerful. In Indian mythology, there is a great elephant in the heavens that carries the armies of the gods when they go into battle to destroy the demigods. Wisdom is like this powerful, destructive elephant because it annihilates your misapprehension of persons and other phenomena as being intrinsically existent. Maitreya said,

> All signs of conceptuality
> are destroyed by this discernment.
> [*Ornament of the Mahayana Sutras*, 18.18]

The third branch is diligence or effort. This is the effort to get where you want to go: liberation. It is diligence that pushes you to get out of samsara and attain emancipation. Therefore, it is called the branch, or cause, of "departure." Maitreya analogizes effort to a special horse, another of the symbolic possessions of ancient royalty. In ancient times, a good horse was the best way to get somewhere quickly. Effort will help you quickly attain the supramundane knowledges. Without diligence you cannot gain knowledge or realizations.

The fourth branch, joy, is the delight of those practicing on the path of seeing. They have joy in their realization and practice. This is the "beneficial limb" in that joy is the benefit of meditation practice. You see that what you have done is of great benefit. You feel happy about this. Maitreya uses the royal symbol of a precious jewel as an analogy for this. The glittering brightness of royal jewels gave rulers a particular kind of pleasure. When you have the light that is the direct realization of reality, it gives you joy. With this joy, you are motivated to increase your spiritual practice.

> Because it increases the light of the Dharma
> joy brings continual development.
> [*Ornament of the Mahayana Sutras*, 18.59]

Three of the seven branches of the path to enlightenment—great agility, meditative concentration, and equanimity—are in the category called "not being mental afflictions." A lack of mental afflictions can be looked at from three angles: the cause for a lack of mental affliction, where this lack of mental affliction exists, and the nature of being unafflicted. The first of the branches in the category, the fifth branch, called great agility, is considered to be a cause for a lack of mental afflictions. It is a suppleness, flexibility, or dexterity of the mind and body. Here your mind and body are in harmony, they hardly seem separate. Before the path of seeing, sometimes your mind is relaxed in meditation, but your body is not; sometimes your body is settled but your mind is not. This joint suppleness of mind and body is a cause for being undisturbed, unafflicted, and without suffering. Hence, it is one of the three limbs of being without mental afflictions. If you have this agility, the unpleasant circumstances resulting from the mental afflictions are destroyed. It makes you very comfortable. Comparing agility to the precious royal symbols, Maitreya says that agility is like a precious queen who provides bliss and happiness to the king. She removes all unpleasantness and discomfort.

> Because it frees you from all obstacles,
> you obtain bliss through agility.
> [*Ornament of the Mahayana Sutras,* 18.60]

The next branch, meditative concentration, is where you find a lack of mental afflictions. During meditative concentration there are no mental disturbances. In that sense, it is where no mental afflictions occur. If you remain in meditative concentration, you will progress on the path to liberation. It is the cause for going higher and higher, and becoming better and better. The comparison to the royal symbols is made to a minister who manages the people of the realm. Farmers, merchants, and workers provide all necessities for the country and the royal court. They make food, clothes, jewelry, and so forth. A skillful minister makes sure all this comes about. In a similar way, meditative concentration brings all desirable spiritual goals.

> Meditative concentration produces the result
> that is the object of your spiritual desire.
> [*Ornament of the Mahayana Sutras,* 18.60]

The last of the seven branches of enlightenment is equanimity. Equanimity is the third limb in the category of being without mental afflictions. Here equanimity refers specifically to the amount of effort required to maintain your meditation. It has the nature of being free of the extremes of too much effort and losing your concentration completely. Your effort is perfectly in balance. Maitreya analogizes equanimity to the royal symbol of the commander of the army. A commander is responsible for making sure the four divisions of the ruler's armed forces are trained, well supplied, and ready to go into action whenever the king wishes.

> Through equanimity, everything
> remains just as you wish.
> > [*Ornament of the Mahayana Sutras*, 18.61]

The Union of Śamatha and Vipaśyanā

Another way to describe how to achieve emancipation specifically in regard to the path of seeing is the union of wisdom—vipaśyanā—and the specific type of meditative concentration called śamatha. Śamatha is the ability of the mind to remain focused on an object of observation with complete freedom from distraction and mental laxity for as long as desired. This effortless mental flexibility and control is accompanied by physical and mental pliancy and bliss. (There is no word in English that accurately indicates this mental ability. A literal translation of the Tibetan as *calm abiding* or a gloss as *single pointed concentration* are too limited.)

Śamatha and vipaśyanā are two separate techniques, but when used together they result in emancipation. Note that in the next verse Nāgārjuna uses the broader term, meditative concentration, to indicate the subset of śamatha.

> 107. Without wisdom, there will be no meditative
> concentration.
> Without meditative concentration there is no wisdom.
> Someone who has them both shrinks cyclic existence
> to the size of an ox's hoof-print.

Meditative concentration alone, without wisdom, will not lead to complete emancipation. But without the mental concentration of śamatha, wisdom alone is dry and will not lead to emancipation. Both of them are necessary. They need to be practiced in union to remove the mental afflictions and attain emancipation. Tsongkhapa said,

> The effortless, flexible, and controlled mental focus of śamatha
>   alone
> isn't seen to have the ability to cut the root of samsara.
> Also, no matter how much you analyze using wisdom
> that lacks the tool of śamatha, the afflictions will not be
>   overcome.
> [*Condensed Points of the Stages of the Path*, 35]

Wisdom here refers to understanding the individual and general characteristics of all phenomenal things. Everything that exists has a conventional individual identity; for example, a body, a feeling, and a table all have their own characteristics. The four realities for āryas also have their own individual characteristics. If something didn't have its own characteristic identity, it wouldn't exist. For example, a rabbit horn—which does not exist at all—is simply imaginary, whereas things that exist are known though valid knowledge of their characteristics. Wisdom also includes the understanding of the general characteristics of phenomena. For example, all produced phenomena are impermanent; all contaminated things have the nature of suffering; and everything is empty of having a self. These are general characteristics that pertain to all phenomena in these categories. So, when you are examining the body, or any other phenomena, you must understand its individual characteristics and also its general characteristics. Within the general characteristics, you meditate on the reality of suffering, the reality of the cause of suffering, the reality of liberation, and the reality of the path to liberation You meditate on the relationship between the two sets of cause and effect: ignorance, the mental afflictions, and karma are the causes of suffering; the path is the cause of liberation. Wisdom understands what is right and wrong: it distinguishes the cause of suffering from the cause of nirvana. The highest wisdom of this latter type is the wisdom that understands emptiness, the ultimate reality of all things.

Without the highest kind of wisdom that understands reality you will not have real, proper meditative concentration. Why? The reason is that wisdom removes confusion, incorrect perceptions of subject and object, and wrong views. Only when you correctly understand phenomena exactly as they are, can you properly focus upon your object of concentration. Also, without śamatha—a mind that effortlessly and flexibly has controlled focus upon its object for as long as you wish—you cannot have a direct realization of emptiness. In order to understand ultimate reality clearly and directly you first need to develop conceptual understanding, in other words, inferential wisdom. You need śamatha to transform that conceptual understanding into a direct realization that properly understands ultimate reality. So, both meditative concentration and wisdom are necessary for attaining nirvana.

Any practitioner who has properly joined meditative concentration and wisdom in their practice can cross over the ocean of samsara and reach the shore of liberation. Their direct realization of emptiness dries out the ocean of samsara. For this practitioner, samsara has become very small; the former vast ocean is now as tiny as a puddle in the footprint of a cow. They can easily step over this puddle to cross to the other side. But the samsaric ocean is huge for those who do not have the union of meditative concentration and wisdom. This type of person still holds phenomena to be truly real in the way that they appear. That ignorance, holding things to exist in a way that they do not, gives rise to the other mental afflictions and karma. And that results in the ocean that is suffering rebirth.

Supreme wisdom is to directly, precisely, and exactly understand the lack of intrinsic existence of the self of persons and the self of phenomena. This lack of inherent existence—the two types of selflessness—is what we call emptiness. Only the wisdom understanding emptiness has the power to directly cut the root of samsara. Even bodhicitta, patience, love, compassion, the understanding of impermanence, and knowing the nature of suffering are not direct antidotes to samsara. These are good thoughts. They are meritorious and indirectly work as antidotes to samsara. However, they are indirect because the root of samsara is the ignorance that holds things to absolutely, ultimately, really, and truly exist. The other types of wisdom and positive attitudes are not the direct opposite of the ignorance that believes in intrinsic existence. Only the wisdom that directly understands that things do not exist this way can destroy it. Therefore, Dharmakīrti said in the *Commentary on Valid Cognition* (2.222ab), that to get rid of the apprehending egoistic view you must understand that the object of that egoistic view does not exist. In other words, you have to understand emptiness to eliminate the ignorance that is the root of cyclic existence. A direct realization of emptiness is like the sharp blade of the axe that cuts down a poison tree. But the blade needs a structural holder, a handle, and someone to use the axe for the tree to be cut down. The other meritorious attitudes, love and compassion etc., are like the other parts of the axe and the woodcutter who wields the axe. Meditative concentration is like the person who firmly wields the axe in the right place. Without that, the blade of the axe isn't effective. Thus, you can't say that concentration, love, compassion, and so forth do not cut samsara at all, even though they don't directly cut it out from the root. You need all these things together.

What does meditative concentration do? It temporarily subdues, reduces, or gives you some distance from the desire realm mental afflictions. Mātṛceṭa wrote in *Praise in Honor of One Worthy of Honor* that both Buddhists and non-Buddhists can develop meditative concentration. By joining that concentration to a form of wisdom that recognizes the faults and good qualities of successively lower and higher states of existence, non-Buddhists too can attain the highest state in samsara, the peak of existence in the noncorporeal realm. But because they have not eliminated the mental afflictions from the root, when the right conditions are present the mental afflictions arise again, just as in the depths of winter there are no flowers or green grass, but when conditions change in the spring, the seeds and roots of flowers and grass bring forth their results again.

> Those uninterested in your teachings
> are people blinded by ignorance.
> They may reach the peak of existence
> but suffering arises again, and existence continues.

> Followers of your teachings
> may not have attained those dhyānas,
> but they remove themselves from cyclic rebirth
> even under the eyes of the demons.
> [*Praise in Honor of One Worthy of Honor*]

You must be clear about what analytical meditation you join to śamatha. Sometimes people think that training in wisdom is only about attaining a realization of emptiness. But as you've seen, that is not the case. Only the highest form of analytical meditation combined with the meditative concentration of śamatha results in a direct understanding of emptiness. Practitioners who attain śamatha and train in developing the highest wisdom may not attain the dhyānas of the corporeal and noncorporeal realms. They don't use their śamatha to do the comparative analytical meditations that lead you up through the absorptions of the corporeal and noncorporeal worlds to the peak of existence. Instead, they use their meditative concentration to engage in the method to permanently eliminate the mental afflictions. We Tibetans say, you can attain nirvana even while demons are staring at you. This is referring obliquely to the story of how Mara tried to prevent the Buddha from attaining enlightenment. There are evil spirits that try to interrupt religious practice. But when you have a direct realization of emptiness, those spirits or demons cannot affect you.

Every meditation technique fits into the two categories of meditative concentration—here more specifically śamatha—and vipaśyanā, or wisdom. In the beginning you don't have perfect meditations of either type. However, this doesn't mean that when you don't have meditative concentration or a direct realization of emptiness you can't do anything. Before you master these two techniques there is much that you can and should do. You must accumulate lots of merit through the practice of the first of the three higher trainings. You practice ethical discipline because you need a good human life as a basis to develop meditative concentration and wisdom. Even the most beautiful cat or dog cannot develop these. However, most humans act like little cats playing with a dangling rope toy. A cat sees the toy moving. It believes there is something really there to catch, to eat, and to play with. We are similarly confused; we grasp things to be objectively real. So, we need the practice of ethical discipline not only to obtain a high rebirth; once you are human, ethical discipline gives you the room to develop meditative concentration and wisdom. There are different techniques to master in order to develop śamatha and wisdom. You study, learn, and practice them individually. Eventually you can join them together.

In summary, both wisdom and meditative concentration are important and necessary. Without the meditative concentration of śamatha, even the wisdom understanding ultimate reality is not able to cut the root of samsara. Wisdom is shaky without effortless, flexible and stable meditative concentration. And a focused stable mind isn't enough on its own to remove ignorance. Although wisdom is more crucial because it is the direct antidote, Śāntideva said that you should develop śamatha first.

> Having understood that vipaśyanā imbued with śamatha
> is what eradicates the mental afflictions,
> first you should strive to develop śamatha.
> This is accomplished with detachment from the world and joy.
> [*Introduction to the Practice of Bodhisattvas*, 8.4]

Most of the time your mind is attracted to worldly things. It cannot stay on your object of meditation because it is under the power of sensory desire. Your senses all focus outward; they are always attracted to their objects. Meditative concentration looks inward. When you are less attracted to worldly things you can focus your mind. As you practice śamatha you develop clarity, vividness, and the ability to stay calmly on a particular object. You are focused and peaceful. After developing śamatha, you use this ability to delve deeper and deeper into your analytical meditation. This makes your analytical meditation more and more powerful until eventually you have a direct realization of the true nature of reality.

Therefore, those who want to attain emancipation from samsara should first accomplish śamatha. This is what makes the mind suitable and flexible enough to investigate reality. Until you have śamatha your mind is stubborn and stiff because it is under the control of the mental afflictions. Those mental afflictions control you; you do not control your mind. After you have developed śamatha, you can meditate on the two kinds of selflessness: the object side of phenomenal things and the subject side of the person. But where do you start? Candrakīrti said,

> Mentally seeing that all afflictions and faults
> stem from the wrong view of the transitory composite,
> and realizing that the self is the object of this view,
> a yogi will engage in negation of this self.
> [*Entering the Middle Way*, 6.120]

The "transitory composite" is the five skandhas, or aggregates, that comprise your body and mind. They are momentary; not one of them lasts forever. They depend upon each other, upon parts, and upon causes and conditions. They are relative aggregations; they do not exist independently either as individuals or as a composite. That is reality. However, we have an innate wrong view of our aggregates. We see them as if they exist permanently, independently, and intrinsically in their own right without relying upon anything else. We act as if they will remain forever. The egoistic view—the wrong view of the transitory composite—doesn't analyze, it just feels that there is a real, independent *me* that is intrinsically self-existent and permanent. We believe it exists as it appears. All the other mental afflictions arise from this wrong view. Karma comes from the mental afflictions, and from karma all the faults of samsara arise. Your problems, misery, and suffering are faults that you have created. They are not produced from external sources.

Therefore, practitioners need to look at the real nature of the self and aggregates. Do they exist as the innate mind believes or not? No, they do not exist as they appear. How do you get the wisdom that understands this? You first have to recognize that the way you naively hold your self to exist is wrong. So, a practitioner will try to negate their erroneous concept of self using analytical meditation. Here it is very important to reiterate that the emptiness of the self or phenomena doesn't mean nothingness. It means that things don't exist intrinsically. If you don't understand that, you will fall into the mistaken views of nihilism or eternalism. To be free of the two extreme wrong views is the middle way or middle path. You realize that things don't ultimately exist, but that doesn't mean that they don't exist at all. They exist due to causes and conditions, they exist phenomenally, and relatively. There are many analytical meditations that help you to gain this understanding.

Giving Up Consideration of Purposeless Topics

Another way to look at the path is to consider what type of analytical meditations are not part of the path. There are some topics or viewpoints that are not worth considering. These are not helpful to meditate upon because they do not directly or indirectly lead to a diminishment and elimination of suffering. In fact, concentrating on these topics can prevent you from developing the wisdom that leads to liberation.

108. In the world there are fourteen unexpounded views.
The Buddha, kinsman of the sun, declared that
you should not contemplate these
for they will not serve to pacify your mind.

The Buddha declined to answer questions about certain positions posed by non-Buddhist teachers. He kept silent; he didn't say whether that viewpoint was positive or negative. Why? It wasn't because the Buddha didn't know the answer. It was because he understood that these non-Buddhists had a firm belief in an absolute permanent self, and with that view they asked fourteen questions about the qualities of the self. If the Buddha said there was no self, they would have concluded that there was no self at all, and would have fallen into nihilism. If the Buddha said there was a self, but that it did not exist in any of the ways they proposed, they still would hold the self to be absolute and permanent in some manner. The Buddha knew that whatever he said about these issues would be completely misunderstood and lead them to one of the extremes. So, the best he could do for them was to remain silent. Buddhists say his silence is proof of his omniscience. Non-Buddhists might say, "Oh, that Buddha doesn't know much! Look, there are fourteen topics he couldn't discuss." Nāgārjuna specifically says this in another text.

When asked if the world has an end or not,
the Buddha, the conqueror, remained silent.
He didn't speak because he understood that
the questioners could not understand profound reality.

Thus, those who are wise understand
that the omniscient one is all knowing.
[*Precious Garland* 1.73–4ab]

The *Net of Brahma Sutra* in the sutra collection called *Long Discourses* lists these fourteen views as four groups of questions, the first three covering four views, and the last covering two:

1. Are the self and the world permanent, impermanent, both permanent and impermanent, or neither permanent nor imper-

manent? This refers to both your aggregates and the external world in the past. In other words, are your aggregates and the world that existed in the past eternal? Not eternal? Both eternal and not eternal? Or neither eternal nor noneternal?

2. The next group of four refers to the same ideas but in relation to the future. Are your future aggregates and the future external world permanent? Or are they impermanent and will come to an end? Are they both permanent and impermanent? Or neither permanent nor impermanent?

3. This next grouping is in connection to the attainment of nirvana. Will the Buddha continue to exist and come again after his body dies? Will he not come again? Will he both continue and not continue? Will he neither continue nor not continue.

4. Last, we have two questions about the soul, or you could say the self or life essence, and its relationship to the body. Are the self and the body exactly the same? Or are the self and the body completely different.

Actually, all of these questions can be discussed. It just wasn't helpful for those non-Buddhist questioners at that time because of their strongly held beliefs. All fourteen positions are wrong views. On the surface it might seem that some are right and their opposites are wrong. For example, the self and world are not permanent, therefore they are impermanent. That seems right, doesn't it? However, the Madhyamaka view is that these are questions about the ultimate nature of reality. From that perspective, we cannot say that any of these fourteen views are ultimately, intrinsically, or absolutely the case. It is incorrect to say that the self and the world are ultimately and intrinsically impermanent. The self and phenomena are not ultimately and intrinsically permanent, impermanent, both, or neither. Nothing exists intrinsically.

This can seem like a word puzzle. It is something you should think about more. A way to approach it is to consider that the self or soul is simply designated based on the aggregates. People are composed of aggregates, a combination of the body and the various aspects of the mind. The self or soul is just a name attributed to this combination. For example, John. There is no independent John-ness. But we label a combination of body and mind as John. However, there is nothing fundamentally essentially there that is John. Nonetheless, conventionally there is a person called John. A car is the same. There is an engine, a roof, electric system, windows, wheels, etc. We call this combination a car. A car does exist relatively and dependently designated upon all these parts. But we incorrectly attribute some car-ness to this and assume the car is independently and intrinsically real. The self, whether a person or an object, is dependent upon aggregates. The aggregates are also dependent and relative to each other. Since they arise in dependence, they do not intrinsically, naturally, and ultimately exist by way of their own nature. So, while conventionally it is correct to say that phenomena are impermanent, they do not intrinsically exist as something impermanent. Nor do they intrinsically exist as something permanent, both, or neither. Therefore, in his most famous work on the Madhyamaka view, Nāgārjuna said,

> Whatever arises dependently
> is peace by virtue of its very nature.
>   [*Fundamental Verses on the Middle Way*, 7.16]

In other words, anything that is dependent on parts, causes, conditions, and so forth, is without intrinsic existence. It is pure and peaceful in the sense that it is free of inherent, intrinsic, or ultimate existence. Therefore, a base for these imaginary qualities of intrinsic permanence and so forth simply doesn't exist. You do not get any benefit from thinking about the qualities of something nonexistent. It is like thinking about the sharpness, size, and prettiness of a rabbit's horns. Contemplation of these questions about the self and phenomena just leads to wrong views. Thinking that way is like inviting a poisonous snake to bite you. The poison of those wrong views will pervade your mind. Your mental afflictions will arise and increase. You will not find the everlasting peace of nirvana by thinking about these topics. If you approach meditation—whether analytical or meditative concentration—in the wrong way you will misunderstand emptiness in such a way that you fall into the two extremes. This will be a great disaster.

So, what is it right to concentrate upon? You should think about topics that will benefit you. If you want to eliminate suffering and develop wisdom you should think properly about the causes of samsaric suffering and the causes to eliminate that suffering. To explain this the Buddha taught the twelve links of dependent origination in both the forward and reverse order.

The Twelve Links of Dependent Origination

The twelve links of dependent origination describe our samsaric lives from time without beginning up to now and into an unlimited future. Dependent origination is the essential teaching that must be understood in order to become liberated from samsara. When you understand the forward and reverse progression of the twelve links you eliminate ignorance, the cause of samsara. Without ignorance, none of the other links can arise. Thus, you need to learn the forward and reverse progression. Then you analyze them. Then if you meditate on them, you will achieve perfect peace.

What are the twelve links? We will talk about each one in detail, but first here is a summary.

> 109. The Buddha said that from ignorance comes karma;
> from that comes consciousness; from that comes the
> mind and body, from that come the six faculties;
> from these six come contact.

> 110. From contact, sensation arises;
> based on sensation, craving arises;
> from craving, appropriation comes to be;
> from that comes existence; from existence comes birth.

> 111. When there is birth, there will be sorrow, sickness, aging,
> losing what you desire, the fear of death, and so forth.
> There will be a huge mass of suffering.
> By stopping birth, all this will cease.

The twelve links, from ignorance to aging and death, are the mechanics of how samsaric beings cycle in samsara. Each link depends upon the prior link; this is the forward progression. It is the mental affliction side of the twelve links. How can you stop the arising of samsara? How are these links stopped? In order to stop one, you need to stop the preceding one. For example, when you eliminate the link of birth, the link of aging, sickness, and sorrow cannot arise. The reverse progression of the twelve links shows the purification side of causality. This is how you attain nirvana. If you eliminate just some of the links, you might get temporary happiness in the upper realms of the desire realm or the two higher realms. But this won't be permanent emancipation from suffering; it is pleasure that doesn't last. Samsara is like a poison tree. If you cut back its branches and trunk to ground level, no tree will be evident for a while. But if you don't get rid of all the roots, the poison tree will sprout again. What is the root of all the suffering of rebirth? Ignorance. Thus, to get out of samsara permanently you look at the links in reverse order through to the elimination of ignorance. If you remove ignorance, then karma cannot arise nor can any of the other links follow. In short, if you eliminate ignorance all the other links will cease.

The Buddha summarized this is the *Sutra on Dependent Arising:*

> O monks! If this exists, then that will come to be. Because this arises, that will arise. It is like this: conditioned by ignorance, activity—in other words, karma—comes to be. Conditioned by birth, there will be the arising of aging, death, sorrow, lamentation, an unhappy mind, and anxiety. Thus, this huge mass of suffering comes to be.

That was the forward progression. Now the Buddha describes the reverse progression:

> Likewise, by ceasing ignorance, action will cease. When birth ceases, aging death, sorrow, lamentation, an unhappy mind, and anxiety will cease. In this way, this huge mass of suffering will come to an end.

This is logical. It is like saying that if there is a fire, there will be smoke. That is a forward progression. From the conventional perspective, this is usually the case. However, there can be a fire without smoke. For that reason, Dharmakīrti says that you can't use a cause as logical reason in a syllogism. You can say that if the causes are present, it is suitable and possible for a result to arise, but the causes do not prove that the result will definitely occur. For example, is it definite that a farmer will get a good harvest if he removes stones from his field, puts down fertilizer, plants seeds, irrigates, and weeds, all at the right time? No, something could happen—hail, a flood, a freeze, and so forth. But for a crop to grow well, you do need all those causes. Dharmakīrti says there are only three types of valid logical reasons: proof by the effect, proof by identity, and proof through the absence. For example, if you see smoke (the effect), even if you don't see a fire (the cause), you can infer with certainty that there is a fire because without a fire there could not be any smoke. Or, if there is no fire (an absence), there will be no smoke. These are both correct logical reasons. This is the reasoning underlying the reverse progression of the twelve links.

Śāntideva summarized the cycle of the twelve links and said that it is extremely important to understand it.

> Having been trapped by the mental afflictions
> you are snared by rebirth, and
> the lord of death is ready to take you.
> How could you not be aware of your situation?
> [*Introduction to the Practice of Bodhisattvas,* 7.4]

We create karma due to mental afflictions. That is the first trap. Based on that karma you are reborn in one of the six realms, a second trap. You cannot stay as long as you wish in a particular birth; the lord of death always comes. When you will die is not definite. Sometimes you have a very short life. Sometimes it is longer. Some die in utero. Some children die. But even a long life eventually ends in death. We are like animals that are fenced in and about to be butchered. There is nothing the animals can do; they are trapped. If you think about your situation, you will see it is just like this. As soon as you are born it is like you are on death row. You don't know when you will die, nor do you know where you will end up after death. Therefore, every day when you get up in the morning you should think about this. This isn't imagining a fiction. It is reality.

Tsongkhapa also stressed the importance of understanding dependent arising:

If you do not possess the wisdom that understands reality,
even if you have developed renunciation and bodhicitta
you cannot cut the root of samsara.
So, strive in the method to understand dependent arising.
                    [*The Three Principal Aspects of the Path*, 9]

Dependent arising and emptiness are not exactly the same. When you understand one it helps you to understand the other. Understanding that everything is relative and dependent helps you to understand the emptiness of intrinsic existence. Understanding the lack of intrinsic existence helps you to understand that everything is dependent upon causes and conditions. Dependent arising is relative, phenomenal reality; it is how experiences occur in samsara. Emptiness is ultimate reality; it is the lack of intrinsic, absolute, independent existence.

Now we will go into each the twelve links in a bit more detail. You may find the chart in appendix 5 a helpful summary as we go along.

The fundamental root of samsara is ignorance. Thus, it is the first link. Ignorance isn't merely not knowing how the self and all phenomenal things actually exist. Ignorance is also perceiving the self and phenomena in the wrong way and then believing that they exist in that way. We give a name to things that are dependent upon causes, conditions, and parts, and then hold to that named thing as something truly real and permanent. From the Madhyamaka point of view, ignorance in the context of the twelve links is the wrong view of the transitory composite. It is the egoistic view that you—your I or your self—have some kind of inherently real intrinsic existence. Based on looking at your aggregates of body and mind, you are sure that you are an independent entity. You have the egoistic conception, "Me. I really, absolutely exist." Once you have that view, then you become possessive of your body, your possessions, your friends, your country, and so forth. You think of things as *mine*. In this context I am not talking about the ignorance that conceives the possessed objects as intrinsically existent. I am talking about two aspects of the selfish egoistic view. First you think and feel, "I really exist; I am more special than anyone else." Then based on that you think of yourself as the possessor of many things; you possessively think, "This is mine." You get angry if someone insults your body, you think others' bodies are better or worse than yours, you get jealous, prideful, avaricious, frustrated, attached, and have so many other feelings. Thus, when you have ignorance—this wrong way of apprehending reality—the other mental afflictions arise. Therefore, ignorance is the root cause of suffering.

The egoistic view of an intrinsically existent self is neither virtuous nor nonvirtuous. Ignorance itself is qualitatively neutral because it can serve as the base for both virtuous and nonvirtuous states of mind. But this neutral apprehension of yourself as having intrinsic existence gives rise to the derivative mental afflictions. Together ignorance and the mental afflictions are causes in that they are suitable for propelling you to do something. In other words, ignorance pushes you to engage in action. Even virtuous activities—for example, the analytic meditations that result in rebirth in the upper realms, practicing generosity, and so forth—have as their foundation a subtle form of the egoistic view. All your virtuous actions are rooted in the idea of I or me. Your motivation is that you want peace and happiness; it is all about you. Even your motivation to help others is based deep down on the egoistic view. It is good karma, but it is contaminated—or you could say influenced—by ignorance. It is only after a realization of the reality of selflessness that good karma is uncontaminated by ignorance. But for now, before you have a direct realization of emptiness, all your actions are contaminated by ignorance.

The second link is called karma, or activity. This is karma contaminated by the egoistic view. This link is specifically referring to projecting or propelling karma. It is an action that will propel you into a new rebirth when all the conditions are suitable and present. The suitable conditions for the ripening of a specific projecting karma may not occur for eons. A projecting karma is like a seed. When you plant a seed, a plant doesn't pop up immediately. There have to be certain conditions for the seed to germinate and sprout. The conditions, or actualizing causes, for the seed to sprout, always occur immediately prior to germination. The second link is not referring to the actualizing karmic causes. They will be explained later as the eighth and ninth links.

There are three classes of propelling karma: virtuous, nonvirtuous, and invariable. Virtuous and nonvirtuous karmas are variable. Variable karmas are causes for results in the desire realm. Although we commonly say that negative karma leads to birth in the lower realms, and virtuous karma leads to birth in the upper realms, this isn't always the case. Sometimes the result of positive actions ripens in the lower realms. For example, rebirth as a dog is the result of negative action. But a pet dog may be well fed, given treats, a bed, love, and taken to see a veterinarian when it is sick. These nice results in the animal realm arise from virtuous karma. Or you may take a human rebirth as result of virtue, but you may become physically or mentally ill, be disparaged, or become poor. These unpleasant human experiences are the results of negative karma. Or your human experiences may be the results of virtuous karma; for example, being healthy, well liked, and successful. While variable karma causes rebirth and experiences in the desire realm, invariable meritorious karma is the cause to be born in the corporeal and noncorporeal realms. Once you take birth in the dhyānas and absorptions, the result of that good karma is fixed, it doesn't change. There is no mental or physical pain in the two upper realms of samsara. There is invariable, or unchangeable, samsaric peace and happiness—but only for as long as that life lasts. This isn't the ever-lasting peace of nirvana or enlightenment. Every rebirth in samsara has ignorance and the mental affliction of desire as its root cause.

Completing any of the three types of propelling karmas leaves behind an impression or potential. In other words, when all four factors of an intentional action are present, a seed that will bring about a good or bad result in the future is created. Where is this nonmaterial seed left? It is left in the mind. So, the third link is consciousness. Here consciousness is not one of the five sense consciousnesses nor is it just any aspect of mental consciousness According to the Yogācāra school, the other main Indian Mahayana school beside the Madhyamaka, the aspect of mind that stores karmic seeds is the storehouse consciousness, the *ālayavijñāna*. Other Buddhists who are not adherents of the mind-only doctrine say that karma is deposited in a consciousness that continuously flows moment by moment, from the moment of conception to the moment of death, and then to the next rebirth. This is a neutral consciousness; in itself it isn't positive or negative. It is a simple and continuous flow of moments of mind. This neutral consciousness has two aspects: causal and resultant. Causal consciousness is where the karmic seeds are deposited and held as potentials until they meet the right conditions to ripen into results. This consciousness carries those potentials throughout your life, into your next life, and into future lives, until they ripen. No action is wasted. The Vaibhāṣika Abhidharma says that the resultant consciousness is the primary consciousness of the first moment of a new rebirth. In the context of explaining the third of the twelve links, consciousness refers only to the aspect of causal consciousness. The aspect of resultant consciousness at the first moment of rebirth is part of the next link, mind and body.

The first three links—ignorance, propelling karma, and the causal consciousness with its predispositions—are causes that combine to affect your future rebirths. After death and the intermediate state, a prior stream of consciousness enters a particular mother's womb, propelled by the power of a projecting karma contaminated by ignorance. The moment of human conception is when this consciousness joins with the physical combination of a sperm and an egg. All three—consciousness, sperm, and egg—are necessary for conception. Conception, the first result among the twelve links, is the fourth link. Its appellation, "mind and body," refers to the five aggregates. The physical aggregate is the sperm united with the egg. The material combination of a sperm and egg has the nature of the great four elements—earth, water, fire and air, along with their derivative properties of color, shape, taste, smell, sound, and touch and so forth. The other four aggregates, the various forms of primary and secondary concomitant consciousnesses, feelings, and predispositions, are all nonphysical, and are identified as mind. The name of this link has typically been translated as "name and form." But the English term "form" is not correct, for in this context the Tibetan word *zug* (*gzugs;* Sanskrit, *rūpa*) doesn't refer to an object of visual consciousness; it is referring to the body at the moment of conception. Further, the old translation term "name" is also misleading. A name is a word or label. But here the term refers to the four mental aggregates that are the basis for later identifying a person by name. The fourth link refers only to the very moment of conception when the combination of the body and mind first comes to be.

The development of an embryo's physical sensory organs and the mental organ into six functional faculties is the fifth link. The six organs are the subjective aspect of experience. Consciousness is already present in the fourth link, but the mental organ was not yet fully developed. You have to have organs in order to be fully able to experience pleasant or unpleasant sensations, to be able to engage in activities, and have other qualities. There are three things necessary for an experience. You need a sensory organ, like an eye; that organ's corresponding consciousness, in this case a visual consciousness; and an object, a form that can be seen. When these three come together, you see something. Therefore, the next link, the sixth, is contact of these three. Contact refers to the objective side of experience. Continuing with our example of sight, whatever you see, whether it is unattractive, attractive or neutral, leads you to experience some sort of sensation, the seventh link. An attractive object leads to a pleasant feeling; an unattractive object leads to an unpleasant or miserable feeling. The positive, negative, or neutral feelings you have from birth to death are the final result of the first three causes.

Things don't just stop when you have a feeling. When you experience a pleasant feeling, desire or attraction arises; you don't want to lose it and you want more. If you experience a negative feeling, you desire the opposite; you want to be separated from that sensation. In general, throughout life these desires lead you to actually do something. Either you desire something so strongly that you do anything to get it and keep it; or you desire to have the opposite experience so strongly that you get very angry and do whatever you can to push it away. In the context of the twelve links, the desires that arise from sensation, the seventh link, refer specifically to those that arise at the time of death. First there is craving, the eighth link. From craving comes an even stronger form of desire called appropriation, the ninth link. Together, craving and appropriation prepare the activation of a strong prior karmic seed. To germinate a strong prior karmic seed into a rebirth, the necessary conditions are the actualizing causes of craving and grasping close to the moment of death. The karmic seed—link two—is like a farmer's seed that was planted earlier. Craving and appropriation—links eight and nine—are like the moisture, warmth, and everything else it needs for germination. When these three come together, they will immediately, with no interruption, result in your next life. Therefore, the coming together of these three causes is given the name of their result, existence, the tenth link. Your next life hasn't arisen yet, but it is almost there. It is ready to come about.

Your next life arises and develops in the same way described in the earlier links. But here we abbreviate that process and call the eleventh link, birth. The moment of conception is birth; the very next moment you begin to age, experience sickness, undergo the sorrow of not getting what you want, and you will eventually die. All these together are together the twelfth link, aging and death.

The twelve links are a complex chain of interwoven sets of causes and effects. While you are experiencing one set of results, you are creating the causes for another set of results. You may wonder how long it takes to complete a set of the twelve links. A single cycle of the twelve links is most often described as occurring over the course of three lives. Take your life for example. Your life is the result of the first set of three causes—links (1) ignorance, (2) propelling karma, and (3) causal consciousness—that were created in a prior life. Your current human life comprises seven links: four results and three causes. This life began with conception and then development in utero—links (4) mind and body, and (5) the six faculties. Then when your sensory and mental organs and faculties were complete, your subjective sense faculties, consciousness, and objects come together as link (6) contact. You experience this contact as pleasant, unpleasant or neutral—link (7) sensation. These feelings are the final result of this life. Feelings are how you evaluate your life as being good or bad. Up to this point, you have had one set of causes and results. Now you begin another set of causes because your feelings about your experiences result in desire, its corollary anger, and the other mental afflictions. At the time of your death the two types of desire—links (8) craving and (9) appropriation— come together with a prior karma to make link (10) existence. This joining of three causes will immediately result in another rebirth, a third life. This life comprises the last two links of (11) birth and (12) aging and death.

Thus, there are six causes and six effects among the twelve links that occur over the course of three different lives. These three lives are not necessarily sequential. In this life at the time of death you will create the actualizing causes—desire, appropriation, and existence—that combine with a propelling karma that results in your next life. So, your current life and the next life are definitely consecutive because of the actualizing causes. Similarly, the actualizing causes for the life you have now were created in your immediately prior rebirth. However, it is not definite when the propelling causes for your present life and your next life were created. The life during which you created the propelling causes—ignorance, karma, and consciousness—for your present life and your next life could have been created in any prior lifetime from time without beginning. The six results are also experienced over two lives: according to the presentation of the twelve links, four results are in the current life, and two in the next life. From this explanation it may seem like the causes for this life and the next life are different. And it may seem that the results described as this life and those described for the next are different. But remember that this is a complex and extended cycle. During a life, while you are experiencing the results of prior causes, you are creating more causes for future lives. That is why for explanatory purposes, and to reduce repetition, these causes and results are explicitly separated into two sets that occur over the course of three lives. The explicit explanation of this is found in the *Rice Seedling Sutra.*

It is implicit, and important to understand, that every life is the result of six causes that were created before that rebirth; and within every life you experience six results. So, you can talk about the twelve links pertaining to just your current life, but they are from different sets of the links. The six causes for your current life are the first group of three projecting causes (ignorance, projecting karma, and consciousness) from some past life—the immediately prior life or a lifetime from eons ago—and also the second group of three actualizing causes (craving, appropriation, and existence) from the immediately prior life that led without interruption to your present rebirth. Every life also has all six results: from mind and body up to aging and death. Four of these are called projected results because they are the effects of the projecting karma; two of those are actualized results because they are the effects of the actualizing karma. Thus, every life has its own complex set of twelve links that is a combination of two sets of causes and results.

It is through understanding the twelve links that you become convinced of the existence of past and future lives. There is no need to prove the present; you know you are here. But from the present life you can logically infer the existence of past and future lives. In this life you are creating more propelling karma that will ripen eventually as another life. At the time of death, you create actualizing karma that will immediately result in a rebirth. These causes and effects go on continuously without interruption. It is like the ring of light you see when you whirl a sparkler or a lit torch at night. Where is the beginning? Where is the end? You can't see it. You see a complete ring, but it is really a set of discrete moments. This doesn't mean there is no end to saṃsara. But you should understand that if things continue as they have been up until now, the cycle will continue.

Nāgārjuna put it this way:

> Two arise from three.
> From two come seven.

> from seven come three once again.
> The wheel of existence revolves again and again.
> > [*Verses on the Essence of Dependent Arising*]

What are these numbers referring to? The twelve links of dependent origination include three basic things: your mental afflictions, karma, and the result of these two—a suffering rebirth. Mental afflictions, karma, and their results are a cyclic chain that goes around and around. The "three" in the first line of the verse are the links that comprise the mental afflictions: ignorance (link 1), craving (link 8), and appropriation (link 9). The "two" are the links that are karma: propelling karma (link 2) and actualizing karma—in that existence (link 10) is the immediate cause for the next rebirth. The seven are the usual six links that are counted as results: mind and body (link 4), six faculties (link 5), contact (link 6), feeling (link 7), birth (link 11), and aging and death (link 12). In addition to these Nāgārjuna includes consciousness (link 3). Here consciousness refers only to the resultant consciousness. In summary, from the three mental afflictions come two types of karma. From these two types of karma come seven results. As you are experiencing the seven results, the three mental afflictions arise again. This is how the cycle of suffering rebirth goes around. This is dependent origination.

How do you gain freedom from this cycle of suffering? Again, we look at the twelve links because they explain the two types of causality that must be understood: what causes suffering and what causes the elimination of suffering. Through thinking about these properly, you will come to see the ultimate nature of reality.

> 112. Dependent origination is the most cherished and profound
> > teaching in the treasury of the Buddha's instruction.
> > Whoever sees this perfectly sees the Buddha,
> > the supreme knowledge of reality.

There are two realities: ultimate and phenomenal. Generally, these are not identical. However, understanding emptiness through dependent origination is often said to be seeing the reality of nirvana. Someone who understands dependent origination knows that everything only exists dependently. There is nothing additional; nothing exists by way of its own independent intrinsic nature. Seeing this is to see the perfection of buddhahood; the truth body of the Buddha, or *dharmakaya*. The dharmakaya has two aspects: the subject side—perfect wisdom or gnosis; and the object side—what is realized, that the essential nature of everything is the emptiness of inherent existence. The essence of buddhahood is the highest purity of mind that understands ultimate reality without any obstacles. A buddha sees the ultimate nature of reality as clearly as you see something in the palm of your hand. So, the nature of a buddha is the dharmakaya, and this is not different from understanding the reality of dependent origination.

Dependent origination is the most cherished teaching because it is the essence of all the teachings in the scriptures. Because you gain perfect realization of reality through knowledge of dependent origination, it is an explanation of the highest wisdom. Dependent origination is the most profound teaching because when you understand ultimate reality your realization is free of the four extremes of arising. When you incorrectly think things inherently exist, there are four possible ways that things could arise: things arise from their own inherently existent self; things arise from an inherently existent other cause; things arise from both an inherently existent self and an inherently existent other; things arise without any cause whatsoever. Each of these four extremes are incorrect; the only correct view is that everything is dependent. This is very difficult to understand; in that sense, it is profound.

The Buddha taught dependent origination based on the example of a rice seedling. A seed becomes a sprout through a complicated process of dependent causation. We usually don't think that way. We think a real, inherently existent, seed produces a sprout in and of itself. The Buddha said,

> Whoever properly knows dependent origination, knows the
>   Dharma.
> Whoever properly knows the Dharma, knows the Tathāgata.
> [Rice Seedling Sutra 1.4]

This statement isn't about inferential knowledge of dependent origination. It is referring to a direct realization of reality on the path of seeing. You may have a few questions here. Is a realization of dependent origination and emptiness the same? Does this literally mean that when you have a direct realization of emptiness you also have knowledge of buddha? Is the object of ultimate knowledge both emptiness and buddha? The answer to all these questions is, "No, not exactly." When you see the true nature of all phenomena you recognize that the ultimate nature of everything is the same: the emptiness of inherent existence. In that sense, your ultimate nature and buddha's ultimate nature are the same. Conventionally, phenomenally, they are different.

Only the Buddha taught how to understand dependent origination and emptiness. Tsongkhapa praised the Buddha on the basis of this most powerful teaching.

> Among teachers, the one who teaches dependent origination,
> among wisdom, the knowledge of dependent origination.
> Like Indra, the victorious lord of the world,
> you alone are supreme, no one else has this exalted wisdom.
> [*Praise of Dependent Origination*, 37]

Through comprehending dependent origination you come to understand the reality of suffering and the reality of the cause of suffering. These are the first two of the four realities for āryas. Now we move on to a discussion of the latter two of the four realities for āryas: the reality of cessation and the reality of the path to cessation. In this regard Nāgārjuna presents the eightfold ārya path.

The Eightfold Path of the Āryas

The next verse lists the elements of the eightfold path. In order to make the Tibetan meter of the verse work, the order of the eight parts of the path is different from what you may have previously heard.

> 113. The eight limbs of the path are
> right view, livelihood, effort, mindfulness,
> concentration, speech, activity, and right thought.
> Meditate upon these in order attain peace.

This is a very common way to conceive of the path. The eight limbs encompass the three higher trainings of ethical conduct, concentration, and wisdom. The three higher trainings are taught at the beginning of your practice of the path and on the ārya path after you attain the path of seeing up until you attain enlightenment. On the path of cultivation, often called the path of meditation, there is basically nothing other than these three higher trainings. Therefore, the eightfold path is presented in conjunction with the path of cultivation.

In regard to the three higher trainings, the *Question of Brahma Sutra* says,

> The root should be very firm.
> In a peaceful mind there is joy.
> As for the right view and the wrong view,
> possess the first and avoid the latter.

The root, or basis, of the path is training in the ethical conduct of body, speech, and mind. If you keep your body, speech, and mind away from negative conduct, and maintain wholesome conduct, your mind will be suitable for developing a high level of concentration. This will bring you peace in the present, and finally, when combined with wisdom, it will bring the peace of liberation. In general, we say that wisdom is to have the right view. There are two types of views: right and wrong. Right views are, for example, the view understanding the two realities, the four realities for āryas, and so forth. Wrong views include holding the self and phenomena to be truly existent—in other words, that things exist as they appear—that there is no causality, and that there is no buddhahood or nirvana. You should strive to have the right view and to eliminate the wrong views. A view isn't just looking at something or simply having blind faith. It is seeking out a true understanding so that your analysis leads to an unshakeable conviction. The ultimate right view of a superior, or ārya, is a direct realization understanding emptiness. The conventional right view is understanding karmic causality. Both are very important.

The eightfold path fits into the three higher trainings as follows. Ethical discipline refers to physical and verbal actions, so it encompasses three parts of the eightfold path: right livelihood, right speech, and right action. The higher training of meditative concentration includes two parts of the eightfold path: right mindfulness and right meditative concentration. Right view and right thought are the parts of the higher training in wisdom. That leaves one more, effort. Effort is diligence, the opposite of laziness. Effort is part of all three of the higher trainings.

You are practicing the eightfold path on the path of cultivation. The lower schools following the Abhidharma system say that when you attain the level of the ārya path, all eight limbs occur when you are engaged in deep meditation on emptiness or the four realities for āryas. In their view, this form of meditation is a combination of uncontaminated good conduct, concentration, and wisdom. Thus, the higher trainings of ethical discipline, meditative concentration, and wisdom all occur in this meditation.

Now to explain these eight parts of the path in a bit more detail. The higher training of wisdom includes the right view and right thought. These two are different. Right view is the wisdom that understands reality. This arises for the first time as a direct realization of emptiness on the path of seeing. The nature of the wisdom referred to as right view is an understanding of reality that you have directly realized in meditation. When you understand the right view, you want to accurately and appropriately explain to others what you have realized. In order to explain to others what you have understood, you have to engage in a thought process. Right thought is this conceptual process. It includes your motivation to say something. It refers to the thought preceding speech; it is thinking about what to say and how to say it.

Speech can be revelatory to others or nonrevelatory to others. If you say something and someone hears it, that is revelatory speech. Nonrevelatory speech occurs during a yogi's meditation on reality. At that time, they don't say anything out loud, so their speech isn't heard by anyone. However, during their meditation on reality a subtle part of speech occurs when yogis think about how to explain their experience. Therefore, this type of nonrevelatory speech is considered to be right speech in the context of the eightfold path.

Right action is to avoid wrong actions of body, speech, and mind. Although verbal actions are mentioned here too, it is not the same as right speech. As part of this aspect of the path, you avoid wrong speech and engage in positive verbal actions during the post-meditation period. In meditation you are primarily engaging in the practices of concentration and wisdom. That too is considered to be engaging in right action at that time.

Right livelihood is living in a way that is not harmful to others. It means you should eat, drink, and use the things you need for your body in accord with what the Buddha taught. The way you live should be in accord with the Dharma.

Diligence is to make effort in all of these.

The last two parts of the eightfold path are part of the higher training in meditative concentration. Right mindfulness, or recollection, is to keep in mind whatever you are meditating upon. It is to remember your object. Right concentration is to be able to stay with single-pointed focus on your object of meditation for as long as you wish. A distracted mind that flits from one thing to another will not get you to your goal. A needle with two points will not work for sewing.

Some of these eight limbs are primary while others are secondary supporting elements. The eight all together are like a body; each limb has a function. Each part of the eightfold path on the path of meditation also its own function. Maitreya summarized the functions of the eight limbs of practice as follows:

> A limb that ascertains, one that provides understanding,
> three limbs that engender others' faith,
> and the antidotes to what is improper;
> these are the eight limbs of the path.
> [*Distinguishing the Middle from the Extremes,* 4.10]

The function of the right view is to analyze. It ascertains the true nature of the object of meditation. The function of right thought is to motivate you to share the content of what you have realized so that others will be able to understand it.

Three limbs—right speech, right action, and right livelihood—function as parts of a bodhisattva's practice of helping others. These three limbs of the path of practice are parts of ethical conduct. Of course, your own morality is most important as a basis, but these practices also serve to inspire others to have faith in you. If you tell people, "This is right, so do it. That is wrong, so don't do it" you should be doing those things yourself. If you are acting properly, others will take heed of your instruction. If you aren't following your own advice, others will respond to your instruction by saying, "Well, what about you?" Right speech contributes to others developing trust in you because it is telling the truth about what you have realized in an agreeable way. When you do this, others will understand that you are explicating the pure, true view. Right action applies to all behavior: whatever you do, you do properly. You do not harm others in any way. Others will recognize that your conduct is pure. You don't need to tell people that you have pure morality. You simply engage in pure ethical conduct, and it will be obvious to others. There doesn't need to be a lot of discussion about it. When others recognize that your conduct is pure, they will see that your advice is beneficial and they will follow it. Right livelihood is similar. When you obtain your food, clothes, and shelter, just as the Buddha explained you should, it demonstrates that you are not attached to material things. The way you get the simple things you need to survive ensures that others will trust that your livelihood is pure.

The antidotes to what is improper include the remaining three aspects of the path. The function of diligence is making an effort to purify obstacles. With effort you can get rid of all the obstacles. Mindfulness functions to purify secondary mental afflictions because you remember your practice. In this context mindfulness primarily refers to avoiding sinking into the dullness and the excitement that interrupt meditation. You are careful of even subtle incorrect things. The function of meditative concentration is to bring forth special virtuous qualities. Concentration results in normal knowledges and other special achievements like the dhyānas.

These eight should be practiced by those who desire to attain the permanent peace of nirvana.

The Four Realities for Āryas

Now Nāgārjuna moves on to talk about the most important fundamental teaching of Buddhism: the four realities for āryas. The four realities for āryas—the reality of suffering, the reality of the cause of suffering, the reality of the cessation of suffering, and the reality of the path to the cessation of suffering—are the basis of the path to liberation. As mentioned earlier in chapter 2, some contemporary scholars have decided to replace the old translation term, "the four noble truths," with the more correct term, "four realities for āryas." In this context *noble* refers to an individual who has directly realized ultimate reality—an ārya— not to the content or truth of what has been realized. Āryas see reality in a way that ordinary beings do not: āryas recognize the reality of suffering, a cause of suffering, a cessation of suffering, and a path to attain that cessation of suffering. Ordinary beings misperceive and misunderstand these four. For example, ordinary people are experiencing suffering and its causes right now, but they don't recognize it as such. They can see gross mental unhappiness or physical pain. But when they are not in obvious distress, they think they are experiencing pleasure. In fact, most of what they focus upon is the temporary pleasure, happiness, and peace that they experience as humans, demigods, or devas. Furthermore, unlike āryas, ordinary beings don't see the subtle nature of suffering; they don't recognize the suffering of change or the suffering of the pervasive conditioning of karma and the mental afflictions. Although their impure aggregates are imbued with misery, they are attached to their seeming pleasure. In contrast, āryas clearly see that all rebirths caused by karma and the mental afflictions are suffering; they see that the temporary happiness and tranquility experienced in the upper realms is not really peace.

We say that the four realities for āryas incorporate three explanations. The first is the basic character of the realities for āryas—this is an explanation of what each of them are. The second is the function of each reality—this is an explanation of what you do with them. The third part of the explanation is in regard to the completion of them.

We have a saying that originated from the Buddha that serves as an overview:

> Suffering should be realized.
> Its cause should be abandoned.
> Emancipation should be actualized.
> The path to liberation should be practiced.

To say that the reality of suffering should be realized or properly known means that you have to understand the nature of suffering. In this sense, suffering is an object of the path. However, this certainly doesn't imply that suffering is an object that you strive to obtain through practice! The reality of suffering is an effect that a practitioner of the path must fully know. Since you don't want to suffer, you must understand what causes it. You should abandon, in other words completely avoid, the cause of suffering. This means that you should get rid of ignorance and the mental afflictions. The reality of emancipation is the complete cessation of ignorance. This cessation is what you should want to obtain. It should be present as part of your mental continuum. The reality of path is what you should cultivate. In other words, the fourth reality for āryas is what you do on the path in order to attain emancipation.

Maitreya likened a yogi's practice of the four realities for āryas to a sick person's attempts to cure an illness:

> The sickness is to be known;
> the cause of the sickness is to be abandoned;
> health is to be attained;
> and the medicine is to be relied upon.
>   [*Higher System of the Mahayana* 4.52ab]

In other words, a practitioner should realize the nature of their suffering. They should abandon the cause of suffering. They should actualize permanent and joyful freedom from suffering. And, they should properly follow the instructions on the path to freedom from suffering.

To complete or finish the four realities for āryas means that when you reach liberation, you have truly realized the reality of suffering; there is nothing more to realize. You have gotten rid of the causes for samsara, so there is nothing more to abandon. You have obtained cessation, so there is nothing further to actualize. Because you have completely removed samsara there is no need to rely upon any part of the path.

With this as an overview, we can now look more closely at the basic character of the four realities for āryas.

> 114. This rebirth is the arising of suffering.
>   Desire is the all-embracing cause of it.
>   The cessation of it is liberation.
>   The path to achieve that is the eightfold path.

The reality of suffering is cyclic rebirth in samsara. Ignorance, mental afflictions, and impure karma are causes that bring about the result of rebirth. The verse literally says "desire is the all-embracing cause" of rebirth. As I explained earlier, desire, which arises because of ignorance, is the most dominant of the mental afflictions. All the other afflictions can be described as corollaries of desire. The mental afflictions impel you to create karma. So here, "desire" is shorthand for ignorance, all the mental afflictions, and karma. The nature of a birth, wherever you are born due to the power of mental afflictions and karma, is suffering. The details in each realm differ, but the nature of all of them is misery. Being reborn again and again due to the mental afflictions and karma is the reality of suffering.

Dharmakīrti succinctly said,

The aggregates are the misery of revolving in samsara.
[*Commentary on Valid Cognition, 2.147*]

Therefore, in order to comprehend the first reality of the āryas we need to understand a bit more about the five appropriated aggregates. The first aggregate is the physical body, while the other four relate to the mind. The second aggregate is feeling; this is feeling the misery or happiness that usually arises due to physical sensations. Feeling causes you to discriminate between good and bad; discrimination is the third aggregate. It doesn't matter if your distinction is correct or not, either way it leads you to act—the fourth aggregate—and so to create more karma and so future rebirths. The fifth aggregate is consciousness. This is the primary consciousness that is reborn and continues throughout your life. From this comes the egoistic view that identifies I. There are many aspects of mind, but only a few of them are directly addressed within the five aggregates. All the other aspects of the mind, everything that wasn't specified as one of the other three mental aggregates, is included in the fourth aggregate, activity.

The Buddha said that you realize the reality of suffering by seeing what is really there. To investigate suffering in more depth, you meditate upon its four attributes: impermanence, suffering, empty of being an absolute self, and selflessness. Impermanence is the fact that everything is changing moment by moment. From the moment you entered your mother's womb up until now nothing has stayed the same. Things are occasional because they occur as a result of causes and conditions. The attribute of suffering is the fact that all samsaric faults arise from contaminated karma and the mental afflictions. Sometimes the latter two attributes—empty of being an absolute self and selflessness—are counted as one, but they are slightly different. The attribute of being empty is the fact that there is no such thing as a self that is a completely different entity from the aggregates; there is no soul or some absolute self. The attribute of being selfless is the fact that there is no substantial self that is the owner or master of the five aggregates. In other words, there is no inherent external self that has power and control over rebirth. When you realize the reality of suffering you see these four attributes.

Once you realize what suffering actually is, you don't want it to continue. Your aggregates already exist—this is your life. It doesn't make much sense to expend a lot of effort to get rid of an effect that has fully come into being. There isn't much you can do at that point. What you need to do is to get rid of the cause of that type of effect in order to prevent a similar result occurring again in the future. Therefore, you look for the cause of taking a suffering rebirth. The main cause is usually said to be karma and the mental afflictions: rooted in ignorance, the mental afflictions are the cause of karma, and together they result in suffering. There are many, many mental afflictions, but here Nāgārjuna wants you to understand that the main cause of suffering is attachment to yourself, to I or me. Hatred, jealousy and the other mental afflictions arise from this primary mental affliction of clinging to your contaminated aggregates. When desire arises, you become a servant to it. Desire is like the moisture that causes everything to grow. It is like oil that permeates a piece of paper. Desire is deep down in the mind. It spreads everywhere. It is deep and wide. It isn't necessarily sharp and obvious like hatred. In this sense desire is the cause of it all; this is what you should get rid of.

The termination of suffering and its causes is emancipation. Nirvana is the complete cessation of the mental afflictions. Liberation isn't a place; nirvana isn't somewhere you go. It is internal; it is the complete absence of ignorance and the mental afflictions in your mental continuum. The reality of cessation occurs when you permanently stop suffering and the cause of suffering through the practice of meditation. This is what should be obtained.

Are cessation and emancipation the same? Emancipation is the complete removal of all the mental afflictions. Cessations are the sequential and gradual removal of particular mental afflictions. In other words, a cessation is the permanent removal of a portion of the mental afflictions through application of a particular antidote on the paths of seeing and cultivation. You have multiple cessations before complete emancipation. Yogis and great practitioners work to remove the mental afflictions permanently, first on the gross level, then the intermediate level, and finally the subtlest level. Arhats and buddhas have removed them all.

How do you achieve the complete cessation that is emancipation? You practice the path. So far we have discussed six ways to look at the path: (1) you practice the seven branches of the path to enlightenment; (2) you practice the union of śamatha and vipaśyanā; (3) you abandon thinking about topics that have no benefit, (4) you develop the correct view of the forward and reverse progressions of the twelve links of dependent origination; (5) you practice the eightfold path; and, (6) you infuse your mind with the four realities for āryas; in other words, you realize suffering, abandon the cause of suffering, manifest the cessation of suffering, and practice the path to the cessation of suffering.

> 115. Since this is so, you should always
> strive to see the four realities for āryas.
> Even laymen whose laps are filled with riches
> can cross the river of suffering by relying upon wisdom.

The four realities are true from an ārya's perspective because they actually see them as they are. For āryas they are real. If you saw your aggregates as an ārya sees them, you wouldn't be attached to them. The difference in the way that an ordinary being and an ārya see suffering is like the following examples. If a tiny hair is caught in your hand, you don't notice it; but if a similarly tiny hair gets into your eye, you feel it. Another analogy is the comparison of someone who is blind to someone who can see. When āryas look at suffering they clearly see it as it is; ordinary beings are blind to it. A third example is a person who has a wound that doesn't hurt when they leave it alone. However, it is rather stupid for that person to think that they are completely okay. Someone with intelligence knows that if the wound is touched by anything, even a light breeze, it will be sharply painful.

Just as the reality of suffering is a reality known only by āryas, this pertains to the other three realities too. But don't be discouraged. Don't think these four realities are impossible for you to practice because you aren't an ārya. Don't think they are just for advanced yogis and so beyond you. Don't think that you are too busy with work and family. Don't think you are too poor or too stupid. These are just excuses. There are various expressions for someone who has lots of things going on in their life. In English you may say they have a full plate. An Indo-Tibetan way to say it is that you have a lot of stuff in your lap. Nāgārjuna said that even a king—someone who has great responsibility to his subjects and country and who is paid much homage—can try to learn and meditate. With enough effort a king can develop knowledge or wisdom that understands reality. He can become an ārya with a direct realization of ultimate reality. This wisdom is a special weapon. There is no other weapon, no matter how many big guns you may have, to eliminate samsara. Another way to say this is that wisdom is like a powerful boat that can take you across a turbulent river.

Seeing reality directly and clearly is possible if you make an effort. A direct realization doesn't just pop up without a cause; it isn't something that some people naturally have, and others don't.

116. Those who have a direct realization of reality
     didn't fall from the sky or arise from the earth
     as an already perfect harvest.
     In the past, they too were just ordinary beings subject to
        the afflictions.

When yogis have a direct realization of the four realities, they have attained the path of seeing and become āryas. Through development of that realization on the path of cultivation, they attain complete liberation. When you look at them you may think, "Well they did it, but I can't." It seems like they must have some special qualities that you don't. It may seem like they came down to earth from heaven as perfectly realized beings. Or it may seem like a hole suddenly opened in the earth and out popped āryas, arhats, and buddhas as a perfectly ripe harvest. That's not the case. They weren't perfectly realized beings from the beginning. In the past, all of them, even buddhas, were completely under the power of their mental afflictions. They were just like you, born again and again due to karma and the mental afflictions. However, they developed their good qualities by following the advice of their spiritual teachers. They made an effort to seriously practice. Slowly they developed their minds. First they understood only vaguely. Then their conceptual understanding became clearer and clearer. Then finally they gained a direct realization of the phenomenal and ultimate natures of all phenomena: causality and emptiness. With that they were able to eliminate their mental afflictions and attain spiritual goals. These direct realizations are the real path to liberation and enlightenment.

So, take courage. Anybody, including you, can practice the path. If you are interested and make an effort you can obtain a direct realization of the ultimate nature of reality. Discouragement about yourself and your abilities is a great obstacle to spiritual attainments. It prevents you from making an effort. Simply wishing for emancipation is not enough. Just like the great beings of the past and present, you too must exert yourself without being discouraged. This is good advice.

CONCLUDING THE DESCRIPTIONS OF THE PATH TO NIRVANA

Now to conclude the discussion of all those ways to describe practicing the path:

> 117.   There's no need to say much to the fearless.
> The most essential and helpful instruction is
> "Control your mind!"
> The Buddha said, "The mind is the root of the Dharma."

If you are without fear you will not be discouraged. You will be free of negative feelings about yourself. You won't feel guilty, ashamed, or inadequate. If you are fearless, you will be enthused and energetically practice the path. The most important aspect of practice is to tame your mind. Your mind is like a wild horse or a wild elephant. A wild animal is powerful; it can cause a lot of damage. An animal trainer has to actively work to tame such an animal. He has to train the animal to eliminate its bad behavior and encourage it to engage in positive behavior. Eventually he doesn't have to do anything; the animal is under control and can do difficult things for its owner.

What does it mean to control your mind? To subdue your mind means that you do not create the causes for samsara and instead create the causes for liberation. If your mind is controlled, all your physical and verbal actions will be appropriate. If your mind is uncontrolled and wild, all your physical and verbal actions will be incorrect. Through taming your mind, you refrain from nonvirtue and engage in the ten virtues. A tamed mind brings the highest peace. Śāntideva put it this way:

> If the elephant of my mind was
> completely bound by the rope of mindfulness,
> all my fear would cease to exist
> and all virtues would come into my hands.
> [*Introduction to the Practice of Bodhisattvas*, 5.3]

Right now, if you are an ordinary being, your mind is as difficult to control as a wild elephant. You think about your present concerns, what you want and what you don't want. You justify doing negative things to others in order to achieve your goals. Under the influence of desire, hatred, ignorance, and the other mental afflictions your mind goes the wrong way. Your body and speech are subject to your mind. What the mind wants, the body and speech do. They could go in an evil direction that is harmful to yourself and others, or they could go in a positive direction to help yourself and others.

It is important to understand what actually will get you what you want. So first you study the spiritual teachings in order to learn about what is right and what is wrong. Then you think seriously about what you have learned. To apply the instructions, you need to be mindful of what your mind is doing. Only then can you prevent yourself from doing evil and instead create the causes that will bring you happiness and peace. Both temporary and permanent happiness and peace arise from mental training. If you tame your mind, all your fears about what will happen in this life and what will happen in your future lives will cease. It will bring you the temporary result of a high rebirth. You will come to have a body and mind that are not affected by illness. You will live in a good environment where teachings and teachers are present. If both positive internal and external circumstances come together, virtue naturally comes into your hands. This is why the Buddha said that the mind is the root of all his teachings.

> The mind brings forth the world;
> the mind is what draws it into being.
> Only the qualities of the mind
> control whatever comes to be.
> [*Connected Discourses*, 1.7.2(62)]

And in addition:

A tamed mind is good.
A tamed mind brings happiness.
[*Collection of Indicative Verses* 31.1cd]

Your mind is the root of everything, good or bad, that happens to you. Everything in the world, all the lower and higher realms of rebirth, occurs due to contaminated karma and the egoistic self-cherishing mind. It may seem odd to say that trees and flowers have their root in the mind. But karma is very extensive. The maturation result of karma is internal. But there are also karmic results that are similar to the cause, and these can be in connection to the external world. Your environment and the external circumstances that you experience are also rooted in your past actions.

To conclude his exposition of the common path, Nāgārjuna said that if you can practice everything that was explained here you will attain liberation. But if you can't do it all now, at least try to practice some part of it.

118.   To properly practice all the teachings that I have given
       is difficult even for monks, even more so for you.
       But you should practice some portion of them.
       Training in these qualities will make your precious life
           useful.

Even someone who has renounced the activities of this life would find it difficult to practice all these techniques completely at one time. This is even more the case for laypeople. Nevertheless, you can do some of these practices. Some of them are suitable for you. You should learn what is right and what is wrong. You should do whatever it is possible for you to do. You may not be able to do everything, but do as much as you can. There are so many faults you can work on eliminating; you can try to give up killing, stealing, lying, and so forth. If you can't work on them all at once, work at what you can. You can work on developing your positive mental, verbal, and physical qualities. As much as you can, try to help others, develop compassion, and become accustomed to the positive side. If you live your life this way, abiding in the Buddhist teachings, your life will be useful. You will gradually achieve higher and higher spiritual goals. So please, engage in this way of practicing the common path.

11. The Uncommon Path

THE LOWER AND HIGHER VEHICLES share much in common. Everyone—laypeople, monks and nuns, those desiring their own liberation, and those desiring complete enlightenment in order to benefit others—engages in the common practices. Because the result of the Mahayana path is different from and superior to the result of the path of the lower vehicle, there are additional practices required to complete the path of the higher vehicle. To conclude this text, Nāgārjuna briefly explains the result of enlightenment and gives advice on how to practice the uncommon elements of the path to achieve that goal.

What is the distinction between the lesser and greater vehicles? How do you know if your Dharma practice is part of the Hinayana or Mahayana? This isn't a matter of what country your teachers come from or what school of philosophical thought you follow. It depends upon your motivation. Practice of the Hinayana is motivated by a desire to look out for yourself. You are tired of your own suffering; you don't want to experience misery anymore; you want your own freedom from samsara. Hinayana practitioners will do whatever they must, no matter how difficult, to attain their own liberation.

This doesn't mean that a Hinayana practitioner never thinks about others. Hinayana yogis practice the four immeasurable thoughts. They think, "How nice it would be if all beings were free of misery and the causes of misery; how good it would be if they all had happiness and the causes of happiness; how fine it would be if all beings attained emancipation; and how nice it would be if all beings had equanimity free of desire and hatred." Hinayana practitioners develop these wonderful thoughts, but just wishing that other sentient beings were free of suffering and so forth is a relatively narrow concept. Mahayana practitioners develop the common limitless thoughts, but then in addition they take on the responsibility to make sure that all living beings are free from suffering, and have happiness, peace, and freedom. Mahayana practitioners can't bear the fact that others suffer in samsara. They want to free others from suffering even more than they want their own happiness. They train their minds to develop universal compassion and love. They do not exclude a single being. They want everyone, not just themselves, to be free from suffering and to have the highest peace and happiness of enlightenment. They take on the responsibility of making sure that all sentient beings attain this state. That is their goal. So, the difference between the Hinayana and the Mahayana is whether the goal of your spiritual practice is for just yourself, or does it also include all beings.

So how are you going to free all beings—not just yourself and maybe a few special friends—from suffering and place them in happiness? You need to equip yourself to do this. You need to view all others as equal. You can't make them equal externally in all respects, but you can view them all as equal objects of your love and compassion. What else do you need? You must have freed yourself from samsara in order to confidently tell others how to do it. Also, you must have omniscient knowledge so that you can see the best way to help others. There is no other way to have all these qualities other than attaining buddhahood yourself. As a buddha you can fulfil your goals of universal love and universal compassion. You will have completed the path to liberation so you will know how to show the path to others. You will be omniscient so you will know exactly what to do to help every other being. Your mind and actions will be perfect in every way. The desire to attain buddhahood yourself in order to save all other sentient beings from the misery of samsara is what we call bodhicitta.

Just wanting to become a buddha isn't necessarily bodhicitta. Sometimes people want to attain buddhahood because they desire to be omniscient, perfect, powerful, and attain a high spiritual state. This is still seeking a goal for yourself, so it is not bodhicitta. Bodhicitta, also called the "mind of enlightenment" or "awakening mind," is based on universal love and compassion for others. Through these practices you come to cherish others more than yourself; you see that the freedom of so many is more important than your own individual freedom. Actual bodhicitta is the thought, "I want to free others from cyclic rebirth; I want them to attain enlightenment. I will take on the responsibility to do this." This thought must arise spontaneously and continuously in your mind. In other words, bodhicitta is the spontaneous desire to attain perfect enlightenment because that is the only way you can truly be of benefit to other beings. Your primary purpose is to free others from the misery of samsara and lead them to enlightenment yourself. You don't just pray that someone else will take care of it.

What do you do when bodhicitta arises in your mind? You work to purify your negative actions. You see that your negative actions don't have repercussions just for yourself, but that they will affect others negatively too. Because your negative actions block your attainment of enlightenment, they destroy the possibility of you having the ability to truly help others. Even the smallest virtuous actions you do when you have bodhicitta become vastly meritorious. Why? Because your actions won't just benefit you, they will also benefit all others. Without the attitude of bodhicitta, there is no way to fulfil others' goals. You can do a lot without being a buddha, but your actions aren't perfect. Practicing a vast amount of generosity, working to be a great yogi, and so on, are very virtuous actions. But if they are not motivated by bodhicitta they will be of limited benefit to others. Practicing virtue for the purpose of attaining enlightenment in order to help other living beings is the Mahayana attitude.

This is why we call practice of the path motivated by bodhicitta the great vehicle. The goal is huge: it is enlightenment. This is much greater than just liberation from samsara. Further, the object of Mahayana practice isn't just one person, it is all sentient beings. There is no limitation. You are determined to do whatever must be done so that every sentient being in existence will attain their goals. That is why in some Mahayana texts, both sutra and tantra, you may find instructions that seem contradictory to earlier prescriptions and prohibitions on the common path. Sometimes it may seem that bodhisattvas, those with bodhicitta, do things that are forbidden on the common path. You have to see these texts and actions in context. A bodhisattva is like a devoted mother. She doesn't just think about herself. She will act in a way that helps her children, even if her actions seem harsh. She sometimes has to discipline her children, prevent them from doing something, or block them from having something that they want. It is the same for bodhisattvas.

Just as alchemy changes iron into gold, bodhicitta transforms ordinary actions into virtues that help other beings. With bodhicitta, even eating a mouthful of food or taking a rest can be very virtuous. You have to maintain your life in order to use it. To be able to help others, you engage in activities that are necessary for your own survival. Although some things you do may look like they are for your own enjoyment, if you have actual bodhicitta they actually are for the benefit of others. With bodhicitta, every moment of every day, even sleeping, can be a great practice of virtue. But someone who hasn't trained their mind in bodhicitta and then imitates the external, ordinary looking activities of a bodhisattva, is not doing the same thing at all. Once you have bodhicitta and are practicing the Mahayana path, and even one moment of practice multiplies the amount of merit you create by the number of sentient beings. Then you will be able to quickly attain buddhahood and help others.

When you have developed bodhicitta you become a bodhisattva and enter the Mahayana path. This doesn't mean that before you have spontaneous bodhicitta you don't learn, practice, and think about others. It takes training to become a Mahayana practitioner. You must create many wholesome actions. Even without bodhicitta, you can think that your actions are for the benefit of others, not just for your own selfish purposes. In order to be able to enter the Mahayana path you must be very fortunate. To be fortunate means that you created virtues in the past that led you to engage in further practice of virtue. Your prior wholesome actions created the potential that make doing positive actions now much easier. It takes a great deal of merit to be able to practice the bodhisattva deeds.

In other texts you will find a lot of detail on how to become a Mahayana practitioner, what makes you a Mahayana practitioner, and what makes a practice a Mahayana practice. Nāgārjuna gives only the briefest of summaries in this text. He begins by recommending two activities to practice on the Mahayana path: rejoicing in your own and others' merit, and dedicating that merit to the attainment of enlightenment.

119. Rejoice in the merit created by all beings
          and also in your own good actions of body, speech, and
              mind.

> By dedicating these to the attainment of buddhahood
> you will obtain a mass of virtues.

Look at all the wonderful things that have been done in the past by buddhas, bodhisattvas, arhats, ordinary beings, and even yourself. Think about what they, and you, are doing in the present and will do in the future. When you recite the *King of Prayers,* a section of the *Flower Array Sutra,* you admire your own merit and the virtues of five other types of beings: the deeds of the buddhas in the ten directions; the bodhisattvas' practice of the perfections; the virtuous actions of the two types of Hinayana practitioners, pratyekabuddhas and śrāvakas, both those who have attained arhatship and those who are still working toward that state; and the positive things that all other sentient beings who have not yet entered any of the Buddhist paths have done. It is all marvelous; you should admire it.

Ordinarily you may admire some people, but you get jealous of others, and you don't care what some other people do. But positive actions, no matter who does them and no matter whether they are big or small, should give you joy. They should please you in the way that a father is pleased when his children do something good. Truly admiring and rejoicing in the virtuous actions of others is the best way to make a huge amount of merit with only a little effort. One of the perfection of wisdom sutras says that although it looks like it would be impossible, you could potentially calculate the number of molecules that make up all the mountains in the world. In contrast, there is no way to measure the amount of merit that you create by admiring the virtuous actions of other beings. It is inconceivably vast. Remember the example of the beggar who rejoiced in a king's offering of a meal to the Buddha and his disciples. At the end of the day, the Buddha said that the beggar had created far more merit than the king. The beggar just sat by the palace gate, but he sincerely admired the actions of the king. He thought how wonderful it was that the king had this opportunity and made these offerings, and he prayed that someday he might be able to do it too. In contrast, the king had a worldly attitude; he wanted fame and renown for what he did.

So, while you are comfortably lying down think about the wonderful actions of buddhas, bodhisattvas, spiritual teachers, and other people. Rejoice in their positive actions. Don't be jealous of them. Don't put yourself down and think you can't create merit too. Think about what you have done from this morning up until now and be happy about the positive things you have done. Rejoice in the good things you have done in the past. You must do this from the heart. Be glad you were able to do a positive action through one of your three doors: a physical action, a verbal action, or developing a loving compassionate attitude. When you admire even a small virtue the merit increases and stabilizes.

Rejoicing in others' virtues may not seem so hard to do. It looks like an easy practice to create a tremendous amount of merit. You are creating merit even though you haven't done a particular practice by admiring that others have done it and wishing you could do that too. But admiration without jealousy isn't so easy to generate properly. And, you have to be careful that rejoicing in your own virtuous actions doesn't become conceit.

There are two important points in any action: having a good motivation at the beginning and dedicating your completed action for a special purpose at the end. You dedicate your merit to preserve it, so that it doesn't easily get used up. Dedication means to wish that the positive actions you have done become the causes for achieving a certain goal. You have been told that you should engage in morality and dedicate that merit so that you will have a good life in the future. But this is a mundane level of dedication. It is ordinary to want to be happy, healthy, well-loved, rich, and so forth. But don't dedicate your merit with expectations for this life or purely for yourself in future lives. With that attitude you may be successful from a worldly point of view, but not spiritually. If your mind is dominated by selfishness or a worldly egoistic attitude, then everything you do will be ruined from the spiritual point of view.

Your dedication should be for a spiritual goal. You can dedicate your action so that you attain a good life for further spiritual practice. Or, you could dedicate your merit for your own emancipation from suffering. A Mahayana dedication is based on the aspiration of bodhicitta. For example, after Mahayana practitioners have given a bit of food to a person or animal, they dedicate that act of generosity by thinking, "By giving this, in the future may I be able to feed all beings who are hungry." Or, "By doing this may I be able to become a buddha in order to benefit all other sentient beings." This mixes a small action with the desire to attain enlightenment. The traditional analogy is that it is like mixing a drop of water into the ocean. That one drop lasts as long as the ocean. Perhaps easier to understand is the example of putting a little bit of milk in a large mug of coffee.

The milk is there for as long as there is coffee. Dedicating your actions toward the goal of attaining enlightenment for the benefit of all sentient beings will make that merit last as long as it takes you to reach enlightenment. If you don't dedicate a virtuous action, the meritorious result of even a great action can get used up quickly.

In your dedication you can even specify where you don't want your merit to go. You can think, "May whatever virtues I have done not be the cause for my fame or renown; may they not be the cause for a god's life in heavens; may they not be the cause for an ordinary happy human life. May these merits be dedicated without any samsaric expectation." All dedications should include a goal beyond the mundane. Milarepa would dedicate the merit of those who came to offer him a bit of food or some other small thing. He would pray that their action would be the cause for them to attain enlightenment. He would also pray that by eating that food he too would be able to attain enlightenment for the benefit of others as soon as possible. He combined the merit of the person making the offering with his own prayer so that it became a much more powerful and lasting cause.

If you don't know what to say to dedicate your merit, you can recite some lines from the *King of Prayers*:

> I dedicate all the virtue that I have created
> so that I might train on the path followed
> by Mañjuśrī who knows reality's true nature,
> and by Samantabhadra who understands it too.
>
> I dedicate all the roots of my virtue in the way that
> the buddhas of the past, present and future
> praised as the best way to dedicate them.
> I dedicate them in order to complete good deeds.
>
> [*King of Prayers,* 53–54]

As you recite these verses you are thinking, "I don't know much, but I don't want to waste the little bit of merit I've created. So may my virtue be dedicated along the lines of whatever these great bodhisattvas and all the buddhas have done." This increases your merit. It preserves your merit through future lives. And your merit will bring you many interim results, not just enlightenment. When a farmer plants a field, he is wishing for—

dedicating his work—toward a harvest. But along the way he gets sprouts and plants with leaves and stems. This is similar to dedicating your actions for your attainment of enlightenment. You will get many good things as ancillary results.

Creating and dedicating merit is so important that all recitations, whether sutra or tantra, include seven elements: prostrating, offering, confession, rejoicing, requesting spiritual beings to give teachings, requesting that they live a long life, and dedicating the merit. Four of these limbs create merit: prostrating, offering, requesting teachings, and requesting that teachers remain in the world. Rejoicing increases that merit. Confession purifies past evil actions so that the merit you have created will be effective. Dedication preserves and saves all that merit.

Nāgārjuna focused on rejoicing in virtue as the means to create merit and dedication as the means to preserve and focus it. But remember, merit alone is not enough to enter and practice the Mahayana path; merit alone cannot result in the attainment of enlightenment. In addition to merit, you need wisdom: you must have a direct realization of the emptiness of the self of persons and the self of phenomena. You must understand that things do not exist as they appear; in other words, that nothing has an independent intrinsic identity. Merit and wisdom together are necessary to eliminate all the mental afflictions and attain the permanent cessation of enlightenment. Merit and wisdom are like a fire-drill that you use to produce a fire. You can't produce a fire with just the stick, or just the base, or by just rubbing the stick and base together for a short time. As a Buddhist practitioner you need to accumulate both merit and wisdom. Together these two accumulations are like a wish-granting jewel because they will grant your wish of perfect enlightenment as soon as possible so that you can benefit all sentient beings.

> 120. Through that you will become a master of yoga
>   for innumerable rebirths in the worlds of gods and men.
>   You will provide relief to multitudes of frail living beings
>   with deeds like those of Ārya Avalokiteśvara.

You may live an almost innumerable number of lives as a bodhisattva until you attain buddhahood. Your dedicated merit will be the cause for you to obtain a life as a human or god. In those two types of rebirths you can continue to practice the path. You develop familiarity and skill in the bodhisattva practices just as the bodhisattva Avalokiteśvara did over a series of lives. There are many stories in the sutras about how his activities helped weak and miserable living beings. There are so many ways to help others, not just one. With a bodhicitta motivation he manifested in many ways in order to benefit ordinary beings who were engulfed in misery. We should aspire to act in the same way.

> 121. In your rebirths you will dispel
>   sickness, aging, desire, and hatred.
>   Then you will be like Amitābha in a buddha-field:
>   a protector of the world with an infinite lifespan.

A bodhisattva only acts with the goal of perfectly saving others. Because bodhisattvas and buddhas manifest in many different ways, you can't be sure if someone is, or is not, a bodhisattva or a buddha. They may seem angry or foolish. They may appear as an animal or even as your enemy. Unless you have supranormal yogic knowledge that sees what someone actually is, you may have a wrong perception. They may be a buddha, but you don't see it. Therefore, you should be careful how you act toward others. Your interactions with others are like a pit filled with extremely hot coals totally covered by a deep layer of ash. You just see soft gray ash, but if you step on it you will fall into the pit and be burned. Similarly, you must be careful because you don't know whether someone is actually a bodhisattva or a buddha. If you act negatively toward them, if you have bad thoughts toward them, you will create and be burned by very, very bad karma. There is a story about Nāropa. He heard about the great master Tilopa and wanted to get teachings from him. He went in search of him. On his travels he saw a filthy old man, only half dressed, who had caught a fish in a stream and was eating it raw. This disreputable looking person was actually the great master Tilopa, but who could have known that?

A practitioner develops more and more ability to assist others on each successive level of the bodhisattva stages. A tenth-stage bodhisattva is almost the same as a buddha. Such a bodhisattva has a special power to teach individuals according to their needs and abilities. After a long time of acting only for the benefit of other sentient beings you will attain enlightenment. We say that a buddha has a measurelessly long lifespan because they do not suffer death as a result of karma and the mental afflictions. In that sense, a buddha is immortal. You should pray to become a buddha like this in order to save all other sentient beings.

To summarize, you want two things. First, you want to be able to improve the mind streams of other sentient beings so that they have permanent happiness and freedom from suffering. Second, in order to fulfil your goal of benefitting sentient beings you wish to become a buddha. In order to attain the qualities of a buddha you must create a great deal of merit. This is how you practice the path and attain the result. After you attain buddhahood there is nothing left for you to do except to help other beings attain emancipation. Now you are able to actually help sentient beings. You have omniscience, and perfect compassion and love. You know what activities to do and how to do them to best lead all others to liberation.

In the next verse Nāgārjuna says that to achieve their goals a bodhisattva primarily practices three things: wisdom, morality, and generosity. This is similar to the three higher trainings of wisdom, ethical conduct, and meditative concentration that were explained earlier. In this framework, bodhisattvas develop wisdom because it is the wisdom understanding reality that eliminates both the mental afflictions tying them to samsara and the more subtle obstacles to the omniscience of complete buddhahood. Based on wisdom they practice pure conduct. Bodhisattvas don't practice ethical conduct only out of fear of falling into samsara themselves; their conduct is designed to benefit others. Therefore, they practice generosity of all sorts; they give material things and the Dharma without any reserve. Through extending their practice of perfect, stainless wisdom, ethical conduct, and generosity throughout the worlds of the heavens, on earth, and underground, they are able to help sentient beings. In this way they can lead others to nirvana.

> 122. Through extending the stainless eminence of your wisdom,
>   morality, and generosity throughout the heavens, the sky,
>   and on earth,
>   you engage in pacifying those who enjoy sense pleasures:
>   humans on earth and the superb youths of the god realms.

123. Having attained the state of a lord of the victors—a
       buddha—
      you calm many weak and ignorant beings' fear, birth, and
       death.
      May you attain the fearless, unadulterated, faultless state
      of the peace simply called "gone beyond sorrow."

This is the final verse of Ācārya Nāgārjuna's letter to his friend King
Sātavāhana.

DEDICATION OF THE MERIT CREATED BY THIS EXPLANATION

Texts such as Nāgārjuna's *Letter to a Friend* make the attainment of enlightenment possible. As long as the Buddha's teachings exist, and as long as
there are good explanations of the scriptures in the world, sentient beings
have a savior and protector. Even though the Buddha himself isn't present,
his teachings continue to bring wisdom to living beings. Therefore, it is
very important that there are pure spiritual teachings in the world. These
teachings are a refuge.

The complete path to enlightenment taught by the Buddha is like
medicine a doctor has prescribed for our illness. The Buddha said,

> I explained the excellent Dharma.
> But if you do not practice it properly,
> you are like a sick person carrying medicines on your back;
> they will not cure you of disease.
>   [*King of Concentrations Sutra* 4.24]

If instead of taking the medicine, we just carry it around, we won't be
cured of our disease: suffering. Putting the Dharma teachings into practice is the means to remove all suffering and its causes. But if we don't
take it seriously and follow the instructions, we can't be cured. You have
to know that the teaching itself is of value. You have to study, learn, and
understand. Then you seriously put that into practice.

If evil prevails in the world, it will make the Dharma fade until it seems
to disappear. Then all sentient beings will degenerate because they will lose

access to learning the Dharma that pacifies misery. The mental afflictions are like demons who shoot us with arrows. These arrows look like beautiful flowers, but they are poisoned and make us engage in evil actions. This destroys all our merit and happiness. Without these teachings it is if we are ill and have no medicine or it is as if we are in the dark and cannot see. With the teachings present, it is as if the sun is shining in a clear sky. It is the shining light of the Dharma that shows sentient beings the way out of misery and suffering.

Therefore, may the merits that arise from the effort that went into the composition of this explanation of Nāgārjuna's text blossom like a beautiful white lotus. May whatever merit that has been created benefit other sentient beings. May it carry them across turbulent river of wrong views. May it free them from these wrong views so they all go to a state of perfect emancipation. You too should dedicate the merit you created by reading this text.

I think it would be good to end with the dedication prayer that concludes the *Preparatory Practices Recitation* composed by Jampal Lhundrup.

> From my collections of merit and insight, vast as space,
> that I have amassed by making an effort on this for a long time,
> may I become the chief leading buddha for all those
> whose mind's wisdom eye is blinded by ignorance.
>
> Until I reach that state, in all my lives
> may I be held in your loving compassion, O Mañjuśrī.
> May I find the best complete sequential path of the teachings,
> and may I please all the buddhas by practicing it well.
>
> May I clear away darkness from the minds of all beings
> using the points of the path as I have discerned them
> and skillful means drawn forth by strong compassion.
> May I uphold the Buddha's teachings for a very long time.
>
> With my heart going out with great compassion
> may I reveal this treasure of happiness and aid
> in every place that the supreme precious teachings
> have not yet spread, or have spread but since declined.

By the marvelous, good actions of buddhas and bodhisattvas,
and also my practice of the graduated path,
may the buddhas' deeds be nourished for a long time
in order to bring peace to those who desire liberation.

May all humans and nonhumans who eliminate adversity
and create conducive conditions for practicing the excellent
    paths
never be parted in any of their lives
from the purest path praised by the buddhas.

Whenever someone makes effort to act in accord
with the ten-fold Mahayana virtuous practices[29]
may they always be assisted by the mighty Dharma protectors,
and may oceans of good fortune spread out all around.

Appendix 1. The Root Verses of Letter to a Friend

1. It is right for someone naturally suited to virtue
    to study this short text that I have composed.
    These special verses will lead you to aspire to the virtues
    which arise from the teachings of the Sugata.

2. The wise venerate statues of the Sugata
    no matter their quality, even those made of wood.
    Likewise, this poetry of mine may be poor
    but do not scorn it for it expresses the holy Dharma.

3. The words of the Great Sage are exquisite.
    Even if you have understood them,
    doesn't something made of white plaster
    become even whiter in winter moon-light?

4. The Jina taught six recollections:
    Buddha, Dharma, Sangha, generosity, morality, and the gods.
    You should be mindful of the good qualities
    of each one of these.

5. You should always adhere to the ten paths:
    the ten virtuous actions of body, speech, and mind.
    Refrain from intoxicants and likewise
    take true delight in a virtuous livelihood.

6. Knowing that wealth is ephemeral and insubstantial,
   exert yourself to properly engage in generosity
   toward the ordained, brahmins, the poor, and friends.
   There is no better friend for your future than generosity.

7. You should practice morality that is unimpaired,
   not degraded, unsullied, and free from contamination.
   Just as the earth supports all animate and inanimate things,
   ethical conduct is the foundation for all good qualities.

8. Develop the immeasurable perfections: generosity, ethical
       discipline,
   patience, enthusiastic perseverance, meditative stabiliza-
       tion, and wisdom.
   You will become a supreme victor after crossing
   to the far shore of the ocean of samsaric existence.

9. Someone who reveres their father and mother is noble.
   The gods and spiritual teachers will be with them.
   Their respectful attitude will bring them fame,
   and in future lives they will have a high rebirth.

10. To avoid harming, stealing, engaging in sex, and lying.
    To not drink alcohol or crave food at improper times.
    And to eschew the pleasures of a high seat,
    singing and dancing, and adornments.

11. When you have taken these eight precepts
    you are emulating the arhats' moral behavior.
    Keeping these vows on a sabbath day bestows upon men
        and women
    the attractive bodies of the desire-realm gods.

12. See the following as enemies: stinginess, cunning, deceit,
    desire, laziness, conceited pride, lust, hatred,
    and arrogance about the superiority of your race,
    body, learning, beauty, and power.

13. Conscientiousness is the source of the nectar of
         immortality.
     Therefore, the sage said heedlessness is the source of death.
     Thus, in order to increase your virtuous deeds
     please, always be respectfully conscientious.

14. Someone who was heedless earlier,
     but changes and becomes conscientious,
     is as lovely as the moon freed from clouds;
     just like Nanda, Aṅgulimāla, Ajātaśatru, and Udayana.

15. Because there is no austerity like patience
     you should not give anger a chance to rise.
     The Buddha said that by eliminating anger
     you will obtain the state of being a nonreturner.

16. "This one criticized me, that one defeated me,
     this one stole my wealth." Repeating this
     is holding onto resentment. It produces strife.
     Those without resentment sleep easily.

17. You should understand that thoughts are like
     drawing figures on water, in earth, or in stone.
     For mental afflictions the first is best.
     For aspiring to the Dharma, the last is the best.

18. The victor said there are three types of ordinary speech:
     pleasing, truthful, and improper. Respectively,
     these three are like honey, a flower, and filth.
     The last type of these should be abandoned.

19. There are four types of beings:
     those who go from light to light,
     from dark to dark, from light to dark,
     and dark to light. Be like the first.

20. Understand that people are like mangos:
     some are unripe but appear to be ripe,
     some are ripe but appear to be unripe,
     some unripe ones appear unripe, some ripe ones appear
          ripe.

21. Don't gaze upon another's wife. However,
     if you do look, think of her as your mother,
     sister, or daughter, according to her age.
     If lust arises, contemplate the body's impurity.

22. Protect your wavering mind as if it were
     your education, child, treasure, or life.
     Renounce sensory pleasures for they are like
     poisonous snakes, weapons, enemies, and fire.

23. The Buddha said that objects of the senses lead to ruin
     and should be discarded like kimpāka fruit.
     Their iron chains bind those in the world
     to the prison of cyclic existence.

24. When the wise compare those who conquer
     the six unstable and constantly wavering senses
     with those who triumph over enemy hosts in battle,
     they see that the former are the great heroes.

25. Look at a youthful woman's body
     without any attractive embellishment.
     It has a foul odor; filth is emitted from nine orifices;
     It is like a pot full of garbage; it is hard to fill; and it is
          covered with skin.

26. Know that someone desiring sense objects
     is like a leper tormented by maggots.
     He resorts to using fire to find comfort,
     but there is no relief to be found.

27. In order to directly see ultimate reality
    properly condition your mind to all things.
    There is no other Dharma
    with greater good qualities than this.

28. A person may come from a high family, be learned, and
        attractive,
    but if they lack wisdom and morality, they are not worthy
        of respect.
    In this regard, if they have these two good qualities, vener-
        ate them
    even if they lack other positive attributes.

29. The eight worldly concerns are: gain and loss,
    pleasure and pain, praise and blame, fame and disrepute.
    The knower of the world says you should be indifferent
    to them and not let them occupy your mind.

30. Do not commit any evil actions for the sake of
    brahmins, monks and nuns, deities, your guests,
    your parents, or even your queen and retinue.
    They will not share the resulting experience in hell!

31. Doing an evil deed will not instantly
    cut you as if slashed by a sword;
    the result of your evil deeds
    will become apparent at the time of death.

32. The Buddha taught that there are seven riches:
    pure faith, conduct, generosity, learning,
    a flawless sense of modesty, decorum, and wisdom.
    Know that other common types of wealth are worthless.

33. Gambling, joining crowds to see shows,
    laziness, relying on evil companions,
    liquor, and roving at night lead to lower realms
    and a loss of reputation. So, give up these six!

34. "Contentment is the best type of wealth,"
taught the Teacher of gods and humans.
So always be content. If you are satisfied
you are wealthy even if you lack material riches.

35. O faithful one! To have many possessions is misery.
Those with few desires are not like that.
Nāga kings have as many headaches
as they have heads.

36. Avoid a wife with any of these three qualities:
a murderess associated with your enemies;
a tyrant contemptuous of her husband; or
a thief who steals even the smallest things.

37. A strong woman who is as easy-going as your sister,
as affectionate as a helpful loving friend, and
as supportive as your mother or a servant,
should be honored as your family's deity.

38. Recognize that food is like medicine.
Eat without desire or anger;
do not eat out of vanity, hatred, or egotism.
You should eat only to maintain your body.

39. Virtuous Lord! Properly use your entire day
and the first and last periods of the night.
Sleep with mindfulness between these two,
and then even your time of repose will not be fruitless.

40. Constantly and perfectly cultivate love,
compassion, joy, and equanimity.
Even if you do not attain the highest goal
you will obtain the bliss of the Brahma realms.

41. The four dhyānas are total abandonment
of sensory experience, joy, pleasure, and discomfort.

Through them you obtain the same good fortune as the
    god realms
of Brahmā, Ābhāsvara, Śubhakṛtsna, and Bṛhatphala.

42. Five attributes determine the strength of good or evil
      deeds:
those done constantly, with a strong motivation, lacking an
      antidote,
and in relation to the two bases of the highest good
      qualities.
Therefore, strive to engage in the practice of virtue.

43. A pinch of salt can change the taste
of a little water, but not the entire Ganges River.
You should know that the same applies to
minor negative actions and vast roots of virtue.

44. Recognize that excitement and regret, malice,
sluggishness and sleepiness, yearning sensory desire,
and doubt are the five obstacles
that steal the riches of virtue.

45. The five supreme dharmas are: faith, perseverance,
recollection, meditative concentration, and wisdom.
Strive in earnest for these. They are called
the strengths, the powers, and what takes you to the peak.

46. Conceit will not arise if the antidote
is considered again and again. Think,
"I am not exempt from sickness, aging, death,
separation from my loved ones, and subjugation to my
      karma."

47. If you desire a high rebirth or liberation
you must become familiar with the right view.
Someone with the wrong view may do good deeds
but they will experience horrific results.

48. Understand that in fact humans are
    suffering, impermanent, without a self, and impure.
    Those who have not established these four recollections
    adhere to the four wrong views and fall to ruin.

49. It was taught that physical things are not the self,
    the self does not possess physical things,
    the self does not dwell in physical things, nor do physical
        things dwell in the self.
    Understand that the four remaining aggregates are similarly
        empty.

50. The aggregates do not arise randomly, nor do they arise
        from time.
    They do not arise from a primordial nature, nor from their
        own essence.
    They do not arise from God, nor do they arise without a
        cause.
    Know that they arise from ignorance, karma, and craving.

51. Know that the three shackles binding you to samsara
    and blocking the gate to the city of liberation are:
    clinging to asceticism as a superior practice,
    having a perverted view of yourself, and doubt.

52. Emancipation depends upon you alone;
    no one else can do anything to help.
    So, endeavor to pursue the four realities for āryas
    through learning, morality, and concentration.

53. Always train in higher ethical conduct,
    higher wisdom, and higher concentration.
    There are more than 250 precepts for the ordained;
    all are included in these three higher trainings.

54. My lord, the Buddha taught that mindfulness
    of the body is the one path to follow.

Hold it and guard it tightly.
Losing mindfulness destroys all Dharma.

55. Your life is tenuous due to many harmful things;
it is as unstable as a bubble tossed by the wind.
Why, it is quite amazing that you breathe
in and out when you wake from sleep!

56. This body will end up as ashes, dry dust, or putrid filth.
You should understand that this body has no essence;
it is destroyed, it dissolves,
it decomposes, and disintegrates into pieces.

57. The earth, Mount Meru, and the oceans
will be incinerated by seven suns.
Not even dust will remain from the environment,
So, what needs to be said about weak, puny humans?

58. Since everything is impermanent and without a self,
there is no protection, savior, or resting place.
Therefore, O great one, turn your mind away from samsara
for it is like a banana tree; it has no essential core.

59. It is more difficult for an animal to be reborn as a human
than for a sea turtle to find a single yoke
floating on an ocean. So, O mighty king,
practice the Dharma to make this life bear fruit.

60. Someone who has taken a human rebirth
and performs evil deeds is more stupid than
someone who has a bejeweled golden vessel
and fills it up with vomit.

61. You reside in a place that is conducive,
you rely upon holy individuals, you are devout,
and you have previously accumulated merit.
You are in possession of these four great wheels.

62. The Buddha said that reliance on a spiritual friend
     is the way to completely fulfil a virtuous life.
     Many who relied on the victorious one obtained peace.
     Therefore, rely upon holy beings.

63. To be born as someone holding wrong views,
     as an animal, a hungry ghost, or in the hells,
     or where there are no teachings of the Buddha,
     as a barbarian in a remote place, or as someone unintelli-
         gent and dense,

64. or as a long-life god; any rebirth of this sort
     is one of the eight defective states lacking opportunity.
     You must find the leisure that is free of these;
     strive to turn away from rebirth.

65. My Lord, to become disgusted
     with samsara, the source of so much suffering,
     pay heed to some of its faults: frustrated desires,
     death, sickness, aging, and so forth.

66. Your father becomes your son, your mother becomes your
         wife,
     people who are your enemies become your friends,
     and the reverse occurs as well. Therefore,
     in samsara there is no certainty.

67. Every being has drunk more milk
     than the four great oceans could contain.
     More than that is still yet to be drunk
     in the subsequent samsaric rebirths of ordinary people.

68. The pile of bones from each individual's lives
     equals or surpasses the height of Mount Meru.
     There is not enough soil on earth to make enough
     juniper berry-sized pellets to count those in your maternal
         line.

69. Indra, who is revered throughout the world,
    falls to earth through the force of karma.
    A monarch of the entire universe
    will become a low servant in samsara.

70. After blissfully caressing the breasts and hips
    of celestial maidens for a long time, once again
    you are stroked by machines in hell
    that crush, slash, and tear you unbearably.

71. Consider that after living for a long time on Mount Meru's
        summit
    and enjoying the ground softly yielding to your feet,
    once again you will be struck by the unbearable suffering
    of the Firepit and Swamp of Filth hells.

72. After going to play in lovely parks,
    enjoying and escorting divine women,
    you will arrive in the forest with leaves of swords
    and your legs, arms, nose, and ears will be cut off.

73. After living in the realm called Gently Flowing Stream
    where there are goddesses with lovely faces, and golden
        lotuses grow,
    you will once again fall into the caustic boiling water
    of the hell called River Without a Ford.

74. After having the great pleasure of being a desire realm god
    and having Brahmā's bliss free of all gross desire,
    you again endure unceasing suffering
    as kindling in the fires of the Avīci hell.

75. When you have obtained the state of being the Sun or
        Moon
    the light of your body illumines the entire world.
    But once again you can return to enveloping darkness
    so thick you cannot see your outstretched hand.

76. Three types of virtue are the lamplight that dispels
     the causes for suffering that you have created.
     Take these up or you will be alone in darkness
     so deep it is not affected by the sun or moon.

77. For beings who engage in evil deeds
     there will be unrelenting misery in these hells:
     Reviving, Black-line, Intense Heat,
     Crushing, Screaming, Incessant, and so forth.

78. Some are crushed like sesame seeds,
     others are ground as fine as flour.
     Some are cut to pieces with blazing saws,
     others are hewn with unbearably sharp axes.

79. Likewise, others are forced
     to swallow liquid molten metal.
     Some are completely impaled upon
     blazing hot barbed iron spears.

80. Some throw their hands toward the sky
     as vicious iron-fanged dogs tear at them.
     Others are helpless while pecked by crows
     with sharp iron beaks and terrible claws.

81. Some writhe on the ground and wail
     as thousands of worms, beetles, deer-flies,
     and black bees bite into them
     leaving huge wounds that are agonizing when touched.

82. Some are immersed in blazing hot mud
     and constantly burned with their mouths agape.
     Some are dumped headfirst into iron cauldrons
     and boiled like dumplings bobbing up and down.

83. As soon as an evildoer ceases to breathe
     he will instantly experience the hells.

Someone who hears of this immeasurable suffering
and isn't afraid has a diamond-hard nature.

84. If it is terrifying to see pictures of the hells,
    or to hear, recollect, read about, or encounter statues of
        them,
    what need is there to say anything
    about actually experiencing that maturation of your karma?

85. Among all the types of pleasure,
    the extinction of craving is the highest bliss.
    Similarly, among all the types of suffering,
    the suffering of Avīci is the worst.

86. The pain of being violently stabbed three hundred times
    by sharp spears in a single day during this life
    doesn't equal or even approach a fraction
    of the smallest of the miseries in the hells.

87. Even if you experience for a billion years
    this extremely unbearable misery,
    you will not be freed from that life
    until those negative deeds are exhausted.

88. The seeds of these fruits of nonvirtue
    are negative actions of body, speech, and mind.
    Therefore, you must skillfully make an effort
    to never engage in the slightest wrongdoing.

89. When you take rebirth as an animal,
    you endure various kinds of misery: being killed, bound,
    and beaten. The unbearable experience of eating each other
    awaits those who have abandoned the virtue that brings
        peace.

90. Some are killed because people want
    their pearls, wool, bones, flesh, or skin.

These helpless beings are forced to work
by being beaten, kicked, whipped, and goaded.

91. The hungry ghosts endure incessant misery
caused by their unfulfilled desires.
They undergo terrible suffering
of hunger, thirst, cold, heat, exhaustion, and fear.

92. Some with mouths like the eye of a needle
and stomachs like mountains suffer hunger.
They do not have the ability to eat
even the tiniest scraps of discarded filth.

93. Some are naked, their bodies are just skin and bones,
and as dried out as the top of palm tree.
Some have mouths from which flames blaze at night.
Sand falls into their burning mouths as food.

94. The lowest types of ghosts cannot find
even filth like pus, blood, or excrement.
They attack each other and eat the pus
discharged from festering wounds on their throats.

95. For them, the summer moonlight feels hot
and the winter sunlight feels cold;
trees are completely empty of fruit;
just their gaze makes rivers go dry.

96. They experience unrelenting misery.
Their bodies are tightly bound by
the karmic noose of evil deeds.
Some do not die for five or ten thousand years.

97. Why do hungry ghosts experience various
types of misery that have but one taste?
The cause is taking delight in stinginess.
The Buddha said miserliness is ignoble.

98. In the higher realms, the suffering of death
is greater than the vast pleasures enjoyed there.
Thinking this way, upright people
do not crave the transitory higher realms.

99. The complexion of their bodies becomes unattractive,
their seats become uncomfortable, their flower garlands
    wilt,
their clothing develops an unpleasant odor,
and their bodies sweat as they never had before.

100. These are the five signs of imminent death in the god
    realms.
They arise for the gods who live in the heavens
similar to the way signs of impending death
arise for humans who reside on earth.

101. If those who are transmigrating from the god realms
have no remaining store of merit,
then without any control they will become
either a hell being, a hungry ghost, or an animal.

102. The demigods naturally resent the gods' splendor.
This causes them great mental anguish.
They are intelligent, but these beings' obscurations
prevent them from seeing reality.

103. Because samsara is like this,
there is no such thing as a pleasant rebirth.
Whether it be as a god, human, hell-being, ghost, or
    animal,
you should know birth is a crucible of great harm.

104. If your hair or clothing were to suddenly catch fire
you would try to put it out immediately. But give that up
and make an effort to end rebirth in samsara due to karma.
There is no greater purpose than this.

105. Pure ethical conduct, wisdom, and meditative stabilization
      lead to nirvana—immaculate peace and control.
      This state is ageless, deathless, eternal, and separate
      from earth, water, fire, air, and the sun and moon.

106. There are seven branches of the path to enlightenment:
      mindfulness, ascertainment of phenomena, diligence,
      joy, great agility, meditative concentration, and equanimity.
      These amass the merit needed to attain nirvana.

107. Without wisdom, there will be no meditative
          concentration.
      Without meditative concentration there is no wisdom.
      Someone who has them both shrinks cyclic existence
      to the size of an ox's hoof-print.

108. In the world there are fourteen unexpounded views.
      The Buddha, kinsman of the sun, declared that
      you should not contemplate these
      for they will not serve to pacify your mind.

109. The Buddha said that from ignorance comes karma;
      from that comes consciousness; from that comes the
      mind and body, from that come the six faculties;
      from these six come contact.

110. From contact, sensation arises;
      based on sensation, craving arises;
      from craving, appropriation comes to be;
      from that comes existence; from existence comes birth.

111. When there is birth, there will be sorrow, sickness, aging,
      losing what you desire, the fear of death, and so forth.
      There will be a huge mass of suffering.
      By stopping birth, all this will cease.

112. Dependent origination is the most cherished and profound
      teaching in the treasury of the Buddha's instruction.
      Whoever sees this perfectly sees the Buddha,
      the supreme knowledge of reality.

113. The eight limbs of the path are
      right view, livelihood, effort, mindfulness,
      concentration, speech, activity, and right thought.
      Meditate upon these in order attain peace.

114. This rebirth is the arising of suffering.
      Desire is the all-embracing cause of it.
      The cessation of it is liberation.
      The path to achieve that is the eightfold path.

115. Since this is so, you should always
      strive to see the four realities for āryas.
      Even laymen whose laps are filled with riches
      can cross the river of suffering by relying upon wisdom.

116. Those who have a direct realization of reality
      didn't fall from the sky or arise from the earth
      as an already perfect harvest.
      In the past, they too were just ordinary beings subject to
          the afflictions.

117. There's no need to say much to the fearless.
      The most essential and helpful instruction is
      "Control your mind!"
      The Buddha said, "The mind is the root of the Dharma."

118. To properly practice all the teachings that I have given
      is difficult even for monks, even more so for you.
      But you should practice some portion of them.
      Training in these qualities will make your precious life
          useful.

119. Rejoice in the merit created by all beings
      and also in your own good actions of body, speech, and
            mind.
      By dedicating these to the attainment of buddhahood
      you will obtain a mass of virtues.

120. Through that you will become a master of yoga
      for innumerable rebirths in the worlds of gods and men.
      You will provide relief to multitudes of frail living beings
      with deeds like those of Ārya Avalokiteśvara.

121. In your rebirths you will dispel
      sickness, aging, desire, and hatred.
      Then you will be like Amitābha in a buddha-field:
      a protector of the world with an infinite lifespan.

122. Through extending the stainless eminence of your wisdom,
      morality, and generosity throughout the heavens, the sky,
            and on earth,
      you engage in pacifying those who enjoy sense pleasures:
      humans on earth and the superb youths of the god realms.

123. Having attained the state of a lord of the victors—a
            buddha—
      you calm many weak and ignorant beings' fear, birth, and
            death.
      May you attain the fearless, unadulterated, faultless state
      of the peace simply called "gone beyond sorrow."

Appendix 2. Sanskrit, Translations, and Commentaries on Nāgārjuna's Letter to a Friend

Sanskrit

The Sanskrit original of Nāgārjuna's *Suhṛllekha* has recently been found and published in the following:

Dngos grub tshe ring. 2020. *Tal la'i lo mar bris pa'i rgya dpe bris ma bshes spring skor gyi dpe bsdur zhib 'jug.* Khrin tu'u: Bod ljongs bod yig dpe rnying dpe skrun khang.

Szántó, Péter-Dániel. 2021. "The *Suhṛllekha* of Nāgārjuna *editio minor* 2.0." Academia.edu.

The Sanskrit commentary by Mahāmati, *Vyaktapadāsuhṛllekhaṭīkā*, is not known to be extant

Chinese translations of the root text

Because Chinese and Tibetan translations are the basis for contemporary translations of this text into English, the most basic of these source language texts are listed prior to English versions.

Guṇavarman. Translated in 431 under the title *Bodhisattva Nāgārjuna's Essential Teaching in Verse for King Chan tuo jia. (Long shu pu wei chan tuo jia wang shuo fa yao ji).* Taishō 1672.

Saṅghavarman. Translated in 434 under the title *The Essential Teaching in Verse Recommended to all Kings. (Quan fa zhu wang yao ji)*. Taishō 1673.

Yijing. Translated in 637 under the title *Bodhisattva Nagarjuna's Exhortation in Verse for the King. (Long shu pu sa quan jie wang song)*. Taishō 1674.

Tibetan Translations of the Root Text

Sarvajñadeva and Tibetan reactor-translator Ka ba dpal brtsegs. Translated in the ninth century under the title *Letter of a Friend. (bshes pa'i spring yig)*. P5682 vol. 129

The Tibetan Translation of Mahāmati's Commentary

Mahāmati. *Vyaktapadāsuhṛllekhaṭīkā*. Sanskrit not extant. Translated into Tibetan under the title *An Extensive Explanation of the Words of* Letter of a Friend. (*bshes pa'i spring yig gi rgya cher bshad pa tshig gsal ba*) by Indian Abbot Sarvajñadeva and Tibetan redactor-translator Bande dpal brtsegs. P5690 vol. 129.

Selected Tibetan Commentaries

Bka' 'gyur Rin po che Klong chen Ye shes rdo rje (1897–1975). *Slob dpon 'phags pa klu sgrub kyi bshes pa'i spring yig gi mchan 'grel shal rgyun bdud rtsi'i zegs ma.*

Dkyil zur Blo bzang sbyin pa (1821–1891). *Bshes pa'i springs yig gi rnam bshad 'phags pa'i dgongs pa kun gsal zhes bya ba bzugs so.*

'Jam' mgon 'Ju Mi pham rgya mtsho (1846–1912). *Bshes spring gi mchan 'grel padma dkar po'i phreng ba.*

Red mda' ba Gzhon nu blo gros (1349–-1412). *Bshes pa'i springs yig gi 'grel pa don gsal.*

Rong ston Shes bya kun rig (1367-1449). *Legs par bshes pa'i springs yig gi rnam bshad thar lam bde ba'i them skas zhes bya ba.*

ENGLISH TRANSLATIONS AND COMMENTARIES

Beale, Samuel. 1892. *Suh-ki-li-lih-kiu: The Suhṛllekha or "Friendly Letter" Addressed to King Sadvaha*. London: Luzać.

Berzin, Alexander. Undated. *Letter to a Friend*. studybuddhism.com

Dharmamitra. 2009. *Letter from A Friend: A Bodhisattva's Advice to An Indian King on Right Living and the Buddhist Path = The Suhṛllekha: An Epistle Composed for King Śatakarṇī*. Seattle, WA: Kalavinka Press.

Dorji, C.T. 2001. *Saint Nagarjuna's Letter to King Gautamīputra*. Delhi: Prominent Publishers.

Kangyur Rinpoche Longchen Yeshe Dorje. 2013. *Nagarjuna's Letter to a Friend: With Commentary by Kyabje Kangyur Rinpoche*. Padmakara Translation Group, translators. Boston & London: Snow Lion.

Karma Thinley, Rinpoche. 2009. *The Telescope of Wisdom: A Condensed Interlinear Commentary on the Great Master Nagarjuna's The Letter to a Friend*. Bristol, UK: Ganesha Press.

Kawamura, Leslie. 1975. *Golden Zephyr: Instructions from a Spiritual Friend*, (Translation of *Suhṛllekha*, by Nāgārjuna and *Bshes spring gi mchan 'grel padma dkar po'i phreng ba* by 'Jam mgon 'Ju Mi pham rgya mtsho.) Emeryville, CA: Dharma Publishing.

Khantipalo, Bhikkhu. 1966. "The Letter of Kind-Heartedness of Ācārya Nagarjuna." In *The Wisdom Gone Beyond: An Anthology of Buddhist Texts*. 13–44. Bangkok: Social Science Association Press of Thailand for the Social Science Review.

Lobsang Tharchin, Geshe and Artemus B. Engle. 1979. *Nāgārjuna's Letter with Commentary by Venerable Rendawa Zhön-nu Lo-drö*. Dharamsala: Library of Tibetan Works and Archives.

Lozang Jamspal, Ven., Ngawang Samten Chophel, Ven., and Peter Della Santina. 1996. *Nāgārjuna's Letter to King Gautamīputra, with Explanatory Notes Based on Tibetan Commentaries*. Delhi: Motilal Banarsidass.

Santina, Peter Della. 2002. *Causality and Emptiness: The Wisdom of Nagarjuna*. Singapore: Buddhist Research Society.

Sumati Manjushri, Vagindra Dhyāna, and Vagindra Kalyana. 1982. *The Letter of a Friend*. Singapore: Singapore Buddha Sasana Society.

Sonam, A. 1961. *Suhṛllekha*. Sarnath: The Pleasure of Elegant Sayings Printing Press.
Wenzel, Heinrich. 1886. "Nagarjuna's Friendly Epistle." *Journal of the Pali Text Society*, 6–32.

Appendix 3. Five Obstacles to Developing Śamatha and Their Eight Antidotes

Five Obstacles	Subtype of Obstacles	Stage of Practice	Eight Antidotes	
Laziness	laziness of not wanting to practice	prevents starting practice	1. faith 2. admiration	
	laziness of procrastination	prevents starting practice	3. diligence	
	laziness of feeling incapable	prevents starting practice	4. flexibility / dexterity	Perseverance
Forgetting the instructions		prevents starting practice	5. recollection / mindfulness of the instructions	
Mental laxity and excitement		during practice	6. introspection	
Failing to apply the antidotes to laxity and excitement		during practice	7. Applying the antidotes to tighten or loosen concentration	
Unnecessary application of the antidotes to laxity and excitement		during practice	8. Ceasing to apply the antidotes	

Appendix 4. The Seventeen Levels (Dhyānas) of the Corporeal Realm

———◆———

ALL LEVELS ARE inhabited by corporeal gods. The levels within a dhyāna are due to the intensity and duration of practice on the preparatory stages. The chart reads with the highest level at the top.

Level of Dhyāna		English	Tibetan	Sanskrit
Fifth	5	Unexcelled	'Og min	Akaniṣṭha
	4	Great Insight	Shin tu mthong	Sudarśa
	3	Sublime Light	Gya nom snang ba	Sudṛśa
	2	Without Distress	Mi gdung pa	Atapa
	1	The Slightest	Mi che ba	Abṛha
Fourth	3	Great Fruition	'Bras bu che	Bṛhatphala
	2	Increasing Merit	Bsod nams 'phel	Puṇyaprasava
	1	Cloudless	Sprin med	Anabhraka
Third	3	Extensive Virtue	Dge rgyas	Śubhakṛtsna
	2	Immeasurable Virtue	Tshad med dge	Apramāṇaśubha
	1	Lesser Virtue	Dge chung	Parīttaśubha
Second	3	Clear Radiance	'Od gsal	Ābhāsvara
	2	Immeasurable Radiance	Tshad med 'od	Apramāṇābha
	1	Lesser Radiance	'Od chung	Parīttābha

Level of Dhyāna		English	Tibetan	Sanskrit
First	3	Great Brahma	Tshangs pa chen po	Mahābrahmaṇa
	2	Priests of Brahma	Tshangs pa mdun na 'do	Brahmapurohita
	1	Heaven of Brahma	Tshangs ris	Brahmakāyika

Appendix 5. The Seven Branches of the Path to Enlightenment

	Name	Description	Maitreya's categorization	Symbolic possession of a Universal Ruler
1	Mindfulness	To continuously recollect your object / recollecting what you have learned	Supportive branch or cause for maintaining and increasing your practice of virtue	Precious wheel
2	Ascertainment of Phenomena	Wisdom that distinguishes between the way things appear and their ultimate nature	Essential branch because it is a direct realization of ultimate reality	Great elephant
3	Diligence	Assiduous pursuit of virtuous actions to achieve your goal	Branch of departure or going forth from samsara	Special horse
4	Joy	Happiness due to practice on the path of seeing	Branch that is the benefit of meditation practice	Precious jewel
5	Great Agility	Flexibility of the body and mind so that you can practice as long as you wish	Branch that is not a mental affliction: the cause for being undisturbed and unafflicted	Precious queen

	Name	Description	Maitreya's categorization	Symbolic possession of a Universal Ruler
6	Meditative Concentration	Single-pointed concentration without distraction of dullness or excitement	Branch that is not a mental affliction: where you find the lack of mental affliction	Skillful minister
7	Equanimity	A balanced amount of effort in maintaining concentration	Branch that is not a mental affliction: the nature of being unafflicted	Army Commander

Appendix 6. The Twelve Links of Dependent Origination

Three lives: not necessarily sequential.

Life 1: Three causes: ignorance, propelling karma, and consciousness (these could be created anytime in the past series of lives).

Life 2: Four results: mind and body, six faculties, contact, feeling. And three causes: craving, appropriation, and existence.

Life 3: Two results: birth, aging and death (life three immediately follows life two).

Two lives: all six causes are created in one life immediately followed by a life encompassing all six results.

One life: can be understood to encompass all twelve links in that you experience all the results and create all the causes for future rebirths.

	Name	Description	Cause/Effect	3 Lives			2 Lives		Nāgārjuna's categorization from *Verses on the Essence of Dependent Origination*
				1	2	3	1	2	
1	Ignorance	Wrong view of the transitory composite: the egoistic view	Propelling cause	✓			✓		Mental affliction
2	Karma	Actions contaminated by the egoistic view	Propelling cause	✓			✓		Karma
3	Consciousness	Continual flow of moments of mind holding karmic seeds	Propelling cause	✓			✓		Result: consciousness at time of conception only; not causal consciousness
4	Mind and Body	Conception	Projected result		✓			✓	Result
5	Six Faculties	Development of embryo to have six functional faculties/organs	Projected result		✓			✓	Result
6	Contact	Coming together of an organ, consciousness, and object	Projected result		✓			✓	Result
7	Sensation	Felt reaction to contact	Projected result		✓			✓	Result
8	Craving	At time of death, desire that arises from sensation	Actualizing cause		✓		✓		Mental affliction

	Name	Description	Cause/Effect	3 Lives			2 Lives		Nāgārjuna's categorization from *Verses on the Essence of Dependent Origination*
				1	2	3	1	2	
9	Appropriation	At time of death, more intense desire	Actualizing cause		✓		✓		Mental affliction
10	Existence	Coming together of karmic seed, craving, and appropriation immediately prior to next life	Actualizing cause		✓		✓		Karma
11	Birth	A new rebirth	Actualized result			✓		✓	Result
12	Aging & Death	The moments during that rebirth	Actualized result			✓		✓	Result

Glossary

Abhidharma (*chos mngon pa*). The Abhidharma, one of three major sections of the Buddhist canon, contains texts that systemize and classify the essence of the Buddha's teachings found in the sutras. This body of commentarial texts is encyclopedic in that it deals with Buddhist ontology, psychology, cosmology, the operation of karma, the path to liberation, and the nature of its stages and attainments. *See also* **Tripitaka.**

afflictions. *See* **mental afflictions.**

aggregates. *See* **five aggregates.**

anātma (*bdag med*). The emptiness, or lack, of an independent, inherently existent self. *See also* **śūnyatā.**

arhat (*dgra bcom pa*). A person who has attained nirvana, the final goal of the Hinayana path. It is the fourth of the four spiritual fruit: stream winner, once-returner, nonreturner, and arhat.

ārya (*'phags pa*). A person who has achieved a direct realization of emptiness (*śūnyatā*), the true nature of all phenomena. Literally, *ārya* means *noble* or *superior. See also* **ordinary individual.**

ārya stage (*'phags pa'i lam*; Skt: *āryamārga*). Stages of the path including and subsequent to the first moment of the path of seeing, where one achieves a direct realization of emptiness, the true nature of all phenomena.

Avīci (*mnar med pa*). The lowest level of the eight great hot hells, in which there is the greatest unremitting suffering.

bardo (*bar do*). The intermediate state between death and the next rebirth.

bhikṣu (*dge slong*). Fully ordained monk.

bhikṣuṇī (*dge slong ma*). Fully ordained nun.

bodhicitta (*byang chub kyi sems*). The altruistic mind of enlightenment. The desire to become a buddha in order to benefit other sentient beings caught in the misery of samsara. The mark of entering the Mahayana path is when the wish to attain enlightenment in order to benefit other sentient beings is continuous and spontaneous.

bodhisattva (*byang chub sems dpa'*). A person who has entered the Mahayana path. Such beings have a continuous, spontaneous wish to attain enlightenment in order to benefit other sentient beings.

body-mind continuum. See **five aggregates**.

buddha (*sangs rgyas*). A fully enlightened being. Someone who has attained their own liberation from samsara as well as perfect omniscience.

calm abiding (*zhi gnas*). See **śamatha**.

cessation (*'gog pa*). The permanent elimination of a particular mental affliction or obstacle to omniscience through the cultivation of a direct realization of the ultimate nature of reality. Nirvana is the cessation of all rebirth under the power of ignorance and the mental afflictions.

conventional truth. See **phenomenal reality**.

corporeal realm (*gzugs khams*; Skt: *rūpadhātu*). Along with the desire realm and the noncorporeal realm, this is one of the three realms of samsaric existence. Its basic divisions are four levels of meditative stabilization (dhyāna). Each of the first three levels has three levels, and the fourth has eight levels; a particular type of corporeal-realm god resides on each of these seventeen levels. In these realms a being's body still has some corporeality. Even the lowest dhyāna is more subtle than the desire realm, and each higher level is more subtle than the preceding levels.

cyclic existence. See **samsara**.

dependent origination (*rten 'brel*; Skt: *pratītyasamutpāda*). In general, all phenomena exist due to causes and conditions. In particular, the term refers to the twelve links of dependent origination. Briefly, from the combination of karma and delusions you take rebirth, then due to ignorance you create more karma, and then you die and take rebirth again.

desire realm (*'dod khams*; Skt: *kāmadhātu*). One of the three realms of existence in samsara. There are six realms within the desire realm: three lower realms—hell beings, hungry ghosts, and animals—and three higher realms—humans, demigods, and gods.

deva (*lha*). Deities or gods. In Buddhism, those beings called gods have extremely pleasurable and long lives, but they are still caught in samsara, either in the desire realm or the corporeal and noncorporeal realms. Their lives are not permanent, and they do not have the power to end their own or others' cycle of misery.

Dharma (*chos*; Skt: *dharma*). The teachings of the Buddha and his followers.

dharmadhātu (*chos kyi dbyings*). Sphere of phenomena; in other words, emptiness.

dhyāna. See **meditative stabilization**.

egoistic view (*'jig tshogs la lta ba*; Skt: satkāyadṛṣṭi). The view of the transitory collection. The apprehension and belief that your five skandhas—the impermanent factors of body and mind—have an intrinsic identity.

eight vows of individual liberation. See **prātimokṣa**.

eight worldly concerns (*'jig rten chos brgyad*; Skt: aṣṭalokadharma). Also known as the eight worldly dharmas. Preoccupation with gain and loss, pleasure and pain, praise and scorn, and fame and ill repute. These four pairs encapsulate the concerns of ordinary people who desire to attain the first in each pair and avoid the second.

emptiness (*stong pa nyid*; Skt: *śūnyatā*). The ultimate nature of all phenomena: their lack of inherent existence.

enlightenment (*byang chub*; Skt: *bodhi*). The ultimate spiritual goal for Mahayana practitioners: the state of buddhahood. A buddha's mind is purified of all obstacles and their causes and is omniscient—knowing every aspect of reality. Enlightenment has the qualities of perfect love, compassion, and the intention and ability to help others attain liberation.

equanimity (*btang snyoms*; Skt: *upekṣā*). There are three different uses of the term equanimity on the Buddhist path. The first is in the context of developing śamatha where it refers to leaving the mind alone when it is functioning properly. The second use of the term is when discussing the three basic types of feeling: unhappiness, happiness, and a neutral, equanimous feeling. The third type of equanimity is in the context of the preparatory practice of the four limitless thoughts: equanimity, compassion, love, and joy. Limitless or immeasurable equanimity means being even-minded, free from desire or hostility toward living beings.

ethical discipline (*tshul khrims*; Skt: *śīla*). The first of the three higher trainings and the second perfection.

faith (*dad pa*; Skt: *prasāda*). Tibetan teachers explain three levels of faith. The first is clear or pure faith (*dang ba'i dad pa*), a sincere, but rather superficial, trust and happiness to practice the Dharma. The second and stronger type of faith is the faith of conviction (*yid ches kyi dad pa*) founded on some background knowledge, seeing the logic of the matter, and bringing personal experience to bear. As our logical and experiential understanding increases, we produce the third and strongest kind of faith, irreversible faith (*phyir mi ldog pa'i dad pa*).

five aggregates (*phung po lnga*; Skt: *pañcaskandha*). The five physical and mental components of a rebirth: the physical body, feeling, discrimination, activity, and consciousness.

five paths (*lam lnga*; Skt: *pañcamārga*). The five consecutive paths leading to or culminating in enlightenment. These consist of (1) the path of accumulation (*tshogs lam*; Skt: *saṃbhāramārga*), during which one begins to amass the accumulation of merit and wisdom that will ripen in enlightenment; (2) the path of preparation (*sbyor lam*, Skt: *prayogamārga*), so named because one is preparing for a direct realization of emptiness; (3) the path of seeing (*mthong lam*; Skt: *darśanamārga*), during which one sees emptiness directly and nonconceptually for the first time; (4) the path of cultivation (*sgom lam*; Skt: *bhāvanāmārga*) during which one repeatedly familiarizes oneself with emptiness, thereby gradually eliminating the obstacles connected with each stage of development; and (5) the path of no further training (*mi slob lam*; Skt: *aśaikṣamārga*), in which there is no longer any need to abandon further obstacles or develop new realizations. At this point the final fruit of the different spiritual journeys is achieved; those who have followed the Mahayana path of the bodhisattva attain perfectly complete buddhahood, while those who have followed the Hinayana path attain arhatship.

five powers (*stobs lnga*, Skt: *pañcendriyāṇi*). In the context of the path system five mental competencies are called powers or strengths (*stobs lnga*, Skt: *pañcabalāni*): faith, perseverance, recollection, meditative concentration, and wisdom. According to the lower Abhidharma system they are called *powers* when practiced on the path of accumulation and *strengths* when practiced on the path of preparation. According to the higher Abhidharma system, both the powers and strengths are practiced on the path of preparation. The five practices keep their individual names on each successive level, but the name of their category changes from power to strength in order to indicate their increasing efficacy.

five strengths. See **five powers.**

four immeasurables. See **four limitless thoughts.**

four limitless thoughts (*tshad med bzhi*, Skt: *caturapramāṇa*): (1) compassion (*snying rje*; Skt: *karuṇā*)—thinking how wonderful it would be if all sentient beings were free from misery; (2) love (*byams pa*; Skt: *maitrī*)—thinking how wonderful it would be if they all possessed happiness; (3) equanimity (*btang snyoms*; Skt: *upekṣā*)—thinking how wonderful it would be if they all were harmonious, having equanimity toward each other, without hatred or desire; and (4) joy (*dga' ba*; Skt: *muditā*)—thinking how wonderful it would be if all beings obtained the highest happiness of liberation from samsara.

four noble truths. See **four realities for āryas.**

four realities for āryas (*'phags pa'i bden pa bzhi*; Skt: *caturāryasatya*). What most readers will know as the "four noble truths." In this context *noble* refers to an individual who has directly realized ultimate reality—an ārya—not to the content, or truth, of what has been realized. There are sixteen aspects of these four realities taught as a means to contemplate the meaning of each reality in depth and counter specific wrong views. The reality of suffering: suffering, impermanence, emptiness, selflessness. The reality of the cause of suffering: cause, origination, intense arising, condition. The reality of cessation of suffering: peace, cessation, perfection, true freedom. The reality of the path to cessation: path, appropriate, effective, truly delivering.

geshe (*dge bshes*). A contraction of geyway sheynyen (*dge ba'i bshes gnyen*), which means virtuous friend, spiritual friend, or guru. In the Gelug school of Tibetan Buddhism it is the title bestowed on those scholars who complete the course of study at one of the three great monasteries.

great compassion (*snying rje chen po*; Skt: *mahākaruṇā*). The desire to take responsibility to free all sentient beings from suffering.

Hinayana (*theg dman*; Skt: *Hīnayāna*). The spiritual path leading to the attainment of nirvana, understood as individual liberation from suffering.

ignorance (*ma rig pa*; Skt: *avidyā*). A lack of realization of the ultimate nature of all phenomena; the innate belief that things exist as they appear—as substantial, independent, self-sufficient entities.

intermediate state (*bar do*). The state one enters after death and before one's next rebirth.

intrinsic identity (*rang gi mtshan nyid*; Skt: *svalakṣaṇa*). If something, or someone, were to exist from its own side, independently of the mind that conceives it, independently of its parts, and independently of its causes, it would exist by way of its own intrinsic identity.

inherently existent (*rang bzhin gyis grub pa*; Skt: *svabhāvasiddhi*). If something had its own independent and intrinsic identity or essence it would be inherently existent. Nothing exists in this way.

kalpa (*bskal pa*). Four billion, three hundred and twenty million years, commonly referred to as an eon.

karma (*las*). Literally, "action." The actions of ordinary sentient beings are contaminated by ignorance. Every contaminated action of body, speech, and mind plants a seed of potential on the mental continuum that will eventually ripen into experience. There are four types of results: (1) maturation result is a rebirth, (2) and (3) are results similar to the cause in that you will have experiences that are similar to the cause that produced it, and (4) environmental result is the quality of the place where you live. The uncontaminated action of buddhas do not result in rebirth and suffering.

kāya (*sku*). Bodies of the buddha: dharmakāya, saṃbhogakāya, and nirmāṇakāya, also known as the wisdom, enjoyment, and emanation bodies. These three can be coalesced into two: the dharmakāya, or perfect mental body, and the rūpakāya, or the perfect physical body. The rūpakāya includes the saṃbhogakāya, and nirmāṇakāya.

kleśa. See **mental afflictions**.

lamrim (*lam rim*). Literally, the "stages of the path." The lamrim method, formalized by Je Tsongkhapa, is a progressive system of practices and meditations organized to lead the practitioner from the very beginning of the spiritual path, through the middle phase, and ultimately all the way to buddhahood.

league (*dpag tshad*; Skt: *yojana*). A unit of distance measuring four thousand arm-lengths, about four and a half miles.

Lord of Death (*'chi bdag gshin rje*; Skt: *Yama*). A personification of death itself.

Madhyamaka (*dbu ma*). A Mahayana school of philosophy based on the writings of Nāgārjuna. It is called the "Middle Way" school because it teaches the doctrine of emptiness (śūnyatā) as a middle position between the extremes of nihilism and inherent existence.

Mahayana (*theg chen gyi lam*; Skt: *mahāyāna*). The spiritual path leading to the goal of perfect buddhahood. The Mahayana disciple wishes to become a buddha so that they can help free all other beings from suffering.

maturation result (*rnam smin gyi 'bras bu*). The main result of the ripening of a karmic seed. The maturation result is the type of rebirth you take and is distinguished from the environmental results and results corresponding to the cause, which together determine the variety of experiences one meets while in that particular type of rebirth.

meditative concentration (*ting nge 'dzin*; Skt: *samādhi*). A virtuous mind that stably abides on its object without distraction to other objects. The second of the three higher trainings. This is a broad category that encompasses effortless and flexible single pointed concentration (*zhi gnas*; *Skt śamatha*) and other types of concentration.

meditative stabilization (*bsam gtan*; Skt: *dhyāna*). A general term for meditative focus. It is the term used to indicate the fifth of the six perfections and also for the four levels of existence in the corporeal realm.

mental afflictions (*nyon mongs*; Skt: *kleśa*). Mental states stemming from ignorance, such as desire, aversion, jealousy, and so forth that are obstacles to attaining liberation from samsara. These mental states obscure the mind from seeing reality in its true nature and motivate actions (karma) that cause one to continue to be born in cyclic existence. Other translations of this term include "disturbing emotions," "afflicting emotions," "afflictions," and "negative mental states." See also **obstructions to liberation.**

merit. Often used as a synonym for virtue. Virtue has more of the flavor of the positive action itself whereas merit has more the flavor of the positive potential of that action deposited in one's consciousness.

mindfulness (*dran pa*; Skt: *smṛti*). A mental factor that functions to hold the mind to its object. It is not allowing the mind forget about its object or move away from it. Another sense of mindfulness is the quality of mind that does not forget which objects are suitable to engage in and which should be avoided. See also **six recollections**.

mundane path (*'jig rten pa'i lam*; Skt: *laukikamārga*). A method of temporarily subduing the mental afflictions through the practice of joining śamatha to meditations on the faults of the level of existence one is trying to transcend and the good qualities of the level of existence one is trying to attain. This method is common to both Buddhists and non-Buddhists and can lead to the highest level of meditative absorption in the noncorporeal realm, but it does not eliminate afflictions from the root.

nāga (*klu*). Demigods with the head and upper torso of a human and the lower body of a snake who generally live underground or in lakes and rivers. They are sometimes considered to be part of the animal realm.

nirmāṇakāya (*sprul sku*). The emanation body of a buddha. The nirmāṇakāya takes various forms that can be perceived by our limited senses. It is the person that we see as the Buddha in our world. Various qualities of enlightenment manifest as thirty-two major marks and eighty minor marks adorning the emanation body. The saṃbhogakāya and the nirmāṇakāya are together called the form body (*rūpakāya*) of a buddha.

nirvana (*mya ngan las 'das pa*; Skt: *nirvāṇa*). One's own permanent liberation from samsara; freedom from all suffering; the attainment of an arhat; cessation of ignorance; permanent liberation from uncontrolled rebirths caused by ignorance and karma; permanent freedom from suffering; and peace.

nirvana with remainder (phung po lhag ma dang bcas pa'i mya ngan las 'das pa; Skt: *sopadhiśeṣanirvāṇa*). When as a result of their practice śrāvakas and pratyekabuddhas free themselves from samsara, for the rest of that lifetime they still have a body that was created by karma from prior lives. The "remainder" is the body; it is the last vestige of a Hinayana arhat's connection to samsara. See also **nirvana without remainder** and **parinirvāṇa**.

nirvana without remainder (*phung po lhag ma med pa'i mya ngan las 'das pa*; Skt: *anupadhiśeṣanirvāṇa*). At the time of death, śrāvakas and pratyekabuddhas who had attained nirvana in their lifetime are completely freed from any kind of subtle misery associated with a body. From then on, they will be free from all samsaric qualities and can remain in peace forever unless stimulated to practice the Mahayana path for the benefit of other beings. See also **nirvana with remainder** and **parinirvāṇa**.

noncorporeal absorptions (*gzugs med snyoms 'jug*; Skt: samāpatti). The four noncorporeal absorptions are successive levels of the noncorporeal realm.

noncorporeal realm (*gzugs med khams*; Skt: *ārūpadhātu*) Along with the desire realm and the corporeal realm, this is one of the three realms of samsaric existence. Beings in this realm do not possess material form; the noncorporeal realm is without a physical dimension. Until recently many scholars translated this term as "formless realm."

nonreturner (*phyir mi 'ong ba*; Skt: *anāgāmin*). Third of the four spiritual fruits: stream winner, once-returner, nonreturner, and arhat. When an ārya has removed all nine desire realm afflictions on the supramundane path, that yogi becomes a nonreturner. Such a being is no longer compelled by karma and the mental afflictions to be reborn in the desire realm.

objects of knowledge (*shes bya*; Skt: *jñeya*). All things that can be known are included in three categories: obvious things, which can be observed directly with the senses; objects that are slightly hidden, which cannot be detected with the senses but can be logically inferred based on sensory information; and very hidden phenomena, which can neither be observed directly nor inferred from ordinary beings' observations, but must be provisionally believed in out of faith in higher beings' perceptions.

once-returner (*lan cig phyir 'ong ba*; Skt: *sakṛdāgāmin*). Second of the four fruits of spiritual practice: stream winner, once-returner, nonreturner, and arhat. When a person has removed six of the nine desire realm afflictions, they are called a once-returner because only one more rebirth is required to remove the final three desire realm afflictions.

ordinary individual (*so so skye bo*; Skt: *pṛthagjana*). A being who has not had a direct realization of ultimate reality. In contrast, an ārya, or superior being, has directly realized ultimate reality.

pāramitā. See **perfections.**

parinirvāṇa (*yongs su mya ngan las 'das pa*). Final nirvana, the state entered when a buddha's human life ends. According to the Mahayana tradition, a buddha's parinirvana is significantly different from the nirvana without remainder attained by śrāvaka and pratyekabuddha arhats. Śrāvaka and pratyekabuddha arhats have removed all the mental afflictions and have attained a state of peace free from samsaric rebirth. Buddhas have removed all the mental afflictions as well as the subtle obstacles to omniscience; they are embodied as the four kāyas.

path of accumulation. See **five paths.**

path of cultivation. See **five paths.**

path of no more learning. See **five paths.**

path of preparation. See **five paths.**

path of seeing. See **five paths.**

path of no further training. See **five paths.**

perfections (*pha rol tu phyin pa*; Skt: *pāramitā*). The activities of practitioners on the Mahayana path after they have developed bodhicitta. The perfections are commonly listed as six: generosity (*sbyin pa*; Skt: *dāna*), ethical discipline (*tshul khrims*; Skt: *śīla*), patience (*bzod pa*; Skt: *kṣānti*), perseverance (*brtson 'grus* ; Skt: *vīrya*), concentration, or meditative stabilization (*bsam gtan*; Skt: *dhyāna*), and wisdom (*shes rab*; Skt: *prajñā*).

phenomenal reality (*kun rdzob kyi bden pa*; Skt: *saṃvṛtisatya*). This is reality as seen from the perspective of ordinary well-educated persons in samsara. Conventionally existent things are determined to exist when they meet three criteria: (1) they are commonly established for people, (2) they are not contradicted by a conventional avenue of knowledge, and (3) they are not contradicted by reasoning that investigates the final nature of things. To ordinary people things appear to have an intrinsic identity, and those without a direct realization of ultimate reality believe that they exist as they appear. Āryas do not assent to this appearance; although in post-meditation periods they perceive phenomenal things to have an intrinsic identity, they understand that phenomenal things exist relatively, dependent on causes, parts, and conceptions. See also **two realities.**

prāṇa (*srog*). The vital energy wind in the body.

prātimokṣa (*so so thar pa*). The "vows of individual liberation" laid out in the Vinaya and forming the basis of Buddhist ethics. There are eight types of prātimokṣa vows: (1) eight-part upoṣadha vows are one-day vows for the laity; the next two, (2) upāsaka and (3) upāsikā vows, are vows for laymen and laywomen taken for life; the next two, (4) śrāmaṇera vows for men and (5) śrāmaṇerī for women, are novice vows taken when you enter a religious order; (6) bhikṣu and (7) bhikṣuṇī are full ordination vows for men and women. (8) The eighth type of prātimokṣa vow is only for women. It is an additional level between śrāmaṇerī and full bhikṣuṇī.

pratyekabuddha (*rang sangs rgyas*). Often translated as "solitary realizers" because in their last lifetime prior to attaining liberation they stay alone—they do not interact with a teacher. Prior study and practice over many lives enable them to be silent and solitary during their last life, in which they attain the state of a Hinayana arhat.

pūjā (*mchod pa*). To worship; to do what pleases the buddhas and bodhisattvas.

pure land (*dag zhing*; Skt: *kṣetraśuddhi*). A buddhafield; an environment of unimaginably excellent qualities, far beyond our ordinary conception, attained as the result of the accumulation of merit.

reality. See **two realities.**

renunciation (*nges 'byung*; Skt: *naiṣkramya*). Intense interest in attaining freedom from suffering because of utter disgust with all of samsara.

rūpakāya (*gzugs sku*). The form body of a buddha, composed of the sambhogakāya and nirmāṇakāya. See also **nirmāṇakāya** and **sambhogakāya.**

sambhogakāya (*longs sku*). The enjoyment body of a buddha. This is the perfected form in which a buddha attains enlightenment, the ultimate physical body, completely absorbed in enjoyment of the Mahayana Dharma. It is always present but is only perceptible to advanced-level bodhisattvas. See also **rūpakāya.**

samādhi. See **meditative concentration.**

śamatha (*zhi gnas*). A form of samādhi. This is the ability of the mind to remain focused on an object of observation with complete freedom from distraction and mental laxity for as long as desired. This effortless mental flexibility and control is accompanied by physical and mental pliancy and bliss.

samsara (*'khor ba*; Skt: *saṃsāra*). The uncontrolled taking of rebirth under the force of ignorance, karma, and the mental afflictions.

Sangha (*dge 'dun*; Skt: *saṅgha*). Assembly, community. Conventionally, this refers to a group of at least four fully ordained monks or nuns. It also refers to anyone, lay or ordained, who has attained a direct realization of the ultimate nature of reality.

śāstras (*bstan bcos*). Literary works explaining religious topics and commenting on the sutras. Refers primarily to the works of the classical Indian masters.

selflessness. See **anātma.**

śīla (*tshul khrims*). Ethical discipline. The first of the three higher trainings and the second of the six perfections.

single-pointed concentration. See **śamatha.**

six recollections (*dran drug*; Skt: *ṣaḍ-anusmṛti*). Also called six reflections, six mindfulnesses, or six remembrances. These are the subjects you keep in mind in order to have faith. The six foci of faith are: Buddha, Dharma, Sangha, generosity, morality, and the gods.

skandhas. See **five aggregates.**

spiritual attainment (*dngos grub*; Skt. *siddhi*). Special powers that result from both Buddhist and non-Buddhist spiritual practices. With effort even ordinary people can achieve these powers. See also **supranormal knowledge.**

śrāvaka (*nyan thos*). Literally, "hearers"; practitioners striving for their own liberation from samsara. They receive this name because—unlike pratyekabuddhas—they rely on listening to their teachers' instructions through the course of their spiritual practice.

Śrāvakayāna (*nyan thos lam*). The path of practice for śrāvakas. A more accurate term for the Hinayana.

stream winner (*rgyun du zhugs pa*; Skt: *strotāpanna*). The first of the four spiritual fruits: stream winner, once-returner, nonreturner, and arhat. A śrāvakayāna practitioner attains the state of a stream winner by having a direct realization of the four realities for āryas. Mahayana practitioners attain this fruit by having a direct realization of emptiness.

suffering (*sdug bsngal*; Skt: *duḥkha*) The three basic types of misery: ordinary suffering (*sdug bsngal gi sdug bsngal*; Skt: *duḥkhadukhatā*), the suffering of transformation (*'gyur ba'i sdug bsngal*; Skt: *vipariṇāmad-*

ukḥatā), and the suffering of being created by causes and conditions (*khyab pa 'du byed kyi sdug bsngal*; Skt: *saṃskāradukḥatā*).

sugata (*bde bar gshegs pa*). An epithet of a buddha meaning "one who has reached the highest bliss" and "the one who is gone well."

supramundane path (*'jig rten las 'das pa'i lam*; Skt: *lokattaramārga*). The method of practice, unique to the Buddhadharma, leading to the direct realization of emptiness, which destroys karmic seeds from the root.

supranormal knowledge (*mngon par shes pa*; Skt: *abhijñjā*). Six by-products of meditation. They are miraculous powers, clairaudience, knowledge of others' thoughts, recollection of former states, knowledge of death and rebirth, and knowledge that the mental afflictions have been terminated.

śūnyatā (*stong nyid*). Suchness, or emptiness; the true nature of all phenomena; the absence of inherent existence.

sutra (*mdo*; Skt: *sūtra*). One of three major sections of the Buddhist canon, containing the general discourses of the Buddha, largely dealing with topics of meditation. See also **Tripiṭaka**.

tathāgata (*de bzhin gshegs pa*). The term the Buddha used to speak of himself after his enlightenment. It means "he who has gone thus on the path of all the buddhas."

three higher trainings (*lhag pa'i bslab pa gsum*; Skt: *triśikṣā*). Ethical discipline, meditative concentration, and wisdom. They are called "higher" because they lead to nirvana or buddhahood. These three higher trainings together constitute the fourth reality for āryas, formerly called the truth of the path. See also **four realities for āryas**.

Three Jewels (*dkon mchog gsum*; Skt: *triratna*). The Buddha, Dharma, and Sangha to which all Buddhists go for refuge.

three realms (*khams gsum*; Skt: *tridhātu*). The three realms of existence. See **desire realm, corporeal** and **noncorporeal realms**.

Tripiṭaka (*sde snod gsum*). The Buddhist canon, consisting of the three "baskets" (*piṭaka*) of Sutra, Vinaya, and Abhidharma.

twelve links. See **dependent origination**.

two truths. See **two realities**.

two realities (*bden gnyis*; Skt: *satyadvaya*). Reality can be accurately viewed from two perspectives: phenomenally and ultimately. Ultimate reality is emptiness: things do not exist in the way that they appear to ordinary people; things appear to be intrinsically existent, but they are not. However, things exist, just not in the way that we ordinarily think that they do. Phenomenal things exist dependent on causes, parts, and designation. Phenomenally existent things are determined to exist when they meet three criteria: (1) they are commonly established for people, (2) they are not contradicted by a conventional avenue of knowledge, and (3) they are not contradicted by reasoning that investigates the final nature of things. Commonly translated as "two truths."

ultimate reality (*don dam bden pa*; Skt: *paramārthasatya*). The emptiness of inherent existence, śūnyatā.

ultimate truth See **ultimate reality**

Vajrayana (*rdo rje theg pa;* Skt. *Vajrayāna*). A subset of the Mahayana path employing powerful meditation techniques to attain enlightenment as quickly as possible.

Vinaya (*'dul ba*). One of three major sections of the Buddhist canon, containing the scriptures dealing with ethical conduct. See also **Tripiṭaka**.

vipaśyanā (*lhag mthong*). Superior wisdom; highest insight. An analytical meditation that when combined with śamatha eventually produces a direct realization of ultimate reality—the antidote to ignorance.

vows of individual liberation. See **prātimokṣa**.

wisdom (*shes rab*; Skt: *prajñā*). Perfect wisdom is realization of the ultimate nature of all phenomena; it is direct comprehension of emptiness, the lack of inherent existence of a personal self and phenomena. Wisdom is the third of the three higher trainings and the sixth perfection.

worldly concerns. See **eight worldly concerns**.

Yama. See **Lord of Death**.

yoga (*rnal 'byor*). Spiritual discipline, control.

yogi (*rnal 'byor pa*). An assiduous religious practitioner. Because they put the various teachings into strict daily practice, yogis and yoginis (the feminine form of the word) often adopt an ascetic lifestyle.

Notes

1. Although there is still some debate about who precisely this king was, most contemporary Western scholars have identified him as Gautamīputra Śātakarṇi. Ruegg 2010, 13–15; Ichimura 2001, 106–30; Jamspal et al 2008, xiv.
2. Tharchin 1979, 5.
3. Jamspal et al 2008, xiv.
4. Dietz 1983, 60; Ruegg 2010, 113–14; Tharchin 1979, 11.
5. Mabbett 1998, 338; Tharchin 1979, 12.
6. Mabbett 1998, 342; Ruegg 2010, 119.
7. Unless words have been adopted into the English lexicon this text employs Sanskrit diacritics and the Wylie transcription system for Tibetan.
8. Pāsādika 1986, 203.
9. Dietz 1983, 59–72.
10. Szántó 2021, 10.
11. See appendix 1 for a list of translations into Tibetan, Chinese, and English. I am particularly indebted to Geshe Lobsang Tharchin and Artemus B. Engle's translation of the root text and Rendawa Shonu Lodro's fourteenth-century commentary.
12. Dietz 1983, 64; Jamspal 2008, xv.
13. Dietz 1983, 61 references some of the works that quote the text.
14. Szántó 2021, 1.
15. Readers may refer to the first section of the Bibliography for works cited by Geshe Sopa.
16. The Sanskrit term *sugata* (*bde bar gshegs pa*) is an epithet for a buddha. It is usually translated as "one who has gone to bliss." In other words, a being who has both abandoned all flaws and realized all that is to be known. There is also the implication that their *going* is good for the world. There are many epithets for buddhas that are meant to inspire followers with a shade of understanding of certain qualities of an awakened being. The purpose of these epithets is increased devotion. The term *special verses* is a loose translation to indicate stanzas written in the complex and rare āryāgīti meter. See Dietz 1995, 65.

17. The title of this important text by Śāntideva has been translated in numerous ways: *A Guide to the Bodhisattva Way of Life, Engaging in the Bodhisattva Deeds, The Way of the Bodhisattva, Entering the Path to Enlightenment, The Path of Light,* and is sometimes simply left in Sanskrit as *Bodhicaryāvatāra.* I have chosen to use a more literal translation of the title in this book: *Introduction to the Practice of Bodhisattvas.*

18. As Western knowledge of Buddhist philosophy has advanced, scholars have replaced the old translation terms *conventional truth* and *ultimate truth* with *phenomenal reality* and *ultimate reality,* respectively.

19. Note that throughout this text unless otherwise specified the term *mindfulness* is used in the traditional manner where it means to remember and recollect your object without forgetting it. This is different from the contemporary usage of *mindfulness* meaning awareness of the present.

20. There are three realms in samsara: desire, corporeal, and noncorporeal. Beings are born into these realms as a result of their karma. The lowest of these three is the desire realm, which has six sub-realms within it: hells, hungry ghosts, animals, humans, demigods, and gods. The desire realm gods, even Indra and Brahma, are born and die like all sentient beings trapped in samsara. All beings in the two upper realms are superior to humans and desire realm gods and so can be considered to be gods or celestial beings. There is an increasing level of subtlety as the levels in the realms progress upward. In the corporeal realm the beings still have some, but very subtle, physicality. This is completely gone in the noncorporeal realm. The old terms for the two upper realms were *form* and *formless realms.*

21. Jina (*rgyal ba*) is another epithet for a buddha, having the connotation of *victor.* A buddha has conquered the four *maras,* or demons: the mara of the aggregates; the mara of the mental afflictions; the mara of the lord of death; and the mara of the sons of the gods. The last mara symbolizes craving for pleasure. These internal demons are explained differently in sutra and tantra contexts.

22. The following section describing the qualities of a buddha roughly follows the ancient formula praising Śākyamuni Buddha. This often chanted hymn is translated into English as, "To the founder, the endowed transcendent destroyer, the one gone beyond, the foe-destroyer, the completely perfected full awakened being, perfect in knowledge and in good conduct, the one gone to bliss, the knower of the world, the supreme guide of human beings to be tamed, the teacher of gods and human beings—to you, the completely and fully awakened one, the endowed transcendent destroyer, the glorious conqueror, the subduer from the Śākya clan, I prostrate, make offerings, and go for refuge."

23. "Third reality for the āryas" here translates what most readers will know as the third of the four noble truths. Although this change in terminology may seem difficult at first, *four noble truths* is a misleading translation. In this context *noble* refers to an individual who has directly realized ultimate reality—an ārya—not to the content or truth of what has been realized. Āryas see reality in a way that ordinary beings do not: āryas recognize the reality of suffering, the reality of a cause of suffering, the reality of a cessation of suffering, and the reality of a path to attain that cessation of suffering. Ordinary beings misperceive and misunderstand these four things; they are not reality for them.

This translation choice is discussed in detail in chapter 10 in the section titled *The Four Realities for Āryas*.

24. The title of this particular text, *Uttaratantra Mahāyānottaratantraśāstra,* has often been rendered as the *Sublime Continuum*.

25. There is an exception to clockwise circumambulation in some Buddhist practice. The mother tantras advocate counter-clockwise circumambulation and making offerings starting on the left rather than from the right. Bön practitioners likewise circumambulate counter-clockwise.

26. See chapter 2, commentary on verse 5 lines a-b.

27. For a complete description of how to purify karma by employing the four opponent powers see Geshe Sopa's *Steps on the Path to Enlightenment,* volume 2, pp 148–74.

28. The five paths are further discussed in the commentary on verse 105 in chapter 10.

29. In Maitreya's *Distinguishing the Middle from the Extremes* these ten activities are listed as: copying texts, making offerings, charity, study, reading, memorizing, explaining, reciting aloud, contemplating, and meditating.

Bibliography

Sutras

Collection of Indicative Verses. Udānavarga. P992 vol. 39.
Condensed Perfection of Wisdom. Prajñāpāramitāsaṃcayagāthā. P735 vol. 21.
Connected Discourses. Saṃyutta Nikāya. Pali Canon, Sutta Piṭaka.
Extensive Sport Sutra. Lalitavistarasūtra. P763 vol. 27.
Flower Array Sutra. Gaṇḍavyūhasūtra. P761 vol. 25–26.
Great Sutra on the Final Nirvana. Mahāparinirvāṇasūtra. P787 vol. 30.
Heap of Jewels Sutra. Ratnakūṭa. P760 vol. 22.
Heart Sutra. Prajñāpāramitāhṛdaya. P160 vol. 6.
King of Concentrations Sutra. Samādhirājasūtra. P795 vol. 31.
Minor Precepts of Religious Discipline. Vinayakṣudrakavastu. P1035 vol. 103.
Monastic Discipline Sutra. Prātimokṣasūtra. P1031 vol. 42.
Net of Brahma Sutra. Brahmajālasūtra. P1021 vol. 40.
Question of Brahma Sutra. Brahmaparipṛcchāsūtra. P825 vol. 33.
Question of the Nāga King Anavatapta. Anavataptanāgarājaparipṛcchā. P823 vol. 33.
Rice Seedling Sutra. Śālistambasūtra. P876 vol. 34.
Sutra on Dependent Arising. Pratītyasamutpādasūtra. P878 vol. 34.
Sutra on the Distinctions of Karma. Karmavibhaṅgasūtra. P1005 vol. 39.
Question of Surata Sutra. Surataparipṛcchāsūtra. P760 vol. 24.

Ten Teaching Sutra. Daśadharmakasūtra. Found in the *Heap of Jewels* collection of Sutras. P760 vol. 22.

Wheel of Dharma Sutra. Dharmacakrasūtra. P1003 vol 39.

INDIAN AND TIBETAN TREATISES

Āryadeva. *Four Hundred Stanzas. Catuḥsataka.* P5246 vol. 95

Āryaśūra. *Garland of Birth Stories. Jātakamālā.* P5650 vol. 128

————. *Tale that is a Jewel Casket of Good Advice. Subhāṣitaratnakaraṇḍakakathā.* P5668 vol. 129

Asaṅga. *Compendium of Determinations. Viniścayasaṃgrahaṇī.* P5539 vol. 110

Candragomin. *Letter to a Student. Śiṣyalekha.* P5683 vol. 103

Candrakīrti. *Entering the Middle Way. Madhyamakāvatāra.* P5261 vol. 98

Dharmakīrti. *Commentary on Valid Cognition. Pramāṇavārttika.* P5709 vol. 130

Dhārmika Subhūtighoṣa. *String of Lights: A Compilation of Bodhisattva Practices. Bodhisattvacaryā[saṃgraha]pradīparatnamālā.* P5332 vol. 102

Jampal Lhundrup ('Jam spal lhun grub). *Preparatory Practices Recitation. Byang chub lam gyi rim pa'i dmar khrid myur lam gyi sngon 'gro'i ngag 'don gyi rim pa.*

Lozang Chokyi Gyaltsen, Panchen (Blo zang chos kyi rgyal mtshan). *Guru Pūjā (A Method of Offering to the Guru, The Profound Path entitled the Indivisibility of Bliss and Emptiness). Zab lam bla ma mchod pa'i cho gab de stong dbyer med ma bzhugs so.*

Mahāmati. *Extensive Commentary on Letter to a Friend. Vyaktapadāsuhṛllekhaṭīkā. Bshes pa'i spring yig gi rgya cher bshad pa tshig gsal ba.* P5690 vol. 129.

Maitreya. *Higher System of the Mahayana. Uttaratantra* or *Ratnagotravibhāga.* P5525 vol. 108

————. *Ornament for the Mahayana Sutras. Mahāyānasūtrālaṃkāra.* P5521 vol. 108

————. *Distinguishing the Middle from the Extremes. Madhyāntavibhāga.* P5522 vol. 108

————. *Ornament for Realization. Abhisamayālaṃkāra.* P5521 vol. 108

Mātṛceṭa. (Aśvaghoṣa). *Praise in One Hundred and Fifty Verses. Śata-pañcāśatkastotra.* P2038 vol 46

———. *Praise in Honor of One Worthy of Honor. Varṇārhavarṇa-stotra.* P2029 vol. 46

Nāgārjuna. *Fundamental Verses on the Middle Way. Mūlamādhya-makakārikā.* P5224 vol. 95

———. *Letter to a Friend. Suhṛllekha.* P5682 vol. 129

———. *Praise of the Supramundane. Lokātītastava.* P2012 vol. 46

———. *Precious Garland. Ratnāvalī.* P5658 vol. 129

———. *One Hundred Stanzas on Wisdom, Prajñāśataka.* P5414 vol. 103

———. *Sixty Stanzas on Reasoning. Yuktiṣaṣṭikā.* P5225 vol. 95

———. *Verses on the Essence of Dependent Arising. Pratītyasamut-pādahṛdayakārikā.* P5236 vol. 95

Śāntideva. *Introduction to the Practice of Bodhisattvas. Bodhicaryā-vatāra.* P5272 vol. 99

Tsongkhapa. *Condensed Points of the Stages of the Path. Byang chub lam gyi rim pa'i nyams len gyi rnam gshad mdor bsdus te brjed byang du byas pa.*

———. *Great Treatise on the Stages of the Path. Skyes bug sum gyi rnyams su blang ba'i rim pa thams cad tshang bar ston pa'i byang chub lam gyi rim pa.*

———. *Praise of Dependent Origination. Sangs rgyas bcom ldan 'das la zab mo rten cing 'grel bar 'byung ba'i sgo nas bstod pa.*

———. *Three Principal Aspects of the Path. Lam gyi gtso bo rnam gsum.*

Vasubandhu. *Treasury of Knowledge. Abhidharmakośa.* P5590 vol. 115

Secondary Sources

Dietz, Siglinde. 1983. "The Author of the Suhṛllekha." In *Contributions on Tibetan and Buddhist Religion and Philosophy. Proceedings of the Csoma de Körös Symposium held at Velm-Vienna, Austria, 13–19 September 1981, vol. 2* (Wiener Studien zur Tibetologie und Buddhismuskunde, Heft 11), edited by E. Steinkellner and H. Tauscher, 59–72. Vienna: Arbeitskreis für tibetische und buddhistische Studien Universität Wien, Indo-Iranian Journal.

Gyan druk chog nyi (rGyan drug mchog gnyis). 1988. "Life and Teachings of Acarya Nagarjuna." *Lives and Thoughts of the Eight Great*

Masters. Buddhist Himalaya. I.I: Gakken Co. Ltd. Originally published 1972. Gangtok, Sikkim: Namgyal Institute of Tibetology.

Ichimura, Shōhei. 2001. *Buddhist Critical Spirituality: Prajñā and Śūnyatā*. Delhi: Motilal Banarsidass.

Jamspal, Lozang, Ngawang Samten Chophel, and Peter Della Santina, translators. 2008. *Nāgārjuna's Letter to King Gautamīputra, with Explanatory Notes Based on Tibetan Commentaries*. Delhi: Motilal Banarsidass.

Li Rongxi and Albert A. Dalia, translators. 2006. *Lives of Great Monks and Nuns*, BDK English Tripitaka translation series vol. 76. Numata Center for Buddhist Translation and Research.

Lindtner, Christian. 1983. "Nagarjuna's Vyavaharasiddhi." In *Contributions on Tibetan and Buddhist Religion and Philosophy. Proceedings of the Csoma de Körös Symposium held at Velm-Vienna, Austria, 13–19 September 1981, vol. 2* (Wiener Studien zur Tibetologie und Buddhismuskunde, Heft 11) edited by E. Steinkellner and H. Tauscher, 147–160.Vienna: Arbeitskreis für tibetische und buddhistische Studien Universität Wien, Indo-Iranian Journal.

———. 1987. *Nagarjuniana: Studies in the Writings and Philosophy of Nāgārjuna*. Delhi: Motilal Banarsidass.

Mabbett, Ian. 1998. "The Problem of the Historical Nāgārjuna Revisited." *Journal of the American Oriental Society* 118, no. 3: 332–46.

Pāsādika, Bhikkhu. 1986. "Review of *Die buddhistische Briefliteratur Indiens* by Siglinde Dietz." *Indo-Iranian Journal*, 29.3: 203-207.

Ramanan, K. Venkata. 1987. *Nagarjuna's Philosophy: As Presented In the Maha-Prajnaparamita-Sastra*. Delhi: Motilal Banarsidass.

Ruegg, David Seyfort. Edited by Tom J. F. Tillemans. 1981. *The Literature of the Madhyamaka School of Philosophy in India*. Wiesbaden. Otto Harrassowitz.

———. Edited by Tom J. F. Tillemans. 2010. *The Buddhist Philosophy of the Middle: Essays on Indian and Tibetan Madhyamaka*. Studies in Indian and Tibetan Buddhism. Boston: Wisdom Publications.

Santina, Peter Della. 2002. *Causality and Emptiness; the Wisdom of Nagarjuna*. Singapore: Buddhist Research Society.

Szántó, Péter-Dániel. 2021. "The *Suhṛllekha* of Nāgārjuna *editio minor* 2.0." Academia.edu. https://www.academia.edu/61531143/The_Suhṛllekha_of_Nāgārjuna_editio_minor_2_0.

Westerhoff, Jan Christoph. 2019. "Nāgārjuna." *The Stanford Encyclope-dia of Philosophy* (Spring 2019 Edition). Edited by Edward N. Zalta. https://plato.stanford.edu/archives/spr2019/entries/nagarjuna.

Index

About the Authors

BORN IN THE TSANG REGION of Tibet in 1923, Geshe Lhundub Sopa was both a spiritual master and a respected academic. He rose from a humble background to complete his geshe studies at Sera Jey Monastic College in Lhasa with highest honors and was privileged to serve as a debate opponent for the Dalai Lama's own geshe examination in 1959. He moved to New Jersey in the United States in 1963 and in 1967 began teaching in the Buddhist studies program at University of Wisconsin–Madison. In 1975, he founded the Deer Park Buddhist Center in Oregon, Wisconsin, which was the site of the Dalai Lama's first Kalachakra initiation granted in the West. He was the author of several books in English, including the five-volume comprehensive teaching *Steps on the Path to Enlightenment*. Geshe Lhundub Sopa passed away on August 28, 2014, at the age of ninety-one. His Holiness the Dalai Lama composed a prayer of request for the swift return of Geshe Sopa.

UNDER THE GUIDANCE of Geshe Lhundub Sopa, Beth Newman received a PhD in South Asian languages and literature from the University of Wisconsin–Madison. She has edited a number of books for Geshe Sopa and other Tibetan masters. She is the translator of *The Tibetan Book of Everyday Wisdom* and *The Tale of the Incomparable Prince*. Currently living in Madison, Wisconsin, she continues to work to make the Tibetan Buddhist tradition accessible to Western readers.

About Wisdom Publications

Wisdom Publications is the leading publisher of classic and contemporary Buddhist books and practical works on mindfulness. To learn more about us or to explore our other books, please visit our website at wisdomexperience.org or contact us at the address below.

Wisdom Publications
199 Elm Street
Somerville, MA 02144 USA

We are a 501(c)(3) organization, and donations in support of our mission are tax deductible.

Wisdom Publications is affiliated with the Foundation for the Preservation of the Mahayana Tradition (FPMT).